Protecting the Vulnerable

Protecting
the
Vulnerable

A Reanalysis of Our
Social Responsibilities

Robert E. Goodin

The University of Chicago Press
Chicago and London

Robert E. Goodin is a senior lecturer in government at the University of Essex. An associate editor
of *Ethics*, he is the author of *Political Theory and
Public Policy* and one of the editors of *Nuclear De-
terrence: Ethics and Strategy*, both published by the
University of Chicago Press.

The University of Chicago Press, Chicago 60637
The University of Chicago Press, Ltd., London

Printed in the United States of America

94 93 92 91 90 89 88 87 86 85   54321

Library of Congress Cataloging in Publication Data

Goodin, Robert E.
  Protecting the vulnerable.

  Bibliography: p.
  Includes index.
  1. Social justice.   2. Responsibility.
I. Title.
HM216.G56   1985   303.3′72   85-1127
ISBN 0-226-30298-9

To My Mother and Father
who taught me the concept

Contents

Acknowledgments

This book was written under the auspices of the Social Justice Project, an exciting interdisciplinary venture of the Research School of Social Sciences at the Australian National University (ANU). First and foremost I must record my debt to my colleagues there, and especially to our most excellent director, Pat Troy, for providing such a congenial and stimulating working environment. I also thank the Fellows of the Research School in general and its director, Max Neutze, in particular for their lively and continuing interest in this work.

The arguments in this book were powerfully shaped and reshaped by tea-room conversations over many months with ANU philosophers Stanley Benn, David Braddon-Mitchell, Steve Buckle, Keith Campbell, Fred D'Agostino, Jerry Gaus, Knud Haakonssen, Rich Hall, John Passmore, Val Routley Plumwood, Wojciech Sadurski, Maureen Sheehan, Jack Smart, and Richard Routley Sylvan. Among the floating company of ANU scholars, political scientists (especially Peter Self and Peter Wilenski), sociologists (especially Dorothy Broom and Frank Jones), economists (especially Frank Cowell and Fred Gruen) and historians (especially Stuart Macintyre and Barry Smith) have also left their marks.

Most of all, I should record my very special debt to four friends and collaborators, Diane Gibson, Julian Le Grand, Philip Pettit, and Patricia Tulloch, each of whom is engaged in important research closely paralleling my own. Their advice and encouragement have proven invaluable at various crucial points in this project. Inevitably for an Antipodean author, I am also very much indebted to distant friends who responded generously to postal badgering. Exceptionally useful comments have come in this fashion from Brian Barry, Sissela Bok, Jim Fishkin, David Miller, and Onora O'Neill.

The arguments of this book were previewed at a special conference convened by the Social Justice Project in October 1982. Tom Campbell, John Kleinig, and Carole Pateman commented most helpfully there, and Kleinig followed up with virtually a line-by-line commentary on the first draft of the manuscript as a whole. Portions of these arguments have also been aired at the universities of Auckland, Canterbury, Otago, and Victoria (thanks to a generous grant from the New Zealand Vice-Chancellors' Committee); at the University of Melbourne; in various venues around ANU; and late in the day, at the University of Chicago. All those discussions were helpful in isolating gaps in my reasoning. Among those whose comments have had the greatest impact are David Braybrooke, Derek Browne, Jim Flynn, Alan Gewirth, Russell Hardin, David Novitz, Marian Sawer, Christine Swanton, David Tucker, and Jeremy Waldron.

This book was rewritten for one last time during a term spent visiting the California Institute of Technology. There, Dick Arneson, Toby Page, Norman Schofield, and Jim Woodward brought yet another diverse range of expertise to bear on the topic of this book. Two Cal Tech colleagues made very special contributions. I am grateful to Alan Schwartz for casting a lawyer's eye over the manuscript and saving me several embarrassments; and Brian Barry once again offered a constant stream of excellent advice.

A particular note of thanks goes to our very efficient secretary at the Social Justice Project. This is the first book I have not typed entirely myself. With someone like Norma Chin around, that could become a most pleasurable habit. At Cal Tech, I am indebted to Kathryn Kurzweil for various vital last-minute rescues.

Synopsis

We all acknowledge special responsibilities toward our families, friends, clients, compatriots, and so forth. That we should do so is one of our firmest moral intuitions (chap. 1).

These special responsibilities are relatively strong moral claims. Their demands will typically override those of any general positive duties we may have to aid others at large. It may be wrong to commit murder to feed our own children, but most people would say it is right to satisfy our own children before giving food to needier neighbors (chap. 2).

The moral basis of these special responsibilities is traditionally analyzed in terms of self-assumed obligations, which substantially restricts their scope: we voluntarily commit ourselves to only a limited range of people (chap. 3).

Examining several cases closely, however, suggests it is the *vulnerability* of the beneficiary rather than any voluntary commitment per se on the part of the benefactor which generates these special responsibilities (chap. 4).

Many more people are vulnerable to us—individually or collectively—than we have made any commitments to, in any sense. We (individually or collectively) have the same sort of strong responsibilities toward all those who are vulnerable to our actions and choices (chap. 5).

This argument provides grounding for, inter alia, broader notions of interpersonal, international, intergenerational, and environmental responsibilities than are ordinarily acknowledged (chap. 6).

Some vulnerabilities—and hence the responsibilities growing out of them—are natural, inevitable, and immutable. Others are created, shaped, or sustained by current social arrangements. While we should always strive to protect the vulnerable, we should also strive to reduce the latter sort of vulnerabilities insofar as they render the vulnerable liable to exploitation (chap. 7).

Do not tell me, as a good man did to-day, of my obligation to put all poor men in good situations. Are they *my* poor? I tell thee, thou foolish philanthropist, that I grudge the dollar, the dime, the cent I give to such men as do not belong to me and to whom I do not belong.

—Ralph Waldo Emerson, "Self-Reliance"

A selfish, contracted, narrow spirit is generally abhorred, and is esteemed base and sordid. But if a man's affection takes in half a dozen more, and his regards extend so far beyond his own single person as to take in his children and family; or if it reaches further still to a larger circle, but falls infinitely short of the universal system, and is exclusive of being in general; his private affection exposes him to the same thing, viz., to pursue the interest of its particular object in opposition to general existence: which is certainly contrary to the tendency of true virtue.

—Jonathan Edwards, *The Nature of True Virtue*

Now it appears, that in the original frame of our mind, our strongest attention is confined to ourselves; our next is extended to our relations and acquaintance; and 'tis only the weakest which reaches to strangers and indifferent persons. This partiality, then, and unequal affection . . . make us regard any remarkable transgression of such a degree of partiality, either by too great an enlargement, or contraction of the affections, as vicious and immoral. This we may observe in our common judgments concerning actions where we blame a person, who either centres all his affections in his family, or is so regardless of them, as in any opposition of interest, to give the preference to a stranger, or mere chance acquaintance. From all which it follows that our uncultivated ideas of morality, instead of providing a remedy for the partiality of our affections, do rather conform themselves to that partiality, and give it an additional force and influence. The remedy, then, is not derived from nature but from *artifice;* or more properly speaking, nature provides a remedy in the judgment and understanding, for what is irregular and incommodious in the affections.

—David Hume, *A Treatise of Human Nature*

1

Which Brother's Keeper?

The greatest obstacle to achieving social justice is, and always has been, limited social resources. As Hume (1777, 145) says, questions of distributive justice arise only under conditions of "moderate scarcity." Were there enough resources to provide everyone "with whatever his most voracious appetites can want, or luxurious imagination wish," then the "jealous virtue of justice would never once have been dreamed of."

According to the conventional wisdom, the same scarcity that gives rise to the problem of social justice in the first place also constrains a society in its pursuit of that goal. But here the referent has subtly shifted. The scarcity now in view has social as well as natural components. It is one thing to ask what resources are available in society overall; it is another to ask what resources society is willing to make available for purposes of pursuing justice. Hume (1777, 146), again, reminds us that there would be little point in discussing social justice unless people displayed "limited benevolence." They must be sufficiently sensitive to the interests of others to be moved by such discussions at all but not so naturally generous as to render all such appeals superfluous.

No one blames philosophers for the scarcity of natural resources. But the scarcity of social resources devoted to the pursuit of justice—the limit we place on our benevolence—does have philosophical as well as psychological underpinnings. The aim of this book, most broadly conceived, is to shake these foundations and thereby help extract a larger share of social resources for just causes.

Working within the constraints set by natural scarcity, the greatest practical obstacle to achieving as much justice as resources permit is, and always has been, the supposition that each of us should "cultivate his own garden." Moral philosophers correctly identify "particularity" as the principal enemy of justice. They err, however, in focusing too narrowly upon its most base form. Their attention is usually concentrated on ways in which our particular self-interest blinds us to the interests of others, and no doubt they are right that "self-love" is a serious stumbling block. But there is another more honorable form of particularity that is equally prevalent and probably more pernicious.

It is our *particular obligations* that all too often blind us to our larger social responsibilities. Whatever claim the world at large may have upon us, it inevitably takes second place behind the claims of particular others: our families, friends, colleagues, clients, compatriots, and so on. These are people who are connected to us in special ways; and the rights, duties, and obligations arising out of those special relationships always seem to take priority. Duty, even more than charity, begins at home. Strangers ordinarily get, and are ordinarily thought to deserve, only what (if anything) is left over.

People's sphere of social concern seems always to have been circumscribed in some such way. "Defending one's own is the rule long before justice becomes an issue" (Bok 1978, 149). Certainly it is true that among "primitive" peoples even the most minimal moral virtues "are practiced almost exclusively in relation to the men of the same tribe." Charles Darwin goes on to observe

> No tribe could hold together if murder, robbery, treachery, etc., were common; consequently such crimes within the limits of the same tribe "are branded with everlasting infamy"; but excite no such sentiment beyond those limits. A North-American Indian is well pleased with himself, and is honored by others, when he scalps a man of another tribe; and a Dyak cuts off the head of an unoffending person, and dries it as a trophy. . . . In a rude state of civilization the robbery of strangers is, indeed, generally considered as honorable. (Darwin 1874, chap. 4)

Little more could be expected from those in a "rude state of civilization." But "civilized" man manages hardly better. His moral universe extends to include mostly just his near neighbors. Recall, for example, how from the seventeenth century forward local magistrates in England were empowered to remove from their parishes any newcomers who might become a public burden; when the New Poor Law eliminated that power in 1834, it was not because of any expanding notions of moral responsibility but merely for the sake of economic efficiency and free markets in labor (Pinker 1979, chap. 10).

In the United States, such provincialism persisted throughout the next century. Right up until the Great Depression, state poor laws restricted relief to "residents," usually of more than one year's standing; "transients" were given only the most miserly interim assistance and sent on their ways. One of the cruelest cases on record involved a man who arrived in Chicago with frostbitten feet and who was sent on his way before they were properly healed. When, this having led to the amputation of both feet, he sued, the courts exonerated the Chicago officials, saying they owed this man no more than he had been given (Heisterman 1934; Abbott 1940, 133–55, 232–57). The same principles were enunciated by Justice Cardozo (1915, 164) in his judgment on a World War I New York law prohibiting the employment of aliens on public works projects:

> To disqualify aliens is discriminatory indeed, but not arbitrary discrimination, for the principle of exclusion is the restriction of the resources of the state to the advancement and profit of the members of the state. . . . The state, in determining what use shall be made of its own moneys, may legitimately consult the welfare of its own citizens rather than that of aliens. . . . In its war against poverty, the state is not required to dedicate its own resources to citizens and aliens alike.

Although this no longer represents official legal doctrine in the United States, even for aliens (Blackmun 1971a, 371), there is still astonishingly widespread support for such policies among the population at large. According to one survey, more than 70 percent of respondents, even among the lowest income groups, favored denying state unemployment benefits to those who had moved to the area only recently and without the promise of a job (Erskine 1961, 665).

To some extent, "the nationalization of welfare . . . opens the neighborhood communities to whoever chooses to come in" (Walzer 1981, 9). Provincialism of one sort, however, is overcome only by provincialism of another. Walzer, echoing the received wisdom of his own age, goes on to observe that "neighborhoods can be open only if countries are closed." In short, the most that "civilized" man has managed to do is "to extend his social instincts and sympathies to members of the same nation," the tribe writ large, and only for certain limited purposes at that (Darwin 1874, chap. 4). Yet he has the audacity to congratulate himself on such a meager accomplishment.[1]

Even economists, not on the whole famous for their moral sensitivity, have been known to remark upon the peculiar narrowness of moral vision produced by such particularism. Stanley Jevons presents a particularly striking case in point:

> When it was stated that the Australian aborigines in the north of Queensland were being shot like kangaroos, or poisoned wholesale by strychnine, one solitary member of parliament went so far as to ask the Government whether this was true. The Government replied that they did not know, but would make inquiries, and nothing more has been heard of the matter to the present

---

1. Jonathan Edwards (1765, 88) pinpoints the source of this error: "When private affections extend themselves to a considerable number, we are ready to look upon them as truly virtuous, and accordingly to applaud them highly. Thus it is with respect to a man's love to a large party, or a country. For though his private system contains but a small part even of the world of mankind, yet being a considerable number, they—through the contracted limits of his mind, and the narrowness of his views—are ready to engross his sight, and to seem as if they were all. Hence, among the Romans, love to their country was the highest virtue; though this affection of theirs so much extolled, was employed as it were for the destruction of the rest of mankind. The larger the number is, to which that private affection extends, the more apt men are, through the narrowness of their sight, to mistake it for true virtue; because then the private system appears to have more of the image of the universal."

day. Accounts which I have heard of the proceedings in the border districts of Queensland are simply dreadful. These accounts may or may not be true . . . but the point is that English society . . . has never cared even to ascertain whether or not scores of Australian natives are shot like kangaroos, or poisoned by strychnine, like the native dogs. (Jevons 1883, 217–18)

The provincialism represented by this cavalier disregard for distant peoples, even if they are notionally one's own subjects or wards, is, alas, nowise unique to the English.

In many respects, such behavior may seem perfectly understandable. Politically, we are not well organized to respond to people beyond our borders, nor are these people ordinarily in much of a position to bring political pressure to bear upon us to do so. Sociologically, it is only natural that our affections should extend principally to members of our own group (Allport 1954). Indeed, it may well be true that in order to flourish a society must inculcate norms of limited altruism, encouraging its members to sacrifice themselves for the group while at the same time defending the group's collective self-interest above all else (Broad 1953, 281–82; Bok 1978, 149).

Psychologically, too, it seems inevitable that we empathize most strongly with those "of our own kind." Brandt (1976, 450), summarizing the "psychology of benevolence" and its implications for philosophy, concludes that "the basic empathetic/sympathetic response will be motivating when we recognize distress like what we feel ourselves." Conversely, Brandt (1976, 450) finds, "where an object is dissimilar to ourselves, we shall tend to act less sympathetically—whether the dissimilarity is a matter of sex or nationality or race."[2]

Some commentators say that partiality on the part of parents is, in various ways, psychologically necessary for the proper development of a child. As far as the development of a child's personality is concerned, it is said that "the crucial characteristic of the parental role is its *partiality* for the individual child. . . . A developing personality *needs* to perceive itself as especially valuable to somebody: needs to know that to someone it matters more than other children; that someone will go to unreasonable lengths, not just reasonable ones, for its sake" (Newson 1978, 2). Then there is also the need to socialize children into the moral norms of the larger society. "It is because we have specific commitments to specific individuals and groups that we can then go on to recognize the claim of all human beings. . . . It is because we first form ties with parents, siblings and friends that we are subsequently able to

2. The unfortunate consequences of this tendency are effectively traced by William Thompson (1825, 12): "The more ignorant and the more weak . . . the less will there be, or appear to be, of identification . . . ; because the less of resemblance, of equality, the less there will be sympathy; the less power to resist and the less of control, the greater will be the temptation to, the more infallible will be the certainty of, abuse of power."

extend our sympathies to other human beings with whom we are less closely connected" (Norman 1979, 199–200).[3]

Other writers suppose that a "deep attachment" to particular people and projects provides the "substance or conviction in man's life" which is psychologically necessary "to compel his allegiance to life itself" (Williams 1981, 18). "Attachment to self, to things and to persons" is, according to T. S. Eliot (1942, 12), what gives life its meaning, and "the integrity of these cognitive and normative universes depends on the preservation of the boundaries of moral obligation" to which they give rise.[4]

Finally, as a brute biological fact, "the species is sustained and prolonged by sexual drives and family ties which are necessarily to some degree exclusive and particularized" (Hampshire 1982, 154). Indeed, if we are to believe some sociobiologists, our genetic make-up itself may dictate that we confine "reciprocal altruism" narrowly, to our own first cousins at most (Trivers 1971; Ridley and Dawkins 1981; cf. Singer 1981).

Given all this, it comes as no surprise that obligations to close kin and near neighbors do in fact tend to get preferential treatment. But explanation is one thing, justification another. What *is* surprising is the extent to which philosophers have over the years positively endorsed what would on its face appear to be such rank prejudice. Many of them seem to regard these forms of favoritism not as concessions that must be made grudgingly to biological necessity and the flawed human psyche but instead as features of the good society actually to be sought.[5]

---

3. See similarly Grote (1870, chap. 5), Durkheim (1903, 74), Berger (1976, 403–4), and Pinker (1979, 27–28).

4. This is a common claim, advanced by (among others) Berger (1974, 167, 182), Fried (1976, 1068–71), Norman (1979, 193–201), Pinker (1979, 25, 40), Brock (1982, 232), Fishkin (1982, 20–24), Sandel (1982), Winkler (1982, 275, 281–84), and Rorty (1983). While there is surely some truth in the claim, it is probably overstated. Nagel (1982) is right to regard the stronger version as "an audacious and rather original form of motivational blackmail: 'If I have to serve the greatest good of the greatest number or the categorical imperative I might as well be dead!' It's a claim few people could make without bluffing."

5. This view finds its clearest expression in Orwell's "Reflections on Gandhi": "The essence of being human is that one does not seek perfection, that one *is* sometimes willing to commit sins for the sake of loyalty, that one does not push asceticism to the point where it makes friendly intercourse impossible. . . . Sainthood is . . . a thing that human beings must avoid. . . . In this yogi-ridden age, it is too readily assumed that 'non-attachment' is not only better than a full acceptance of earthly life, but that the ordinary man only rejects it because it is too difficult: in other words, that the average human being is a failed saint. It is doubtful whether this is true. Many people genuinely do not wish to be saints, and it is probable that some who achieve or aspire to sainthood have never felt much temptation to be human beings" (Orwell, 1949, 467; see similarly Wolf 1982). Of course, the mere fact that people do not often embrace it is no evidence that the ideal of sainthood is morally suspect.

Among the philosophers making only the more modest sort of claim are Parfit (1978, 285–92; 1979a, 396–97), Bennett (1981, 89) and Singer (1981, chap 6). Parfit in particular is quite clear that your obligations to your friends, etc., do *not* override your obligations to strangers: in

Particularism has been a long and constant refrain among applied moralists. In his classic codification of Jewish law, the *Mishneh Torah,* Maimonides prescribes that

> A poor man who is one's relative has priority over all others, the poor of one's own household have priority over the other poor of his city, and the poor of his city have priority over the poor of another city, as it is said, *Unto thy poor and needy brother, in thy land* (Deut. 15:11). (Maimonides 1168, bk. 7, treatise 2, chap. 7, sec. 10)

Cotton Mather (1710, 35, 41) similarly counsels the Puritans of Massachusetts in their "duties to do good," asking, "The charity we are upon, why should it not begin at home? . . . Particularly, let us begin with our domestic relations, and provide for those of our own house." Having discussed the primacy of our duties to our blood relations, Mather (1710, 57) goes on to discuss the subsidiary duties owed to neighbors, who also "stand related unto one another." And with this Mather concludes his catalogue of duties that people in general have to one another as he turns to the peculiar responsibilities of people in particular roles—magistrates, ministers, physicians, lawyers, schoolmasters, and so forth.[6]

This prejudice in favor of the people who stand in some special relationship to us reverberates throughout modern moral philosophy. Consider the following examples:

1. Sir David Ross maintains that

> The essential defect of the "ideal utilitarian" theory is that it ignores, or at least does not do full justice to, the highly personal character of duty. If the only duty is to produce the maximum of good, the question who is to have the good—whether it is myself, or my benefactor, or a person to whom I have made a promise to confer that good on him, or a mere fellow man to whom I stand in no special relation—should make no difference to my having a duty to produce that good. But we are all in fact sure that it makes a vast difference. (Ross 1930, 21)

2. This has been a central theme in Bernard Williams's ongoing attack on

---

Taurek's (1977, 296) case, it is *not* morally laudable to sacrifice five strangers in order to save one friend. Parfit goes on to observe, however, that the temptation to protect friends at the expense of strangers is psychologically very strong. Hence, he describes the act of saving strangers when friends, etc., are at risk as "supererogatory"—morally desirable but above and beyond the call of duty. Others however take the stronger line, insisting that it is morally preferable (and not just morally forgiveable) to opt for saving your friend in such situations (Winkler 1982, 274 ff.). Indeed, Parfit himself elsewhere adopts a line concerning the agent relativity of duties that will often lead him, along with all these others, to this stronger conclusion (Parfit 1979b, 557).

6. Pragmatically, he may well have been right to cut off duties at that point; given the geography and available technology, perhaps neighbors were the most you could hope to aid effectively. It is clear from context, however, that Mather saw himself making a moral rather than merely pragmatic point when handing down these prescriptions.

utilitarianism: "The moral point of view," as conceived by utilitarians and Kantians alike, is "characterized by its impartiality and its indifference to any particular relations to particular persons" (Williams 1981, 2). Be this as it may, Williams, like Thomas Nagel (1970, 129–30; 1980, 119–26) before him, insists that we must nevertheless carve out a special place, morally speaking, for a person to pursue his own particular "projects."[7] These projects include, among other things, commitments "to oneself, one's family, one's friends" (Williams 1973, 110; cf. MacIntyre 1983, 122).

3. On this point Richard Wasserstrom (1975, 4) is particularly firm:

> As a parent one is entitled, if not obligated, to prefer the interests of one's own children over those of children generally. That is to say, it is regarded as appropriate for a parent to allocate excessive goods to his or her own children, even though other children may have substantially more pressing and genuine needs for these same items. If one were trying to decide what the right way was to distribute assets among a group of children all of whom were strangers to oneself, the relevant moral considerations would be very different from those that would be thought to obtain once one's own children were in the picture. In the role of a parent, the claims of other children vis-à-vis one's own are, if not rendered morally irrelevant, certainly rendered less morally significant. In short, the role-differentiated character of the situation alters the relevant moral point of view enormously. (See similarly Wasserstrom 1984)

4. Derek Parfit (1979b, 556) expresses similar sentiments:

> Most of us believe that there are certain people to whom we have special obligations. These are the people to whom we stand in certain relations—such as our children, parents, pupils, patients, members of our own trade union, or those whom we represent. We believe we ought to help these people in certain ways. We should try to protect them from certain kinds of harm, and should try to give them certain kinds of benefit. Common-sense morality largely consists in such obligations. Carrying out these obligations has priority over helping strangers. (See also Parfit 1983b, 35–36; 1984, 95, 485)

---

7. By "be this as it may," I mean to capture Williams's own ambivalence about the source and status of such considerations. They may be purely pragmatic; certainly it is hard to focus clearly on your own projects when the world at large is constantly intruding with equally legitimate demands (Fried 1978, 37–38; Walzer 1981, 3; Fishkin 1982, 20–24, 75, 154–55). There is also the psychological dynamic to which Williams (1981, 18) himself alludes: "unless such things [as deep attachments to particular persons and projects] exist there will not be enough substance or conviction in a man's life to compel his allegiance to life itself." There is, finally, an even stronger logical link, ignored by Williams but brought out by Grote (1870, 94): "Just as, intellectually, reason . . . deindividualizes [men], truth being common, . . . while error is individual: so morally, the growth of virtue is a gradual deindividualization of men as to the purpose of their action also, substituting common purposes for private ones, and carrying sympathy to such an extent that individual interests will really vanish. Reason is the same for all, and the application of the principle of reason to morality abolishes the notion of self." Fried (1976, 1070) suggests something of this when he writes that "there remains a circle of intensity which through its emphasis on the particular and the concrete continues to reflect what I have identified as the source of all sense of value—our sense of self" (see similarly Sandel 1982; Rorty 1983).

5. John Mackie (1977, 167, 157–58), having found reasons for rejecting moral absolutism, is dissuaded from going all the way over to "simple consequentialism" primarily by considerations of these special relationships. "One may have the right, or the duty, to look after *one's own* children (or other relatives) in preference to persons who, apart from this relationship to oneself, would have equal claims."

6. Joel Feinberg (1980, 202) similarly remarks that "generally speaking, our duties to persons close to ourselves in space and time, kind and relation, tend to have a greater stringency than our duties to creatures who are more remote in those respects. I have a greater duty to my immediate family than to my remote relatives, to my friends than to strangers, to countrymen than to foreigners."

7. Jonathan Bennett (1981, 78), too, says that "I hold myself entitled to give extra weight to a cost or benefit which is to accrue to someone with a special relation to me. The most special relation of all is identity—I am entitled to put the thumb on the moral scales on behalf of my own interests—but I extend this to my offspring, my parents, my closest friends, and so on" (see similarly Scheffler 1982).

8. For yet another example, Michael Walzer (1970, chap. 1) argues that one's narrower obligations—to "parties, congregations, sects, movements, unions or clubs"—often take precedence over one's broader obligations. These narrower obligations give rise to a "duty to disobey" more universalistic demands. According this sort of priority to small-group attachments leads Walzer (1981, 1) to conclude that "the idea of distributive justice presupposes a bounded world, a community within which distributions take place, a group of people committed to dividing, exchanging, and sharing, first of all among themselves."[8]

9. The general point is perhaps best expressed by Stephen Toulmin (1981, 35) in his remarks on "the tyranny of principles": "In our relations with casual acquaintances and unidentified fellow citizens, absolute impartiality may be a prime moral demand; but among intimates a certain discreet partiality is, surely, only equitable, and certainly not unethical. So a system of ethics that rests its principles on 'the veil of ignorance' may well be 'fair,' but it will also be—essentially—an ethics for relations between strangers."[9]

Over a century ago, Henry Sidgwick identified the challenge of commonsense morality on precisely this point as the first challenge that utilitarianism,

---

8. Walzer does go on to say, "It is possible to imagine such a group extended to include the entire human race, but no such extension has yet been achieved. For the present, we live in smaller distributive communities." The balance of his essay and his subsequent book (Walzer 1983) is, however, devoted to arguing that until and unless what Walzer (1981, 21) calls people's "sense of relatedness and mutuality" fortuitously undergoes a dramatic expansion, it is right and proper that we should so limit our distributive concerns.

9. For one way of formalizing these judgments, see Sen (1982).

or any other universalistic moral theory, had to meet.[10] In both practical terms and philosophical ones, it remains so to this day.

It is not just moral universalism which is at stake, however. Social justice itself needs to be rescued from the consequences of such particularism. Even avowed particularists agree that "it is unjust," in some sense, "to view friends as having special claims; for since friendship is, and is bound to be, very unevenly distributed, the rights which it confers will also be unevenly distributed" (Telfer 1970–71, 236). So, too, will there be some skewedness in the distribution of the resources of families, neighbors, colleagues, and compatriots. Advocates of particularism typically concede that justice is the loser, and they regret that fact.

As far as advocates of particularism are concerned, "the only possible answer" to this criticism, which they also regard as a perfectly *adequate* answer, "is that . . . the utility of a practice is high enough to compensate for the fact that some measure of injustice is involved in it" (Telfer 1970–71, 236). They join Charles Fried (1976, 1070) in saying, "Truly I must be ready to generalize outward all the way. That is what justice consists of. But justice is not all of morality." Certainly not. I aim to show, however, that it has a larger role than Fried allows. Here I shall be arguing that the most coherent theory available to explain our special responsibilities to family, friends, and so on also implies that we must give far more consideration than particularists allow to at least certain classes of strangers.

M y argument in this book proceeds by trying to bring our considered moral judgments, our moral principles, and our relevant background theories into what has been called a "wide reflective equilibrium" (Rawls 1951; 1971, secs. 4, 9; 1974, 7–10). The nature of this procedure is to "start both with some *prima facie* acceptable general principles, and with the mass of *prima facie* acceptable detailed moral judgments, and where they do not fully agree adjust either or both until the most satisfactory coherent compromise is reached" (Mackie 1977, 105). Simple coherence apart, what makes one of these compromises more "satisfactory" than another is that we draw upon an independent set of "relevant background theories" in order to "advance philosophical arguments intended to bring out the

10. "Common Sense . . . seems . . . to regard it as immediately certain . . . that we owe special duties of kindness to those who stand in special relations to us. The question is, on what principles . . . we are to determine the nature and extent of the special claims to affection and kind service which arise out of these particular relations of human beings. . . . The different answers given to this fundamental question will obviously constitute the main difference between the Intuitional and Utilitarian methods" (Sidgwick 1874, 242). This is, in fact, the first topic Sidgwick addresses in trying to reconcile Utilitarian and Common Sense morality in his *Methods of Ethics* (bk. 4, chap. 3). Other recent critics who attack universalistic moral theories on these grounds include especially Schrag (1976), Blum (1980), Kekes (1981), Oldenquist (1982), Winkler (1982), and Cottingham (1983).

relative strengths and weaknesses of the alternative sets of principles''
(Daniels 1979, 258).

Quite what this procedure will, if successful, prove remains a moot point.
Some commentators give the method a quasi-scientific interpretation, treating
moral intuitions as data points and suggesting that we fit moral theories to the
data just as in any ordinary scientific endeavor. According to this interpretation, the object of the exercise is to establish the ''objective truth'' of the
moral theory thus validated (Sidgwick 1874, bk. 4, chaps. 3–5; Ross 1930,
40–41). Talking in terms of objective truth, however, raises all sorts of embarrassing questions about the status of the intuitions going into the process in
the first place. A theory thus tested can aspire to the status of objective truth
only if the data itself can. In the case of moral intuitions, especially, any such
claim must be highly suspect (Mackie 1977).

I prefer to regard the reflective-equilibrium process as a method designed to
resolve problems that arise within the shared moral code of a given society.
That code itself may be no more than a negotiated order, making no pretense
to any larger objective truth. But it does inevitably contain some inconsisten-
cies, which it is the task of the reflective equilibirum to iron out. Seen in this
light, reflective equilibrium is essentially a political process aimed at negotiating a few ''points outstanding'' within the framework of a larger, preexisting
negotiated social order. Hence, I propose to use the reflective-equilibrium
procedure for the relatively modest and uncontentious task of merely ''teasing
out the implications of [our collective] views'' about what is right and wrong
(Raz 1982, 310–11).

Interpreted in this way, the results of the reflective-equilibrium process do
not *prove* anything one way or the other. Some independent reasons must
always be given, some ''background theories'' always appealed to, in support
of any ethical propositions that the reflective equilibrium might suggest to us.
But the reflective equilibrium is nonetheless a most useful device for
motivating changes in the received ethical wisdom.

In part, the reflective-equilibrium process will lead us to reject considered
moral judgments that simply do not fit with the rest of our theoretically inte-
grated judgments. A more important consequence, however, is the way in
which the reflective equilibrium can lead us to accept some new, nonintuitive
moral judgments. The moral theory that best explains the moral judgments
which we do intuitively make also typically commits us to similar judgments
concerning situations that are theoretically indistinguishable but which, pre-
analytically, we would be inclined to judge differently. By showing us what
lies hidden within our ordinary moral judgements, reflective-equilibrium procedures can thus lead us to acknowledge commitments that we would otherwise have shunned.

Leading people to acknowledge broader commitments is the goal of this
book. I shall not be rejecting our intuitions. I shall not be arguing that we have

no responsibilities toward those with whom we enjoy "special relation-ships." That would be absurd. Nor for that matter shall I deny our firm intui-tions that our responsibilities toward them tend to be particularly strong ones.[11]

What I *shall* be doing is trying to ratchet up from our intuitions about special responsibilities. I shall, in other words, be arguing that there is noth-ing so very special about them. That is not to say that special duties are just particular instantiations of some more general duties. It is instead to say that both sorts of duties derive from fundamentally the same sorts of moral consid-erations. For the same reasons we recognize the one we must recognize the other.

What is crucial, in my view, is that others are depending upon us. They are particularly vulnerable to our actions and choices. That, I argue, is the true source of all the standard special responsibilities that we so readily acknowl-edge. The same considerations of vulnerability that make our obligations to our families, friends, clients, and compatriots especially strong can also give rise to similar responsibilities toward a much larger group of people who stand in none of the standard special relationships to us.[12]

Occasionally these further responsibilities fall upon each of us individually. More commonly they fall upon all of us collectively and are devolved upon particular individuals only by virtue of the collective arrangements we have made (implicitly or explicitly) for discharging those collective respon-sibilities. Either way, however, these additional responsibilities have the same source and, depending on circumstances, perhaps even the same strength as the special responsibilities we have always regarded as particularly binding.

---

11. Some do, most especially Godwin (1793, bk. 2, chap. 2). In the "famous fire cause" in which he served as "counsel for the Archbishop Fenelon versus [his] own mother," he insists that we have no stronger duty to reward our *own* benefactor or to rescue our *own* mother than someone else's. Godwin's argument is that we should reward benefactors on account of the "goodwill" they have displayed. "But the merit of this disposition," Godwin observes, "is equal, whether the benefit were conferred upon me or upon another. . . . My benefactor ought to be esteemed, not because he bestowed a benefit upon me, but because he bestowed it upon a human being." (For a more subtle development of a similar point, see Edwards 1765, chap. 1.) Godwin says the same of our kin: "My brother, or my father may be a fool or a profligate, malicious, lying or dishonest. If they be, of what consequence it is that they are mine? . . . What magic is there in the pronoun 'my,' that should justify us in overturning the decisions of impartial truth?"

12. In this, I am pursuing the traditional strategy. "Historically, the idea of a common humanity has [long] been articulated by taking a particular relationship and showing how it can be ex-tended. The Stoics asserted that the whole world is a *polis,* a community in which every human being is a citizen. In Christian ethics the question 'Who is my neighbour?' is answered by showing how anyone can, in principle, stand in that relation to me; or again, it is asserted that all human beings are children of the same divine father. The same idea of universal brotherhood and sisterhood is taken up by working-class, feminist, and socialist movements, and within those traditions we also find the idea of class solidarity extended into a basis for internationalism, since 'the workingmen have no country' " (Norman 1979, 200).

The basic argument of this book, then, is that our social responsibilities are broader than we might ordinarily be inclined to suppose. Specifically, my argument is that "general social responsibilities"—responsibilities with respect to undifferentiated others, of a sort that we might ordinarily be inclined to shun—are to some extent implicit in the "special responsibilities" which we ordinarily are so anxious to embrace.

Mine is not fundamentally a historical exercise. Casual reflection upon the history of philosophy does, however, suggest that readers will be coming to my discussion from one of four broadly distinct ethical traditions. It may be useful for me to outline in advance my proposed responses to the anticipated reactions of each of these four types of reader.

First, there are the traditionalists—or, in their more modern guise, the intuitionists. They would resist the suggestion that there is any particular logic at all underlying the standard list of special responsibilities. Traditionalists-cum-intuitionists regard those as being handed down by a historical tradition (or a higher being or a sixth sense or some such) whose working is inherently mysterious to us.[13] That is one good way of denying my argument and resisting its larger implications. For if each special responsibility really were *sui generis,* a law unto itself and not derivative from any larger ethical principle, then committing ourselves to any one special responsibility (or to any set of them) would not commit us to anything beyond that. And much the same would be true on the weaker version of the traditionalist-cum-intuitionist's argument, which holds merely that there is no *single* thing that is common to all those standard special responsibilities. If there were an irreducible multiplicity of ethical principles underlying all those responsibilities, then (unless those underlying principles were remarkably well ordered) it would not be at all clear what if any further responsibilities would follow from those principles.

These are serious challenges to my argument. I shall say little that is directly addressed to them, however. The reason is simply that the best way to refute either version of the traditionalist-cum-intuitionist's claim is to show that there *is* some unified, coherent ethical principle from which all those special responsibilities can plausibly be derived. The first challenge argues that there is no general account at all; the second, that there is no single, coherent account. Both are automatically refuted when in chapter 4 I show that the vulnerability model I offer provides just such an account of all those special responsibilities that we traditionally acknowledge.

The burden of this argument will obviously have to be carried by chapter 4 below. For now, I merely want to emphasize that I am not assuming in advance that there has to be a single, coherent explanation for all these diverse ethical phenomena. That is something to be proven, not something simply to

---

13. For a critique of the intuitionist line on special responsibilities, see Pettit and Goodin (1985).

be presumed. My argument is not that all these special responsibilities should necessarily fit into some larger pattern but merely that they all do and that certain things follow (at least presumptively) from that fact. Once I have shown that all those special responsibilities that we do acknowledge fit the vulnerability model, the burden shifts to my opponents to explain why we should not accept all the other responsibilities that that selfsame model implies. They might be able to produce an answer, although I am unable to see what it might be. But surely at this point the logic of the argument requires them to produce an answer. Failing that, they would be obliged to follow the vulnerability model where it leads, which is, as chapter 6 shows, to a broader notion of social responsibility than the one currently embraced.

If the traditionalist represents the most primitive form of moral consciousness, the voluntarist represents the Enlightenment reaction. On his analysis, described more fully in chapter 3 below, special responsibilities derive their moral force from the fact that they have been voluntarily self-assumed. Self-assumed responsibilities are indeed special in a number of ways. Unlike general moral responsibilities, they are not timeless: they did not exist until we created them; and at least in some cases we may be able to terminate (discharge or extinguish) them. Furthermore, and more to the present point, self-assumed responsibilities are not universal. General moral rights and duties are the same for everyone. Special moral responsibilities, in contrast, are assumed *by* specific people *with respect to* specific other people (Hart 1955, 188).

Finally, and most importantly in the present context, self-assumed responsibilities are said to be special in the sense of being especially binding. In chapter 2 this feature is discussed more fully. For now, suffice it to say that at the very least the special responsibilities we have created provide an additional reason for action, over and above any that might arise from our general moral duties.[14] This necessarily entails some watering down of our general moral responsibilities: our limited stock of time, attention, and resources must now be divided among some extra claimants; and honoring our special obligations therefore means defaulting to some greater or lesser extent on our other more general ones.[15] The upshot is that the select few whom we have brought

14. Our special responsibility to repay a benefactor is "specially binding," according to Sir David Ross (1930, 30), because "a benefactor is not only a man, calling for our effort on his behalf on that ground, but also our benefactor, calling for our *special* effort on *that* ground."

15. Bernard Williams (1981, 18) acknowledges that since "such things as deep attachments to other persons will express themselves in the world in ways which cannot at the same time embody the impartial view," they inevitably "run the risk of offending against it" (see similarly Sandel 1982, 179). Jonathan Edwards complains bitterly of this. In a passage reminiscent of Rousseau's (1762b, bk. 2, chap. 3) analysis of "partial associations," Edwards (1765, chap. 2) protests that "he that is influenced by private affection, not subordinate to a regard to being in general, sets up its particular or limited object above being in general; and this most naturally tends to enmity against the latter . . . even as the setting up another prince as supreme in any kingdom, distinct from the lawful sovereign, naturally tends to enmity against the lawful sovereign."

into special relationships with ourselves get more than would be their due under our general moral obligations, and everyone else gets less. On the model of self-incurred obligations, all of this looks perfectly legitimate.

This is a powerful challenge to my argument, and I shall devote the bulk of this book to meeting it. I propose to attack the voluntarist's argument at what I regard as its strongest point. Presumably what makes his argument so attractive is that it promises to allow us to hold onto our strong intuitions about our special responsibilities while at the same time sparing us any more general ones. As I shall show in chapter 4, however, the voluntarist account does not underwrite anything like all the standard special responsibilities in anything like their present form. That discovery forces an awkward choice upon the voluntarist: either he can stick to his theory and maintain that our special responsibilities really do stop far short of where we ordinarily suppose; or else he can capitulate, subsuming his theory within my larger vulnerability model and conceding that our social responsibilities really do extend well beyond those we presently recognize. Either response leads to consequences that are, to some extent, counterintuitive. But conceding broader responsibilities seems to do far less violence to our ordinary moral intuitions and associated background theories—especially since, as shown in the discussion of promises and contracts (chap. 4), the vulnerability model subsumes and supplements the voluntarist's model rather than repudiating it altogether.

Third and fourth are a pair of post-Enlightenment schools, loosely associated with utilitarianism and Kant. I need say little to persuade utilitarians or their closer cousins to embrace either my principle of protecting the vulnerable or the broader political conclusions that follow from it. Anyone starting from those premises will regard the injunction to "protect the vulnerable" as just a special case of the injunction to "maximize utility" (or "maximize distribution-weighted utility" or "maximize the primary goods of the worst-off"). And anyone starting from such premises will, similarly, be independently predisposed to embrace all the broader responsibilities that are shown, in chapter 6, to follow from the principle of protecting the vulnerable.

It is the Kantian, and the nonconsequentialist more generally, who might be thought to be harder to reconcile to the present argument. That is not so much because Kantians would necessarily take violent exception to the practical implications of my argument: after all, Kant himself advocates a duty of mutual aid. The biggest sticking points for the Kantian would be with the derivation and the fundamentally consequentialistic structure of my principle. The point of protecting the vulnerable is precisely that in doing so we produce good consequences (i.e., promote the welfare of the vulnerable people we are protecting). Of course, such an emphasis upon consequences would necessarily be an anathema to any thoroughgoing *anti*consequentialist. But few nonconsequentialists are as radical as all that: they do not deny consequences any role whatsoever in moral reckoning; they merely deny them an exclusive role. Hence, all I have to do to square my analysis with nonconsequentialists of this more ordinary stripe is to show that the consequentialistic considerations implicit in the principle I am advocating are broadly consistent with the nonconsequentialistic constraints that characterize standard Kantian-style moralities. That, as I show in chapter 5, is likely often to be true.

In short, the two major ethical traditions that would staunchly resist my efforts at broadening our social responsibilities can be shown to be inferior to the vulnerability model in their account of the special responsibilities that we already acknowledge. The other two major traditions prescribe roughly the same broadening of our social responsibilities as the vulnerability model, and arguably for roughly the same reasons. This is the claim that I shall attempt to sustain throughout the next several chapters.

Of course, there is nothing absolutely conclusive in showing that my arguments can stand up to all the major sorts of challenges that can be anticipated from all the major traditions. There might always be a new twist on an old theme, or a new theme altogether might emerge. But such a demonstration at least puts a heavy burden upon those who would shun the broader responsibilities my argument imposes to produce some dramatic new justification for their position.

2

A Hierarchy of Moral Duties

W hat worries me, what prompts me to write this book, is the way in which special responsibilities tend to ride roughshod over our general duties to aid unspecified others. The bulk of the book is devoted to arguing that that should not be so, or that it should not be so to anything like the extent it is today. Before arguing that it should not be so, however, I need first to establish that it is so. This chapter is, accordingly, devoted to fixing the place of that proposition in the existing philosophical literature.

O ne explanation of why, traditionally, it is thought that special duties should take priority over general duties of aid builds on the distinction between duties arising out of considerations of *justice* and those arising out of *charity* or *benevolence*. Discharging our special responsibilities, especially insofar as those responsibilities are seen to have been voluntarily self-assumed, is ordinarily regarded as a matter of justice. Duties falling under that heading are duties to specific other individuals, who may legitimately enter claims against us for the particular performances that are their due. Denying those claims would constitute a clear case of injustice to identifiable individuals.

Such positive duties as we have to assist others in general are, in contrast, ordinarily analyzed as duties of charity or benevolence.[1] These are, in the terms Kant takes from natural (and ultimately Roman) law, "imperfect" duties, duties owed to no claimant in particular. "Duties of charity . . . require us to contribute to one or another of a large number of eligible recipients, no one of whom can claim our contribution from us as his due" (Feinberg 1980, 144).[2] A person who never makes any charitable contributions at all would

---

1. Notice the remark of Philippa Foot (1978, 45): "A culpable failure to come to the aid of someone whose life is threatened is normally contrary, not to justice, but to charity. But where one man is under contract, explicit or implicit, to come to the aid of another, injustice too will be shown." A contractual obligation is, of course, a classic case of a special responsibility according to the conventional wisdom. For a powerful critique of the "charity" model, with particular application to international distributive justice, see Nagel (1977).
2. See also Mill (1863, chap. 5), Brandt (1959, 439), and Lyons (1982, 46–48).

certainly be morally deficient. (Even then, we would describe him as "immoral" but not, strictly speaking, "unjust.") In declining to contribute to any particular needy individual, however, he would be entirely within his rights, and guilty of neither injustice nor even impropriety.[3] No particular individual can claim to have been wronged even by a person's decision never to perform any acts of charity at all or by his decision to perform them for one person rather than another. After all, no one has any legitimate claim either to that particular resource or against that particular person.

Perhaps for the simple reason that there are legitimate claimants who stand to be disappointed in the case of justice but not in the case of charity, duties of justice are ordinarily thought to take precedence over those of charity. Only after all the claims of the former have been met may we properly turn our attention to the latter. In Sidgwick's (1874, 242) phrase, "Benevolence begins where Justice ends."

It is all well and good in theory to say that charity should pick up where justice leaves off. The crucial question then, however, becomes exactly where justice *does* leave off; and my objection is precisely that the peculiar notion of "justice" at work here has been expanded so far that the notion of "charity," so called, hardly ever gets a chance to operate. Subsuming "special responsibilities" under the heading of justice vastly expands the range of claims that enjoy this kind of priority. If justice takes precedence over charity, and meeting all our special responsibilities is a matter of justice, then there might be (and, typically, there will be) very few resources left for charity to dispense.[4]

Perversely enough, meeting our special responsibilities might even be thought to *extinguish* our charitable obligations. These, after all, are imperfect duties. We only have to make a few donations to any of a large class of eligible recipients in order to discharge them. What makes recipients "eligible" is left typically unclear. What is clear, however, is that eligibility is not strictly confined to the neediest. While some of the eligible recipients may be more needy than others, donations to any of those who count as eligible will suffice to discharge these obligations of charity. Now, under some circumstances anyway, donating to the neediest people with whom we enjoy special relationships—our neediest relatives, neighbors, clients, or compatriots—may be regarded as discharging this general obligation to give to the needy. Thus, special obligations not only take priority over our general duties of charity but may even, in this way, take the place of them.

---

3. See, e.g., Anscombe (1967), Taurek (1977, 297ff.), and Fried (1979).
4. Perhaps claims of justice do not have *absolute* priority over claims of charity. It is nonetheless clear that the former weigh much more heavily than the latter, at least according to the conventional wisdom. Even in a court of purely moral appeals, few juries would regard it as an adequate defense against charges of breach of contract to say that the money was paid instead to someone who needed it more.

A more elaborate analysis of the way in which special duties tyrannize over general ones would draw upon the distinctions between general duties and special obligations on the one hand and positive and negative duties on the other. These categories cut across one another, yielding the four cells of table 1.

Table 1   Varieties of Moral Duties

	Negative duties	Positive duties
General duties	I	IV
Special obligations	II	III

The best brief discription of the distinction between general duties and special obligations comes from Hart's classic essay, "Are There Any Natural Rights?" which was responsible for introducing these terms into the modern moral lexicon. Hart writes,

> When rights arise out of special transactions between individuals or out of some special relationship in which they stand to each other, both the persons who have the right and those who have the corresponding obligation are limited to the parties to the special transaction or relationship. I call such rights special rights to distinguish them from those moral rights which are thought of as rights against (i.e., as imposing obligations upon) everyone. (Hart 1955, 183)

The distinction between positive and negative duties basically amounts to "a distinction between what we owe people in the form of aid and what we owe them in the way of non-interference" (Foot 1978, 27). Negative duties are ones that oblige us to "refrain from some act which would operate to the prejudice" of someone else; positive duties are ones that oblige us to undertake "some positive act" to benefit another (Salmond 1957, 283). Positive duties are duties to help; negative duties are duties not to harm.[5]

According to the traditional wisdom, within the class of general duties negative duties are much more strict and binding than positive ones. In terms of the classification in table 1, duties of class I are far stronger than those of

---

5. In his reinterpretation of John Stuart Mill, Lyons (1982, 50), rightly emphasizes that there is an important distinction between "acts for the positive benefit of others" and "positive acts for the benefit of others." In the latter case, the benefit might merely be "the prevention or elimination of harm." The conventional wisdom is grievously at fault in equating "positive acts" with the production of "positive benefits" and "negative acts" (i.e., omissions) with the "prevention of harm." Actually, a great many "positive acts" might be required to prevent harm and a great many "negative acts" to produce positive benefits. (See similarly Bennet 1981, 72ff.; 1983.) This is just one of many ways the conventional wisdom mistakes a morally unimportant distinction (between positive and negative acts) for a morally significant one (between providing positive benefits and merely preventing harm). I shall return to this point in the closing pages of this chapter.

class IV. This is particularly apparent from the way the law tends to enshrine negative duties but not, generally, positive ones.

The relative supremacy of negative over positive duties has long been established. Among the "absolute duties . . . such as oblige all men antecedently to any human institution," Pufendorf (1672, bk. 1, chap. 1, sec. 1) ranked "first and noblest" the requirement "that no man hurt another."[6] By Sidgwick's day, this had become a central tenet in the modern liberal faith:

> Freedom from interference is really the whole of what human beings, originally and apart from contracts, can be strictly said to *owe* to each other: at any rate, the protection of this Freedom (including the enforcement of Free Contract) is the sole proper aim of Law, i.e. of those rules of mutual behaviour which are maintained by penalties inflicted under the authority of Government. (Sidgwick 1874, 274)

Whether or not it is the "sole proper aim of Law," this is clearly thought to be the first task that should be performed by any system of social order. Nonmaleficence—the duty not to harm others—constitutes the common thread linking criminal and civil (especially tort) law, both historically and analytically (Maine 1861, chap. 10; Devlin 1965, 26–27). Modern lawyers may regard it as an exaggeration to say, as does Blackstone (1783, vol. 4, p. 5), that "every public offense is also a private wrong and somewhat more"; but an essentially individualistic concept of harm does nonetheless lie at the core of the criminal law (Kleinig 1978). Indeed, as Hart (1955, 175) brilliantly demonstrates, "forbearance . . . from the use of coercion or restraint" is the fundamental background norm against which all our other rights are set.

While negative duties not to harm others are well ensconced in the law, positive duties to help others are only rarely enjoined. Jurists tell us

> There is no distinction more deeply rooted in the common law and more fundamental than that between misfeasance and non-feasance, between active misconduct working positive injury to others and passive inaction, a failure to take positive steps to benefit others, or to protect them from harm not created by any wrongful act of the defendant. (Bohlen, 1908, 219; see also Weinrib 1980, 250–58)

Modern textbooks still quote approvingly Macaulay's "Notes on the Indian Penal Code":

6. This idea is, of course, ancient in its origins. Yet it only seems to have come fully to life in early modern political theory. Pufendorf's argument for this proposition is also strikingly modern: "It is the most necessary of human duties, in as much as the life of society cannot possibly be maintained without it. For suppose a man to do me no good, and not so much as to transact with me in the common offices of life, yet provided he do me no harm, I can live with him under some tolerable comfort and quiet. . . . It is at the same time the most easy [duty] to be performed, consisting for the most part purely in a negative abstinence from acting" (Pufendorf 1672, bk. 3, chap. 1, sec. 1).

> It is . . . most highly desirable that men should not merely abstain from doing
> harm to their neighbours, but should render [them] active services. . . . In
> general, however, the penal law must content itself with keeping men from
> doing positive harm . . . . We must grant impunity to the vast majority
> of . . . omissions, . . . and must content ourselves with punishment only
> when they are distinguished from the rest by some circumstances which mark
> them out as peculiarly fit objects of penal legislation. (Macaulay 1837, 497;
> quoted in Williams 1961, 3–4)

Legal principles sometimes constitute an inadequate guide to our real moral
commitments. That may well be so in the present case. Certainly, moral philosophers are less comfortable than lawyers in saying that there is *no* duty to
render positive assistance to others in need. Perhaps we have no moral "duty
of rescue" where that would entail exposing ourselves to grave dangers, but
surely we have a "duty of *easy* rescue" (Weinrib 1980). Although we may
have no moral duty to be a Very Good (much less a Splendid) Samaritan, we
are morally bound to be a Minimally Decent Samaritan (Thomson 1971). On
this point, moral intuitions seem to have shifted little from the early modern
times.[7]

While recognizing some general duties of beneficence that the law would
not acknowledge, moral philosophers nevertheless concede that the duty of
nonmaleficence is "of a more stringent character . . . . Even when we have
come to recognize a duty of beneficence, the duty of nonmaleficence is recognized as a distinct one, and as *prima facie* more binding" (Ross 1930, 21–
22). Ross offers a pair of examples to motivate this conclusion: "We should
not in general consider it justifiable to kill one person in order to keep another
alive, or to steal from one in order to give alms to another." In Philippa
Foot's twist on these examples:

> Most of us allow people to die of starvation in India and Africa, and there is
> surely something wrong with us that we do; it would be nonsense, however, to
> pretend that it is only in law that we make the distinction between allowing
> people in the underdeveloped countries to die of starvation and sending them
> poisoned food. There is worked into our moral system a distinction between
> what we owe people in the form of aid and what we owe them in the way of
> non-interference. (Foot 1978, 26–27)

Such reasoning leads philosophers to conclude that "our morality takes it to

---

7. Notice, for example, the words of Pufendorf (1682, bk. 1, chap. 8): "Especially it is regarded
as contemptible malignity and inhumanity, not to bestow willingly upon others those blessings
which can be accorded without loss, trouble or labor to ourselves. . . . Thus it is not right to
waste food, after we have sated ourselves, nor to stop up a spring, or hide it, after we have had
enough to drink, nor to destroy aids to navigation or road-marks after we have used them. Here
belong moderate alms bestowed by the rich upon the needy; also that kindness which is shown
with good reason to travelers, especially when some misfortune has overtaken them; and other
things of the sort." See similarly Sidgwick (1874, 253), Singer (1972), Walzer (1981, 2–3), and
Fishkin (1982, chap. 8).

be worse to harm someone than to refuse to help someone," and to consider this proposition to be one of the first facts that any moral theory must attempt to explain (Harman 1975, 13). In morals as well as in law, then, negative duties seem far stronger than positive ones.

Negative duties seem decisively to outweigh positive ones where general duties are concerned, but do not appear to do so where special obligations are involved.[8] "Unlike the general public, : . . special classes of persons such as bodyguards, firemen or doctors"—those who have some special responsibility for rendering positive assistance—"are not within their rights if they merely refrain from interfering and do not try to sustain life" (Foot 1978, 50–51). If you have a duty to act, or merely to prevent certain results from occurring (Fletcher 1976), and fail to do so, then "blame becomes particularly appropriate" (Fitzgerald 1967, 136; see also Hughes 1958). To use Macaulay's legalistic examples:

> A. omits to give Z. food, and by that omission voluntarily causes Z.'s death. Is this murder? . . . It is murder if A. was Z.'s gaoler, directed by the law to furnish Z. with food. It is murder if Z. was the infant child of A., and had therefore a legal right to sustenance. . . . It is murder if Z. was a bedridden invalid, and A. a nurse hired to feed Z. . . . It is not murder if Z. is a beggar, who has no other claim on A. than that of humanity.

> A. omits to tell Z. that a river is swollen so high that Z. cannot safely attempt to ford it, and by this omission voluntarily causes Z.'s death. This is murder, if A. is a person stationed by authority to warn travellers attempting to ford the river. It is murder if A. is a guide who had contracted to conduct Z. It is not murder if A. is a person on whom Z. had no other claim than that of humanity. (Macaulay 1837, 495)

Just as a person is legally blameworthy if he omits to discharge his special legal obligations, so too would he be deserving of severe moral censure if he failed to discharge his special moral obligations (Pufendorf 1672, bk. 3, chap. 1, sec. 4; Foot 1978, 24). Both in law and in morals, failing to discharge a positive duty when you have some special responsibility for doing so constitutes an "onerous offense" rather than as a "mere omission." Where those special responsibilities give rise to both positive and negative duties, neglecting one kind of duty seems to be neither necessarily better nor necessarily worse than neglecting the other. In the terms of table 1, duties of classes II and III are more or less on a par. Neither type systematically outweighs the

---

8. Sharply distinguishing between general duties and special obligations here helps us to avoid the difficulties which Davis (1980) finds in Foot's (1978, 29) rather obscure comment that "it clearly makes a difference whether our positive duty is a strict duty [i.e., arising out of a special responsibility] or rather an act of charity: feeding our own children or feeding those in faraway countries."

other.[9] This finding will prove to be of particular importance in the argument in chapter 5 below.

So far I have been discussing priorities *within* the categories of general duties and special obligations, respectively. Now we must look *across* those categories. First, let us consider the relative priorities of our special obligations and the stronger type of general duties: negative duties not to harm other people. Here the answer is fairly apparent. "It is not . . . permissible to commit a murder to bring one's starving children food" (Foot 1978, 28). Even if strong special responsibilities were at stake, our negative duty not to harm others in general would ordinarily take priority over any positive duty to aid specific others.[10]

Now, this priority is not quite categorical. Nancy Davis (1980, 187), replying to Foot's example, remarks, "We tend to think that it is permissible to steal a loaf of bread . . . to get the starving children fed." But such cases are rare.[11] Besides, the exception Davis claims is really quite weak. Notice that it is merely *permissible,* not obligatory, to steal the bread to feed the children. When you have the food or the money to buy it, then omitting your positive duty to feed your children constitutes murder, just as surely as if you had poisoned them; but if you lack the resources, you are excused from that positive duty (Macaulay 1837, 494–95). Certainly at law, and most probably morally as well, it is not obligatory (even in a prima facie sense) to feed your children if you have to steal in order to do so. At most it might, as Davis says, be permissible. The children may still get fed. Indeed, given what we know of the psychological dynamics of parenthood, it would be most surprising if

9. Special negative duties are often results oriented (being duties not to harm someone) rather than action oriented (being duties not to do something). It is the latter, "agent-centered restrictions" on *actions*, that Scheffler (1982) argues against.

Special negative duties might be a subspecies of agent-centered prerogatives; i.e., they might be imposed by virtue of the agent's exercising his prerogatives to assume those duties (as, e.g., when signing an employment contract obliging him not to reveal company secrets). However, they cannot all be assimilated to agent-centered prerogatives in this way. The parent's duty not to harm his own child is not imposed by virtue of any voluntary self-assumption, nor is it merely a duty imposed on parents to see to it that children per se (their neighbors' as much as their own) are not harmed. These sorts of special negative duties really are agent-centered restrictions, and ones which cause far more trouble for Scheffler's thesis than the standard deontological niceties about "clean hands" which he dismisses so easily.

10. Indeed, it is doubtful that special relationships have any bearing at all upon negative duties. A murder is a murder whether the deceased is cousin, compatriot, or a stranger (Haksar 1979, 41–42). Parfit (1983b, 36) argues similarly that, although "the U.S. government ought in general to give priority to the welfare of its own citizens, . . . this does not apply to the infliction of grave harms. Suppose this government decided to resume atmospheric nuclear tests. If it predicts that the resulting fallout would cause several deaths, should it discount the deaths of aliens? Should it therefore move the tests to the Indian Ocean? It seems plausible to claim that, in such a case, the special relations make no moral difference."

11. In the elipsed portion of the quotation, Davis (1980, 187) adds parenthetically "or perhaps even to break an arm." Most people, I daresay, would think that is going too far. Nozick (1974, 66) regards arm breaking as precisely the sort of thing we want moral side constraints to protect us against. His intuitions on this point seem by far the more standard ones.

people did not take advantage of this permission. Here, however, it is the moral rather than psychological strength of duties which concerns us. In moral terms, it is safe to say that general negative duties of class I in table 1 weigh far more, albeit not infinitely more, heavily than either the positive or negative special obligations of classes II and III.

For my purposes, it is the final comparison that is of most interest: how do our positive duties to aid others in general stack up against our special responsibilities to help or protect from harm specific individuals with whom we enjoy special relationships? The general principle, enunciated by Parfit (1979b, 556; 1984, 95, 485) is that "carrying out these obligations . . . to the people to whom we stand in certain [special] relations . . . has priority over helping strangers." In Dickens's *Bleak House* (Pinker 1979, 3–4), Mrs. Jellyby's "telescopic philanthropy," which led her to help distant Africans while neglecting her own children, made her the object of ridicule. Philosophers quite agree that she should be ridiculed. To use an example owing to Bernard Williams, if you were in a fiery air crash and able to pull out only one other victim, you should save your own child rather than the distinguished surgeon sitting on the other side of you.[12]

Some commentators go so far as to say that in cases in which your special obligations to family or friends are greatly at stake, any general obligation you may have to strangers becomes purely supererogatory: it is above and beyond the call of duty. For some commentators this is merely a matter of moral realism, of tailoring our principles to fit man's limited psychological capabilities (Parfit 1979b); for others, it seems to be a positively desirable feature of our moral system (Fried 1979). Such cases, the latter say, constitute "instances of laudable loyalties." "What is loyalty," they ask, "if not a special sort of favoritism—the singling out of a subset of the population that one is justified or perhaps even obligated to count as being of greater importance than persons generally?" (Gorovitz 1977, 134)[13]

Thus, in terms of the categories of table 1, both the positive and negative

---

12. Hare (1981, 138) reports Williams's teasing him with his example in a broadcast debate, and Williams (1981, 17–18) has committed himself in print to much the same proposition. Here Williams is, of course, merely updating Godwin's (1793, bk. 2, chap. 2) example of a burning house, taking the side of the mother over that of Archbishop Fenelon. Blum (1980, 49–51) adapts the example as follows: "Suppose that I am in a train crash in which many people are injured, including my best friend (but not myself). I am certainly generally justified in giving my first attention to my friend." The convenient thing about wrecked trains, for these purposes, is that they do not explode; Blum can therefore make his principle more appealing by insisting that you then go back and help strangers. Still, he does insist that "it is . . . inappropriate for us at the outset to apportion our help impartially—solely according to need—ignoring the fact that one of the persons is our friend." That presumably means that Blum thinks you should allow nonfriends to die while giving prior attention to less seriously injured friends, rather as Williams seems to suggest. In his notes on an earlier version of my manuscript, John Kleinig (pers. com. 1983) has asked (I suspect only half jokingly), "What are friends for?"

13. See also Orwell (1949, 366–67), Blum (1980), Oldenquist (1982), and Winkler (1982).

special duties of classes II and III are ordinarily thought to weigh far more heavily that the positive duties of class IV to aid others in general. "This priority is not absolute," as Parfit concedes. "We may not believe that I ought to save my child from some minor harm rather than saving a stranger's life. But I ought to protect my child rather than saving strangers from somewhat greater harms" (Parfit 1979b, 556; 1984, 95, 485).

Close inspection of Parfit's phrasing, however, reveals what a limited qualification he is offering. Note especially the comparative confidence with which he makes each of these two judgments. When a stranger's life is at stake, the most Parfit can say is that "we *may* not believe" that it is wrong to allow my child to suffer some slight injury; when only somewhat greater harm to strangers is in prospect, Parfit is quite sure that "I *ought* to protect my child." Thus, it seems clear in Parfit's mind that the priority of special obligations over general positive duties, while not *quite* absolute, is very strong indeed. Here he seems to be broadly in accord with conventional moral judgments. Ordinarily, it would be deemed the height of irresponsibility for me to subject my children to any appreciable risk of serious bodily harm in order to save others from even a very much greater risk of similar fates. No yachtsman with all his family on board should sail into treacherous waters to save others who are drowning, and so on.[14]

Quite serious consequences follow from all this. Creating these special responsibilities has not merely introduced another consideration to be weighed alongside all our preexisting moral duties. That would be bad enough: it would skew our moral concerns, boosting the entitlements of those with whom we enjoy special relationships and reducing those of people with whom we do not. What is worse is that the special obligations are particularly strong; they usually (if not quite always) outweigh our general duties to aid unspecified others. Our general duties are not merely forced to share our limited moral resources with some extra new claimants but to share with— and, far more often than not, yield to—particularly voracious new claimants. In this way, special responsibilities typically tend to deflect us badly from our ordinary moral course. That would be no bad thing provided that some convincing moral justification could be offered for special responsibilities with

---

14. Haksar (1979, 38–41) tries to be even more noncommittal in discussing this priority. He writes: "Other things being equal you have greater duty towards your child than towards mine"; and "Other things being equal one's positive obligations to one's own countrymen are greater, just as your obligations to give food to your child is much greater than any obligation that you may have to give food to my child other things being equal." This, however, yields only a very weak ordering of our obligations. Other things are rarely equal, and all the hard, interesting cases come where they are not. Haksar's comment that our special obligations are not only "greater" but "much greater" is revealing. It suggests that he has in mind a weighting, not just a ranking, of obligations and that in that schema positive special obligations weigh far more heavily than positve general ones.

such priority. It is the argument of this book, however, that there is no such justification.

The problem, then, is that according to the conventional moral wisdom negative duties not to harm others "trump" special duties, which in turn trump positive duties to aid others. My aim is to raise the status of these latter duties and, in that way, to prevent our duties to aid others in general from being overridden by our special duties to particular others quite so systematically as that conventional wisdom suggests. This goal can be accomplished in either of two ways: negating the distinction between positive and negative duties or assimilating positive general duties to the stronger form of special duties.

The more radical approach would be to try to undercut the distinction between positive and negative duties. Often conclusions appear to be based upon certain commonsensical notions of what an act consists in (e.g., bodily movements); these distinctions clearly cannot withstand close philosophical scrutiny. It is far from clear that champions of the distinction can offer tenable substitutes. If omissions are analytically indistinguishable from acts, then the distinction between positive and negative duties also collapses (Davis 1980). Were we to consider "the act of withholding a benefit" to be just as much of an act as "the act of retracting a benefit," then every positive duty to provide someone with a benefit could be described, equivalently, as a negative duty not to perform the act of withholding benefits.

Even if it were possible to establish an analytic distinction between acts and omissions, positive and negative duties, what moral importance attached to that distinction per se would remain unclear. What *is* clear is that various other considerations of undeniable moral significance are commonly, but only contingently, associated with harmful acts (breaches of negative duties) rather than with omissions (breaches of positive duties to provide aid). Once all these other considerations are factored out, there may be little or nothing of moral significance left in the original distinction.[15]

If it *can* be shown that acts and omissions, negative and positive duties, *are* morally equivalent, then we will have to adjust our preanalytic intuitions accordingly. We will have to treat positive and negative duties equally, which means either weakening our prohibitions on harming others or strengthening our insistence on helping them. Presumably we are sufficiently persuaded of the importance of not harming one another that if confronted with that choice,

15. Breaches of negative duties (i.e., immoral acts) typically constitute a failure to discharge obligations, whereas breaches of positive duties (i.e., omissions) merely constitute failures to perform supererogatory acts. Immoral acts actually make someone worse off, omissions merely mean that someone has failed to gain more than he previously had; and assuming diminishing marginal utility, it is more important to people to avoid losing $X than it is to gain $X. Furthermore, breaches of negative duties tend to cause harms more directly, whereas the harms resulting from breaches of positive duties tend to be more indirect (Goodin 1982b, chap. 1; see also Glover 1977, chap. 7; Bennett 1981; 1983; Lichtenberg 1982).

we would be driven to the solution of strengthening positive duties. The status of duties to aid would thereby be elevated, just as I desire.

Kleinig (1976) effectively pursues this strategy in his argument for Good Samaritan laws, which would make it legally obligatory for us to aid others in distress, at least whenever we could do so without endangering ourselves (see similarly Lichtenberg 1981; 1982). The knee-jerk philosophical response to arguments like Kleinig's is, however, to rally to the defense of the distinction between acts and omissions, between negative and positve duties (Mack 1980). That defense seems to me ill grounded. Surely we could, by building on Ryle's (1973) arguments, show that at least some omissions constitute "active non-doings" and hence might be rendered punishable as criminal offenses. The philosophical ruts that are sure to be encountered in pursuing any such strategy, however, are so deeply worn that it hardly seems worth trying to pursue it directly.

Here I shall adopt the other approach to trying to upgrade positive duties. For the moment, I shall not quarrel with the conventional assumption that negative general duties "trump" special ones and that special ones "trump" positive general ones. What I argue, instead, is that many of those duties which we would have regarded as merely positive duties to aid others in general turn out upon further analysis to be indistinguishable at root from special duties. Both types of duties, I argue, are predicated on the vulnerability of one party to another. In this way, I put many so-called positive general duties morally on a par with our allegedly stronger special duties to our families, friends, and so forth.

In Kleinig's (1976, 383) terms, I am going after Bad Levites—those who, in the Biblical parable, breach their special responsibilities (there, to help fellow Levites)—rather that after merely Bad Samaritans, who breach no more than a general duty to aid others in need. I expand the number of people to whom we owe moral duties that are theoretically indistinguishable from our classically special duties. I hope thereby to show that what would ordinarily be described as merely ungenerous acts are actually far worse than that. They show us to be Bad Levites rather than merely Bad Samaritans.

The same strategy can also effectively undermine the putative priority of duties of justice over duties of charity or humanity. For the sake of argument, I shall assume once again that there is a real distinction here: to say that something is unjust is to say that it is wrong for certain distinctive sorts of reasons quite unlike those on which claims of a lack of charity or humanity are based.[16] My strategy will not be to deny the analytic distinction but instead to deny that any moral importance attaches to it. My aim will be to show that precisely the same sorts of considerations that make duties of justice morally binding—considerations relating to the particular vulnerability of one person

16. As is argued by, e.g., Campbell (1974), Passmore (1979), and Barry (1982, 226).

to another—also give rise to far more extensive duties of charity or humanity. The effect of that is to put duties like charity or humanity morally on a par with those of justice and to say that (depending on the circumstances) charity can be every bit as compelling as justice, narrowly construed.[17]

17. It is often remarked, but always in passing, that saying that duties of humanity are analytically distinct from duties of justice is not to say that they are necessarily any the less strong for that reason alone. Indeed, we "may even . . . be led to give priority to humanity over justice in those cases where they conflict" (Campbell 1974, 16; see also Barry 1982, 226). Thomson (1971, 63) makes a similar distinction in discussing the rights of a fetus to the use of its mother's body: "we would conclude that she is self-centered, callous, indecent, but not unjust, if she refuses. The complaints are not less grave; they are just different." Hart (1958, 83), in arguing that that bundle of notions associated with the concept of justice (rights, obligations, duties, etc.) represents merely one realm of moral discourse, similarly concedes that we need to look to some other realm altogether for concepts befitting "the blacker moral offenses." Such concessions are often made, but curiously enough their implications are never thoroughly worked through.

3

Grounds of Special Responsibilities

L ike all propositions of common-sense morality, the supposition that we have special responsibilities toward some people but not toward others is rooted most firmly in our intuitions about concrete cases. It may be hard to characterize these special responsibilities in any general terms, but "the mere enumeration of them is not difficult." Sidgwick's list would probably still seem pretty standard:

> We should all agree that each of us is bound to show kindness to his parents and spouse and children, and to other kinsmen in a less degree: and to those who have rendered services to him, and any others whom he may have admitted to his intimacy and called friends: and perhaps we may say to those of our own race more than to black or yellow men, and generally to human beings in proportion to their affinity to ourselves. And to our country as a corporate whole we believe ourselves to owe the greatest sacrifices when occasion calls . . . : and a similar obligation seems to be recognized, though less definitely and in a less degree, as regards minor corporations of which we are members. And to all men with whom we may be brought into relation we are held to owe slight services, and such as may be rendered without inconvenience: but those who are in distress or urgent need have a claim on us for special kindness. (Sidgwick 1874, 246)

It is not particularly difficult to detect some larger patterns in this compendium. Each writer offers his own slightly different scheme for grouping these various common-sense duties into a few more general categories. By merging the proposals of various authors, however, we arrive at the following sort of standard list:

1. "Duties arising out of comparatively permanent relationships not voluntarily chosen, such as Kindred and in most cases Citizenship and Neighbourhood" (Sidgwick 1874, 248; Hart 1955, 187)

2. "Those of similar relationships voluntarily contracted" (Sidgwick 1874, 248), be they bilateral as in the cases of commercial contracts (Feinberg 1980, 130–31) and friendship (Sidgwick 1874, 248), or unilateral as in the cases of promises (Ross 1930, 31; Hart 1955, 184; Feinberg 1980, 131) and the authorization of another to act on one's behalf (Hart 1955, 187)

3. "Those that spring from special services received," such as duties of gratitude reciprocating a benefactor's past assistance (Sidgwick 1874, 248; Ross 1930, 21; Hart 1955, 185–86; Feinberg 1980, 133), or analogously, reparation compensating victims for past wrongs (Ross 1930, 21; Feinberg 1980, 133)

4. "Those that seem due to special need, or duties of Pity" (Sidgwick 1874, 248)

The question remains what, if anything, all these responsibilities have in common. One answer might be Nothing. Logically, it is perfectly possible that each of these special responsibilities is *sui generis* or that all of them are derived from an irreducible multiplicity of ethical principles. The suggestion that that is in fact the case constitutes the traditionalist-cum-intuitionist challenge to my argument (chap. 1). The best way to meet that challenge is simply to do what these opponents claim cannot be done, namely, offer a single, coherent account of all those special responsibilities that we traditionally/intuitively acknowledge.

Here I focus, instead, upon the second challenge canvassed in chapter 1, the voluntarist challenge. That model, too, purports to offer a single, coherent account of all the standard special responsibilities. The voluntarist account is, I shall show in this chapter and the next, not as satisfactory as mine couched in terms of vulnerability. If either the voluntarist account or my own is true, however, the traditionalist-cum-intuitionist account must be wrong.

There are various reasons for taking as my principal foil the model that traces people's special responsibilities to some previous voluntary acts of will on their part. One reason is purely professional: voluntarism is the major competing philosophical doctrine. From the Enlightenment onward, this concept has dominated the moral stage.[1] It is hardly surprising, then, that when they have turned to the task of analyzing special responsibilities, moral philosophers have naturally tended to talk in terms of self-assumed obligations. That is, in any case, the pattern firmly established by Hart (1955) in his seminal paper "Are There Any Natural Rights?"—and, as I shall show below, it has remained the conventional philosophical wisdom to this day.

I have a practical political motive as well as a professional philosophical one in choosing as my principal foil the model of self-assumed obligations. That model, apparently virtually alone among all those that might account for our special responsibilities, would seem to justify our embracing those special responsibilities and those alone. The model of self-assumed responsibilities offers an alluring rationale for shunning any general social responsibilities over and above those we have explicitly or implicitly assumed. The best way

1. See Pateman (1979) for a brilliant analysis of the protracted attempt to analyze political obligation in these terms.

to show that it is wrong to shun general social responsibilities in this way is to show that it is wrong to suppose that all special responsibilities are necessarily self-assumed. Thus, in this and the next chapter I shall be arguing that the model of self-assumed obligations fails even to account for some of the most important features of the special responsibilities which we do ordinarily acknowledge. That means that the price of shunning any more general social responsibilities on these voluntaristic grounds is repudiating many of the special responsibilities that we are firmly convinced we should honor.

I t is to be expected that some special responsibilities will fit one of the two basic patterns, the vulnerability model or the model of self-assumed obligations, better than the other. "Facts" that are central to and well explained by one model will naturally be peripheral to and poorly explained by the other (Quine 1961, 42–46). Hence, it is important where you start, "which cases you take as clear and central and which as difficult and exceptional" (Barry 1979a, 630).

The "fact" that is most central to the standard analysis is that promises are firmly believed to create moral obligations. In modern moral philosophy, a promissory obligation is taken to be the paradigm case of a moral obligation. Other obligations are regarded as "obligations" at all (as opposed to "duties" more generally) only by analogy to promissory obligations. According to the conventional account, "obligations arise from claims validated by commitments" (Sesonske 1957, 49), the prime example of which is an oath, promise, or other solemn undertaking.

Promissory obligations are also ordinarily presumed to constitute the paradigm case of special responsibilities. Promissory obligations are obligations par excelence. Promissory obligations are also special obligations. They are commitments *by* specific people *to* specific people, and they require different performances from different people depending on the individuals' promises to one another. Promises create a metaphorical "bond" between two particular individuals, the promiser and the promisee, of just the sort that exists between people linked by special responsibilities (Hart 1961, 85). Furthermore, in the paradigm case of an obligation construed along these lines, "a prior transaction, the promise . . . , is the source of the relationship" (Brandt 1964, 386–87).

Hence, it is hardly surprising that Hart (1955, 183) should suppose that "the most obvious cases of special rights are those that arise from promises" and that he should base his whole analysis upon that supposition. In modern moral philosophy, Hart's (1955, 183–84) pioneering discussion of special rights and duties remains the locus classicus. It deserves to be quoted at length:

> By promising to do or not to do something, we voluntarily incur obligations
> and create or confer rights on those to whom we promise; we alter the existing

moral independence of the parties' freedom of choice in relation to some action and create a new moral relationship between them, so that it becomes morally legitimate for the person to whom the promise is given to determine how the promisor shall act. . . . The simplest case of promising illustrates two points characteristic of all special rights: (1) the right and obligation arise not because the promised action has itself any particular moral quality, but just because of the voluntary transaction between the parties; (2) the identity of the parties concerned is vital—only *this* person (the promisee) has the moral justification for determining how the promisor shall act. It is *his* right; only in relation to him is the promisor's freedom of choice diminished. (Hart 1955, 183–84)

Having established the promissory obligation as the paradigm case of special rights and duties, Hart goes on to discuss various "attenuated" cases. First is the situation in which a person unilaterally surrenders his rights to someone else, authorizing him to act on his behalf. Next are situations in which special rights and duties arise out of what Hart terms "mutuality of restrictions." Others would call these duties of fair play, gratitude, or indebtedness. These obligations differ from ordinary debts mainly in that they are not explicitly contracted for ahead of time.

The final and most peripheral case of special rights and duties is, for Hart, that of "a special natural relationship, as the case of parent and child" (Hart 1955, 187). Here the relationship to the paradigm case of promissory obligations is really very attenuated indeed. Hart apologizes for including the case at all, explaining that it is merely "worth mentioning because some political philosophers have had recourse to analogies with this case as an explanation of political obligation." Besides, Hart says, it is interesting to note that "even this case has some of the features we have distinguished in special rights, viz., the right arises out of the special relationship of the parties (though it is in this case a natural relationship) and not out of the character of the actions" (Hart 1955, 187). The language is clearly loaded: it is the fault of the case for not fitting Hart's model rather than that of the model for not fitting the case. Load the language as he will, Hart can hardly conceal the poorness of fit.

Taking promissory obligations as the most central instance of special rights and duties—and familial obligations as the most peripheral—leads Hart to believe that *voluntary commitments* of some sort or another must underlie all special obligations. In discussing the paradigm case of promissory obligations, Hart emphasizes that these are obligations "we voluntarily incur" (Hart 1955, 183). In the extended applications of his model, he acknowledges only minor qualifications to this general rule.

Hart concedes, for example, that "not all [special] obligations to other persons are deliberately incurred" (Hart 1955, 185). Some, such as those arising from promises, might be. But not so duties of fair play: you may have an obligation to reciprocate another's sacrifice even if you did not mean to incur this obligation. Nor, for that matter, did you mean to incur your special obligations to make restitution to those you have wronged. Still, having conceded that ''not all [special] obligations to other persons are deliberately incurred,'' Hart proceeds to reaffirm his main point: ''I think it is true of all special duties that they arise from *previous voluntary actions*'' (Hart 1955, 185, emphasis added). The special duties that arise from our having benefited from the actions of others, for example, arise only if we voluntarily put (or kept or left) ourselves in a position to benefit. It is this voluntary act on the part of the beneficiary which differentiates between the benefits which give rise to duties of repayment and those, merely foisted upon ''innocent bystanders,'' which do not (Nozick 1974, 95; cf. Pufendorf 1672, bk. 6, chap. 2, sec. 4). The same is true of duties of restitution: nobody is blamed for or required to compensate anyone for damage he has done involuntarily.

Elsewhere, Hart concedes that there are ''moral duties attached to an office or role in social life.'' These ''differ most notably'' from promissory obligations ''in that the particular duties attached to these roles (a husband's duty to support his wife, the father's to look after his children) are not conceived of as truly created by the deliberate choice of the individual'' (Hart 1958, 103). If these be contracts, they are most peculiar ones, because there is no opportunity to negotiate terms. Nevertheless, Hart assimilates these special role duties to his voluntaristic model by saying that they ''are conceived of as *assumed* by entry upon the particular role, so that one who takes up the role is thereby specially committed to discharging these duties'' (Hart 1958, 104). Of course, the word that Hart chooses to emphasize—''assumed''—has a strong voluntaristic flavor, its principal meaning, according to the *Oxford English Dictionary*, being ''to take upon oneself.''

Hart's characteristically cagey discussion abounds with qualifications, exceptions, and ambiguities. As his analysis has passed into the conventional wisdom, however, most of these have been stripped away. John Rawls (1958, 178), for example, accepts without question or qualification that ''special rights and duties . . . depend on previous actions voluntarily undertaken.'' More dramatically, Judith Jarvis Thomson (1971, 65) asserts quite bluntly: ''Surely we do not have any such 'special responsibility' for a person unless we have assumed it, explicitly or implicitly.'' Thus, according to the conventional wisdom, which Hart has done so much to shape, special rights, duties and responsibilities are thought to be incurred in consequence of some voluntary commitment of the person involved. In the shorthand that I shall adopt here, special responsibilities are said to be voluntarily self-assumed.

W e were warned in advance that the model of self-assummed responsibilities would fit some cases better than others. Of the four categories of special responsibilities introduced above, this model fits the second particularly well (''duties of relationships voluntarily contracted,'' such as commercial contracts, promises, friendships, and authorizations); and the third, perhaps tolerably well ("duties that spring from special services received," such as those of gratitude or reparation). It appears to fit the first category badly ("duties arising out of comparatively permanent relationships not voluntarily chosen, such as Kindred"); and the fourth, not at all ("duties that seem due to special need"). How serious these failings are depends upon the success of voluntarists' efforts, discussed in the next chapter, to assimilate these apparently hard cases to the promissory model; and surely the failings of any one theory must be judged in light of those of the alternative theories available. Still, the badness of fit constitutes a prima facie cause for concern with this model.

To the model of self-assumed obligations I counterpose one that builds upon the notion of *vulnerability*. I develop this more fully and explore its wider implications more carefully in chapters 5 and 6, respectively. For now, it is enough to sketch its broad outlines.

These two alternative accounts of our special responsibilities, the self-assumed-obligations and vulnerability models, bear stark witness to the importance of where you start. The model of self-assumed obligations starts from the premise that you should keep your promises. With that principle as its central tenet, however, the model is ill equiped to account for the intuition, which is every bit as compelling, that we owe something special to our own children. In my alternative model, I take that intuitive obligation as the central case, and I proceed to build a theory of our special responsibilities around it.

Consider carefully the plight of the infant. "Is there anything," Rousseau (1762a, bk. 2) asks, "so weak and wretched as a child, anything so utterly at the mercy of those about it, so dependent on their pity, their care, and their affection?" Indeed, biologists remark that the most salient feature of the human infant is its severe and protracted vulnerability. Man is more helpless for more of his life than virtually any other species. Somebody must be assigned the special responsibility of looking after the young. Who that is will, of course, be a matter for social determination: typically it will be the biological parents, at least in the first instance; but sometimes it will not. Whoever is picked out, however, the more basic point remains that those special responsibilities flow fundamentally from the child's special vulnerabilities.[2]

All this points to the more general proposition that your special responsibilities derive from the fact that other people are dependent upon you and are particularly vulnerable to your actions and choices. What seems true for chil-

---

2. "Whatever the grounds of the rights of dependency, they must be to certain sorts of care and support from others. In the case of children, the duties which correspond to these rights must in the first place be the duties of particular caretakers, whether natural parents or otherwise" (O'Neill 1982). The grounds for assigning those duties to the biological parents, at least in the first instance, are that "the right to beget or to bear is not unrestricted, but contingent upon begetters and bearers having or making some feasible plan for their child to be adequately reared by themselves or by willing others."

dren in particular also seems to be true for other kin, neighbors, countrymen, and contractors. To some greater or lesser extent, they are all especially dependent upon you to do something for them; and your varying responsibilities toward each of them seem roughly proportional to the degree to which they are, in fact, dependent upon you (and you alone) to perform certain services.[3]

In terms of the above classification of special duties, the vulnerability model gives pride of place to those of the fourth sort: duties to aid those in special need. The norm of beneficence, properly construed, does indeed require the "rich and powerful . . . [to] give to certain categories of people, [i.e.,] to the less powerful or the particularly vulnerable: to children, to the mentally and physically handicapped, to the poor, to the infirm aged" (Gouldner 1973, 280; see similarly Campbell 1974, 15; Barry 1982, 219–20). What the vulnerability model emphasizes is not just their special need, however, but also your special ability to help. That is the crucial factor in imposing the duty upon you in particular.

This is a much more plausible explanation of our special responsibility to help those urgently in need of assistance. In applying models of self-assumed obligations, we would be looking for some sort of tie between the people involved. Consider, however, Flathman's (1972, 214) compelling counterexample: "If the seriously injured A instructs B (a perfect stranger but the only person about) to call an ambulance for him, neither the legitimacy of A's request nor B's obligation to comply with it depends on B's consent." What is crucial is that B is the only person in a position to render assistance; A is utterly dependent upon B. Under such conditions, B has special responsibilities to which he did not consent and which are not self-assumed in any sense of the term. As Annette Baier (1980, 179) observes, "The relations that form a moral community, and which . . . give rise to obligations, all concern dependency and interdependency. Some of these dependency relations are self-initiated, but the most fundamental ones are not." It is dependency and vulnerability rather than voluntary acts of will which give rise to these, our most fundamental moral duties.

Notice, furthermore, that my vulnerability model can also explain the cul-

---

3. Even the infamous Social Darwinist William Graham Sumner (1883, 162–63) concedes this point. "Every honest citizen of a free state," he writes, "owes it to himself, to the community, and especially to those who are at once weak and wronged, to go to their assistance and to help redress their wrongs. Whenever a law or social arrangement acts so as to injure any one, and that one the humblest, then there is a duty on those who are stronger, or who know better, to demand and fight for redress and correction. When generalized this means that it is the duty of All-of-us (that is, the State) to establish justice for all, from the least to the greatest, and in all matters. This . . . is no new doctrine. It is only the old, true, and indisputable function of the State." Of course, the "injustice" Sumner (1883, 34) would have us remedy is violation of his principle "that each man is guaranteed the use of all his powers exclusively for his own welfare," i.e., the "injustice" of redistributive taxation. It is, however, nonetheless significant that he focuses upon our *peculiar* responsibility to protect the weakest and humblest, however oddly he may conceive that class.

tural relativity of special responsibilities. "When we compare the customs and common opinions now existing among ourselves in respect of such claims with those of other ages and countries," the diversity is enormous. The varying norms of hospitality were the first examples to strike Sidgwick (1874, 246). "In earlier ages of society a peculiar sacredness was attached to the tie of hospitality, and claims arising out of it were considered peculiarly stringent: but this has changed as hospitality in the progress of civilization has become a luxury rather than a necessity." Travel has become less precarious. Travellers are now less vulnerable to the ravages of nature and less dependent upon random hosts for shelter.[4] Hence, we no longer feel under any special responsibility to shelter each and every vagrant who turns up on our doorstep. "A similar change might be traced to the commonly recognized duty of children to parents," Sidgwick (1874, 247) suggests. Where there is no collective provision for the care of the aged, a special duty falls upon their children to do so; to the extent that communities now make adequate collective provision to meet the needs of the aged (through pensions, etc.), these special duties fall away. In short, the cross-cultural diversity in people's special responsibilities might be explained by the enormous diversity that exists among societies with regard to people's vulnerabilities and available options for coping with them.

T here are various ways in which special obligations might arise, corresponding to the many different ways in which people might be vulnerable to or dependent upon others. That variety, however, should not blind us to what is common throughout: it is always vulnerability of one sort or another that gives rise to special obligations.

I want to argue not so much that the model of special obligations as being voluntarily self-assumed is wrong than that it is radically incomplete (though of course its very incompleteness leads to error in many important instances). Special obligations do arise out of our voluntary commitments. But what makes those obligations morally binding, I argue, is the vulnerabilities that those commitments engender; and those vulnerabilities are only one of many

---

4. Macaulay (1837, 537) makes a similar point: "In England it would be unnecessary to provide a [criminal] punishment for a stage-coachman who, however maliciously or dishonestly, drive[s] on, leaving behind a passenger whom he is bound to carry. The evil inflicted is seldom very serious. The country is everywhere well inhabited. The roads are secure. The means of conveyance can easily be obtained. . . . But the mode of performing journeys and the state of society in this country [i.e., India] are widely different. It is often necessary for travellers of the upper classes, even for English ladies, ignorant perhaps of the native languages, and with young children at their breasts, to perform journeys of many miles over uninhabited wastes, and through jungles in which it is dangerous to linger for a moment, in palanquins borne by persons of the lowest class. If, as sometimes happens, these persons should, in a solitary place, set down the palanquin and run away, it is difficult to conceive a more distressing situation than that in which their employer would be left." That is why he suggests that an exception should be made in such cases to the general principle that "a mere breach of contract ought not be an offense [against the criminal code], but only to be the subject of a civil action."

forms of vunerability to which we should morally respond. Thus, the vulnerability model is a more general one, capable of subsuming and transcending the model of self-assumed obligations.

Chapter 4 is devoted to demonstrating the superiority of the vulnerability model over the model of self-assumed obligations through a case-by-case analysis of various commonly acknowledged special responsibilities. A shorter and perhaps even stronger argument can, however, be couched in more general terms. The orthodox model presupposes that any special responsibilities must have been assumed voluntarily. What motivates an agent to assume them is left unspecified. It may be altruism, but there is nothing within the model that requires it to be; at least occasionally, the commitments a person makes are predicated upon hard calculations of narrow advantage. It is in cases of this latter sort that the implications of the two models diverge dramatically and the vulnerability model demonstrates its superiority decisively.[5]

Suppose that two people are in a bargaining situation in which each has something the other wants. Suppose further that there is a great disparity in bargaining power between them: the first is dependent upon the second for his livelihood, let us say, while the second regards what he wants in return as a mere luxury. Suppose, finally, that the stronger party is no altruist: he is prepared to be moved by moral arguments, but he does not automatically internalize the pains and pleasures of the other person. In these circumstances, the outcome of ordinary bargaining is painfully obvious. Even if each party gets more out of the deal than he could have expected acting independently, the benefits will be far from evenly divided: the greater advantage is certain to go to the stronger party. The "Matthew effect" once again prevails: to those that have still more is given. Any special obligations voluntarily incurred in the course of this bargaining will likewise tend to benefit disproportionately the party enjoying the initial advantage. The stronger transforms bargaining power into promissory claims and thereby legitimizes his domination of the weak. This is "exploitation" par excellence (Coleman 1983; Feinberg 1983).

Perhaps the most poignant examples come in connection with sentimental relationships. In these, "the one who cares less can," and often does, "exploit the one who cares more" (Ross 1921, 136). In the exchange model of social life,

> The individual who is less deeply involved in a love relationship . . . is in an
> advantageous position since the other's greater concern with continuing the
> relationship makes him or her dependent and gives the less involved individual

---

5. Contemporary philosophers discuss this divergence most commonly in connection with the distinction between two models of reciprocity, a Humean model of actual reciprocal advantage versus a Kantian model of imagining oneself in the other's shoes for purposes of moral evaluation. See, e.g., Danielson (1973), Barry (1978), and Richards (1983, 132–33).

power. . . . This power can be used to exploit the other; the woman who exploits a man's affection for economic gain and the boy who sexually exploits a girl who is in love with him are obvious examples. (Blau 1964, 78)

According to the model of self-assumed obligations, it is not only predictable but also perfectly permissible that the person who cares less should exploit the person who cares more.

As an empirical proposition, that analysis may well be right. Such behavior is, unfortunately, all too common. As a moral proposition, however, that conclusion is surely in error. There can be little doubt that anyone who exploits a lover in such a way deserves the description "cad." The same principle seems to hold for a wide range of dependency relationships. When, for example, a natural disaster has cut off communications between a community and the outside world and left the population totally dependent upon one grocer for all its supplies, it would clearly be morally reprehensible for the grocer to take advantage of that dependency and engage in price gouging.

Consider the case of a desperate Irish farmer who has no hope of finding another leasehold should he lose the one he has and who therefore must agree to renew his present lease on any terms he is offered. T. H. Green (1881, 372), reflecting upon such a situation, remarks, "There is no clearer ordinance of that supreme reason, often dark to us, which governs the course of man's affairs, than that no body of men should . . . be able to strengthen itself at the cost of others' weakness."

This is a very common theme indeed. William Thompson (1825, xi–xii) offers precisely this argument for women's rights: "the more physical advantages Nature has given man, the *less* excusable is he in superadding factitious advantages, by the abuse of strength, to those which are natural and unavoidable." Henry Shue (1981, 135) offers the same sort of analysis of the responsibility of the United States government to prevent firms from exporting hazardous products or activities to unwitting Third World countries: "Why should I defend defenseless human beings? . . . The question answers itself. . . . Because they are human beings and they are defenseless." George Bernard Shaw (1965, 77), reflecting upon "infantile docility and juvenile dependence," similarly maintains that "there is no viler crime than to abuse them, [and] there is no greater cruelty than to ignore them."

Likewise, in peasant societies or machine politics, "patrons" who use their superordinate positions to exploit their "clients" rather than caring for them are widely perceived to have violated a fundamental moral precept of the system (Scott 1975; 1976). The same is true even in international politics. An imperial power that takes advantage of its position of strength to extract all it can from its "dependencies," rather than protecting and fostering their growth, is regarded as having betrayed whatever moral claim it might have had to rule over its empire (Lewis 1841).

One way to respond to all this would be to say that the model of self-assumed obligations is only applicable under certain tightly°specified circumstances, namely, those in which the parties have approximately equal bargaining power. Only then, perhaps, do self-assumed obligations have any binding moral force. That restriction would certainly save the model from the above embarrassments—and from many similar ones to be discussed in chapter 4 below. Such a limitation to the model would, however, radically restrict the range of its application: a number of relationships would lie outside its scope, including many of those that give rise to what we ordinarily regard as our very strongest special duties. Thus, a model of self-assumed obligations that is circumscribed tightly enough to be plausible is necessarily incapable of explaining what most needs to be explained.

With the vulnerability model, in contrast, the moral force of precisely those special responsibilities can be readily explained. On that analysis, a strong moral duty on the part of the stronger to protect the weaker follows from precisely the same facts that in ordinary economic bargaining would enable the one to exploit the other. Economically, you could drive a very hard bargain indeed with someone who is utterly dependent upon you. Morally, it would be utterly outrageous to do so. The simple fact that a person is so very vulnerable to you imposes upon you special responsibilities in respect of him. You have done nothing that would be remotely construed as voluntarily assuming these responsibilities. Indeed, you could have easily bargained your way out of them. Morally, however, the fact that you could have done so is completely irrelevant.

To cap off this preliminary demonstration of the power of my vulnerability model of social responsibilities, notice its continuing impact on the legal system. Here I shall focus upon decisions of the United States Supreme Court in three very different areas and eras.

For the first and most recent example, reflect upon the plight of terminally ill cancer patients. In terms of ordinary bargaining games, these patients are in a very vulnerable position indeed. Having virtually no alternatives, they are more than willing to grasp any snake oil offered them; and their desperation is such that they are willing to pay just about any price for it. Either of two conclusions might follow from these facts. One is that drug manufacturers have no responsibility to ensure that drugs administered to the terminally ill are "safe and effective," since the patients themselves are only too happy to waive any such right. As the United States Court of Appeals for the Tenth Circuit concluded, "Since those patients, by definition, would 'die of cancer regardless of what may be done,' . . . there were no realistic standards against which to measure the safety and effectiveness of a drug for that class of individuals" (quoted in Marshall 1979, 547). The patients were therefore denied the ordinary protections of the Federal Food, Drug and Cosmetic Act of 1938. Drugs, such as Laetrile, which might be useless or worse could be sold to them with impunity. That is where the model of self-assumed responsibilities, conjoined with the logic of bargaining, would inevitably lead.

The Supreme Court, however, recoiled from that conclusion. The Court saw that for the same reason that the lower court thought that *anything* could be done to the terminally ill (their options being so terribly grim), these patients were actually deserving of *special* protection:

> If history is any guide, this new market would not be long overlooked. Since the turn of the century, resourceful entrepreneurs have advertised a wide variety of purportedly simple and painless cures for cancer, including linaments of turpentine, mustard, oil, eggs, and ammonia; peatmoss; arrangements of colored floodlamps; pastes made from glycerin and limburger cheese; mineral tablets; and "Fountain of Youth" mixtures of spices, oil and suet. (Marshall 1979, 555)

"This historical experience" of the merciless exploitation of those who were desperate and vulnerable was sufficient to persuade the Court that we had to be "determined to protect the terminally ill, no less than other patients, from the vast range of self-styled panaceas that inventive minds can devise" (Marshall 1979, 558).

The conclusion must necessarily be damning to models of self-assumed obligations. People should not be morally at liberty to strike any old bargain they can with each other about their respective rights and duties. If one party is in a position of particular vulnerability to or dependency on another, the other has strong responsibilities to protect the dependent party.[6] These responsibilities both precede and constrain any bargain between the parties over what rights and duties they may voluntarily assume. Thus, it is vulnerability rather than some voluntary act of will which gives rise to special responsibilities of the most basic kind.

For a second example of the influence of the vulnerability model upon United States jurisprudence, consider the case of *Wyman v. James,* 400 U.S. 309 (1971). This action arose when Mrs. James, a recipient of public assistance under the Aid to Families with Dependent Children (AFDC) program, refused to allow a caseworker to come for a "home visit," as was required by the program's regulations. When payments were stopped, Mrs. James sued, arguing that the home visit would have constituted an unreasonable search of the sort prohibited by the Fourth Amendment.

The Court decided against Mrs. James on two grounds. First, the social

6. Furthermore, this is not necessarily a paternalistic proposition. It most probably reflects the preferences of the people themselves concerned; while it certainly is true that when put in a position of weakness they would rationally choose to succumb to the other's demands, it is equally true that they would usually prefer not to be put in that position in the first place. The fact that families of kidnap victims pay out the demanded ransom does not prove that they would not prefer that the assets of families of kidnap victims be automatically frozen so that kidnappers could never hope to collect ransom (Schelling 1963).

worker's home visit was thought to be more of an interview than a search. Second, even if it were a search, the Fourth Amendment would prohibit only *unreasonable* searches. Foremost among the many arguments Justice Blackmun (1971b, 318) offers for believing that the search would not be unreasonable is the need to protect the vulnerable child:

> The public's interest . . . is in protection and aid for the dependent child whose family requires such aid for that child. The focus is on the *child,* and further, it is on the child who is *dependent.* There is no more worthy object of the public's concern. The dependent child's needs are paramount, and only with hesitation would we relegate those needs, in the scale of comparative value, to a position secondary to what the mother claims as her rights.

In liberal theory, we ordinarily regard rights as "trumps," overriding every other consideration. And in the United States, especially, constitutional rights are ordinarily regarded as the most powerful trumps imaginable. Yet here we have the Court admitting that the need to protect the vulnerable should trump the trumps.

For a final example of the vulnerability model at work in United States jurisprudence, consider the much older Indian problem. Official doctrine long held that the United States government owed a special duty of care to the American Indian tribes, partly because of the treaties that the government entered into with them but even more importantly because of the *dependency* of the Indians upon the government for protection. In the landmark case of *Cherokee Nation v. Georgia,* 5 Peters 1 (1831), Chief Justice Marshall (1831, 17) suggests that Indians should be regarded as "domestic dependent nations." As he goes on to explain, "they are in a state of pupilage; their relation to the United States resembles that of a ward to his guardian. They look to our government for protection; they rely upon its kindness and its power; appeal to it for relief to the wants; and address the president as their great father." Throughout the long period between Reconstruction and the New Deal, the "doctrine of the dependent ward" prevailed (Barsh and Henderson 1980, chap. 8). The Supreme Court continually traced the power and the duty of the federal government to protect Indians to their dependency relationship. Thus, for example, in *United States v. Kagama,* 118 U.S. 375 (1885) the Court held the following:

> These Indian tribes *are* wards of the Nation. They are communities *dependent* on the United States; dependent largely for their daily food; dependent for their political rights. . . . From their very weakness and helplessness . . . there arises the duty of protection, and with it the power. This has always been recognized by the Executive and by Congress, and by this Court whenever the question has arisen. (Miller 1885, 384; see similarly Matthews 1886, 28)

With this doctrine as with so many others, the promise obviously far outstripped the performance. Eventually it became clear that the doctrine of the dependent ward was being used as a device not for helping Indians but for tyrannizing over them; and it was rejected accordingly. I shall return to such problems in chapter 7. For now, however, what is important to note is the way in which vulnerability and dependency on the one side give rise to moral, and perhaps legal, responsibilities on the other. The only way to avoid the responsibilities would be to eliminate the vulnerabilites.

4

The Standard Cases Reanalyzed

There are some special responsibilities that virtually all of us acknowledge daily, without hesitation but also without justification. This chapter is devoted to exploring what, if any, ethical principles can account for those preanalytic moral judgments. I discuss, in turn, special responsibilities associated with promises and contracts; business relations (employees, clients, and consumers); professional roles (especially doctors and lawyers); families; friends; and benefactors.

It is my thesis that all of these special responsibilities are best analyzed through a model that derives one party's responsibilities from the other's vulnerabilities. I shall be implicitly taking issue with those who deny that any single, coherent model can account for all those standard responsibilities; and I shall be explicitly taking issue with those who would construe them all as voluntarily self-assumed. A story told in terms of self-assumed obligations, while explaining most of those special responsibilities in broad outline, leaves many of their most important details completely unexplained. The vulnerability model provides a more complete explanation. Indeed, it actually explains the moral force of self-assumed obligations themselves; in this way, the model of self-assumed obligations can be subsumed within the vulnerability model and shown to be a special application of those more wide-reaching principles.

Promises and Contracts

In the model of self-assumed obligations, promises and their legal analogues, contracts, constitute the paradigm cases of special responsibilities. It is my thesis that these obligations can also be explained, and in certain crucial respects better explained, by using the notions of vulnerability and reliance.

A long history and a rich literature surround the notions of promise and contract. Naturally, there are plenty of precedents for, and stock rejoinders to, the sort of analysis I shall offer. Mine is similar in important respects to that of Hobbes (1651) and Hume (1739; 1777); Adam Smith, in his lectures on jurisprudence, seems to have gotten closer to my argument still;[1] among contemporaries, Hodgson (1967) and McNeilly (1972) seem to have hit it pretty much on the head. It would be tedious to rehearse the history in full. Instead, I shall merely borrow those bits that are relevant to my own discussion, without pretending to give a complete account of the many other fascinating controversies that have sprung up over the years.

The essence of the notions of promise and contract, as ordinarily conceived, is that "the parties' duties to each other are just those they have assumed and no more" (Fried 1981, 76). The usual justification for the enforcement of those bonds, and only those bonds, is couched in terms of "the will binding itself . . . Parties are bound . . . because they have chosen to be" (Fried 1981, 3). Promising, philosophers note, is "among the strongest . . . devices for *commitment* provided by the English language" (Searle 1969, 58); and commitment is a powerfully voluntaristic notion. Thus, the obligations that follow from promises and contracts are usually thought to be voluntary obligations par excellence. Certainly no one can be under what we would, strictly speaking, call a promissory obligation unless he has performed the appropriate ritual for incurring it and had done so voluntarily.

Promissory obligations necessarily follow from a voluntary act of will, and that alone. That is the conventional wisdom. Coerced contracts are everywhere unenforceable. Indeed, many moralists would go so far as to say that promises must be not only voluntary but also intentional.[2] Such moralists would be reluctant to counsel the enforcement of promissory obligations people did not actually intend to incur. In the case of "express contracts," they would require that the words be "spoken with understanding of what they signify"; in the case of implicit contracts, they would require that the "sign" from which they are inferred "sufficiently argues the will of the contractor" (Hobbes 1651, chap. 14; see also Grotius 1625, bk. 2, chap. 13). Innocently scratching your nose at an auction should not render you liable to a contractual obligation to buy an ugly stuffed moose, and so on. Whether or not we want to add this requirement of intentionality, promises and contracts clearly must, at the very least, represent acts of will that are truly voluntary.

What I shall question here is whether and to what extent such promissory

---

1. "A promise is a declaration of your desire that the person for whom you promise should depend on you for the performance of it. Of consequence the promise produces an obligation, and the breach of it an injury" (Smith 1766, chap. 1, sec. 9). According to a modern formulation, "we must not so act as to disappoint the reliance of others when we have intentionally or knowingly induced them to rely upon us" (MacCormick 1972, 70).

2. The argument that we should ignore the contractors' private intentions and focus instead on the express terms of their contract, as those terms would conventionally be understood, is crucially couched in terms of the reliance people place in words as conventionally construed. "It is not . . . enough for [one party] to plead ignorance of the conventions for him to escape from his obligation," as Miller (1976, 70) argues. "As social beings we have a duty to make ourselves familiar with the conclusions that others will draw from our behaviour, in cases where the behaviour has a standard significance."

obligations are necessarily obligatory. On the model of self-assumed obligations, of course, promises must be binding: any promise (being by definition a
voluntary act of will) necessarily carries special obligations in consequence;
and only promises, or acts that are substantially similar in this respect, carry
such obligations. On the alternative model that I shall be advocating, neither
proposition is necessarily true: it is not necessarily true that promises always
entail special obligations, nor is it necessarily true that only promises can
entail such special obligations. Promises *usually* carry special obligations, but
only because other people are usually relying upon you to discharge them. It
is their vulnerability far more fundamentally than any voluntary act of will on
your part, which explains the moral force of the promissory obligation.
When, as occasionally happens, no one is relying upon you to keep your
promise, then virtually no moral force attaches. Conversely, whenever there
are people relying upon you to do something (and you know, or should know,
of their vulnerability to your actions and choices), you have the same sort of
special obligation. Those obligations are, then, independent of any promises
or other voluntary acts of will on your part.

P romising is nothing more than a device for coordinating behavior: it
   serves merely to reduce some of the uncertainty that would otherwise surround human action. To promise is to make others a pledge and to
offer your "honor" as hostage. The point of literally handing over hostages is
to guarantee your own performances. So too with promising: it enables others
to form firm expectations about your behavior.[3] Insofar as they matter at all,
promises matter morally only because someone else is depending on you to do
as you have promised. As Mill (1863, chap. 5) wrote: "When a person, either
by express promise or conduct, has encouraged another to rely upon his continuing to act in a certain way—to build expectations and calculations, and
stake any part of his plan of life upon that supposition—a new series of moral
obligations arises on his part towards that person." What makes promises
special is not so much that they represent a voluntary act of will on your part
but rather that the expectations about your behavior thereby engendered form
crucial components in the plans of others.

Taking this position invites the immediate reply that surely obligations cannot be imposed upon you by just *any* old expectations others have about your
conduct. Surely, it will be said, we must add something to ensure that those
expectations are somehow "reasonable." As Fried (1980, 1863), for exam-

---

3. Roscoe Pound (1945, 18, 20) makes the same point about contracts, supposing that that
differentiates them from promises when in fact it is a feature shared by both contracts and
promises: "The oldest and most general idea in the development of contract is not one of
enforcing promises. It is one of enforcing security for performance. Thus, hostage and pledge are
the ideas from which we must begin the history of contract on the secular side. . . . It seems well
established that originally hostages were delivered bound, and the whole terminology of the law
of obligations preserves the memory of this starting point."

ple, insists: "To claim compensation for harm suffered in relying on someone, a person must show that his reliance was somehow justified. Without this requirement a person could thrust obligations on others willy-nilly by merely asserting that he will rely—or, worse yet, that he has relied—on them to perform some burdensome act."

Philosophers here traditionally evoke the distinction between making a promise, on the one hand, and merely stating an intention or making a prediction (which, too, can engender expectations), on the other. According to the standard analysis, however, expectations based on stated intentions or predictions are not legitimate, and there is no moral reason for fulfilling them.[4]

It may well be true, as a purely linguistic point, that you are under no *obligation* to honor your stated intentions or predictions. That is just the way we use the word: if there is no "promise" or similar solemn undertaking given, there is no obligation (Hart 1958). Obligations do not exhaust the universe of moral reasons for action, however. It would be wrong to assume that, just because you have no obligation so to act, there is no moral reason for your behaving as you said you would (Warnock 1971, 100–1).[5]

Here as elsewhere, moral intuitions seem hopelessly contaminated by the very moral theories which are supposed to be validated by reference to them. Consequently, it might be best to confine our attention to the law, regarding it merely as a codification of (some, if not all) moral sentiments widely shared in our community. In law, and presumably morals as well, if you knowingly allow a person to act on the assumption that you are going to do something which you then choose not to do, you are obliged either to disabuse him of that illusion or to do as he expects. Otherwise, you would be liable (legally as well as morally) for any losses he suffered from relying upon erroneous expectations you allowed to persist.[6] This is the doctrine of "estoppel," which

---

4. See, e.g., Grotius (1625, bk. 2, chap. 11, sec. 2), Smith (1766, chap. 1, sec. 9), Searle (1969, 178), Warnock (1971, 100–101), and Fried (1981, 10–11).

5. Where mere predictions or statements of intention are concerned, moral reasons to honor them do not disappear; they are merely weaker. Those formulations entail less firm commitments and should therefore reasonably engender less heavy reliance on the part of others. "The crucial distinction between statements of intention on the one hand and promises on the other lies in the nature and degree of commitment or obligation undertaken in promising," as Searle (1969, 178) himself says. A promise implies 100 percent certainty; stating an intention or making a prediction merely communicates a high probability. Surely we are also morally liable for getting others' hopes up, especially insofar as their relying on those expectations causes them to incur costs or foreclose options.

6. Imagine Harry saying to John: "I am almost certain to offer you a lift to town tomorrow. In the circumstances it would be far wiser for you to rely on me than make alternative arrangements, but remember—I do not promise anything. I am merely advising you." Raz (1972, 99) correctly infers from this case that you can intentionally induce reliance without making a promise, and MacCormick (1972) is wrong to think otherwise. Surely, however, we should go on to say that, owing to John's reliance, Harry has an obligation to get him to town tomorrow if John has no other way of getting there. That obligation has precisely the same moral basis (i.e., reliance) as promissory obligations, although of course it is not itself based on a promise. It is weaker than a promissory obligation only because of the element of uncertainty introduced by the phrase

looms so large in both tort and contract law. In its most general form, the doctrine holds that

> 1) A person who is not otherwise liable as a party to a transaction purported to be done on his account is nevertheless subject to liability to persons who have changed their positions because of their belief that the transaction was entered into by or for him, if
>   A) he intentionally or carelessly caused such belief, or
>   B) knowing of such belief and that others might change their positions because of it, he did not take reasonable steps to notify them of the facts. (Seavy 1958, sec. 8B)

The phrase "change of position" in this formulation can mean almost anything: "payment of money, expenditure of labor, suffering a loss or subjection to a legal liability" (Seavey 1958, sec. 8B).

This doctrine of estoppel provides grounds for all sorts of legal actions. We are legally entitled to enforce "gratuitous undertakings."[7] Under the famous section 90 of the *Restatement (Second) of the Law of Contracts* (Braucher and Farnsworth 1981, sec. 90), dramatically upgraded from the first *Restatement* (Lewis 1932, sec. 90), we are entitled to enforce "promises reasonably inducing action or forbearance" merely on account of the other's reliance upon them: "A promise which the promisor should reasonably expect to induce action or forbearance on the part of the promisee or a third person and which does induce such action or forbearance is binding if injustice can be avoided only by enforcement of the promise."[8] In the law of torts similar rules apply against misrepresentation or negligence in the performance of an undertaking to render services.[9]

The general philosophical lesson to be drawn from these rather arcane principles of law would seem to be this: Guaranteeing the reasonableness of ex-

---

"almost certain." John's reliance therefore was, or should reasonably have been, less than complete.

7. "One who by a gratuitous promise or other conduct which he should realize will cause another reasonably to rely upon the performance of definite acts of service by him as the other's agent, causes the other to refrain from having such acts done by other available means is subject to a duty to use care to perform such services or while other means are available, to give notice that he will not perform" (Seavey 1958, sec. 378).

8. Cf. Williston (1932, secs. 75 and 90); see generally Gilmore (1974) and, for English parallels, Atiyah (1979, 776–78).

9. Section 872 of the *Restatement (Second) of the Law of Torts* holds that: "If one person makes to another person a definite misrepresentation of fact concerning the ownership of property or its disposition, knowing that the other intends to act in reliance on it, and subsequently does act or makes a refusal that would be tortious if the statement were true, the first person is subject to liability to the other as if the statement were true, provided that the other in reasonable reliance upon that statement has so changed his position that it would be inequitable to deny an action for the act or refusal." Section 323 holds that: "One who undertakes, gratuitously or for consideration, to render services to another which he should recognize as necessary for the protection of the other's person or things, from his failure to exercise reasonable care to perform his undertaking, if . . . the harm is suffered because of the other's reliance upon the undertaking" (Prosser 1965).

pectations is one great strength of the model of self-assumed obligations. Whenever you have voluntarily incurred the obligations, it *must* be reasonable that you should be held to them. Voluntariness is surely not the only basis of reasonable expectations, however. It would be equally reasonable to form expectations on the basis of statistically well-grounded predictions about your behavior, or, in cases in which others could not be expected to have intimate knowledge of your personal quirks, on statistically well-grounded predictions about the behavior of "people like you" or of "people in general."[10] Hence, the fact that the obligations have been voluntarily assumed may be a sufficient guarantee of their reasonableness, but not a necessary one.

The effect of this argument is to break out of the "chicken and egg" problem that arises if we say that "X ought to keep his promise because Y is relying on it" and that "Y is relying upon it because X ought to do it" (Warnock 1971, 99). I am suggesting that there may be various other reasons, quite apart from X's antecedent moral duties (much less X's promissory obligations), for Y to have good cause to rely upon X's performance. And Y's reliance, based on any of these various grounds, would be perfectly reasonable and provide a strong (albeit not necessarily conclusive) reason for X to behave in the way Y expects.

The one thing that does seem to be necessary (although not necessarily sufficient) to guarantee the reasonableness of the expectations relates to notions of reliance: surely we think it is reasonable to demand that X's behavior be shaped by Y's expectations about X's behavior only on the condition that X knows that Y is relying on X to behave in some particular way.[11] That is what much of the apparatus of traditional contract law is all about. The whole point of the ritual of offer and acceptance, consideration and bargaining is merely to ensure that each party knows that the other is relying on him, and what pre-

---

10. Similarly, and equally damaging to promise-based analyses, it would be reasonable to expect people to behave in accordance with non-promise-based legal and moral obligations. "For instance, a person who buys a new house, in reliance upon the proper performance by the local authority of its duties of ensuring compliance with the Building Regulations, may have a remedy against the authority for malperformance even though they give no promises" (Atiyah 1979, 2).
11. That it might not be sufficient is demonstrated by cases like this: Suppose you write to a millionaire whom you have never met, advising him that you expect him to bestow a gift of $100,000 upon you and that you are relying to your detriment upon that expectation. Even after he knows of your expectations and your reliance, we would ordinarily say no obligations grow out of that fact. He would be perfectly entitled to ask, "Why should my liberty be constrained by the harm you would suffer from the disappointment of the expectations you choose to entertain about my choices?" (Fried 1981, 10). From the point of view of advocates of the model of self-assumed obligations, what lets the millionaire off the hook is the fact that he has not made any promises, has not invited your reliance, and hence has not assumed any obligations toward you. From my point of view, the unreasonableness of your expectations might let him off the hook also, but I would analyze the notion of unreasonableness in terms of the *groundlessness* of your expectations: there was simply no reason of any kind for your believing that the millionaire was going to bestow the money upon you, not just no reason that was couched in terms of his prior commitments.

cisely each is expecting of the other. Paradoxically, the counterexamples typically produced against the reliance model all point to this very conclusion. Suppose, it is asked, someone overhears you stating your intention to do something and as a result, and without your knowledge, relies upon you to do it? Then, his reliance notwithstanding, you can hardly be said to owe him anything. What if you actually did tell him you were going to do such and such, but you were clearly just joking? Then again, his reliance notwithstanding, you have no obligation to make good the costs of his misunderstanding (Fried 1981, 10–11). The solemn ritual attending contract formation is basically just a device for making sure each party knows of the other's expectations.[12]

Advocates of the model of self-assumed obligations, of course, have their own explanations for the importance attached to offer and acceptance, consideration and bargaining. For this school, the explanation, dating from Holmes's lectures on the *Common Law,* would be that these conditions are required in order to underwrite the motivation necessary for the person's will to bind itself, and thus for the person voluntarily to incur the obligations in question (Gilmore 1974; Fried 1981, chaps. 3, 4). Notice, however, that we can dispense with all this ordinary apparatus merely by affixing a seal to the contract (Braucher and Farnsworth 1981, secs. 95–96). The ritual affixing of a seal clearly does nothing to guarantee the sort of a balanced bargain which might motivate contractors voluntarily to bind themselves; and the fact that this ritual can fully substitute for the other (offer, acceptance, consideration, bargaining) clearly suggests that the real point of the other is not to guarantee that the bargain reflects the true wills of the parties, either. What is crucial, it seems, is the formality and solemnity of the ritual. The real point of both sets of ritualized performances is merely to make sure that each party knows that he is doing something serious; more specifically, the point is to make sure that each party knows that the other is depending upon him and precisely what the other is depending upon him to do.

I have said that there are two crucial tests that should guide our choice between the two models of special responsibilities. One is whether there can be any obligations without promises or quasi-promises. Within the model of vulnerability the answer is yes; within that of self-assumed obliga-

---

12. In the comment on section 90 of the *Restatement (Second) of the Law Contracts,* concerning "promises which have reasonably induced action or forebearance," it is stipulated that "the promissor is affected only by reliance which he does or should foresee, and enforcement must be necessary to avoid injustice. Satisfaction of the latter may depend on the reasonableness of the promissee's reliance, . . . on the formality with which the promise is made, [and] on the extent to which the evidentiary, cautionary, deterrent and channelling functions of form are met by the commercial setting or otherwise" (Braucher and Farnsworth 1981). Grotius (1625, bk. 2, chap. 11, sec. 3; bk. 2, chap. 13) similarly describes "formality as an indispensable sign of deliberate intent."

tions, it is no. The other test is whether there can be any promises without obligations. Within the model of vulnerability, the answer again is yes; within that of self-assumed obligations, it is no.

The discussion of estoppel has revealed that obligations are generated by reliance as well as promises. Of course, promises are often also involved, as in section 90 of the *Second Restatement of Contracts* (Braucher and Farnsworth 1981) or in cases of "gratuitous undertakings." But sometimes reliance alone generates the obligations. Section 8B of the *Second Restatement of Agency* (Seavey 1958) explicitly does *not* require that the beliefs upon which vulnerable parties rely be "intentionally" or even "carelessly" induced. Under paragraph 1B of that section, quoted above, to become liable it is sufficient that a person knew that the vulnerable party has the belief and will act to his detriment on that belief. (The connective between paragraphs 1A and 1B is "or," not "and.") A reporter for the American Law Institute (Seavey 1958, sec. 8B) comments as follows: "When one realized that another is or may come under a misapprehension as to the authority of his agent or the ownership of his property—a misapprehension for which he is not at fault—his duty to give information is a duty of care." Thus, there can be special obligations without promises or any other voluntary acts of will. Score one for the vulnerability model.

The results of the second test are less clear-cut. The vulnerability model here has us looking for promises without obligations. This might be said to fly in the face of analytic necessity: a promise, by its very definition, must impose an obligation (Searle 1969, chap. 8). Although I think this analysis is incorrect, I shall not bother to dispute definitions, because as it happens, even in the vulnerability model promises also usually impose obligations of a rather weak sort for rule-utilitarian reasons.[13] I argue, instead, that there can be promises carrying *no very strong* moral obligations. That, in combination with the earlier finding that there can be obligations without promises, should suffice to undermine models that attach great importance to self-assumed obligations.

I shall be making a crucial distinction between the existence of a promise, on the one hand, and the moral importance attached to a promise, on the other. I shall *not* be claiming that without reliance (much less the intention of inducing reliance) a promise will not exist. Of course it will. Once you have gone through all the right motions which, according to the rules governing our social practices, constitute making a promise, a promise most certainly exists. That is true whether or not anyone then relies upon it (Raz 1972, 99).

But saying a promise exists is not necessarily to say that, morally, it pro-

---

13. Sometimes they do not, as in cases of promising the impossible, the wicked, or perhaps even just the unnecessary. Those exceptions, however, are common to both models and cannot be used as the basis for choosing between them.

vides an important reason for action. Suppose that you have promised to do something but that it really does not make one bit of difference to anyone whether or not you do it. Then I think we can say, perfectly consistently, both (1) that you have promised and (2) that you have no compelling moral reason for honoring the promise.

Here again, our moral intuitions are likely to vary, depending on which theory we embrace. Those who are not under the sway of any particular philosophical theory would, however, surely concur with Kronman's (1981, 408–9) assessment:

> When we consider a case of pure promise, a case in which every vestige of reliance has been stripped away so that nothing but the promise remains, our intuitions flicker and fail to provide any clear support for the view that Fried (1981) defends [namely, that we should honor our commitments regardless]. Only where there has been reliance on the promise do our intuitions incline us strongly in the direction of enforcement.

To prevent us from "cooking" the evidence upon which our choice between rival theories is to be based, however, let us again focus upon law as the formal codification of our community's standard moral intuitions. There, too, the legal equivalent of a promise—a contract—exists just so long as you have performed all the right rituals. Reliance is no more analytically necessary for the existence of a contract than it is for the existence of a promise. Contracts also analytically imply obligations; hence you can have obligations even if it makes no difference to anyone whether or not you discharge them. Although the existence of the contract (and hence the obligation to discharge it) cannot be doubted, the strength of the contract most certainly can be doubted. The varying strengths of contractual obligations are reflected most directly in the varying damages that would be assessed for their breach. Indeed, there is no other measure of—indeed, no other sense that could be attached to the notion of—the strength of a contractual obligation, qua contractual obligation, except the damages that would be assessed for its breach.[14] Damages *are*

---

14. At this point, David Miller (pers. com. 1983) queries whether damages really reflect the relative strengths of the obligations, since "the point of damages, after all, is simply to restore the position of the injured party [rather than as] punishment for the defaulter. The question is, do we think that the degree of wrongdoing varies with the amount of compensation necessary?" I can only reply that in the law of contract there is no other sense attaching to the notion of wrongdoing (Braucher and Farnsworth 1981, chap. 16, introductory comments). Miller's talk of punishment takes us outside contract law, for punitive damages are assessed for breach of contract only when "the conduct constituting the breach is also a tort for which punitive damages are recoverable" (Braucher and Farnsworth 1981, sec. 355). Even in tort law, merely nominal damages are usually awarded when "no harm has been caused by the tort or the amount of harm is not significant"; only where the defendant has engaged in particularly "outrageous conduct" will further "punitive damages" be assessed, even in tort law (Prosser 1965, secs. 907–17). If the quantum of punishment rather than the quantum of compensation were the right measure of the strength of an obligation, then we would have to conclude that contractual obligations are utterly without force: for it is the criminal law that inflicts penalties intended as punishments, and breach of contract is virtually never a criminal offense (Williams 1961, sec. 224).

calculated (just as according to the vulnerability model they should be) on the basis of the extent to which others are depending upon your performance.[15]

That damages are determined by the extent of others' dependence is crucial to my case for the superiority of the vulnerability model of contractual and promissory obligations. The law of contract mirrors the vulnerability model in assessing the strength of the contractual tie, and hence the damages that would be awarded in case of breach, as a function of the extent to which one party is depending upon the other's contractually bound performance. In the limiting case, if *A* breaks a contract with *B* and *B* suffers no (compensatable, calculable) loss as a result, then courts will award *B* a judgment of only token damages. The *Second Restatement of Contracts* emphasizes this point: ''If the breach caused no loss or if the amount of the loss is not proved under the rules stated in this chapter, a small sum fixed without regard to the amount of loss will be awarded as nominal damages'' (Braucher and Farnsworth 1981, sec. 346). The provision of the British law of contracts is identical: ''Damages for breach of contract are designed to compensate the plaintiff for damage, loss or injury he has suffered through that breach. Where the plaintiff has not, in fact, suffered any loss by reason of the breach, he is nevertheless entitled to the verdict, but the damage recoverable by him will be purely nominal (usually £2)'' (Guest 1979, 549).

Now, of course, the question remains why courts assess even that paltry sum in damages.[16] I have argued that contracts and promises have moral weight merely because others are depending on them; and, *ex hypothesi,* in this case nobody is. The explanation I propose basically follows rule-utilitarian lines (Kronman 1981, 411): there is a certain value attached to promis-

---

15. That last phrase is intentionally vague, designed to straddle both ''expectation interests'' and ''reliance interests.'' Opponents of the model of contracts as self-assumed promissory obligations, with whom my sympathies obviously lie, mistakenly suppose that their countermodel necessarily implies that the proper measure of damages must be the reliance interest, i.e., the amount of unrecoverable expenses the plaintiff has already incurred pursuant to the contract. Surely the right measure of damages is instead the expectation interest, i.e., how well off the plaintiff would have been had the contract been honored, as is emphasized by both Fried (1981, 5, 17–21) and the *Restatement (Second) of the Law of Contracts* (Braucher and Farnsworth 1981, sec. 347). This conclusion is, however, perfectly consistent with my rejection of ''contract as promise.'' The crucial point is that reliance interests, properly construed, include opportunity costs, i.e., the gains *X* could have realized by signing a contract with *Z* which he had to forgo when signing instead a contract with *Y*. Assuming anything like a perfect market, *X* could have contracted for the same goods on the same terms with any number of other people instead of *Y*, at least some of whom would (unlike *Y*) have honored the contract. Then *X*'s reliance interests, analyzed in terms of opportunity costs, equal his expectation interests. I am grateful to Alan Schwartz (pers. com. 1984) for this point.

16. In the *Restatement (Second) of the Law of Contracts,* a comment on section 90 suggests that it often is ''the *probability* of reliance [that] lends support to the enforcement of the executory exchange'' where neither a benefit interest nor a reliance interest can be found (Braucher and Farnsworth 1981, emphasis added; see similarly Fuller and Perdue 1936–37). Often that will be true, also; but I would not want to rest my whole case on that fact alone, since we can surely find some instances where reliance on it is utterly improbable.

ing and contracting as institutions, quite apart from their value in any particular instance. The reason that those institutions have that value is that they enable us to fix firm expectations about what others will do (Hodgson 1967). Contracts and promises are thus useful devices for enabling us to depend on one another; we do not have to worry about other people's trying to second-guess our actions and vice-versa, as we might have to in act-utilitarian societies. Purely "executory" contracts, ones on which no one is relying, are nonetheless enforced so as to protect the larger institution that is so useful in protecting expectations and facilitating private planning (Atiyah 1979, 420–21). While in the case of a purely executory contract there is one sense in which no one is relying on that particular contract being kept, there is a larger sense in which we all are. Our deeper dependency upon the institutions of promising and contracting thus explains why, within my model, contracts and promises remain (slightly) obligatory even when no one is depending upon them specifically. It also explains why in such cases the obligation and the attendant penalty is so slight: no single breach of contract or promise will do very much to undermine the institution as a whole.

Business Relations

In theory, untrammelled contract underlies all business dealings. In practice, however, many of the most important special obligations businessmen have to their employees and customers, their clients and consumers have no obvious basis in contracts. Some terms and conditions are read into the contracts, even if they are absent on their face. Others we refuse to enforce, even if they are clearly stipulated. A close inspection of such extra-contractual constraints upon business relationships sheds important light upon their real moral bases.

Constraints on contractual dealings are, of course, prima facie inconsistent with the model of self-assumed obligations: people should be able to incur or to avoid any obligations they wish, as long as all parties to the contract agree. Constraints, however, make perfectly good sense within the model that traces special responsibilities to the peculiar vulnerabilities of the parties involved in the relationships.

A person's views on the particular moral obligations of businessmen seem unusually sensitive to his attitude toward the practice of business in general. Corporate apologists go to extraordinary lengths in denying the most basic moral responsibilities; populists demand most unreasonable obligations. On balance, the legal code appears once again to be the best guide to the settled norms of our larger moral community in this matter. This is a conservative guide, to be sure; here, as elsewhere, the law requires rather less than morality might demand. For my purposes, however, the errors probably will not matter much, since I am trying to show merely that the vulnerability model can account for our special responsibilities in broad outline.

L et us start with the employment relationship, which was classically discussed under the heading of "masters and servants." The servitude originally in view was of a particularly nasty sort. Grotius (1625, bk. 2, chap. 5, sec. 30) concludes a discussion of slavery with the observation that "there are also varieties of incomplete slavery, such as that . . . of men hired for pay." Hobbes (1651, chap. 20), too, treats the master-servant relation as an instance of "despotical domination," legitimated (as, classically, was slavery itself) by the "consent of the vanquished, extracted under the guns of the victors." Pufendorf's (1682, bk. 2, chap. 4) discussion of masters and servants also rapidly narrows to a discussion of the proper treatment of slaves. "In the case of a slave who has voluntarily assigned himself to a man in perpetual slavery, the master owes him a constant supply of food and other things necessary to life," Pufendorf concludes; and practice in slave societies seems to have been surprisingly faithful to these precepts (Stampp 1963, chap. 7; Genovese, 1974, 75–86). These same moral conclusions—namely, that "his master assumes full responsibility for meeting all of [the servant's] essential needs"—were carried over to various less dramatic instances of the master-servant bond, such as apprenticeship, indenture, and domestic servitude (Demos 1970, 107–9; MacDonnell 1908).[17]

This initial focus upon the master-slave relation as the paradigm case of servitude had another carry-over: what is peculiar to the plight of slaves, and what seems so clearly to give rise to their masters' duties in respect of them, is their utter helplessness and complete dependence upon their masters for protection and sustenance.[18] The early Victorian moralist Sir Arthur Helps (1845, 28, 39) traces "the duties of the employer to the employed" to the fact that employees are "entrusted to [his] care," whether they be "servant, ap-

17. This conclusion might also rest on some notion of a "just wage," which by this time had come merely to mean a subsistence wage (Atiyah 1979, 524). Blackstone (1783, bk. 1, chap. 14), denying any natural-law basis to the master-slave relationship, nonetheless refuses to put the rights and duties of masters and servants on a purely contractual basis. "By service all servants and labourers, except apprentices, become entitled to wages," he writes. But only in the case of domestics are these "according to their agreement." For "labourers or servants in husbandry," wages were to be "according to the appointment of the sheriff or sessions." Their decisions were, presumably, to be based on calculations of a "just" (i.e., subsistence) wage. This effectively ties the obligations of the master/employer to the vulnerabilities of the servants/employees—and in rather a more flexible way than that suggested by the analogy to slaves. Alas, this tradition was eclipsed throughout the next century and a half.
18. Note that the master's duties with respect to his slaves are the same whether or not he acquired them through any voluntary act of will on his part. Someone who has inherited slaves he does not want is, of course, free to sell (or free) them; but until he does, he has the same duties with respect to his unwanted slaves as does someone who assumed the role and duties of a slave-owner completely voluntarily.

prentice or hired labourer." A "duty of attention to the welfare of your dependents" falls upon you, Helps argues, "whether you are a manufacturer, master workman, owner of land, or private individual." In law, too, "acute helplessness" long continued to be a factor used to establish a master's duty, under the criminal code, to provide assistance to personal servants domiciled in his house (Kirchheimer 1942, 631). The fundamental principle of law, relaxed in its application only at the margins,[19] holds that "The master's duty extends no further than to take care not to expose the servant to unnecessary risks from sources over which the master having exclusive control has the sole ability to protect the servant, and, from which the servant, being ignorant of the true condition of affairs, is unable to protect himself by withdrawing the service" (Bohlen 1908, 235).

This principle carries several important consequences for the terms and conditions of work. Duties of the master/employer arising under it include, for example, "supplying safe tools and appliances, a safe place to work, a sufficiency of not obviously incompetent fellow-servants, a safe system of rules and regulations where the complicated nature of the business makes it necessary for the servant's protection and . . . efficient superintendence" (Bohlen 1908, 325–26). Now, of course, these obligations might *also* be contractual ones. Assuming that a good trade union exists, it is entirely likely that some such requirements would be built into the employment contract. But the crucial point from my perspective is that the requirements need not be contractual to be enforceable. Even in the absence of any formally self-assumed obligations, some safety obligations are nonetheless imposed upon the master/employer (Bohlen 1908, 238–39).

The real basis of the obligations toward the servant/employee is not the voluntary act of will on the part of the master/employer, but rather the "inability on the part of the servant to provide for himself [and] the . . . complete dependence upon the care of the master" (Bohlen 1908, 238). This fact is particularly apparent from the limits that were traditionally placed on the scope of these duties. The protections, originally designed for slaves, were initially extended only to specific classes of employees who, owing to special features of their jobs, found themselves in a similar state of almost complete dependence on their employers. Seamen constituted the classic example.[20]

---

19. A duty of care may be imposed in anticipation of a state of acute helplessness, and not merely in response to one. As Kirchheimer (1942, 631) remarks, "The duty to help, particularly to provide adequate medical care, is established in order to prevent a state of acute helplessness and should not merely provide a belated remedy."

20. "The very nature of their employment causes them to be during the voyage entirely under the control and at the mercy of the master of the vessel, and to visit foreign ports where if cast adrift ill and without resources and very possibly ignorant of the language, they would be utterly helpless, while the master is able to cause the sailor to be properly cared for. . . . [Hence] the duty recognized in the maritime law as resting upon a vessel and its owner to provide sufficient food, and in America at least, medical attendance to its seamen. . . . There appears to be

Others included servants "of tender age," who were helpless and hence dependent upon their masters for support. The same was true for servants working in isolated sites; if these workers could neither procure the necessities of life locally nor carry them in with them, they were dependent upon their employer to provide them, and he was duty-bound to do so. In what is perhaps the limiting case of duties growing out of dependence, "one who imprisons another, though legally, is bound to provide his prisoner with necessaries" (Bohlen 1908, 238).

During the eighteenth and early nineteenth centuries, "changes in social conditions led to a decline in the old paternalism involved in the master and servant relationship" (Atiyah 1979, 523). The most important change was that the servant ceased to be utterly reliant upon the good offices of any particular master. He could negotiate better terms with his present employer, change jobs, or if indigent and incapacitated, seek assistance from the state. Since employees in the factory or workshop were no longer absolutely dependent on their employers, as was the servant-cum-slave, they were denied the legal protections traditionally afforded to him. It was the worker's responsibility, insofar as he was able, to protect himself.[21] Thus, for example, one English court held that "a master is not guilty of manslaughter in failing to supply food and lodging to a servant who was *sui juris* and was free to leave the master's house and was not coerced by threats of ill treatment to remain" (Bohlen 1908, 238). Such arguments, of course, attribute more power of self-protection to employees than they actually enjoyed. They were hardly "free" to leave the employ of one master where there were no others who would hire them (i.e., the hypothesized perfect labor market often did not exist); and the protections afforded by poor laws were of course grossly (and intentionally) inadequate. Furthermore, employees who were unorganized and individually

recognized a further duty on the part of a ship to its sailors, to make all reasonable efforts to rescue them if they fall overboard from any cause whatsoever. . . . The very nature of the employment is subjecting the sailor to grave risk of just such peril, and his helplessness and the master's ability to protect him is manifest" (Bohlen 1908, 237).

21. Even during the heyday of "freedom of contract" ideologies, obligations were still imposed upon employers where employees were genuinely unable to protect themselves; and, interestingly, one of the most important grounds for releasing employers from such obligations was that workers could increasingly turn to the public (rather than their masters) for relief. Consider the case of the employer's duty to provide emergency medical assistance. "When . . . the servant is employed to do hazardous work in a place or under circumstances making it evident that he must look solely to his master for such immediate and urgently required care and attention as can only be rendered on the spot, . . . it is the duty of the master's representative upon the spot to make a *bona fide* effort to relieve him. This duty . . . arises only out of absolute necessity. It would not exist when . . . the servant though injured could provide medical aid for himself or could turn for relief to the public authorities primarily charged with the care of the indigent sick. It would arise out of the emergency and expire with it. It would not require the master to support, care for and provide medical attention for his servant till cured. . . . It would . . . bind the master only to render the servant such immediate aid as was possible on the spot and transportation to a point where he could be properly cared for, either by himself, or by the public" (Bohlen 1908, 240).

powerless were free only in the most formal sense to negotiate terms and conditions with their employers. As Engels (1845, 201) protests: "The employer is absolute law-giver; he makes regulations at will, changes and adds to his code at pleasure, and even if he inserts the craziest stuff, the courts say to the working man: 'You were your own master; no one forced you to agree to such a contract if you did not want to, but now, when you have freely entered into it, you must be bound by it.'" Even those who do not regard this as a necessary feature of the capitalist mode of production are nonetheless forced to concede that as things stood in early Victorian England, "the generality of labourers, in this and most other countries, have as little choice of occupation or freedom of locomotion, are practically as dependent on fixed rules and on the will of others, as they could be on any system short of actual slavery" (Mill 1848, bk. 2, chap. 1, sec. 3).

The history of modern labor law is characterized by the increasing recognition of the inability of isolated employees to protect themselves. In essence, the problem is one of coordination: the nature of the bargaining game would allow employers to impose grossly disadvantageous hours and conditions upon their unorganized employees (Mill 1848, bk. 5, chap. 11, sec. 12; Goodin 1976; Elster 1978).

The most direct response to the problem of coordination among workers might seem to be to unionize. Certainly workers are highly vulnerable to the actions and choices of their union leaders; and it follows, on my theory, that those leaders have strong special responsibilities with respect to their members. Some evidence suggests that unions are, in fact, highly effective not only in equalizing bargaining power between employers and employees but also in improving both the safety and the efficiency of the production process by pooling shop-floor information from their members (Freeman and Medoff 1982).

Collective bargaining is obviously a contractualist response to the problem of protecting vulnerable workers. Trade unions negotiate contracts that impose various obligations upon the employer to protect the health and safety of his workers. From the employer's perspective, those obligations are thereby self-assumed. Notice, though, that typically the state does not trust collective bargaining to protect completely the health and safety of workers. In various respects it directly regulates the hours and conditions of labor; and in so doing, it circumscribes (and, indeed, overrides) any private agreements made between employers and employees themselves. Thus, even with their consent it is illegal to employ people for less than the minimum wage. Similarly, "in tort law, there has been a tendency to reduce or minimize the importance of consent as a critical factor in the imposition or non-imposition of liability. The defence of *volenti non fit injuria*, for example, widely used in early cases of injured workmen, . . . has almost entirely disappeared in modern [English] law" (Atiyah 1979, 730). Some such logic also pretty clearly underlies the

United States Occupational Safety and Health Act of 1970 (PL 91-596; 84 STAT 1590). That act makes it the duty of "each employer . . . [to] furnish to each of his employees employment and a place of employment which are free from recognized hazards that are causing or are likely to cause death or serious physical damage to his employees" (sec. 5[a][1]). The act also commits the government to discharge its secondary responsibilities to vulnerable workers by promulgating (and enforcing against both employers and employees alike) occupational safety and health standards (Ashford 1976).

T he same pattern can be traced in the responsibilities of businessmen for the safety of their customers. The traditional rule was said to be that of *caveat emptor*, placing the onus on the customer to inspect the goods he purchased. The obligations of businessmen were said to be limited to those that were expressly stated in the contract of sale, and they were said to be owed only to the users of their products who were party to that contract (or in "privity" with those who were). Thus, in the landmark case of *Winterbottom v. Wright*, (1842) 10 M & W 109, 152 Eng Rep 402, a passenger who was injured when a carriage broke down was prevented from recovering damages from negligent manufacturers because he had not been party to the contract of sale of the carriage (Atiyah 1979, 464–79; Epstein 1980, chaps. 2–3).

An undue focus upon the rule of *caveat emptor* would, however, be misleading; that was the rule of a peculiar period, and a relatively brief one at that.[22] Those engaged in providing public services had traditionally been held to a much stricter standard. In the *Second Restatement of Torts* it is pointed out that

> Since the early days of the common law those engaged in the business of selling food for human consumption have been held to a high degree of responsibility for their products. As long ago as 1266 there were enacted special criminal statutes imposing penalties upon victualers, vintners, brewers, butchers, cooks, and other persons who supplied "corrupt" food and drink. (Prosser 1965, sec. 402A, comment B)

Indeed, in his 1537 treatise *De Natura Brevium*, the earliest authoritative

---

22. Hamilton (1931, 1169), searching for the historical antecedents of the doctrine of *caveat emptor*, concludes: "The raw materials of a judicial doctrine of caveat emptor were scant enough. An excerpt or two from Fitzherbert or whoever wrote his books, a neat distinction between the civil and the common law pried from its context in Coke, a persuasive but doctored line of Latin lifted from a venerable text, the prescribed tests for the validity of a declaration in deceit, the dubious support of a handful of none too relevant cases—and that was all. But the words were there, ready to bear the ideas of a later age; and interpretation, the great creator, was to prove equal to the occasion," come the late eighteenth century. Alan Schwartz (pers. com. 1984) tells me that his unpublished study of early United States commercial law suggests an even simpler explanation: *caveat emptor* applied only in the period when most vendors were, in fact, merchants who transshipped goods manufactured abroad; but as soon as manufacture became indigenous, producers were promptly held responsible for the quality of their wares.

abridgement of the common law, Sir Anthony Fitzherbert supposes that inn-keepers are under almost an "absolute duty of affording full protection to the guest and his property"; and other tradesmen such as carpenters and farriers are held to be under an only slightly weaker duty "of care in the conduct of the business to secure the safety of its patrons" (quoted in Bohlen 1908, 225; see also Prosser 1965, sec. 314A). Indeed, in one of the earliest authoritative statements of the rule of *caveat emptor* in the common law, Coke himself emphasizes that under the civil (i.e., statute) law "every man is bound to warrant the thing he selleth or conveyeth, albeit there be no express warranty, either in deed or in law" (quoted in Hamilton 1931, 1165). In Great Britain throughout the nineteenth century, ostensibly the heyday of "freedom of contract" ideologies, there were increasingly stringent attempts at protecting consumers in the areas of food and drink, weights and measures, hallmarking and assay, merchandise marks, usury, licensing doctors, and transport (Atiyah 1979, 544–60). Given all this, Atiyah (1979, 479) concludes,

> the early nineteenth century saw little more than a brief flirtation with the doctrine of *caveat emptor*; from the beginning this flirtation had to contend with serious opposition from judges who still believed that it was part of the job of the Courts to see that contracts were fair; and by the 1860s, at least in contracts of sale of goods, these judges had won out and the flirtation was over. The common law had, in large part, returned to the traditions of eighteenth-century Equity when the fairness of a contractual exchange was still an important part of contract law.

United States courts, though lagging considerably behind the British in this respect, eventually followed suit.

In contemporary law (presumably mirroring contemporary morals) the businessman is recognized to have far greater responsibilities toward his customers. This "special liability of a seller of products for the physical harm to users or consumers" is set out in the *Restatement (Second) of the Law of Torts* (Prosser 1965, sec. 402A):

1) One who sells any product in a defective condition unreasonably dangerous to the user or consumer or to his property is subject to liability for physical harm thereby caused to the ultimate user or consumer, or to his property, if
   a) the seller is engaged in the business of selling such a product, and
   b) it is expected to and does reach the user or consumer without substantial change in the condition in which it is sold.

2) The rule stated in Section 1 applies although
   a) the seller has exercised all possible care in the preparation and sale of his product, and
   b) the user or consumer has not brought the product from or entered into any contractual relations with the seller. (See similarly ALI 1976, sec. 2–314)

For present purposes, what matters is the basis for these responsibilities rather than their details. A case can be made for calling them contractual. Early jurists, attempting to breach *caveat emptor* defenses, described these obligations as arising out of "implicit warranties," and hence self-assumed contractual duties. "The warranty gradually came to be regarded as a term of the contract of sale, express or implied, for which the normal remedy is a contract action" (Prosser 1971, 635). That was little more than a tactical maneuver, however, for "the obligation is imposed on the seller not because he assumed it voluntarily, but because the law attaches such consequences to his conduct irrespective of any agreement" (Prosser 1971, 635).[23]

Perhaps the best evidence for not interpreting the duties of seller to buyer as duties of contract is the fact that the parties are not permitted to contract *out* of them (Epstein 1980, chap. 5). In the United States, the landmark case in this area is *Henningsen v. Bloomfield Motors, Inc.*, 32 NJ 358, 161 A2d 69 (1960). It is now standard practice for United States courts to invalidate the attempts of tenants to waive their right to withhold rent payments if the property they rent fails to meet minimum standards of habitability; and in many places the law imposes nonwaivable "cooling-off periods" for consumer transactions (Kronman 1983, 764). Similarly in Great Britain, there are "statutes enforcing the liability of transport undertakings for the safety of their passengers irrespective of contractual clauses purporting to exclude or restrict them" (Kahn-Freund 1967, 640).[24]

Those rules, and many like them, are justified by reference to the peculiar vulnerability of the customer. In *Henningsen v. Bloomfield Motors, Inc.*, the court argued that a single customer was in no position to negotiate in detail contractual terms with a large firm. Irish emigrants were in no position to bargain hard with shipowners over the terms of their passage to America; so in 1842 Parliament protected them by setting a prescribed form of contract, unalterable by the parties themselves (Atiyah 1979, 554). And so on.

One of the most striking applications of the reasoning based on the concept of vulnerability is the assignment of responsibilities to operators of public transportation for the safety of their passengers. This duty to protect passengers from all foreseeable dangers arises "because the passenger, by placing himself in the charge of the company, confined by the very necessities of the transportation to its car, and being in effect imprisoned therein has no

23. This leads Prosser to recall approvingly an anonymous note in the 1929 *Harvard Law Review* to the effect that "A more notable example of legal miscegenation could hardly be cited than that which produced the modern action for breach of warranty. Originally sounding in tort, yet arising out of the warrantor's consent to be bound, it later ceased necessarily to be consensual, and at the same time came to be mainly in contact" (quoted in Prosser 1971, 634).

24. Initially, this principle seems to have applied principally to personal-injury cases; in other cases, a disclaimer on the part of the vendor or a waiver on the part of the purchaser sufficed to release producers from liability for product defects. But the principle has now been extended far beyond that, as the example of "nonwaivable cooling-off periods" suggests.

power to avoid such dangers, and must look to his carrier to keep him out of the range of them'' (Bohlen 1908, 234). The same sort of logic also underlies the unusually harsh rule imposing ''strict liability'' for faulty products upon the seller, whether or not the sellers were guilty of negligence. In early cases, concerning the purity of food and drink, it was held that producers owed a very strict duty of care to consumers (Epstein 1980, 30–40). In a typical case, *Hertzler v. Manshum,* 228 Mich 416, 422, 200 NW 155, 156 (1924), the duty was justified in terms of ''the imperative need of consumers of foodstuffs to rely upon the care of the manufacturers thereof, and the inability of consumers . . . to detect injurious impurities or poisonous substances therein.'' Extensions of this rule of strict producer liability beyond the area of foodstuffs were similarly justified by reference to the peculiar vulnerability of consumers. Notice, for example, the language in the leading case of *Greenman v. Yuba Power Products Inc.*: ''The purpose of [strict] liability is to insure that the costs of injuries resulting from defective products are borne by the manufacturers that put such products on the market rather than by the injured persons who are *powerless to protect themselves*'' (59 Cal 2d 57 at 63, 337 P2d 897 at 901, 127 Cal Rptr 697 at 701 [1963]; emphasis added).

All this is most effectively captured in that classic of the American Progressive movement, E.A. Ross's *Sin and Society: An Analysis of Latter-Day Iniquity.* Ross begins by exclaiming, ''Under our present manner of living, how many of my vital interests I must intrust to others!'' He goes on to list the various vulnerabilities implicit in modern life:

> Nowadays the water main is my well, the trolley car my carriage, the banker's safe my old stocking, the policeman's billy my fist. My own eyes and nose and judgment defer to the inspector of food, or drugs, or gas, or factories, or tenements, or insurance companies. I rely upon others to look after my drains, invest my savings, nurse my sick, and teach my children. I let the meat trust butcher my pig, the oil trust mould my candles, the sugar trust boil my sorghum, the coal trust chop my wood, the barb wire company split my rails. (Ross 1907, 3)

Ross proceeds next to observe that ''this spread-out manner of life lays snares for the weak and opens doors to the wicked. Interdependence puts us, as it were, at one another's mercy, and so ushers in a multitude of new forms of wrong-doing'' (Ross 1907, 3–4). The bulk of Ross's book is devoted to investigating the new moral obligations that both he and I think necessarily proceed from such interdependence, and to the new forms of sin associated with their breach.

It is apparent from this brief survey that some of the most important obligations of businessmen to their employees and to their customers are extracontractual. They arise independently of any voluntary acts of will— and indeed maybe even in spite of them, for these obligations cannot be removed even by mutual consent. They arise instead from the vulnerability of one party (employees, customers) to the actions and choices of the other (businessmen). T. B. Macauley's speech in the Parliamentary debate on the Ten Hour Bill is more famous, but a subsequent speaker seems to have come nearer the mark simply when asking, "What was a Legislature for if it was not to protect the weak against the strong?" (Wakley 1846, 1046).[25]

These points relating to the duties of the strong to the weak are nicely summarized by the distinguished English legal commentator Kahn-Freund (1967, 635):

> The labour law of Great Britain shares with that of the other nations in our orbit of civilization two essential jurisprudential features: it is based on the contractual foundations of the obligation to work and of the obligation to pay wages, and at the same time permeated by a tendency to formulate and to enforce an ever-growing number of imperative norms for the protection of the worker, norms which the parties to the contract cannot validly set aside to the detriment of the economically weaker party.

The same is true of consumer protection regulations. "In all these situations," Kahn-Freund (1967, 640) concludes, "the law operates upon an existing contractual relationship, but it moulds this relationship through mandatory norms which cannot be contracted out to the detriment of the weaker party (employee, passenger, customer in general). It is this phenomenon which is characteristic of the legal developments of our time."

Of course, no one is forced to go into business, hiring employees or selling to customers. That is a matter of choice; and only if one chooses that role does one incur the special responsibilities that accompany it. Hence, the special responsibilities of businessmen are, if not exactly contractual (because unalterable and nonnegotiable), at least "self-assumed" in some broader sense.[26] This view of special business responsibilities as self-assumed offers, at best, a partial explanation: it may be used to explain why businessmen have some special responsibilities but not to explain what the responsibilities are or why they should take the unalterable form they so often do. The what and why remain a mystery within the narrower model of self-assumed obligations, whereas the mystery dissolves when the responsibilities are viewed from the broader perspective of the vulnerability model.

---

25. Bowie (1979, 150) offers a variation on this theme: "Another moral reason for business to accept a new contract [with society] might be based on the notion of power. Those constituents of society which have the most in the way of resources should contribute the most to resolving social ills. Since business is either the most powerful force or second only to the federal government, its superior resources impose special obligations upon it."

26. Bowie (1979, 147–48), for example, argues that "the operation of a business . . . is not a matter of right. Rather, the individuals enter into a contract with society. In [re]turn for the permission to do business, the society places certain obligations and duties on the business. . . . The corporation has those obligations which the society imposes on it in its charter of incorporation. In accepting its charter the corporation accepts those moral constraints."

Professional Ethics

Professionals such as doctors and lawyers have special and especially strong obligations to protect the interests of their clients. Not only do they owe these obligations to no one except their clients, but at least occasionally, they must also serve a client at the expense of those who are not their clients. "The professional *qua* professional has a client or patient whose interests must be represented, attended to, or looked after by the professional. And that means that the role of the professional . . . is to prefer in a variety of ways the interests of the client or patient over those of individuals generally" (Wasserstrom 1975, 5; see also Wasserstrom 1984); as Fried puts it, "Doctors and lawyers . . . owe a duty of loyalty to their clients, a loyalty which . . . requires taking the medical or legal interests of that client more seriously than the interests of others in similar or greater need, more seriously, indeed, than formulas of either efficiency . . . or fairness . . . would require or even permit" (Fried 1978, 176; see similarly Fried 1974, chaps. 3–4; 1976, 1061–62).

Why a professional person should have these obligations to his clients, and only his clients, is ordinarily explained in quasi-contractual terms of voluntary undertakings. Here again, the model of self-assumed obligations is thought to apply. Yet closer investigation once again shows the model to be inadequate. The peculiar vulnerability of clients to their doctors, lawyers, and so forth, offers a more satisfactory explanation for both the existence and the peculiar strength of the special professional responsibilities.

Here I shall concentrate on doctors and lawyers as professionals par excellence. Their special responsibilities may well be far stronger (and hence clearer) than those of architects, accountants, or engineers, for example; yet the source and structure of all special professional responsibilities are surely the same. I shall continue to look to the law as the principal guide to our settled moral intuitions; but in the case of professional ethics, we can also look to the formal codes adopted by the professional associations themselves. Hence, I shall refer from time to time to the "Principles of Medical Ethics" of the American Medical Association (AMA) (1957) and to the "Code of Professional Responsibility" of the American Bar Association (ABA) (1969).

Writers occasionally refer to the relationship between doctor and patient explicitly as a "bilateral contract,"[27] and to the one between lawyer and client as a "contract of employment."[28] As Fried (1974, 78) says, "the structure of these [professional] relations and values presupposes that they are deliberately entered into, chosen, assumed as obligations

27. Jonas (1969, 238), Stevens (1974, 253–34), Fletcher (1976, 704), and Veatch (1981, chap. 5).
28. Pirsig (1970, chap. 2), Fried (1976, 1077).

are assumed.'' There is much indeed in these relationships to suggest something of a contractual tie. As in the classic formula of contract law, clients *offer* employment to professionals, and the professionals agree to *accept* their cases.

Its apparent voluntariness is probably the most important factor in making the relationship between professional and patient/client seem contractual. A patient is notionally at liberty to approach any physician he wants; and a client any lawyer. The official professional ideologies hold that professionals are, by the same token, largely at liberty to accept or reject as client whomsoever they please.[29] "A lawyer is under no obligation to act as adviser or advocate for every person who may wish to become his client," the ABA code (1969, EC 2–26) insists; and "a physician is free to choose whom he will serve" according to the AMA code (1957, chap. 2, sec. 4). Even the law of torts acknowledges that "a physician is under no duty to answer the call of one who is dying and might be saved" (Prosser 1971, 340–41).

Its reciprocity is the second factor giving the professional relationship the appearance of a contract. Doctors and lawyers are "consulting professionals who act . . . on a fee-for-service basis" (Bayles 1981, 13). The professional gets his fee; and the client, his service. So, in the language of contract law, there is "consideration" on both sides.

In various other respects, however, the analogy to a contract is simply inappropriate. Let us dispose of the weakest objections first. The sort of vague "contract" we enter into to obtain the services of a professional person is not nearly specific enough to count as a paradigmatic legal contract. For example, what precise activities are to be performed and when are ordinarily left unspecified. That would seriously undermine the strength of the putative contract in any court of law. This is a rather weak objection, however. Even if it is not a full-blooded legal contract, the transaction might still be analyzed as a kind of "quasi-contract." We need only impute to the patients and clients "standard intentions," rather like those we impute to persons who die intestate when we are disposing of their estates, or those we impute to unconscious patients brought into hospital emergency rooms when we are deciding on their treatment.[30] The binding responsibilities of a doctor or lawyer who has agreed to only a vague contract or none at all might, in this way, be analyzed in terms of the client's "reasonable expectations" of "ordinary procedures" (Fletcher

---

29. Fried (1976, 1062) in particular hammers home the point that professional codes generally have "little or nothing to say about the initial choice of clients or patients. Certainly it is laudable if the doctor and lawyer choose their clients among the poorest or sickest or most dramatically threatened, but the professional ideal does not require this kind of choice in any systematic way— the choice of client remains largely a matter of fortuity or arbitrary choice."

30. "In an emergency which threatens death or serious bodily harm, . . . the surgeon must be free to operate without delaying to obtain consent. . . . He is reasonably entitled to assume that, if the patient were competent and understood the situation, he would consent, and therefore to act as if it has been given" (Prosser 1971, 102).

1968, 68). In the terms of tort law, "the standard of conduct becomes one of 'good medical practice' [or its equivalent in other professions], which is to say, what is customary and usual in the profession" (Prosser 1971, 165, 162).

Three further anomalies, however, are less easily explained away. First, parties to a contract should, if they so desire, be permitted to negotiate between themselves the terms and conditions of their agreement. The terms of the putative contract between professionals and their clients, however, are largely fixed independently of any bargaining between the parties. Professional codes of ethics set out, in effect, a "standard form" of contract of which few provisions can be altered even by mutual agreement, however fully informed it may be, between professional and client.[31]

Second, parties to a contract should be permitted to contract with anyone they want, or with no one if they prefer. This is true, to a certain extent, of professional obligations; and as already noted, the official ideologies of the professions make much of the fact. There are important limits, however, to the freedom of professionals to serve whomsoever they please. The AMA code, having said that "a physician is free to choose whom he will serve," pointedly adds that "he should, however, respond to any request for his assistance in an emergency" (AMA 1957, chap. 2, sec. 4).[32]

Third, parties to a contract should be permitted to terminate the contract whenever they please, upon payment of appropriate damage charges. Professionals, in contrast, are much more constrained in their power to withdraw from a case. The AMA code stipulates that, "once having undertaken a case, the physician should not neglect the patient, nor should he withdraw from the case without giving notice to the patient, his relatives or his responsible friends sufficiently long in advance of his withdrawal to allow them to secure another medical attendant" (AMA 1957, chap. 2, sec. 4). The ABA code similarly provides that a lawyer may withdraw from a case "only on the basis of compelling circumstances." It goes on to say that "Even when he justifiably withdraws, a lawyer should protect the welfare of his client by giving due

---

31. The exceptions alluded to in the text are found in the ABA (1969) code: "a lawyer may reveal confidences or secrets of the client or clients affected, but only after full disclosure" (DR 4-401-C-1); and "except with the consent of his client, after a full disclosure, a laywer shall not accept employment if the exercise of his professional judgment on behalf of his client will be or necessarily may be affected by his own financial, business, property, or personal interests" (DR 5-101).

32. This derives from the fact, pointed out by Bayles (1981, 27), that "professions . . . recognize a responsibility to establish equal opportunity for or equal access to their services. . . . This obligation belongs to professions as a whole and cannot be directly reduced to a similar obligation on the part of individual professionals" in ordinary circumstances. But when in an emergency this particular doctor is the only one in a position to help, the profession's obligation becomes his own. Presumably the only reason this is not mentioned in the ABA code is that analogous legal emergencies seldom arise; the pace of legal proceedings is such that there is always time to find someone else to do the job. Where that is not the case (in remote locations or arcane specialties, for example), the same logic should surely lead us to require lawyers to take any case proffered them, at least as long as it would not require them to do anything illegal or immoral (Bayles 1979, 178).

notice of his withdrawal, suggesting employment of other counsel, delivering to the client all papers . . . and otherwise endeavoring to minimize the possibility of harm" (ABA 1969, EC 3–32). Here tort law stands behind the requirements of the professional codes. In the *Second Restatement of Torts* (Prosser 1965, sec. 323), "negligent performance of an undertaking to render services" is defined as follows:

> One who undertakes, gratuitously or for consideration, to render services to another which he should recognize as necessary for the protection of the other's person or things, is subject to liability to the other for physical harm resulting from his failure to exercise reasonable care to perform his undertaking, if:
> (a) his failure to exercise such care increases the risk of such harm, or
> (b) the harm is suffered because of the other's reliance upon the undertaking.

Where the professional's undertaking has reasonably induced the client to forebear from opportunities to seek alternative sources of assistance, the professional will under the law of torts "be required to exercise reasonable care to terminate his services in such a manner that there is no unreasonable risk of harm . . . , or to continue them until they can be so terminated" (Prosser 1965, sec. 323 and comment C). Thus, a physician is legally under no obligation to stop and treat the victims of a traffic accident.[33] Once having commenced treatment, however, he is not at liberty to discontinue it until the patient is out of danger or until alternative provisions for care have been made.[34] None of this makes much sense in terms of contracts and quasi-contracts.

The above three factors, taken together, suggest that the relationship between professional and client is not (and should not be) viewed as primarily a contractual or quasi-contractual one. The reason lies in the unequal bargaining power of the two parties to the putative contract. Bayles (1981, 64) usefully catalogues these inequalities:

---

33. The morality of the matter may well be—indeed on my vulnerability analysis, would often be—otherwise. Here as elsewhere the law is a very conservative guide to our settled moral intuitions, imposing fewer and weaker obligations than morality might.

34. In the *Restatement (Second) of the Law of Torts,* Prosser (1965, sec. 324) defines the "duty of one who undertakes charge of another who is helpless" as follows:

> "One who, being under no duty to do so, takes charge of another, is subject to liability to the other for any bodily harm caused to him by:
> (a) the failure of the actor to exercise reasonable care to secure the safety of the other while within the actor's charge, or
> (b) the actor's discontinuing his aid or protection, if by so doing he leaves the other in a worse position than when the actor took charge of him."

As Prosser (1971, 348) points out in his own *Handbook of Torts,* that duty is in practice even stronger than the loophole in clause (b) suggests: "It seems very unlikely that any court will ever hold that one who has begun to pull a drowning man out of the river after he has caught hold of the rope is free, without good reason, to abandon the attempt, walk away and let him drown, merely because he was already in extremis before the effort was begun."

First, a professional's knowledge far exceeds that of a client. A professional has the special knowledge produced by long training, knowledge a client could not have without comparable training. Second, a client is concerned about some basic value—personal health, legal status, or financial status—whereas a professional is not as concerned about the subject matter. The client usually has more at stake. Third, a professional often has a freedom to enter the relationship that a client lacks. A professional is often able to obtain other clients more easily than a client can obtain another professional. From this point of view, the bargaining situation is more like that between an individual and a public utility. (See similarly Masters 1975, 25–26; May 1975, 35)

"This relationship of inequality is," Wasserstrom (1975, 16) concludes, "intrinsic to the existence of professionalism. For the professional is, in some respects at least, always in a position of dominance vis-à-vis the client, and the client in a position of dependence vis-à-vis the professional." It is the client's dependence upon the professional, I would argue, that gives rise to strong obligations on the professional's part.[35] Clients are and must necessarily be relying upon professionals to protect them in these crucial ways. Here, as in the case of promises and contracts discussed above, "the factor of reliance . . . that the doctor [or other professional] will render aid means that [he] is . . . obliged to do so," both legally and morally (Fletcher 1968, 66); or as Bernard Williams (1981, 55) similarly remarks, "lawyers and doctors have elaborate codes of professional ethics . . . because their clients need to be protected, and be seen to be protected, in what are particularly sensitive areas of their interests."

Although there are undeniably contractual elements in the relationship between professionals and their clients, a better legal model for the relationship would be that of a "trust." The law does indeed "use such a conception to characterize most professional-client relationships," Bayles (1981, 69) writes.[36] "In a fiduciary relationship, . . . because one party is in a more

35. Kenneth Arrow (1974, 37) finds similar grounds for medical ethics: "The difference in information between the patient and the physician implies that the former has relatively little check on the latter. He may never be in a position to know whether the physician did as well as he could; if the patient knew that much, he would be a physician. . . . It is for this reason that ethical indoctrination of physicians is of such crucial importance." So, too, do Pellegrino and Thomasma (1981, 214, 218, 260) trace the physician's "special moral obligation" to "the patient's special vulnerability." They point out that the relationship between the patient and physician "involves one person who is less free and more vulnerable. That is why the relationship cannot be regarded as a contract or even a covenant. It is not an agreement between two parties more or less equal, more or less free, who can negotiate terms for the delivery of some service or commodity. Medical care is not a commodity one may choose as freely as one chooses automobiles or television sets."

36. Strictly speaking, the law distinguishes between a "fiduciary relation" (such as that between a "trustee and beneficiary, guardian and ward, agent and principal, attorney and client") and a "confidential relation" (such as within "a family relation or one of friendship or such a relation of confidence as that which arises between physician and patient or priest and penitent"). There are, however, similar obligations to protect the interests either of those whose trust or of those whose confidence one enjoys (Scott 1959, sec. 2, comment B; cf. sec. 44, comment C).

advantageous position, he or she has special obligations to the other. The weaker party depends upon the stronger in ways in which the other does not and so must *trust* the stronger party.'' What follows from such a relationship of trust, both in law and in morals, is that ''a person in a fiduciary relation to another is under a duty to act for the benefit of the other as to matters within the scope of the relation'' (Scott 1959, sec. 2, comment B; Frankel 1983).

Tracing professional responsibilities to the vulnerabilities of clients or patients explains certain particular features of professional responsibilities which, within models built around notions of contracts or quasi-contracts, would seem most peculiar. Consider the three anomalies discussed above. The vulnerability of prospective clients explains why parties are held to the standard-form contract set out in professional codes of ethics: otherwise the party in the stronger bargaining position, the professional, might drive an unconscionably hard bargain with the vulnerable client. So, too, does the vulnerability of the prospective client explain why a physician is not free to decline the offer of employment in an emergency: no one else could provide the desperately needed assistance if he did not. So, too, does the vulnerability model explain why professionals cannot withdraw from a case without giving the client sufficient opportunity to obtain other assistance: that would leave the client dreadfully exposed (Fried 1976, 1077).

This analysis of professional responsibilities in terms of client vulnerabilities suggests the following general rule governing the permissibility of a professional's declining to serve a would-be client: a professional ought to be held morally and professionally (if not necessarily legally) responsible to provide assistance in any situation in which, if he did not, someone would be left helpless. Consider the case of the only doctor in an isolated frontier town. Surely he should not be entitled to withdraw from the case of someone too ill to be moved, no matter how much notice he gives of his intention to do so. Neither should he be entitled to refuse to treat that patient in the first place (Reeder 1982, 99).

As a kind of corollary to that rule, a professional should not be entitled to press the claims of his own clients against persons who are helpless. This problem arises particularly in the practice of law. It is the job of the advocate ''to present his or her client's case in the most attractive, forceful light and to seek to expose the weaknesses and defects in the case of the opponent'' (Wasserstrom 1975, 9).[37] That is the nature of the adversary system. That is all well and good, provided that everyone has an advocate who can shield him from the onslaught of others' advocates in court. But what if one party were undefended or inadequately defended? Then he would be very vulnerable indeed to the attacks of the others' advocates. That, in turn, would make it immoral for those attorneys to press their clients' cases as forcefully as other-

37. See similarly ABA (1969, EC 7-1), Nagel (1970, 132), Fried (1978, 189–93).

wise they would, oblivious to the possible impact upon others (Luban 1984a).[38]

More generally, the vulnerability of people in need of professional help but unable to obtain it explains the obligation imposed upon both doctors and lawyers, collectively and to some extent individually, to provide services free or at reduced rates to those who cannot afford the ordinary fees (AMA 1957, chap. 7, sec. 1; ABA 1969, EC 2-17, 2-24, 2-25).[39] The indigent are doubly vulnerable: their poverty puts them especially at risk both medically and legally and at the same time prevents them from obtaining the needed assistance in the ordinary market.

Vulnerability provides a more satisfactory rationale than that of contract or quasi-contract for the form and content of professional responsibilities. Here, as in the case of business responsibilities, it might be argued that the model of self-assumed responsibilities can at least provide a rationale for applying those fixed prescriptions to particular individuals. However, the argument is considerably less plausible as applied to people involved in professions than as applied to people involved in businesses.

Consider first the "undertaking" given by the professional in accepting a particular case (Veatch 1981, chap. 5). The profession as a whole may have a responsibility for serving the group of people in need as a whole; and that responsibility may be, just as I have argued it is, predicated upon the vulnerability of the needy to dangers that only members of the profession can alleviate, rather than upon any collective undertaking on the part of the profession. But there is still the problem of deciding how particular clients should be matched up with particular professionals. Advocates of the quasi-contract model would argue that the problem is resolved through an undertaking on the part of the particular professional to the particular client.

---

38. Wasserstrom (1975, 9, 13) considers the argument that "the lawyer *qua* lawyer participates in a complex institution which functions well only if the individuals adhere to their institutional roles," and concludes: "If the institutions work well and fairly, there may be good sense in deferring important moral concerns and criticisms to another time and place, to the level of institutional criticism and assessment. But the less certain we are entitled to be of either the rightness or the self-corrective nature of the larger institutions of which the professional is a part, the less apparent it is that we should encourage the professional to avoid direct engagement with the moral issues as they arise. And we are, today, I believe, certainly entitled to be quite skeptical both of the fairness and of the capacity for self-correction of our larger institutional mechanisms, including the legal system. To the degree to which the institutional rules and practices are unjust, unwise or undesirable, to that same degree is the case for the role-differentiated behavior of the lawyer weakened if not destroyed."

39. Halberstam (1974, 250) points out that "the law [profession] made no attempt to extend this . . . doctrine to the poor until the 1870s, and little real effort until the 1960s"; and some lawyers still resist such suggestions (Fried 1978, 187). But "unlike the law, medicine has always taken special responsibility for the poor." Indeed, in "the earliest written healing ethic," the Code of Hammurabi, there is a differential fee schedule tailored to the patient's presumed ability to pay (Halberstam 1974, 231–32).

This is not a true undertaking, however. The so-called undertaking is typically predicated upon the most trivial of incidents. Prosser (1971, 345–46) points out that "initiation of the undertaking is commonly found in minor acts, of no significance in themselves and without any effect of their own upon the plaintiff's interests, such as writing a letter or attending a meeting or merely accepting a general agency." There is no pretense that those actions in which we locate the undertaking "argue the will" of the professional to be bound thereby to serve the client.[40] Often all that an action does is establish some unique link between the client and the professional, which in itself can be sufficient to pick him out, among all other professionals, as the one who should discharge the collective duty of the profession to the needy individual.[41] Occasionally this sort of unique link may exist without any sort of undertaking, as in the case in which the only doctor in the area where an emergency has occured is obliged (by the AMA code, if not tort law) to provide service to injured people who are complete strangers to him. In that case it does not look very much like a "voluntary act of will" that connects particular professionals with their particular clients.

On the second level, there is an undertaking when members of a profession accept their roles. Along with those roles come concomitant responsibilities: "doctors, nurses, policemen, firemen, and lifeguards are committed by their *vocational* skills to render aid" in certain circumstances (Kleinig 1976, 383). The reason traditionally offered is that the profession as a whole has undertaken a commitment along these lines to society as a whole and that each practitioner takes that commitment onto himself by joining the profession.[42] "There is a general contract, if you will, between therapists and society, in the context of which particular agreements are made" (Reeder 1982, 98). Professional responsibilities are self-assumed because professional roles are

40. Uttering the words "I promise," though perhaps objectively a trivial incident, at least "argues the will" of the promisee in a way that merely dropping someone a noncommittal note or sitting through a meeting does not. As Hobbes (1951, chap. 14) rightly insists, "implicit signs" can give rise to contractual obligations only if they do "argue the will" of the parties to the contract in this way.

41. Notice this example of an "undertaking" discussed by Fletcher (1978, 615): In the case of *Regina v. Instan* (1893) 1 QB 450, a niece took up residence with an aged aunt and undertook to care for her. When through gross neglect of this duty the aunt died, the niece was convicted of manslaughter. The court's judgment in this case "brought together a number of criteria, including the blood relationship, their living in the same house, a contract to care for the aunt, and the undertaking to do so." Lord Coleridge's rambling opinion hints that any one of these could, independently, have been sufficient for settling the duty of care upon the niece. The real emphasis in his opinion is not, however, so much upon the niece's undertaking but rather upon the fact that the aunt was peculiarly vulnerable to her. What seems decisive for Lord Coleridge is the fact that "the deceased could not get [food] for herself; she could only get it through the prisoner. It was [therefore] the prisoner's clear duty at common law to supply it to the deceased."

42. "Taking on a role is sometimes appropriately viewed as a kind of promising. The process of assuming a professional role often illustrates this. Many professional groups have rituals of initiation that include oaths of allegiance" (Veatch 1981, 84). See similarly Veatch (1972, 536–46; 1981, chap. 5), and May (1975).

self-assumed. "It is the entry into the role which is free. Once one has assumed the role, it binds with the obligations of right and wrong" specified in the professional code (Fried 1978, 168). "In accepting the job, he accepted the standards of that job" (Daniel Lyons 1969, 95). Professional responsibilities can, in this way, be analyzed as ones that professionals have undertaken as part and parcel of that package of rights and duties which they accepted upon assuming their professional roles.

Professional responsibilities are not, however, merely "the price society demands" for allowing professionals their privileges.[43] To argue that they were would be to suggest that there would be nothing wrong with a society that made no such demands on its professionals, and that professionals would bear no such responsibilities if their society did not happen to make such demands on them.[44] That is surely incorrect. People in need of professional assistance necessarily depend for it upon those who have acquired certain professional skills.[45] As I have been arguing, such vulnerability on the one part gives rise to responsibility on the other. In short, neither argument that professional responsibilities are self-assumed because professional roles are self-assumed is particularly promising. The vulnerability component is here very large indeed.

Family

Family life provides some of the clearest examples we have of special moral responsibilities. "Family members are expected to weigh each other's interests more heavily than those of strangers, to provide for each other's needs as they would not for strangers" (Goldman 1980, 4). This is the first example of special responsibilities which most philosophers mention, and it is generally the one of which they speak with greatest confidence.[46]

---

43. "If it is true, as I believe it is, that members of the medical profession have been given 'high rank' and occupy a special place in society, a special definition and application of the noblesse oblige ethic seems justified: honorable behavior encompassing kindness, charity and a desire to promote the welfare of others is considered to be the responsibility of physicians and members of other professions who have been given a special status by society" (Ballantine 1979, 637).
44. That is to say, on this model there is no lower limit on what society must demand. There may be an upper limit on what it can realistically demand, and still get people willing to take up the professions. This, some would say, is the fatal flaw in various proposals for two years of mandatory national service by professionals immediately upon leaving school (Halberstam 1974; Stevens 1974; cf. Bayles 1981, 47–50).
45. To revert to that favorite philosophical example of the drowning man, suppose that someone with a "top lifesaving certificate" simply stood by and watched him drown. "He would be somehow disgraced, for failing to live up to his elite expertise; the obligations of professionalism [therefore] hold . . . even without a contract" (Daniel Lyons 1969, 95). The reason, as Reeder (1982, 99) explains, is that "the special skills are relevant to the distributive question of who should provide help in a particular situation, just as a firefighter's or mountain climber's might be. . . . The duty [to help] falls on whoever, *ceteris paribus*, can do so most efficiently."
46. See, e.g., Nagel (1970, 129–30), Williams (1973, 110), Fried (1974, 70; 1976, 1066, 1071), Wasserstrom (1975, 4), Parfit (1979b, 556), Bennett (1981, 78), and Sen (1982, 19–28).

At first brush, anyway, the special responsibilities growing out of family life do not seem to fit any voluntaristic model. You cannot choose your family in the same way that you can choose your friends or business associates. You are not free to negotiate the terms of what you owe to your family, as you are with ordinary contractors. Such facts make applying the model of self-assumed obligations to family responsibilities appear prima facie inappropriate. Nevertheless, there is a long tradition of trying to force family relationships into a voluntaristic framework. "Even in the case of family relationship," lawyers tell us, "there is present the will of the citizen to become a husband or father, so that even here the relation is, in the last analysis, the creature of voluntary action on his part" (Bohlen 1908, 243; see similarly Fried 1976, 1071); or as philosophers sometimes say, "the husband . . . has unique obligations to his spouse and children, because of his prior actions of promise-making" (Veatch 1972, 542–43).

Contemporary social mores lend increasing credibility to voluntaristic accounts of social life. "The ideology of the conjugal [nuclear] family proclaims the right of the individual to choose his or her own spouse, place to live, and even which kin obligations to accept" (Goode 1963, 19). For once, ideology maps reality: most of us today do choose our own spouses; and as contraceptive technologies are perfected, we do increasingly choose whether or not to become parents, albeit we do not (yet) choose the particular individual that is to be our child.[47]

Of course, the voluntaristic model cannot plausibly accommodate *all* family relationships. No one chooses his own siblings or parents; we merely tumble into these relationships. Then again, we are increasingly doubtful about whether any special moral responsibilities attach to those relationships anyway. Should parents, siblings, or distant kin fall upon hard times, we are increasingly inclined to say—both morally and legally—that they should lodge their claims with the state welfare services rather than with their families.[48] Perhaps, then, where the voluntaristic model fails to work, we have less need for it anyway.

47. These developments may be less modern than they seem. Stone (1977, 272, 415, 422) reports that "by 1660, . . . in all but the highest ranks of the aristocracy it had been conceded . . . that children of both sexes should be given the right of veto over a future spouse proposed to them by their parents. Between 1660 and 1880, . . . there took place the further more radical shift, . . . with the children now normally making their own choices, and the parents being left with no more than the right of veto over socially or economically unsuitable candidates." Similarly with contraception: "between 1675 and 1775 there took place a striking decline in the fertility of the children of the nobility. . . . Just how this reduction of births was achieved is not known for certain, but . . . it is presumed that the principal means was *coitus interruptus,* assisted no doubt by oral, manual and anal sex."
48. See, e.g., Sidgwick (1874, 247), Ginnow and Gordon (1978, vol. 67A, sec. 97; vol. 70, secs. 59–62; vol. 81, sec. 109), Schorr (1980, chap. 2), Graycar and Kinnear (1981), and Sundstrom (1982). This phenomenon, too, may be less new than it seems. Laslett (1970, 52) reports that "recent research has shown the familistic picture of 'elder generations' being able to count on

My argument here, again, will be that special responsibilities follow more fundamentally from special vulnerabilities than from special self-assumed obligations. What gives rise to the duty to act in cases of family relationship (or personal ties more generally) is the "state of mutual reliance" that exists within such relationships (Kirchheimer 1942, 635–36) and the "dependence and helplessness of him who claims that the duty is owing to him" (Bohlen 1908, 227). And what makes expectations of material support particularly "justifiable" in "intimate associations" is the even more important emotional vulnerabilities among the participants (Karst 1980, 648).

T he relationship between husband and wife is ordinarily thought to be very special indeed. I am obliged, both legally and morally, to share with my spouse a great many things that I would not be expected to share with anyone else. Spouses are expected to provide each other with sustenance, spiritual as well as material, far in excess of that which anyone else could reasonably demand of them (Pound 1916). How are we to explain these very special responsibilities?

The received view of marriage is insistently contractual. When he counts the "Conjugal Relation" as primary among "relationships voluntarily assumed," Sidgwick (1874, 254) is merely restating a long-standing presumption. According to Blackstone's *Commentaries* (1783, bk. 1, chap. 15), "our [English common] law considers marriage in no other light than as a civil contract." Locke (1690, sec. 78) similarly holds that "conjugal society is made by a voluntary compact between man and woman"; and Pufendorf (1672, bk. 6, chap. 1, secs. 14, 12) before him referred approvingly to the "common maxim of the lawyers that *consenting and not bedding, makes a marriage,*" reiterating that "the *domination* of one person over another, considered as a *moral entity,* doth not exist without the concurrence of some human act, and . . . the woman for this reason lies under no obligation to obey, before she hath by her own consent, submitted to the rule and authority of a husband."

Of course, we no longer think in terms of a wife subjecting herself to the domination of her husband. Although it has taken a century since Mill (1869, chap. 2) bemoaned the horrors of Victorian marriage laws, the legal "subjec-

---

maintenance of the offspring and kin has been considerably overdrawn. . . . In the past, at least in English history, there can be no doubt that political pressure had to be brought to bear to require children to support their needy parents, and that many such destitute parents were in fact supported by the State through the Poor Law, even if they had grown up, independent children at the time. Nothing like the same political persuasion had to be used to ensure that parents maintained their offspring." This is abundantly clear from Charles Booth's (1892, 106–232) survey of 360 Poor Law unions in England and Wales. Research on the Plymouth Colony in Massachusetts similarly reveals "that small and essentially nuclear families were standard from the very beginning of American history" (Demos 1970, 62).

tion of women" is now easing thoughout the developed world (Glendon 1977). Modern marriage law still imposes reciprocal duties of support and service, however, and these are still analyzed in terms of a marriage contract. Even economists are now getting in on the act. In his *Treatise on the Family*, for example, Gary Becker (1982, 14–15) suggests that

> Since married women have been specialized to childbearing and other domestic activities, they have demanded long-term "contracts" from their husbands to protect them against abandonment and other adversities. Virtually all societies have developed long-term protection for married women; one can even say that "marriage" is defined by a long-term commitment between a man and a woman.

Now, this marriage contract is a most *peculiar* sort of contract, if it is a contract at all: "Its provisions are unwritten, its penalties are unspecified, and the terms of the contract are typically unknown to the 'contracting' parties. Prospective spouses are neither informed of the terms of the contract nor are they allowed any opinions about them" (Weitzman 1974, 1170).[49] Even Lord Devlin (1965, 68) concedes that "the law prescribes the shape and obligations of the contract of marriage," and that "in this respect it may be said that matrimonial law is radically different from the ordinary law of contract which generally leaves the parties free to make such arrangements as they like." Lord Devlin himself supposes that this will be an "especially welcome service in case of marriage, for courtship and legal draftsmanship are unnatural companions" (Devlin 1965, 63). Nevertheless, this very feature goes far toward making the marriage contract a "contract of adhesion" of the sort he bemoans just one chapter earlier in his *The Enforcement of Morals* (Devlin 1965, chap. 3). The terms of the marriage contract, like those of the famous "ticket cases," are set in advance and nonnegotiable. People are offered only Hobson's choice—this or nothing. They must contract on those terms or not at all. Such contracts of adhesion, while binding, are generally regarded as much less binding and more easily overturned than contracts of the more ordinary sort.

Although the content of the role responsibilities lay outside the will of the particular parties, the parties were nonetheless free to accept or reject the roles and all those invariant rights and duties attending them. Marital respon-

---

49. See similarly Ketchum (1977), O'Driscoll (1977, 250), Pateman (1981), and Weitzman (1981). This modern protest is, of course, a pale shadow of William Thompson's (1825, 55–56): "Audacious falsehood! A contract! where any of the attributes of contracts, of equal and just contracts, to be found in this transaction? A contract implies the voluntary assent of both the contracting parties. Can even both the parties, man and woman, by agreement alter the terms, as to *indissolubility* and *inequality*, of this pretended contract? No. Can any individual man divest himself, were he even so inclined, of his power of despotic control? He cannot. Have women been consulted as to the terms of this pretended contract? A contract, all of whose enjoyments . . . are on one side, while all of its pains and privations are on the other."

sibilities might, in this sense at least, be seen as self-assumed ones. Hart (1958, 103–4), for example, pursues this line. He agrees that "a husband's duty to support his wife, the father's duty to look after his children, [etc.] are not . . . truly created by the deliberate choice of the individuals." He insists, however, that they are nonetheless "*assumed* by entry upon the particular role so that one who takes up the role is there specially committed to discharging these duties" (see similarly Hollis 1977).

Of course, the most this move can do is to save the model of self-assumed obligations as a very partial analysis of marital responsibilities. Working within that model, we can (in the way just described) trace the fact that one *has* some such responsibilities to some voluntary act of will on one's own part; but as I shall show below, to explain the *content* of those responsibilities, we must turn to some other principle altogether. The vulnerability model, in contrast, provides a more complete account. It explains not only why one has marital responsibilities but also what those responsibilities require one to do.

In the present case, however, the model of self-assumed obligations probably cannot even do that much. Traditionally, anyway, one of the parties had virtually no choice but to agree to the marriage contract. For men, Hobson's choice might really be a choice: living outside marriage might be a live option. For women in traditional societies, it was not. They had no other way of supporting themselves. "Things are so arranged—knowledge, property, civil as well as political exclusions, man's public opinion—that the great majority of adult women must marry on whatever terms their masters have willed, or starve" (Thompson 1825, 57; see also Pateman 1981).[50] Where that was generally true—and, even today, for those for whom it still is true—the contract was *forced* upon them. A contract concluded under duress has never been held in particularly high esteem. Neither has one that "takes advantage of the weakness of one of the parties." Such agreements are "unfairly one-sided" and hence "unconscionable" (Fried 1981, 74; see further Mill 1869, chap. 2; Leff 1967).

Champions of the contract model, of course, have ready replies to such objections. Their remedy is to base marriage on a *real* contract, variable in its terms and explicitly negotiated between the two parties so as to reflect their "own needs and lifestyle" (Weitzman 1974, 1249; 1981; Shultz 1982). From as early as Locke (1690, secs. 82–84) theorists have argued that various forms of the marriage contract are equally capable of serving the same social purpose and that contracting parties should be allowed simply to choose the form that suits them best (Shanley 1979). Modern feminists have taken up this

---

50. They still have a choice of whom to marry, even if they have no choice of whether to marry or the terms on which they marry. As Mill (1869, chap. 2) rightly protests, however, "To those to whom nothing but servitude is allowed, the free choice of servitude is the only, though a most insufficient, alleviation."

refrain with gusto. It is claimed that once we have increased the range of options concerning terms of contract, partners, and alternatives to marriage, we no longer need fear anyone's being forced into an "unconscionable contract."

Before we follow the contract model to this, its logical conclusion, we should pause to consider whether the reciprocal duties of marriage really do rest on a contract or quasi-contract at all. The *Second Restatement of the Law of Contracts* (Braucher and Farmsworth 1981, sec. 90, comment) contains a salutory warning: "Although marriage is sometimes loosely referred to as a 'contract,' the marital relationship has not been regarded by common law as contractual in the usual sense. Many terms of the relationship are seen as largely fixed by the state and beyond the power of the parties to modify." The rule of law on this point is that: "A promise by a person contemplating marriage or by a married person, other than as part of an enforceable separation agreement, is unenforceable . . . if it would change some essential incident of the marriage relationship." The primary example offered of an "essential (and hence unalterable) incident" of the so-called marriage contract is "the duty imposed by law on one spouse [the husband] to support the other [the wife]" (Braucher and Farnsworth 1981, sec. 90 and associated comment).

Why we insist upon these particular duties being written into the "contract" has, as the reporters in the *Second Restatement* emphasize, nothing to do with the values of contract or self-assumed obligations. Our insistence is grounded instead in more general considerations of what lawyers loosely dub "public policy." Primary among these considerations comprising the "social interests in the family" is the need for "the protection of dependent persons," both dependent spouses and dependent children (Pound 1916, 296). Furthermore, "the obligations incident to family relationship generally [have not] been extended beyond the definite limits of furnishing necessities of life" (Bohlen 1908, 227–28). The duty of maintenance and support is imposed on one set of persons (husbands, parents) only because, and only insofar as, another set of persons (wives, children) are depending upon them.

We insist upon the husband's duty to support his family as firmly as we do because, traditionally, wives have been utterly dependent upon their husbands for material support. As Becker (1982, 27) observes in his *Treatise on the Family*, "Specialization of tasks, such as the division of labor between men and women, implies a dependence on others for certain tasks. Women have traditionally relied on men for provision of food, shelter, and protection, and men have traditionally relied on women for the bearing and rearing of children and the maintenance of the home." Specialization by its nature implies that you will have to depend on others to supply those goods and services in which you do not specialize. In ordinary markets there are, in principle, several people who could supply your needs. The sexual division of labor causes further specialization by making particular individuals of one sex dependent upon particular individuals of the other sex, rather than just on others in general, for the supply of the goods and services in question.

Dependency within marriage, and particularly the dependency of wives on husbands, is a familiar enough phenomenon. Mill (1869, chap. 4) bemoans the fact that the Victorian woman "is not self-dependent; she is not taught self-dependence; her destiny is to receive everything from others." This is partly due to the details of the marriage laws themselves, as early critics— among them, Wollstonecraft (1792), Thompson (1825, 54–107), and Mill himself (1848, bk. 5, chap. 11, sec. 9; 1869, chap. 2)—were all quick to point out. It is, to that extent, circular to justify the details of marriage laws by reference to dependencies created (or at least reinforced) by those self-same laws.

At the same time, however, the weaknesses of the "fairer sex" were also traditionally thought to have some objective basis. According to the sociological theories of the famous Brandeis brief which persuaded the United States Supreme Court to approve laws restricting women's hours of work,

> History discloses the fact that woman has always been dependent upon man. . . . It is impossible to close one's eyes to the fact that she still looks to [man] and depends upon him. . . . She is so constituted that she will rest upon and look to him for protection: . . . her physical structure and a proper discharge of her maternal functions justify legislation to protect her from the greed as well as the passion of man. (Brewer 1908, 421–22)

Even so fierce an advocate of women's rights as William Thompson (1825, x) concedes that two circumstances of nature—"permanent inferiority of strength, and occasional loss of time in gestation and rearing infants"—must "eternally" handicap women in their independent economic pursuits.

Be these allegedly natural facts as they may, there are also undeniable social facts about the division of labor prevailing in any given society. Even though women might have been physically capable of handling jobs outside the home, traditionally few such jobs were open to them (Thompson 1825, xi, 57), and those that were "the very lowest only" and grossly underpaid. For that reason, if none other, women were traditionally dependent for support upon their menfolk (first their fathers, then their husbands or brothers).[51] To a distressingly large extent, this pattern remains little changed to the present day (Cass 1982; Tulloch 1984).

It was this traditional dependency of women upon men for support that gave rise to the responsibilities that figure most centrally in the so-called marriage contract. What clinches my case is the way these reciprocal duties

---

51. Since "inequality from this source does not depend on the law of marriage but on the general conditions of society, as now constituted" (Mill 1869, chap. 2), justifying the terms of marriage laws by reference to this inequality is not strictly circular.

have shifted when, in recent years, the law has come to realize that women are as capable as men of supporting a family.

There is, of course, nothing all that new in the phenomenon of role reversal. Surveying working conditions in mid-nineteenth-century Manchester, Engels (1845, 162) remarks that it "happens very frequently indeed" that "the wife is the bread-winner while her husband stays at home to look after the children and to do the cleaning and cooking." The law has, however, been slow in recognizing this fact. As late as 1968, lawyers could say with some justice that "a reading of contemporary judicial opinions leaves the impression that these roles [of man the provider and woman the homemaker] have not changed over the last two hundred years" (Clark 1968, 181). However, the realization was starting to dawn upon lawmakers as early as the turn of the century. Pound reported that

> A number of states make the separate property of the wife secondarily liable for necessities furnished the family and under such statutes it has been held that where the husband is infirm and incapacitated, necessities furnished to him are included. . . . Under this provision it is held that a proceeding may be maintained directly by an indigent and infirm husband against a wife of means and ability to compel performance of the duty of support. (Pound 1916, 192–93)

The possibility of role reversal, leaving the wife with the duty of support that was traditionally the husband's, is now explicitly recognized in modern laws governing divorce settlements:

> Statutes in several states specifically authorize awards of alimony to husbands. Under such statutes, alimony may be awarded to husbands on the same principles as to wives. Since husbands do not need alimony to the same extent as wives, and are able to support themselves after divorce, alimony is only rarely granted to husbands even when the statutes do authorize it. If the husband is unable to work and the wife has substantial property an alimony order in the husband's favor would be upheld, however. (Clark 1968, 448)

These practices have won the endorsement of the American Law Institute. Its Uniform Marriage and Divorce Act (ALI 1970, secs. 308–9) provides that "the court may order *either or both* parents owing a duty of support to a child to pay an amount reasonable or necessary for his support. . . . The court may grant a maintenance order for *either* spouse." In specifying the conditions under which this is to be done, it makes explicit reference to considerations of dependency. A maintenance order shall be granted to either spouse

> only if [the court] finds that the spouse seeking maintenance: (1) lacks sufficient property to provide for his reasonable needs; and (2) is unable to support himself through appropriate employment or is the custodian of a child whose condition or circumstances make it appropriate that the custodian not be required to seek employment outside the home.

In recent years, it has grown increasingly common for husband and wife to be held jointly responsible for maintenance and support of the household. Assuming both are perfectly capable of earning a living independently, neither is awarded alimony. As the earning power of the wife increases, her responsibility for supporting dependent children (and perhaps even unemployable househusbands) is tending to increase. In short, as dependency relations have shifted, so too have our conceptions of marital duties (Glendon 1977). That powerfully suggests that vulnerabilities rather than contracts have been underlying our thinking about the reciprocal duties of husbands and wives all along.[52]

This is not quite yet a full explanation of the special responsibilities written into marriage laws, however. Saying that women were traditionally vulnerable is not to say *to whom* they were vulnerable. In some cases and in some sense, the woman may have been more vulnerable to persons other than her husband. A rich employer, for example, may be in a better position to help or to harm a woman than an indigent spouse. Nothing I have said so far explains the wife's duties to her husband, either: traditionally, it is she who has been, at least economically, dependent upon him. Moreover, none of this explains why, in the increasingly common circumstance of two coequal wage earners, either marriage partner has any responsibility towards the other.

To round out this analysis, then, we have to take account of dependencies of a nonmaterial nature. The husband is depending upon his wife not so much for household or sexual services (which, assuming a reasonable income, he could always hire from others anyway). Instead, he is depending upon her principally for spiritual and moral support. Household and sexual chores are partly in payment for room and board, perhaps—but surely they are mostly a token of affection.[53] The wife, for her part, likewise depends upon the spiritual and moral support of her husband. The bacon he brings home may not be "merely" a token; it may be welcome, to some extent, regardless of the history or motives that lie behind it. In "good" marriages, though, it is largely a token. It matters more that it is *his* salary than that it is a good salary (Blau 1964, 76–84). The traditional division of marital labor, wherein the husband has provided all the material support and the wife all the emotional

---

52. This, I hasten to add, is not the only possible interpretation. As parties' resources alter, so too do the contracts they strike; and presumably, as the resources characteristically possessed by each party alter, so too do the "standard forms" of contracts of adhesion between such parties alter. Within that model, however, a party whose position improves should be in a stronger position to drive a harder bargain. What we have seen, in fact, is that as women's positions strengthen, their marital *duties*—not their marital rights—increase. Perhaps that, too, could be explained in the contract model if the duties could somehow be construed as the "price" they paid for enjoying more rights or privileges elsewhere. Although women have undeniably come to enjoy a stronger position in various respects, none of these gains seems in any way contingent upon their increasing marital duties. If there is a "package" at all here, it can only be of the very loosest sort.
53. Since they are not the only possible (nor perhaps even the best) tokens, a woman is surely at liberty to abandon her role in the home (or even in bed) and find other ways of expressing that affection.

support, is surely dead or dying; in any case, it has nothing morally to recommend it (Blum et al. 1975, 232–35). Emotional support is, or ought morally to be, reciprocal (Held 1974; O'Driscoll 1977; Pateman 1981). It is that reciprocal emotional vulnerability that does most to vest obligations and responsibilities in the particular individual to whom one is (*de jure* or *de facto*) married (Tulloch 1984).

The "marriage contract," far from constituting the bond that creates the union, is merely the "external embodiment of the ethical bond, which indeed can subsist exclusively in reciprocal love and support" (Hegel 1821, sec. 164; see similarly O'Driscoll 1977, 256; Pateman 1981). The reason marriage partners owe each other what they do is not that they have made each other certain promises in the wedding ceremony. It is instead that they have placed themselves, emotionally and sometimes physically and economically as well, "in one another's power" (Wilson 1978). As the United States Supreme Court has acknowledged, "the importance of the familial relationship to the individuals involved . . . stems from the emotional attachment that derives from the intimacy of daily access" (Brennan 1977, 844). From such extraordinary vulnerabilities follow strong responsibilities of the sort we have always associated with the marriage bond.[54]

F rom marriage spring children. They, too, have always been thought to be the subject of very special responsibilities. The list Blackstone (1783, bk. 1, chap. 16) borrowed from Pufendorf (1672, bk. 4, chap. 2; bk. 6, chap. 2) is standard. First and foremost, parents have a duty "to provide for the maintenance of their children," to provide them with food, clothing, shelter, and so forth, as far as the parents are able to provide that care either on their own or with the assistance of state social services (Kirchheimer 1942, 623). Second, parents have a duty to protect their children from harm. Finally, parents have a moral duty to give their children "an education suitable to their station in life."[55] According to the conventional

---

54. It goes without saying that unmarried couples can be equally vulnerable to one another and therefore have the same moral responsibilities, even if these prove more difficult to enforce legally.

55. See similarly Locke (1690, secs. 56 and 58), Pound (1916, 185–86), and U.N. General Assembly (1959). Not all of these moral duties have always and everywhere been legally enforced. In Blackstone's (1783, bk. 1, chap. 16) day, the duty to protect your children from attack was "permitted rather than enjoined by any municipal laws"; legally, you would be at liberty either to beat up the bully or to run away (see also Bohlen 1908, 241). "The municipal law of most countries" also failed in Blackstone's time to "constrain the parent to bestow a proper education upon his children," although present U.S. state law does now enforce some such duties (Ginnow and Gordon 1978, vol. 67A, secs. 49–59). It is the duty of maintenance to which civil law has attached greatest importance. Indeed, "it carries this matter so far, that it will not suffer a parent at his death totally [to] disinherit his child, without giving his reasons for doing so; and there are fourteen such reasons reckoned up, which may justify such disinherison. If the parent alleged no reason, or a bad, or a false one, the child might set the will aside, . . . [as] a testament contrary to the natural duty of the parent" (Blackstone 1783, bk. 1, chap. 16). This serves to confirm our suspicions that the prime moral duty of parenthood (which is also universally recognized in law in a way the others are not) is to provide for the maintenance of children.

wisdom, all these are duties which parents owe peculiarly to their *own* children, and not merely to children as such.

It is the source of these special parental responsibilities that is here at issue. Traditionally, this has been traced to "their own proper act, in bringing them [children] into the world." Pufendorf (1672, bk. 4, chap. 2, sec. 4), in a passage reproduced verbatim in Blackstone's (1783, bk. 1, chap. 16) *Commentaries,* maintains that "by the act of generation . . . they seem to have voluntarily bound themselves, to endeavour as far as in them lies, that the life which they have bestowed shall be supported and preserved. And thus the children will have a perfect right of receiving maintenance from their parents." Both Mill (1863, chap. 5) and Sidgwick (1874) echo these sentiments. "The parent, being the cause of the child's existing in a helpless condition, would be indirectly the cause of the suffering and death that would result to it if neglected''; and from that fact Sidgwick (1874, 249) derives the special duties of parenthood. Such arguments are still often heard.[56] And today they are all the more appropriate, given the increasing opportunities to choose whether or not to become parents.

> If a set of parents do not try to prevent pregnancy, do not obtain an abortion, and then at the time of birth of the child do not put it out for adoption, but rather take it home with them, then they have assumed responsibility for it, they have given it rights and they cannot *now* withdraw support from it at the cost of its life because they now find it difficult to go on providing for it.
> (Thomson 1971, 65)

"Assuming" responsibilities and "waiving" one's rights in favor of another, of course, require more than mere acts. They also crucially require that the persons involved display certain "mental states." Thus, whether or not parents have voluntarily taken upon themselves special responsibilities through the simple "act of generation" depends in large measure upon whether or not they intended to do so. Holly Smith (1983) raises serious doubts about whether the mental state of a woman who voluntarily engages in sexual intercourse is such that she can be said to have thereby assumed responsibility for the resulting fetus or waived her rights in favor of it. Those doubts could easily be generalized to the responsibilities of parenthood as a whole.

---

56. The act of begetting is presumably what Hart (1958, 103–4) has in mind when describing "the father's [duty] to look after his children" as one which was voluntarily "*assumed* by entry upon the particular role." On this point, less careful writers such as Pollock (1981, 18) are more explicit: "Since parents are responsible for producing a person who cannot see to his own needs, they have a duty to care for their child until he is able to care for himself. The basis for this duty can be seen by considering an analogous case. Suppose that you lock a person in a cell without food or water. If the person dies, you have killed him, because you are responsible for producing his helpless condition. Likewise, parents are responsible for producing a helpless child, and so they are held responsible for killing the child if it dies due to their neglect." For a rather more careful statement see Buchanan (1982, 37).

Even setting to one side those problems with the model of parenthood as a self-assumed responsibility, notice that there are limits on what parents owe to their children. Examining those limits provides important clues as to the real source of parental duties. In Pufendorf's (1672, bk. 4, chap. 2, sec. 4) formulation, "parents lie under a perfect obligation to maintain their children" only "so long as they are unable to maintain themselves." Blackstone, expanding upon this point, emphasizes that

> natural right obliges [parents] to give a *necessary* maintenance to children; but what is more than that they have no other right to. . . . No person is bound to provide a maintenance for his issue, unless where children are impotent and unable to work, either through infancy, disease, or accident; and then is only obliged to find them with necessities. . . . For the policy of our laws . . . did not mean to compel a father to maintain his idle and lazy children in ease and indolence; but thought it unjust to oblige the parent, against his will, to provide them with superfluities, and other indulgences of fortune. (Blackstone 1783, bk. 1, 16; see also Locke 1690, sec. 60; Bohlen 1908, 227–28)

Similarly in modern law and morals, "While the duty to take care of minors of tender age is an unconditional one, there exists no general duty to care for grown-up children, husbands, relatives, and other persons closely connected with the defendant. In these cases, an obligation exists only when a state of destitution and helplessness prevails" (Kirchheimer 1942, 624).

Clearly, it is the child's vulnerability that delimits the scope of the parents' duties. Now, of course, that does not necessarily prove that that was also the initial source of those duties. It would be perfectly possible for one principle to generate the responsibilities in the first place and for another principle to delimit their scope. With the vulnerability model, however, we can aspire to offer a comprehensive explanation of the source and scope of parental responsibilities, whereas with the other models we can offer only partial explanations at best.

According to my thesis, it was the child's vulnerability, rather than the voluntary acts of will of the parents in begetting it, which has been giving rise to the special responsibilities of parenthood all along. The earliest commentators, even those attracted to the model of self-assumed obligations, do comment upon the helplessness of human infants as the grounds of parental power and responsibility. "It is fair that he who is not able to rule himself be ruled by another," says Grotius (1625, bk. 2, chap. 5, sec. 2). "Conjugal society" must be enjoined by "Natural Law," according to Locke (1690, sec. 79), because "the assistance of the male is necessary to the maintenance of their common family, which cannot subsist till they are able to prey for themselves, but by the joint care of male and female." Few of these earlier commentators, however, face up to the full logical consequences of these arguments, namely, that we should reclassify the duties of parents under the more general heading of "duties arising out of special needs," be they special needs of kin or strangers (Sidgwick 1874, 249). The reason that the institutionalized role of parent gives rise to "moral" duties is that people "have a duty to satisfy the needs of those who are dependent on them" (Blustein 1982, 116).

The special needs of the infant are determined by nature. How they are met is ordinarily determined by society. Grotius (1625, bk. 2, chap. 5, sec. 2) supposes that, "naturally no one except the parents can be found to whom such control [and responsibilities] may be committed." But that is empirically untrue. Adoptive parents or kibbutz child minders can perform the same tasks. Hence, what is under discussion here might be better termed the responsibilities of child rearers, be they natural parents or otherwise (Blustein 1979, 117). These are responsibilities which, as Hart (1958, 104) acknowledges,

> may vary from society to society together with a whole mass of associated institutions. . . . The obligation to maintain wife or children may not attach to husband or father in societies that think of it as normal for the wife to work and for children to be provided with support at the public expense. . . . Though wider principles of morality may require a man to look after any child in need of care, the *duty* on a parent to do this springs from the fact that this particular society attaches moral importance to persons occupying such a position doing this.

Perhaps it is true that "normally parents are in a better position to harm their child, not because they have caused the child to exist but because of a set of [social] practices which assign them a special responsibility to care for their needy child" (Blustein 1979, 117). Suppose, however, that a given society makes no allocation of child-care responsibilities whatsoever; it would be wrong to say that no one has responsibility for child care. Rather, parents have primary responsibility to care for their children, or to arrange for someone else to do so, until society makes other arrangements (O'Neill 1979; see similarly Malthus 1826, bk. 4, chap. 8). This is merely because—given their crucial causal contribution to producing this vulnerable child, and in the absence of any further social signposts—parents are the *obvious* candidates to bear such responsibilities. Obviousness comes to have moral significance, in turn, by virtue of the reactions of other people. The nearest person is obliged to rescue the drowning swimmer, for example, because other people will regard him as the obvious person to do so and will wait for him to act. Similarly, in the absence of any specific social mandate, a child's natural parents will be regarded as the obvious bearers of child-care responsibilities vis-à-vis that child, which in practice makes the child most vulnerable to its natural parents.[57]

---

57. Pufendorf (1672, bk. 5, chap. 2, sec. 5) holds that "without the bounds of a commonwealth or in a state of natural liberty, if the parents were not united by any lasting contract, the child is under the care and command of the mother." This is due merely to pragmatic considerations,

Still, even in the absence of social (re)allocations of responsibilities, children may in some sense be more vulnerable to persons other than their parents. Rich neighbors, for example, may be better able than their penurious parents to help or to harm them. Nevertheless, the task falls to the parents in the absence of alternative arrangements made either by themselves or by their society. The reason that we have these peculiar responsibilities for helping our *own* children, when others might make a better job of it, once again has to do with nonmaterial vulnerabilities. Getting money from strangers is not the same as getting it from parents, because in the latter case money betokens something even more valuable—love.[58] Indeed, we regard assistance lovingly given by nonkin—a foster parent, for example, or honorary aunt— as every bit as valuable to the child as that given by ordinary parents (Brennan 1977, 844–85).

N ext, naturally, come the special responsibilities of grown children for their aged parents. All commentators agree that parents are entitled to honor, reverence, filial affection, and so on.[59] Aged and infirm parents are often said also to be entitled, morally if not legally, to material assistance from their children:

> They, who protected the weakness of our infancy, are entitled to our protection in the infirmity of their age; they who by sustenance and education have enabled their offspring to prosper, ought in return to be supported by that offspring in case they stand in need of assistance. Upon this principle proceed all the duties of children to their parents. (Blackstone 1783, bk. 1, chap. 16; Ginnow and Gordon 1978, vol. 67A, sec. 97; vol. 70, secs. 59–62; vol. 81, sec. 109)

Here, we might have thought, is a special responsibility which could not conceivably be said to be voluntarily self-assumed. The child did not ask to be brought into the world. As an infant, it did not ask for sustenance. Even when it became capable of communication, its immaturity would have rendered it

---

such as "it cannot be known who is the father, unless it be declared by the mother" (Hobbes 1651, chap. 20). Contemporary arguments for giving the mother "the exclusive right to consent to the adoption of a child born out of wedlock" repeat this consideration and add others of an equally pragmatic character: the father's whereabouts may not be known by the time the child is born; besides, we would not like to give a former lover generous rights to return to haunt the woman in such ways (Stewart 1978, 404–6). In moral as distinct from pragmatic terms, though, both parents must surely be equally responsible for their offspring. All we lack is a good, practical way of institutionalizing that principle (Locke 1690, secs. 53, 56).

58. "Should I insist that it be *I* who benefits my child, if I knew that this would be worse for him? Some would answer, 'No.' But this answer may be too sweeping. It treats parental care as a mere means. We may think it more than that. We may agree that, with some kinds of benefit, my aim should take the simpler form. It should simply be that the outcome is better for my child. But there may be other kinds of benefit, which my child should receive *from me*" (Parfit 1979b, 557).

59. See, e.g., Pufendorf (1672, bk. 6, chap. 2), Locke (1690, secs. 67–69), Blackstone (1783, bk. 1, chap. 16), Sidgwick (1874, 243), and Blustein (1982, 172–75).

incapable of entering into morally meaningful contractual relations with its parents. Typically, nevertheless, the duties of children toward their parents *are* analyzed in quasi-contractual terms of "reciprocal duty" (Wollstonecraft 1792, chap. 11). Children are said to have a duty to repay their parents for the benefits bestowed upon them by their parents, both in begetting them and especially in raising them. In Locke's (1690, sec. 68) formulation, "[due] return for the benefits received by and from [the parents] is the indispensable duty of the child and the proper privilege of the parents."[60]

However, models of "reciprocity" as the basis of filial duties have some odd implications, quite out of line with what we ordinarily think offspring owe their parents. They imply that what children owe parents varies according to how much parents have previously done for them. Locke (1690, sec. 70) noticed this consequence early and faced up to it bravely: "These obligations to parents, and the degree of what is required of children, may be varied, by the different care and kindness, trouble and expense, which is often employed upon one child, more than another."[61] But that does not square with our ordinary intuitions about filial duties. "The medical assistance grown children ought to offer their ill mothers in old age depends upon the mothers' need, not upon whether they endured a difficult pregnancy, for example" (English 1979, 354). That might not be a particularly apt example, since the magnitude of suffering during pregnancy, although clearly variable, is not within the mother's power to control. Even where the goods in question clearly *were* within the parents' control, however, we would still be most reluctant to say, for example, that children whose parents supported them for twenty-one years have a sixteen percent greater debt to their parents than those who moved out of the family home at age eighteen. Nor do we ordinarily suppose that "one's duties to one's parents cease once an equal quantity of sacrifice has been performed, as the phrase 'discharging a debt' may lead us to think" (English 1979, 354).[62]

---

60. See similarly Pufendorf (1672, bk. 6, chap. 2, Sec. 12) and Hume (1739, bk. 3, pt. 1, sec. 1). This is standardly phrased as a "duty of gratitude." Later in this chapter I distinguish duties of gratitude from duties of reciprocity proper; but there I also argue that the vulnerability model offers a better explanation of both types of duty than does the model of self-assumed obligations.

61. See similarly Blustein (1982, 164). In states where children are legally required to support parents in need, "there is a . . . trend to eliminate . . . the obligations of a child to support the father who deserted him at birth" (Schorr 1960, 23). But it is unclear whether the rationale is that desertion destroys *moral* obligations, or whether it simply renders any attempt at *legal* enforcement of those obligations inappropriate. See more generally Anon. (1928).

62. Proponents of this model, of course, have an easy reply: the benefits parents bestow are incalculable, so the child's debt "can never be cancelled or repaid" (Pufendorf 1672, bk. 2, chap. 2, sec. 12; see also Locke 1690, secs. 67, 68). That, however, is clearly an empirical question. If it were just a matter of how much money parents spent on their children, for example, it might well turn out to be a sum which middle-aged children could in some cases repay fully and with interest. The same is arguably true of debts payable in all other currencies (love, etc.). The only benefit that could plausibly be said to be infinite would be that of "giving them life itself." Neither Pufendorf (1672, bk. 6, chap. 2, sec. 12) nor Locke (1690, sec. 65) want to place that

Reciprocity models of filial duties have another odd consequence, which caught the attention of early commentators. Wicked parents, who bestowed no benefits upon their children, would be able to claim none from them in return. Some commentators happily accept this consequence (Pufendorf 1672, bk. 2, chap. 11, sec. 13). Others balk at it. Blackstone (1783, bk. 1, chap. 16), for example, observes that, except in the case of "spurious issue" (i.e., bastard children), "the law does not hold the tie of nature to be dissolved by any misbehaviour of the parent; and therefore a child . . . is equally compellable, if of sufficient ability, to maintain and provide for a wicked and unnatural progenitor, as for one who has shown the greatest tenderness and parental piety." On balance, Sidgwick (1874, 347) is surely right to say that "we certainly have no clear intuition of what is due to parents who do not deserve gratitude." The fact that the quasi-contractual reciprocity model renders a decisive answer where most of our intuitions are so indecisive must surely count against it.[63]

Reciprocity arguments are also flawed in other more familiar ways. They crucially presuppose that beneficiaries (here, children) are indebted to their benefactors (here, parents) whether or not the benefits bestowed were requested, welcomed, or even voluntarily accepted. Pufendorf (1672, bk. 6, chap. 2, sec. 4) does indeed believe that he who has received benefits from another is under a "silent covenant to contract an obligation of refunding the charges," even if those benefits were foisted upon him "in his absence and without his knowledge."[64] The fallaciousness of such reasoning is now widely recognized.

---

much emphasis upon the simple "act of generation," for fear of underwriting despotic parental control of their offspring.

The best strategy for advocates of the model of self-assumed obligations at this point would be to shift out of the language of reciprocity altogether, and to talk instead in terms of the ostensibly self-assumed duties of gratitude and friendship. This objection would then fall away, since (as I argue below) those sorts of duties do not admit of any very fine calculation. All the subsequent objections would remain, however. Besides, this move merely postpones the moment of truth, since I shall argue below that duties of gratitude and friendship are better explained by the vulnerability model than by the model of self-assumed obligations.

63. One way of saving the reciprocity model at this point would be to argue that the sheer act of begetting produces such enormous benefits for the child that they cannot be cancelled by any amount of subsequent mistreatment by the parent. A person's debt surely can be so large that "all he has, all he can do, cannot sufficiently pay it" (Locke 1690, sec. 90). Applying this principle to relations between parents and children implies, however, that "I have a right to diminish [my children's] happiness, provided I do not turn it into a negative quantity; since . . . without me they would not have existed at all" (Sidgwick 1874, 347; see similarly 248, n. 1). The inference is impeccable, the conclusion absurd. Hence, this constitutes a *reductio ad absurdum* of the reciprocity model of filial duties. Another way to address this issue is to ask to whom an adopted child owes his filial obligations. Most of us would surely concur with Hobbes (1651, chap. 20) and Locke (1690, sec. 65) in saying that, during its minority, "it ought obey him by whom it is preserved"; and, by extension, as an adult its duties would be to protect those who protected it during its minority (English 1979, 354). At most, there might be some residual "duty to honor" its natural parents (Locke 1690, sec. 69).

64. Even Hart's (1955, 185–86) discussion of duties of mutual forbearance admits of such a reading—although it is not, to my mind, the most plausible one. Notice the parallel with the

Like so many other commentators on political obligation (Simmons 1979, chap. 5), Rawls (1971, secs. 18, 52) sees clearly the need to stipulate that "one has voluntarily accepted the benefits of the arrangement or taken advantage of the opportunities it offers to further one's interests" for the receipt of benefits to bind a person. Otherwise, it would count as a gratuitous benefit, on which no return could reasonably be expected and from which no obligations could follow (Seavey and Scott 1937, sec. 2).

The relationship between parents and their children must necessarily be one in which any benefits bestowed upon children count as gratuitous ones. Arguments about our putative obligation to our parents "depends, mainly at least, on uncovenanted benefits conferred on us" (Ewing 1947, 218). Consequently, any talk of a debt owed by children to their parents must be "loose and metaphorical" at most, since "the duty of fair play presumably exists only where benefits are voluntarily accepted within a cooperative scheme, and we can hardly suppose that a child has voluntarily accepted his role in the cooperative scheme of family life" (Slote 1979, 320). There are two fundamental problems with the debt analysis. First, underage children lack the power (legally or morally) to consent to any arrangement whatsoever; that is what is meant by being underage. Second, "the family relationship is not a voluntary one . . . [because] the child cannot [i.e., is powerless, legally and morally] to opt out of it, at least until he reaches a certain age" (Miller 1976, 81).[65]

Related to the reciprocity model is a second and slightly different way of putting the parent-child relationship on a quasi-contractual basis. This builds on the notion of hypothetical consent. Pufendorf (1672, bk. 6, chap. 2, sec. 4), again, maintains:

> The sovereignty of the parents seems . . . to be built on the presumed consent of the children, and consequently on a tacit pact. . . . It being fairly presumed that had [the child], at his coming into the world, been furnished with the use of reason, and made capable of understanding that his life could not be

argument offered by Grotius (1625, bk. 2, chap. 5, sec. 29) for enslaving the children of slaves: "the right of masters over the children of slaves will arise from the furnishing of nourishment and other necessities of life; and so, since the children of slaves have to be supported for a long time before their work can be useful to their masters, and since the services which follow are in return for support in that period, it will not be permissible for those who are born under such an obligation to flee from slavery unless they return adequate compensation for their support."
65. David Richards (1971, 174) concedes this for the case of "young children and infants." They "do not voluntarily accept the benefits of being born or being fed, clothed, nurtured, loved, etc." However, Richards goes on to say that "when the child is older [he] has developed the capacities of rationality and control, and is therefore able to choose not to accept the benefits." If he continues to accept benefits then principles of fairness and gratitude oblige the child "to bear the burdens when his turn comes, i.e., caring for his parents as the institution requires." Certainly a child who flees the family home at the moment he reaches the age of discretion has no obligations to his parents, as this would imply. Neither, I would have said, does one who makes a "clean break" at the age of 25. What is crucial is the matter of "breaking off the friendship," as English (1979) emphasizes and to which Richards himself alludes.

preserved, without the kind provision of his parents, joined with their command over him, he would gladly have yielded obedience on so commodious terms, which consent of his, being rationally supposed, hath the same validity as if it had been openly declared.[66]

Here, Pufendorf is attempting to justify the authority of parents over their young children. The same sort of argument could, however, be easily adapted to impose quasi-contractual duties upon grown children for caring for their parents in old age.

Such arguments are not without difficulties.[67] Still, they are on much stronger footing here than in some applications. Although actual agreements are binding in a way that hypothetical ones are not, hypothetical consent does sometimes provide a sufficient reason for action. In the absence of evidence to the contrary, a doctor who finds an accident victim bleeding to death is justified in presuming his consent to a transfusion, and that hypothetical consent justifies his action. In that case, hypothetical consent reflects the presumed will of the victim "at the time and in the circumstances that the decision was taken" (Dworkin 1977, 152). The cases where hypothetical consent does not justify action are those where this is not true, that is, where the argument takes the following form: "Because a man would have consented to certain principles if asked in advance, it is fair to apply those principles to him later, under different circumstances, when he does not consent" (Dworkin 1977, 152). The position of children is more akin to that of the accident victim. It is their present (albeit inchoate) will to which we ascribe the hypothetical consent.

Arguments based on hypothetical consent nevertheless leave unexplained one important aspect of filial duties, namely, the limitation placed upon them. Parents are entitled to honor, respect, and so forth, whatever their circumstances, simply by virtue of their status (originally, biological; now, more commonly, sociological) as parents. However, "some parents . . . have the additional title of infirm and indigent old age; under which sad condition their children were otherwise obliged to maintain them" materially (Pufendorf 1672, bk. 4, chap. 11, sec. 13). The moral duty to provide material assistance comes into play only "in the infirmity of their age, . . . in case they stand in need of assistance" (Blackstone 1783, bk. 1, chap. 16), "when the feebleness of age comes upon them" (Wollstonecraft 1792, chap. 11), "in case of infirmity or any special need" (Sidgwick 1874, 248), "if

66. This of course "confounds a presumed consent with a tacit one," as Jean Barbeyrac points out in his notes to the 1717 edition (Pufendorf 1672, bk. 6, chap. 2, sec. 4; bk. 3, chap. 6, sec. 2).
67. The tension pulling us both ways on this issue is nicely represented in Blustein's (1982, 183–84) remarks: "When children are older and have the capacity for real choice, they may quite rationally decide that they would rather not have received their benefits at all than be indebted to their parents for having bestowed them on them. . . . Older children's refusal . . . cannot, of course, alter the fact that they did receive those nonobligatory parental benefits while young and did (possibly still do) profit from them. But the freedom to decide when, and to whom, one shall become indebted cannot be abridged in advance by unilateral parental decision."

they are in need" (Pound 1916, 185; Laslett 1970, 51), "when they become sick or infirm" (Slote 1979, 320). The same is true of children's legal duties to support their parents. Statutory law, even where it does impose such a duty, "does not require children to support parents who are not in a penurious condition" (Ginnow and Gordon 1978, vol. 67A, sec. 97; Schorr 1980, 27–28).

In terms of quasi-contracts, it would be hard to explain why the obligation to support parents should be based on the condition of need. After all, according to that model what we owe our parents depends on what they did for us, not on what they now need. That account is implausible in another even more important respect. It is likely that, at least where material assistance is concerned, considerations of present need would lead to allocations opposite to those recommended on the basis of considerations of reciprocity or quasi-contracts. Parents who are indigent in their old age were probably not very well off while their children were growing up; those parents now in need probably gave less, not more, to their children. Consequently, reciprocity and quasi-contracts would generally require children to repay less to needier parents, whereas in practice they are obliged to provide them with more.

Here again, this need not be a knock-out blow to voluntaristic theories of filial responsibilities. We might use one principle to justify the existence of the responsibilities and some other to delimit their scope. This anomaly, however, does make it clear that the voluntaristic analysis is a very partial one at best. Again, within the vulnerability model both aspects can be plausibly explained. The reason *why* children have the responsibilities they do is that their parents are vulnerable to their actions and choices. We can also explain *what* their responsibilities are by talking in terms of vulnerabilities: children are responsible for providing parents with moral support under all conditions (since parents will always be vulnerable to their children in this respect) and with material support when their parents are in need of it. Finally, references to vulnerabilities can also explain the *limit* of those responsibilities: grown children are under no duty to lavish money or gifts on prosperous parents. Within families, as elsewhere, responsibilities are greater where vulnerabilities are greater.[68]

Again, one's *own* children are not necessarily in the best position to help or to hurt one, at least in material ways. Aged and infirm parents might be more vulnerable to rich friends than to penurious children. Here, again, it is the bond of affection that makes the assistance provided by the child special, even if that assistance is quantitatively less than what others might provide (Streib 1958, 52–58; Schorr 1960, 15–17; 1980, 18–19). Some writers go as far as to say that if affection is lacking, then the child is under *no* special obligation

---

68. Notice, for example, that dependent children, who are far more vulnerable to us, get preference according to the laws of inheritance over aged parents "to whom we are much more indebted and engaged" (Pufendorf 1672, bk. 4, chap. 11, sec. 16; Mellows 1977, chap. 12). Obligations, as Laslett (1970) says, flow forward rather than backward. The reason, I suggest, is that forward-looking vulnerabilities tend to be stronger.

to help his aged parents, "beyond his general duty to help those in need" (English 1979, 355). That may be slightly exaggerated, but in spirit it is certainly correct.[69] We ordinarily think children have a special responsibility for aiding their aged parents precisely because their parents are most vulnerable to them; and the most important component of their vulnerability is emotional rather than material.

Bonds of affection also help to explain the importance we attach to that other filial duty, to honor and respect one's parents. In earlier days, societies were particularly insistent upon that duty: in the Plymouth Colony the official penalty for grown children's "cursing or smiting" their parents was death or maiming (Demos 1970, 100). We have ceased trying to enforce the duty in quite that way, but serious social pressure is still brought to bear. The reason is not that the spiteful child is somehow reneging on a debt. The wound goes far deeper than that. It is, instead, much more like betrayal of a friendship.[70] Here it is especially clear that it is emotional rather than material interests that are at stake.

A final problem is with the very terms in which familial transactions are analyzed within contractual models. Such models are, and must be, based on notions of the reciprocal rights and duties among various family members. Debts are incurred, demanded, and discharged. Once discharged, they are obliterated: the slate is wiped clean; the parties stand in exactly the same relation as they did before the debt was incurred. (At most, you might be slightly more inclined to deal again with people you know you can trust to pay their debts.) This seems a very poor way of representing the continuing bonds that constitute a family. That is not just because it suggests something too ephemeral. More importantly, it misses the mutual involvement in each others' lives that leaves parties tied more closely after the "debt" has been discharged than before (English 1979, 354; Heath 1976, 59–60). Ritual exchanges of gifts between family and friends at Christmas, for example, are definitely *not* designed to clear the debt and cancel the relationship. Instead, they renew and reinforce it (Caplow 1982).[71]

---

69. Societies ordinarily settle that general duty upon specific individuals (children) on the grounds of presumed affection (and correlative emotional vulnerability) which, while generally present, is occasionally sadly lacking. For that reason, grown children may have an obligation (both legally and morally) to support needy parents, given that no one else will, even if there is no affection in the relationship.

70. Wollstonecraft (1792, chap. 11) suggests that a parent who has raised his child well, and "endeavours to form the heart and enlarge the understanding of his child . . . acquires all the rights of the most sacred friendship, and his advice, even when his child is advanced in life, demands serious consideration." Both English (1979) and Blustein (1982, 186–93) pursue this friendship analogy further.

71. May (1975, 34) suggests that such relationships be analyzed in terms of a covenant rather than a contract, saying that while "contracts are signed to be expediently discharged, convenants have a gratuitous, growing edge to them that nourishes rather than limits relationships. . . . There is a donative element in the nourishing of convenant—whether it is the convenant of marriage,

Furthermore, the sort of careful and jealous accounting of debts and repayments that characterizes contractual relations seems out of place in family relationships. Friends and family members alike "offer what they can and accept what they need, without regard for the total amounts of benefits exchanged" (English 1979, 353). Family life consists not in bargaining for reciprocal benefits but rather in bestowing gratuitous ones. A child

> believes unquestioningly that he has a right to cherishing, welfare, gratification from his parents, entirely gratuitously, without having to do anything for it, without having to pay. This is in fact the outstanding characteristic of the parent-child relationship, for both father and mother lavish gratification on their children without expecting reward. (Laslett 1970, 74)

If, as ordinarily happens, the parental sacrifices lead to developing bonds of love, affection, and friendship with their children, it is likely that their children will also later make some sacrifice for them. But that reciprocity is incidental, not essential, to the relationship. As Onora O'Neill (1982) complains,

> discussion of the moral basis of life with young children [and family life more generally] is oddly distorted by . . . focusing mainly on the rights of dependent children and the corresponding duties of others. These are the terms in which the breakdown of family life must be sorted out: when something goes awry, we need to clarify against whom it is that a dependent child may have legally or morally enforceable claims for various sorts of service and care. But when things are going well, the adversarial framework of discussions of rights and duties fails to bring out the distinctive moral features of intimately shared lives in which the interests and concerns of each become part of the interests and concerns of others.

Last but certainly not least, contractual models of the family are predicated on notions of exchange: the duties of family life are thought to be reciprocal because each party has insisted upon getting a good return on his own contributions. Actually, of course, family members (like friends) "are motivated by love rather than the prospect of repayment" (English 1979, 355). Anyone who cynically looks upon his own contributions to the family as "investments," motivated merely by the expected returns, is thereby deemed to have

---

friendship, or professional relationship. Tit for tat characterizes a commercial transaction, but it does not exhaustively define the vitality of that relationship in which one must serve and draw upon the deeper reserves of another." The basic trick in convenanting relationships, as May describes them, seems to be giving a bit more than you get in order to ensure the continuation of a relationship which both persons find profitable. This distinction, therefore, merges with Macneil's (1980; see also Hardin 1982a, b) distinction between "relational" and merely "discrete" exchanges. Far from being one-off trades, these exchanges create, reinforce, and sustain certain sorts of relationships between the parties. What must be emphasized, however, is that, at least where family and friends are concerned, these are not just trading relationships that are sustained. The relationships also have an affective component: you care about family and friends in ways you do not about your greengrocer. Within families and friendships, people come to define their own projects, lives, and selves in terms of the others'. This goes well beyond the minimum sort of trust needed to sustain a long-term trading relationship.

perverted or betrayed the relationship. Perhaps, in some sense, love is exchanged for love. If so, it can be exchanged *only* for love. There must surely be separate spheres of exchange and, even within one's own mind, separate spheres of account if love is to remain something special (Goodin 1982b, ch. 6; cf. Becker 1982). Any attempt to exchange love for money would debase the sentiment, turning it into a mere commodity. As Hirsch (1976, 87, 95–101) wryly observes, "bought sex is not the same."

This underlies Hegel's (1821, sec. 75) analysis of the marriage contract as "shameful." Marriage is thereby "degraded to the level of contract for reciprocal use." Marriage may begin with a contract, but its whole point is to "transcend the standpoint of contract" and make marriage partners start thinking in noncontractual terms of "love, trust and the common sharing of their entire existence" (Hegel 1821, sec. 163; see also Pateman 1981).

The same sentiments also seem to underlie the reluctance of United States courts from the days of the Plymouth Colony forward (Demos 1970, chap. 5) actually to *enforce* the reciprocal rights and duties of marriage partners against one another. "Our law has long maintained a 'hands-off' attitude toward inter-spousal disputes" on the grounds that "a marriage is an association emphasizing 'shared commitment' rather than rules" (Karst 1980, 639).[72] For example, recall that the husband's duty to support his wife is deemed so essential by the courts that he is not allowed to contract out of it. Yet, it is one that they rarely enforce:

> In practice, the spousal support obligations of the husband are rarely enforced in an ongoing marriage because the courts are reluctant to interfere with the internal marriage relationship. In the leading case in this area, *McGuire v. McGuire*, 157 Neb. 226, 59 N.W.2d 336 (1953), the wife complained that her husband had not given her any money or provided her with any clothes for the past three years. She alleged that although he was a man of substantial means, he had also refused to purchase furniture and other household necessities, beyond the groceries which he paid for by check. The court refused to consider the wife's complaint, however, because the parties were still living together and it did not want to intrude on the marital relationship. (Weitzman 1974, 1184; see also Ketchum 1977, 272–74)

In another case, *Graham v. Graham*, 33 F. Supp. 936, 939 (E. D. Mich., 1940), an United States court refused to enforce contractual agreements between marriage partners on the grounds that demanding one's contractual due introduces considerations, motivations, and patterns of behavior inconsistent with and destructive to the marriage bond. For another example, conjugal

---

72. Similarly, "invoking the power of the state to bring children to heel is destructive of the values of caring and commitment, intimacy, and self-identification" that are supposed to lie at the center of family life, and is for that reason also eschewed (Karst 1980, 643). See similarly Fishkin (1983, 35–43).

rights are among the most central to the marriage relationship, yet they are legally unenforceable; while tort law permits actions against a third party for "alienation of affections," suits by one marriage partner against another for restitution of conjugal rights have long been obsolete in Great Britain, and in the United States they are entertained in only one state (Pound 1916, 190–91, 195; Ginnow and Gordon 1978, vol. 41, sec. 12).

All of these rights and duties of marriage are, in short, "so peculiarly related to the mental and spiritual life of the individual" as to be unfit for judicial enforcement (Pound 1916, 196; see also Douglas 1965). Sex without love may not be completely worthless, but it certainly is relatively cheap. Just as the courts cannot compel love, neither can parties contract for it.

M y conclusion is that the model of voluntarily self-assumed responsibilities has little place in the analysis of special familial responsibilities. At most it can be used to trace those responsibilities to *roles* that have been voluntarily assumed. Some such approach is suggested by, for example, Hart (1958, 103–4), Rawls (1971, 113) and Blustein (1982, 116).

Many people, however, find themselves occupying familial roles which they have not taken up voluntarily. In many periods, and in some places still, women have no choice but to marry. Some children are conceived involuntarily (through rape) or unintentionally (through defective diaphragms); and of course, no child could have volunteered for his role vis-à-vis his parents. Where roles have not been voluntarily assumed, and role responsibilities cannot therefore have been voluntarily incurred, advocates of the self-assumed-obligation model are left with an unenviable choice: either they must exempt every man, woman, and child who happens to occupy a role involuntarily from ordinary responsibilities attaching to that role; or they must concede that there are some special responsibilities that are not self-assumed. Surely the latter conclusion is more reasonable.

Even where roles have been voluntarily self-assumed, the model that traces responsibilities to that fact alone provides a less than fully satisfactory account. At most, we might be able to point to voluntarily assumed roles to explain *why* spouses or parents have some special responsibilities. That model, however, cannot be used to explain *what* those responsibilities are. To understand some of the most important features of such responsibilities— their content and their largely unalterable form—some separate, nonvoluntaristic account must be given. The vulnerability model is more satisfactory in that it provides a unified account of why people have such responsibilities, what those responsibilities are, and what particular form they take.

Friends

Friends, too, are commonly thought to have certain special responsibilities toward one another. In the language of sociologists, friendship is a "particularistic" relationship.[73] Indeed, "the first element in . . . friendship," philosophically construed,

> is affection, . . . a desire for another's welfare and happiness *as a particular individual*. This desire is . . . to be distinguished from both sense of duty and from benevolence. For those motives prompt us to see others' good in general, whereas we want to say that those who feel affection feel a concern for another which they do not feel for everyone. It is this concern which typically motivates services performed out of friendship. (Telfer 1970–71, 224; see similarly Blum 1980, 44; Ewin 1981, chap. 9; Hampshire 1982, 154; and Cottingham 1983, 79)

As Wasserstrom (1984, 33) says, "Part of the meaning . . . of what it is to be one's friend is that one does and will prefer the interests of one's friend over those of other people. If there were no firm and dependable disposition to do so, that would be a powerful conceptual reason to suppose that one was not even considering a case of friendship at all."

Exactly *what* special duties friends have toward one another is somewhat difficult to establish. Here recourse to the law will not help: the duties of friendship are almost nowhere legally enforceable. There is relatively little in modern philosophical literature (as distinct from exegeses of Aristotle, etc.) on the topic of friendship, either. It is nonetheless clear that we would want to include among the duties of friendship such things as the duty "to help the friend when under attack (physical or verbal) or in need or trouble of any kind; to proffer advice and criticism, not only when asked for but also when not asked for but needed"; and so on (Telfer 1970–71, 231). In general, friendship would involve duties both of care and of affection.[74] That, in turn, suggests that friendship relations are both affective and instrumental, in their effects if not in their intentions.[75] Someone who cultivates a "friendship" purely for material gain would be guilty of a certain kind of fraud: without the

---

73. See, e.g., Parsons and Shils (1951, 81–82), Naegele (1958, 236), and Ramsoey (1968).

74. "Deep caring and identification with the good of the other" is how Blum (1980, 70) characterizes those "aspects of friendship [that] are of great moral worth and significance." We may, and may even be morally obliged to, "befriend friendless, or relatively friendless, people whom we don't really like very much" (Brock 1982, 241). But "befriending"—being a friend to—is crucially distinct from "being a friend of." The crucial affective component of true friendship is missing (Telfer 1970–71, 223).

75. "A service performed as a gesture of friendship . . . can be instrumentally useful, and can also be valuable because it is done by a certain person out of certain motives" (O'Driscoll 1977, 256). Various survey findings reveal the intermixture of instrumental and affective components in friendship relations. For example, 70 percent of the respondents in the United States said that one had a right to expect a businessman friend to tip him off to sell his stocks when financial ruin was in prospect (Stouffer and Toby 1951, 484); and, when asked to imagine themselves proctoring an examination, 20 percent fewer United States university students said that they would report a cheater if he were their roommate and closest friend than if he were a stranger (Stouffer 1949, 713). Cross-culturally, too, "some instrumental obligations . . . always form a basic component of this type of relationship" (Eisenstadt 1956, 90; see also Wolf 1966).

proper sort of emotional involvement, a person cannot truly claim to be a friend. Yet no true friend would deny certain forms of material assistance in times of need. Certain sorts of emotions inevitably lead to certain sorts of actions. (''What kind of friend are you?'' is the question most commonly used to evoke this sentiment.) Hence, friends expect, and have every reason and hence every right to expect, both emotional and material support from one another (Ewin 1981, chap. 9).

T raditionally, the duties of friendship have always been analyzed in terms of voluntary acts of will. As one of the first and best early modern commentators says, ''Our free will has no product more properly its own than affection and friendship'' (Montaigne 1580, 137). We are still very much inclined to suppose that, ''whatever else friendship is, it is . . . a personal relationship freely . . . entered into'' (Cooper 1977, 619).[76] Indeed, it would seem that friendship ''is a voluntary relation par excellence'' (Naegele 1958, 251): the relationship and its attendant obligations *must* be self-assumed. No one can foist friendship upon you. It must be a voluntary mutual undertaking.

There are, however, various ways in which the willfulness (and hence the voluntariness) of the relationship are called into question. One has to do with the involuntariness of the requisite feelings. Friendship, I have said, involves not only performing the right sorts of actions but also performing them for the right sorts of reasons, reasons related to certain types of feelings (affections, emotions, etc.). ''Emotions,'' however, ''cannot be summoned up as motives'' (Paton 1956, 49). No one can choose his feelings; they are and must necessarily be ''essentially by-products,'' things that can emerge only if we do not seek them directly.[77] If, however, we cannot choose our feelings, and if feelings of a certain sort are necessary for true friendship, then the implication is that we cannot choose our friendships.

Telfer (1970–71, 229–30), having considered the above objection, offers the following reply: ''Although the right passions are a necessary condition of friendship, they are not by themselves a sufficient condition. A man who possesses these passions has still to act on them—actually to help instead of merely wanting to, for example—and insofar as he acts he is necessarily making choices.'' Thus, defining friendship as ''friendly acts done for friendly reasons'' will necessarily ''imply *choice* in friendship.'' In this reply, how-

---

76. See similarly Ramsoey (1968, 12), Paine (1969), and Fried (1978, 180).
77. Stocker (1981, 756). See more generally Nagel (1970, 132), Blum (1980, chap. 8), and Elster (1983, chap. 2). Although they spoil the desired effect insofar as the *direct* pursuit of the goal is concerned, intentions might not spoil the effect where the strategy is an indirect one. If ''friendly feelings'' are like that, if they can be successfully pursued through the intentional adoption of indirect strategies, then the duties of friendship might be intentionally (albeit indirectly) self-assumed.

ever, Telfer puts altogether too much emphasis upon "friendly acts" as a defining feature of friendship. Certainly the disposition to perform such actions will inevitably accompany the sort of feelings that define friendship. It is equally certain that friends often go—and Kant says *should* go (Paton 1956, 63–64)—to considerable lengths to avoid asking (or even allowing) friends to do them favors (Paine 1969); seeking favors from friends could be construed as imposing on the friendship. Would we really want to withhold the title of friend until friendly acts have been exchanged, even if all the right feelings and all the right dispositions to help have been present all along? I think not.

Even if we agree to put choice at the center of friendship in this way, that still makes the obligations of friendship self-assumed only in a very indirect way. Notice that that account does not have us choosing our obligations. It does not even have us choosing our friends. (As Telfer [1970–71, 230] says, "we cannot choose to be a friend of just anyone, since the relevant passions cannot be summoned at will.") What it really has us choosing is our *actions*, or more precisely, choosing which of our passions to act upon. Why should choosing one sort of action rather than another constitute any sort of general commitment to one particular person; and even if it does entail a general commitment of some kind, why should that, in turn, entail the diverse range of rights, duties, and responsibilities ordinarily associated with friendship? The basis for these rights and duties requires further explanation. The most plausible explanation, I shall argue below, is couched in terms of the reciprocal vulnerability (emotional and material) of friends who have come to trust and rely upon one another.

There is another way in which we might suppose that friendship is a self-assumed obligation. Telfer (1970–71, 230) argues for what she calls a "weaker version" of the proposition that "a necessary condition of friendship [is] that we should choose our friends," saying,

> the existence of the passions of friendship in both parties, and the practice of both sides of acting on them, once established, [must] be *acknowledged* by the parties. This acknowledgement involves, not so much the *formation* of a policy [of acting in a friendly manner], as endorsement of or consent to a policy which is by then enshrined in practice. This is part of what is meant by *commitment* to friendship. (See similarly Blustein 1982, 187–88)

In primitive societies, it may be true that a few of the very strongest forms of friendship (e.g., blood brotherhoods) are attended by some such formal, public ritual (Eisenstadt 1956). In our own societies, however, friendships are ordinarily initiated and terminated without any elaborate ritual.[78] They just grow up, without any particular acknowledgement (formal or informal, public

---

78. "Friendship . . . seems to be a social relation that allows the loyalties it engenders or requires to be once more suspended without requiring a public announcement to that effect" (Naegele 1958, 251; see similarly Paine 1969).

or private). Usually the most that voluntarists can plausibly claim is that we "tacitly consent" to the continuation of the relationship; and they risk committing a well-known fallacy by positing any very strong responsibilities on the basis of something like that.

There is yet another difficulty in trying to construe friendship as a self-assumed obligation: even if we could voluntarily choose whether or not to become friends with a person, we could not voluntarily pick and choose what duties we would have toward that person. The duties of friendship constitute yet another standard form contract, the content of which is largely fixed independently of the will of the parties and is immune to any attempts on their parts at renegotiation. Any act of negotiating would necessarily destroy the relation, inasmuch as friendship implies the absence of ulterior motives. "The relation is always conceived to have its end in itself, and to be formed primarily for the development of mutual affection between the friends, and the pleasure which attends this" (Sidgwick 1874, bk. 3, chap. 4, sec. 7).[79] That explains why it is inappropriate to keep a close accounting of favors and return favors among friends (English 1979, 252–54).[80] That also explains why within a friendship one cannot negotiate for a "lighter load" of responsibilities than a friend would ordinarily bear.[81] Negotiating behavior implies ulterior motives of a sort that is incompatible with true friendship. This impossibility of negotiating (and most especially, negotiating to alter) the content of the obligations undercuts, in turn, the argument that these obligations are completely voluntary.

There are, then, some serious weaknesses in the model of self-assumed obligations as an account of obligations among friends. Then obligations cannot plausibly be linked to any particular act of self-commitment. Furthermore, the *precise* rights, duties, and responsibilities associated with friendship cannot be shown to follow from any voluntary acts that might be said to form the basis of the friendship. At most, with the model of self-assumed obligations,

79. This is a theme that early modern philosophers such as Montaigne (1580) carried over directly from the ancients, especially Aristotle (Cooper 1977). Sociologically, this remains an important component of friendship norms to this day (Naegele 1958, 25; Ramsoey 1968, 12).

80. This also explains the implausibility of Fried's (1976, 1071) analysis of doctors and lawyers as "special-purpose friends." Friendship, by its nature, is not something that admits of purposes, be they special or general (Paine 1969, 516–17; cf. Blum 1980, 77–80). Matters are only made worse for the friendship model by the fact that the professional, too, has ulterior motives in forming the relationship. "Professionals accept clients for a fee, not out of concern for individuals" (Bayles 1981, 65). Indeed, even Fried (1976, 1075; 1978, 179) acknowledges that "money is usually what cements the lawyer-client relationship."

81. A friendship may, through "mutual understandings" which have grown up gradually between the two friends over the course of many interactions, have come to entail limited liabilities for both parties. There is no way to negotiate directly for this arrangement, however, without radically altering the relationship, and marking the end of the friendship proper. With friendships, just as with contracts, it is the other's expectations rather than your intentions that matter morally. The the model of friendship as a self-assumed obligation would tend to emphasize your intentions, whereas the vulnerability model emphasizes the other's expectations.

we can explain why we owe something special to our friends but not what we owe. Hence, the model is crucially incomplete.

O ne of the principal components of friendship is trust. Friends ordinarily do, and we firmly believe they should be able to, count on one another in various ways and for various things. Sometimes it is primarily a matter of being able to trust friends to keep confidences. This seems to be the primary emphasis among the American adolescents studied by Naegele (1958, 243), but it also figures largely among adults (Paine 1969) and lies at the core of Kant's notion of "moral friendship" (Paton 1956, 54–57). Besides keeping confidences, friendship often also entails being able to trust each other to provide material aid when the occasion arises. This points to Kant's more pragmatic "friendship of need" (Paton 1956, 54–57), which is also evidenced in various studies of contemporary social norms (Stouffer 1949; Stouffer and Tobey 1951). Mutual trust seems to be an absolutely central element in all these forms of friendship.

Trust, in turn, entails "reliance on a disposition of another person" (Fried 1970, 81). Having observed that "the most prominent feature of friendship is . . . 'trust,'" Naegele (1958, 243) goes on to point out that "to trust is to depend—and to become dependent, or at least vulnerable." It is this element of reciprocal vulnerability among friends, I would argue, that gives rise to the reciprocal obligations of friendship.[82] With the model of self-assumed obligations, we would focus on the origins of the relationship of trust, looking especially for some evidence of voluntary commitment. Instead, I suggest that we focus on the consequences of vulnerability, regardless of how it came about.[83]

Friends inevitably have unique opportunities to help or to hurt one another. "In friendship Self is known to the Other more completely than in other relationships. Such openness implies great vulnerability. . . . There is no one who is as vulnerable to the actions of Self as a friend" (Hutter 1978, 12). Friendships, Brock (1982, 227) writes, "involve structured expectations, commitments, and responsibilities. In particular, they involve commitments to do things for and with friends that one is not committed to doing for or with just anyone; we can 'count on' our friends in various ways that we cannot

82. Sidgwick (1874, bk. 3, chap. 4, sec. 7) similarly proposes that we bring "all cases of wrong conduct towards friends . . . under the general formula of breach of understanding." As he points out, "the profession of friendship . . . must imply a greater interest in one's friend's happiness than in that of men in general, it must announce a willingness to make more or less considerable sacrifices for him, if occasion offers. If then we decline to make such sacrifices, we do wrong by failing to fulfil natural and legitimate expectations." See similarly Buchanan (1982, 37).
83. Voluntarily self-incurred obligations might ordinarily be stronger, merely because in such cases people will generally (but not always) have firmer grounds for expecting that others will be relying upon them.

count on just anyone." According to Mill (1863, chap. 5), "the disappointment of [this] expectation . . . constitutes the principal criminality of . . . a breach of friendship. Few hurts which human beings can sustain are greater, and none wound more, than when that on which they habitually and with full assurance relied, fails them in their hour of need."

To be sure, rich strangers might be in a better position to provide material resources; but friends, because of the emotional component inherent in their relationship, can supply each other with certain sorts of goods that are unavailable from mere strangers. Blum (1980, 56–57) is surely right to insist upon "the lack of comparability between what I do for a friend and for a nonfriend. . . . If we go out together to drink or to a film, what pleases my friend is essentially bound up with the fact that the activity is something shared with his friend. What gives the activity the particular kind of meaning and particular kind of pleasure that it has is in important ways bound up with how we relate to and participate in it together as friends." When a friend breaks an important promise, you feel betrayed; when a mere acquaintance does so, you feel only cheated. It is because friends are relying upon one another, not only for material but also (and in many ways more importantly) for affective or emotional support, that they have the special responsibilities they do toward one another (Paine 1969, 507).

To count as true friendship, a relationship cannot be one-way.[84] The definitional requirement of mutuality or reciprocity might seem to suggest that the relationship is quasi-contractual. My preferred interpretation, however, is couched in terms of mutual emotional vulnerability among friends. When you are let down by someone who you know does not return your affection, you may feel deeply disappointed. Still, you have had no reason to expect him to do otherwise. You should be able to expect more from a purported friend who has given every indication of recriprocating your affection. If it is he who lets you down, you are hurt more deeply; you feel betrayed. This greater emotional vulnerability between persons who reciprocate affection explains why their responsibilities should be reciprocal and especially strong. The obligations of friendship consist essentially in mutual consideration for the feelings of the other.

The emotional vulnerability of friends to one another also explains why we are reluctant to institutionalize, much less legalize, the obligations of friendship (Paine 1969, 521). As far as your friends are concerned, it is crucial that you perform the right actions for the right reasons. They value your friendly acts largely (if not wholly) as manifestations of your friendly sentiments.[85]

---

84. See, e.g., Paton (1956, 48–49), Ramsoey (1968, 12), and Telfer (1970–71, 223).

85. "As it is essential to Friendship that the mutual kindly feeling, and the services springing from it, should be spontaneous and unforced, neither the one nor the other should be imposed as a duty." Sidgwick (1874, bk. 3, chap. 4, sec. 7) supposes that this is something "all would . . . admit to a certain extent," even as regards the realm of purly moral duties. He does, however, suppose that in certain limiting cases we want to be able to say "that one friend has

Were we to make friendly actions legally obligatory, that would only confuse the crucial question of motivations. Your friends could no longer be sure whether your friendly action was performed out of friendly sentiments or out of fear of legal sanctions.[86]

Benefactors

The proper relations between beneficiaries and their benefactors is a topic that "has not been discussed very often in recent moral philosophy. Ross (1930) was probably the last major moral philosopher to seriously consider gratitude as a source of moral requirements" (Simmons 1979, 162). It has not always been so. Barely a century ago, Sidgwick (1874, bk. 3, chap. 4, sec. 8) could claim that "where gratitude is due, the obligation is especially clear and simple. Indeed the duty of requiting benefits seems to be recognized wherever morality extends; and Intuitionists have justly pointed to this recognition as an instance of a truly universal intuition." Perhaps few would go so far as Swift's Lilliputians, who reckoned that "whoever makes ill returns to his Benefactor must . . . be a common enemy to the rest of Mankind . . . and . . . is not fit to live" (quoted in Walker 1980–81, 39). Kant, nevertheless, counts ingratitude as one of the three vices which constitute "the essence of vileness and wickedness" (1797, 218). Utilitarians have long agreed. Hume (1739, bk. 3, pt. 1, sec. 1) writes, "Of all the crimes that human creatures are capable, the most horrid and unnatural is ingratitude." Mill (1863, chap. 5) concurs: "few wrongs are greater than this . . . [and] none excite more resentment, either in the person suffering, or in a sympathising spectator."

A benefactor is defined by his behavior: he is one who "renders aid to others" (*Oxford English Dictionary*). Yet the moral obligations of the beneficiary with respect to the benefactor depend not simply on the actions of benefactor but also on his motives. Perhaps anyone who has incurred costs in order to do us a service deserves repayment.[87] If repayment were his only motive in

---

behaved wrongly to another, and to speak as if there were a clearly cognisable [moral] code of behaviour in such relations."

86. This also explains Ramsoey's (1968, 12) observation that "in general, friendship can be . . . expected to occur only when there is a low probability of higher or strongly sanctioned obligations intervening directly between friends." Thus, he supposes that you cannot form "genuine" friendships with your brothers or employees (see similarly Paine 1969, 508, 518–19). According to my argument, the problem is just that your brothers and employees (and, indeed, perhaps you yourself) can never be *sure* that the friendship is genuine, that the actions are motivated by friendship rather than a sense of obligation.

87. "The mere fact that a person benefits another is not of itself sufficient to require the other to make restitution therefor. Thus, one who improves his own land ordinarily benefits his neighbours to some extent," but that does not entitle him to restitution (Seavey and Scott 1937, sec. 1, comment C). Incidental or accidental benefits impose no obligations. We expect beneficiaries to repay a benefactor only if he has gone out of his way with the intention of benefiting them (Sidgwick 1874, 261; Berger 1975; Simmons 1979, chap. 7; Walker 1980–81). In my formula-

performing the service, however, then repayment would be *all* that would be due him. Something more is due to those benefactors whose actions manifest a more diffuse form of goodwill. Here, and here alone, would we properly speak of a duty of gratitude, which entails reciprocating affections as well as services.[88]

F̲ocus first on the more straightforward matter of what beneficiaries owe their benefactors purely by way of material repayment. The rule of law, which here mirrors morality fairly faithfully, is that if the beneficiary has *requested* the benefit then he is indeed obliged to repay his benefactor for it. "It is inferred that a person who requests another to perform services for him or to transfer property to him thereby bargains to pay therefor" (Seavey and Scott 1937, sec. 107).[89] Likewise, if a beneficiary has voluntarily *accepted* benefits, even if initially uninvited, then a quasi-contract has been formed. Mill (1863, ch. 5) writes: "He who accepts benefits, and denies a return of them when needed, inflicts a real hurt, by disappointing one of the most natural and reasonable of expectations, and one which he must at least tacitly have encouraged, otherwise the benefits would seldom have been conferred." Once again the beneficiary is obliged to repay his benefactor. This is merely the widely discussed "duty of fair play," whereby those who voluntary participate in a cooperative scheme for mutual benefit are obliged to reciprocate each other's sacrifices.[90]

Neither law nor morality, however, imposes any obligations to repay benefits you neither invited nor could have rebuffed. "A person who officiously confers benefits upon another is not entitled to restitution thereof" (Seavey and Scott 1937, sec. 2; see also Nozick 1974, 90–95). This, in turn, seems to suggest that these obligations to our benefactors must have been self-assumed, either by our inviting or by our accepting the benefits upon which the obligations are predicated. "A person should not be required to become an

---

tion in the text, "in order to" is meant to suggest intentionality; and "costs" include "opportunity costs." That, in turn, implies that the benefactor has deviated from the course of action he would presumably have otherwise pursued with the intention of helping the beneficiaries.

88. See, e.g., Sidgwick (1874, bk. 3, chap. 4, sec.8), Strawson (1974, 5), Berger (1975), English (1979, 352–54), Simmons (1979, chap. 7), and Walker (1980–81).

89. The appropriate quantum of repayment still suffers from some uncertainty. As the reporters of the *Restatement of the Law of Restitution* state the rule: "ordinarily, the measure of restitution is the amount of enrichment received . . . , but if the loss suffered differs from the amount of benefit received the measure of restitution may be more or less than the loss suffered or more or less than the enrichment" (Seavey and Scott 1937, sec. 1, comment A; see similarly Sidgwick 1874, 261).

90. For example, "when we invite people to parties or to dinner or give them presents, these social benefactions often form part of existing social practices of mutual hospitality. The practices require those who voluntarily accept such benefactions to do a similar good in return" (Richards 1971, 173). See similarly Hart (1955, 185), Rawls (1971, secs. 18, 52), Berger (1975, 300–301), Simmons (1979, chap. 5), and Lyons (1982, 65–67).

obligor unless he so desires'' (Seavey and Scott 1937, sec. 2, comment A) seems to be the operative premise underlying all these obligations.

Yet there are situations in which the duties of beneficiaries to repay their benefactors are not self-assumed. The law of restitution, for example, makes provision for the recovery of certain precontractual benefices under the heading of ''unrealized expectations'': ''A person who transfers property to or to the account of another, manifesting that he is doing this as the offer of a contract or for a specified purpose, is entitled to regain the subject matter if the offer is not accepted or if the purpose is not carried out and if the other has possession or control over the subject matter'' (Seavey and Scott 1937, sec. 56). These benefits were neither invited nor accepted by the recipient; they were foisted upon him. Nevertheless, under this principle the recipient has obligations, in no way voluntarily assumed, to hand back the property.[91]

A much more important class of non-self-assumed obligations to repay benefactors emerges in the exception written into the principle in the law of restitution that holds, ''A person who, without mistake, coercion or request, has unconditionally conferred a benefit upon another is not entitled to restitution *except* where the benefit was conferred under circumstances making such action necessary for the protection of the interests of the other or of third persons'' (Seavey and Scott 1937, sec. 112, emphasis added). The ALI reporters go on to explain that ''a person or his belongings may be in such jeopardy that a stranger is privileged to intervene and to recover for his salvage services. These . . . represent the types of situations in which the unasked-for conferring of a benefit has been regarded as unofficious'' (Seavey and Scott 1937, sec. 112, comment B).

These obligations cannot have been self-assumed in any ordinary sense of the word. *Ex hypothesi*, the beneficiary has neither requested nor even ''accepted'' the help. Yet he has benefited, nonetheless, and is therefore obliged to repay. Perhaps in another sense these might be regarded as *hypothetically* self-assumed obligations. After all, what is crucial in all these cases is that the beneficiary would have agreed to the implicit bargain, or at least that the benefactor had no grounds for supposing that the beneficiary would have refused to agree to it. For example:

> A person who has supplied things or services to another, although acting without the other's knowledge or consent, is entitled to restitution therefor from the other if
> (a) he acted unofficiously and with the intent to charge therefor, and
> (b) the thing or services were necessary to prevent the other from suffering serious bodily harm or pain, and

---

91. Certainly this is so where ''handing back the property'' is a costless activity. We might be more reluctant to make the innocent recipient bear any very heavy costs in returning the unsought benefices.

(c) the person supplying them had no reason to know that the other would not consent to receiving them, if mentally competent; and

(d) it was impossible for the other to give consent or, because of extreme youth or mental impairment, the other's consent would have been immaterial. (Seavey and Scott 1937, sec. 116)

Similarly, a benefactor can claim restitution for expenses incurred in "preserving another's things or credit," or in performing another's "noncontractual duty to supply necessaries to a third party," "to a third person in an emergency," or "to the public" at large (Seavey and Scott 1937, secs. 117, 113–15). Yet in all these rules there is a clause analogous to (c) above. Benefactors can never claim repayment for doing things on behalf of beneficiaries which the beneficiaries clearly would not have done (or wanted done) themselves.

All this seems to suggest that the duties we impose upon beneficiaries to repay their benefactors are at least hypothetically self-assumed. There are, however, various problems with this line of analysis. Questions may well be asked about the moral or legal relevance of purely hypothetical consent, although such consent is probably more relevant in this case than in some others. (Here, as in the case of children above, consent is predicated upon what is presumed to be the present will of the recipient rather than upon his projected will under some hypothetical condition.) More serious questions might be asked about the important shift in the presumption: ordinarily those who claim to have received consent are required to offer evidence for it, whereas here consent is presumed to have been received unless there is evidence to the contrary.

Most important of all, however, is the question of why beneficiaries should be obliged to repay some favors but not others. Presumably, there is much that we would like to receive from benefactors besides the strict necessities of life or assistance in discharging our moral duties. Helping a millionaire make his second million or dousing a fire in someone's holiday cottage are undeniably useful services. Yet, since they involve neither the beneficiary's necessities nor moral duties, a benefactor providing such services cannot (in the absence of formal contracts or quasi-contracts with the beneficiaries) claim recompense for them.

There are two possible explanations for this narrow focus upon necessaries and moral duties in the law of restitution. One, still couched in terms of hypothetical agreement, might be that we can be *sure* that beneficiaries would have consented to the protection of these things, whereas we cannot be certain that they would have consented to anything else. Another explanation is couched in terms of the especially strong vulnerability of beneficiaries in such circumstances to the actions and choices of benefactors. Vital moral or material interests of the beneficiaries are at risk, yet they themselves are helpless to protect those interests. These two explanations are probably just variations on the same theme; the reason we can be so sure that beneficiaries would agree is precisely that they are so vulnerable in areas that touch their vital interests. Hence, there are probably no grounds for choosing between these two explanations. It is nonetheless important to see that the phenomenon admits of either sort of interpretation.

The duty of the beneficiaries to *repay* the benefactors in such circumstances remains to be explained. Within the model of hypothetically self-assumed obligations, the explanation is relatively easy: it is just another quasi-contractual obligation. Within the vulnerability model, the explanation is less straightforward. There we would be looking for some way in which former benefactors were vulnerable to or relying upon their former beneficiaries for some sort of material assistance. In certain respects, this seems implausible on its face. Assuming the weak remain weak and the strong strong, it seems unlikely that benefactors will ever be in a position to require assistance from their former beneficiaries.

Notice, however, two things. First, our duty to help our benefactors, although perhaps ever-present in inchoate form, is far, far stronger (and is arguably only activated at all) in circumstances in which our benefactor "obviously stands in need of it" (Sidgwick 1874, 261; see also Feinberg 1980, 134). This makes little sense in terms of quasi-contracts. There we are obliged to repay debts, regardless of our creditor's relative needs or our relative capacities. However, this feature of our duty toward benefactors makes good sense in terms of vulnerability.[92]

Second, notice that a benefactor is legally entitled to restitution (and perhaps morally as well) only if he made it clear at the time of his action that he *expected* repayment.[93] It is possible that a benefactor will occasionally expect repayment without in any way relying on it; usually, however, he will be relying on it to some greater or lesser extent for various of his other goals and projects. Here, as in the case of contracts and promises more generally, such

---

92. Walker (1980–81, 53) suggests that this may merely be because "it would be wrong . . . not to help the person in distress even if the latter were not his benefactor" (see similarly Daniel Lyons 1969). If so, so much the better for the vulnerability model of special responsibilities. That model generates a general duty to aid those in distress of just this sort. Models of self-assumed obligations do not.

93. "A person who has conferred a benefit upon another, manifesting that he does not expect compensation therefor, is not entitled to restitution merely because his expectation that the other will make a gift to him or enter into a contract with him is not realized" (Seavey and Scott 1937, sec. 57). The same is true of a person offering ostensibly gratuitous gifts "because of his expectation that an existing relationship will continue or that a future relationship will come into existence" (Seavey and Scott 1937, sec. 58). Under section 112, too, "compensation for benefits conferred is denied . . . to persons who do not desire or manifest to have compensation for their services" (Seavey and Scott 1937, sec. 112, comment B).

reliance renders the former benefactor vulnerable to his beneficiaries and imposes duties upon them to repay him for his services.

D uties to reciprocate benefits, such as I have discussed above, must be sharply distinguished from duties of gratitude proper. The former follow from actions done with the express purpose of securing some return service. The latter are done purely out of generosity (Hunt 1975), as a favor which is nowise conditional on some return favor.[94] Under the heading of duties of reciprocity, there is no claim available legally (or perhaps morally, either) to someone who performs an action "manifesting that he does not expect compensation therefor" (Seavey and Scott 1937, secs. 57–58); under the heading of duties of gratitude, a claim is available (morally, although not legally) *only* to people manifesting such intentions. Duties of reciprocation are seen as a species of debt. Duties of gratitude are something else entirely. As Feinberg (1980, 133) persuasively argues,

> gratitude, I submit, feels nothing at all like indebtedness. When a person under no duty to me does me a service or helps me out of a jam, from what I imagine to be benevolent motives, my feelings of gratitude toward him bears no important resemblance to the feeling I have toward a merchant who ships me ordered goods before I pay for them.

Still, duties of gratitude do oblige a beneficiary to repay his benefactor, albeit in a severely constrained form of currency. As Feinberg (1980, 134) describes the case,

> My benefactor once freely offered me his services when I needed them. There was, on that occasion, nothing for me to do in return but express my deepest gratitude to him. (How alien to gratitude any sort of *payment* would have been.) But now circumstances have arisen in which he needs help, and I am in a position to help him. Surely, I *owe* him my services now, and he would be entitled to resent my failure to come through.

The reciprocity that results at the end of the day from such a process might, to some, make this look like a case of paying off a quasi-contractual debt.[95] What the model of vulnerability would emphasize is the fact that, in Fein-

---

94. English (1979, 352–54), in contrast, uses the word "favor" to describe the quasi-debt relationship and talks of "gestures of friendship" when describing the other sorts of actions. Surely in standard usage, "favor" is used to describe a benefit that you confer free and simple, without reserving the right to demand any reward. Far from being merely the offer of a quasi-contract for mutual advantage, a "favor," by definition, is "something given as a mark of favour, i.e., propitious or friendly regard, goodwill" (*Oxford English Dictionary*).

95. Gouldner (1973, 277) suggests some such analysis: "The same action . . . may be referred to and interpreted by the donor in terms of the norm of beneficence at *one* time and the norm of reciprocity at a *later* time. An investment that was originally placed in the account marked 'gifts,' and was written off as a loss, may with the changed fortunes of each party, be reactivated and transferred to the 'accounts payable' ledger."

berg's rendering, "circumstances have arisen in which *he needs help*, and I am in a position to help him" (emphasis added). It is his need, not the promise to repay ostensibly implicit in my having accepted his previous favors, that activates the obligation. Contrast this with the case of a genuine contract: parties can demand what is by right theirs whether or not they need it.

This still does not explain the link between these particular individuals. To be sure, he needs help, and my being in a position to render it makes him vulnerable to me. Still, there might be someone else in an even better position to help him and hence to whom he is even more vulnerable. Why then should it be on *me*, his previous beneficiary, that the duty falls? Here, as in all the cases of familial responsibilities, ties of affection are crucial. Doing someone else a favor is a friendly gesture. You may not see each other for months thereafter; friendship in the ordinary sense might, therefore, never develop. Still, you would normally be expected to harbor warm feelings toward those who have shown you a kindness. Your benefactor should be able to count on that, and on the return kindnesses that would ordinarily follow from such sentiment. It is for this reason that ingratitude is so often regarded as a form of betrayal. Your benefactor has invested in you both materially and emotionally. He is peculiarly vulnerable to you in both these ways, and from those vulnerabilities flow your special responsibilities in respect of him.

Both philosophically and psychologically, there is an affective component built into the notion of gratitude that is absent in relationships of mere indebtedness. Gratitude is a response on the part of a beneficiary to actions which display the benefactor's goodwill toward himself.[96] What all this seems to suggest, in turn, is that such actions are essentially gestures of friendship. The offer of aid, and of friendship, can of course be refused. One way of doing so would be to refuse the aid;[97] another would be to repay it promptly and fully; another, perhaps, would be simply to make it clear to your benefactor at the outset that you regard this as no more than a business proposition. Failing any such disclaimer, however, a benefactor has every reason to believe that friendly relations have been established and that his friendly gestures will be returned in kind.

This explains many of the more curious features of duties of gratitude.

96. Psychologically, this is undeniably crucial. As Strawson (1974, 5; cf. 6, 14) writes, "If someone's actions help me to some benefit I desire, then I am benefited in any case; but if he intended them to benefit me because of his general goodwill towards me, I shall reasonably feel a gratitude which I should not feel at all if the benefit was an incidental consequence, unintended or even regretted by him, of some plan of action with a different aim." The argument here is that the benefactor's goodwill is a crucial factor in determining moral duties as well as psychological responses. "Goodwill" is Walker's (1980–81, 50) choice of phrase; others put the same point in terms of "affection" (Sidgwick 1874, 260; English 1979, 352–54) or "value, respect, concern" (Berger 1975, 301–2).

97. Doing so would mark a person as "ungrateful," rather than as an "ingrate," in Walker's (1980–81, 52) terms. It amounts to a refusal to incur the duties of gratitude in the first place rather than to a failure to discharge duties once you have them.

Notice, for example, that where these are concerned, we generally feel that a careful accounting of debts and repayments is inappropriate. Walker (1980–81, 50) observes that "the grateful return has about it a gratuitous and indefinite quality which aligns it with generosity rather than justice." And Sidgwick (1874, 261) before him pointed out that, "Here, as in other affectionate services, we do not like too exact a measure of duty." The reason is precisely that the relationship is supposed to be an affectionate one. Here, as in the case of families or friends (English 1979, 353; Ewin 1981, chap. 9), anyone keeping close tabs on favors and return favors would betray an instrumental orientation that is inimical to affective relations. Someone who does us favors in expectation of return favors deserves his due return but no more. Someone who does them out of pure generosity deserves much more: our affection and all the material services that might naturally flow from it.

This also explains why it is regarded as improper for a benefactor to *demand* that his beneficiaries show gratitude. Certainly he may "rightly resent the failure to show gratitude," especially where his sacrifice has been substantial (Daniel Lyons 1969, 92; Feinberg 1980, 134). "Other parties may rightly criticize the failure to discharge [the duty of gratitude], and even the person to whom it is owed may be entitled to complain of the insult such a failure represents" (Berger 1975, 300). All of this, however, stops well short of vesting a right in the benefactor to *demand* a demonstration of gratitude. The reason, once again, has to do with the affective, noninstrumental nature of the relationship that underlies true duties of gratitude. Actions performed out of a sense of duty cannot, by their nature, display the sort of regard, esteem, and affection that is supposed to underlie acts of gratitude. Indeed, in demanding his due the benefactor would himself be displaying motives inappropriate to such a relationship. "Such a demand shows the help or gift to be something less than a show of benevolence; it appears to be something done in order to gain favor, and to the extent we feel this to be the case, the duty to show gratitude is diminished" (Berger 1975, 300).

The affective nature of the relationship also explains why it is improper to discharge duties of gratitude (as distinct from duties of recirprocity) by returning the same gifts as we received.

> While some form of reciprocation is requisite, this need not be, and often *ought not to be*, the giving of the same or an equivalent benefit to the grantor. Not only is this not always possible, but sometimes it would destroy the force of the original gift. When someone grants us a benefit because of his concern for us, or because he wishes to make us happy, it can be an insult to return it or to show that we feel obligated to make a like return. The grant was made with no strings attached, with no desire to obligate us. To show that we feel we *are* obligated demonstrates that the gift misfired to a certain extent or, worse, gives reason to think the donee misread the intentions of the grantor. (Berger 1975, 302–3; see similarly Walker 1980–81, 50).

If we were just buying return favors, then the more nearly equivalent the favor and return favor the better. Returning offerings that we meant as offers of friendship constitutes a repudiation of the offer or, if previous behavior implied that such relations had already been established, an actual betrayal of the friendship.

In short, emotional vulnerability can explain the peculiarities of duties of gratitude. A benefactor, having offered friendship and reasonably inferred that the offer had been accepted, is emotionally vulnerable to the actions and choices of his beneficiaries. Perhaps no one can be obliged to feign feelings that he has never had or that he has no longer (Sidgwick 1874, 261). At the very least, however, we *can* expect people to treat those who are emotionally vulnerable to them with special consideration and to try to let them down gently.

Of course, an element of self-assumed obligation remains. Even if you neither invited nor accepted your benefactor's offering, nor perhaps even enjoyed it, you nonetheless allowed certain understandings and expectations to grow up. For that reason if none other, your duties of gratitude might be thought to be self-assumed. That might explain the fact that you have duties of gratitude, but it cannot explain the nature of those duties. Once again, only with the vulnerability model can we explain both aspects.

Conclusion

The upshot of this long survey is that there is a great variety of ways in which people might become vulnerable to one another. Sometimes the relationship seems to arise out of natural necessity, other times out of social conventions, still other times out of voluntary choice. What is clear and constant throughout these many examples is that it is vulnerability, however engendered, that plays the crucial role in generating special responsibilities.

A theory accounting for special responsibilities would have to explain several things: their incidence (who has special responsibilities with respect to whom); their content (what the one is responsible for providing for the other); their context (the circumstances under which these special responsibilities will be activated); and their form, especially the fact that their specific content is so often unalterable even with the explicit consent of both parties.

The model of self-assumed obligations provides a ready answer to some of these questions in some of the examples. With a fair bit of twisting and turning, the model can be used to provide some sort of an answer to several more. But none of its possible variants—contracts, quasi-contracts, or self-assumed role responsibilities—can provide a wholly adequate account of all these features of all the special responsibilities surveyed.[98] Certainly none of them can

---

98. As Kirchheimer (1942, 635–36, 625) sums it up, ''the duty to act may be derived from family relationship or personal ties which create a state of mutual reliance, from a professional or group status, from the mere fact of human coexistence as well as from contractual obligations. . . . The

provide as compact and as coherent an account as the alternative explanation which I have offered, which traces all these special responsibilities to various peculiar vulnerabilities between people, and which indeed subsumes the model of self-assumed obligations through its analysis of promises and contracts. In short, I have shown (*pace* the traditionalist-cum-intuitionist challenge) that a single, coherent model can account for all the special responsibilities we ordinarily acknowledge and (*pace* the voluntarist challenge) that the most plausible such account is couched in terms of vulnerabilities rather than in terms of voluntary acts of will in assuming those responsibilities.

---

question to what degree personal relationships create legal duties to protect one another cannot be determined by construing a fictitious contractual relation as some courts do. Either the relationship between the persons is so strong and manifest that a legal duty may be inferred therefrom or it is not, and the introduction of an implied contract does not produce a relationship not otherwise existing.''

5

Vulnerabilities and Responsibilities

The central argument of this book is that we bear special responsibilities for protecting those who are particularly vulnerable to us. This proposition is reflected, powerfully albeit indirectly, in all those special responsibilities ascribed to us by common-sense morality. These special duties can best be understood in terms of a more general responsibility to protect the vulnerable (as shown in chapter 4). To some extent, the basic proposition has already made its way into common-sense morality. Certainly in the official rhetoric of various British and Australian royal commissions, much is made of our responsibilities to protect the vulnerable.[1] Social psychologists have also found that, at least under certain conditions, people internalize and act upon such norms.[2] The aim here is to systematize and solidify those inchoate intuitions.

My purpose in this chapter is twofold. My primary aim is to provide a more formal statement of the nature of our responsibility to protect the vulnerable. In so doing I shall also be pursuing the secondary aim of examining the deeper philosophical underpinnings of the principle of protecting the vulnerable. In particular, I shall address the nonconsequentialist challenge to my principle by showing that although in form my principle is fundamentally consequen-

---

1.The British Wolfenden Commission, for example, accepts without hesitation that one of the principal public responsibilities—one which is and should be discharged through the criminal law—is "to provide sufficient safeguards against exploitation and corruption of others, particularly those who are *specially vulnerable* because they are young, weak in body or mind, inexperienced, or in a state of special physical, official or economic dependence" (Wolfenden 1957, par. 14, emphasis added; cf. Devlin 1965, 11–12). The Australian Royal Commission on Human Relationships strikes a similar chord: "Just as the child is *vulnerable* to the family, so are families *vulnerable* to the society of which they are a part. Malnutrition, poor housing, unemployment, discrimination are only a few of the pressures which can affect family life and well-being. Therefore society carries a *responsibility* to see that families can function effectively, particularly where the case of children is concerned" (1977, vol. 1, p. 63, emphasis added).
2. The conclusion of a seminal study by Berkowitz and Daniels (1963, 430) is that "many people in our society seek to aid others only because they believe that these others are *dependent* upon them for reward. The perception of the dependency relationship . . . arouses feelings of *responsibility* to those others, and the outcome is a heightened instigation to help them achieve their goals" (emphasis added; see further Krebs 1970, 277–79).

tialistic, in its derivation and its implications my principle is broadly consistent with most standard forms of nonconsequentialism.

Philosophical Foundations

The first step is to clarify the central concepts. According to the *Oxford English Dictionary*, something is "vulnerable" if it "may be wounded," either literally or figuratively; it is "susceptible of injury, not proof against weapon, criticism, etc." Essentially, then, the principle of protecting the vulnerable amounts to an injunction to prevent harms from befalling people. Conceptually, "vulnerability" is essentially a matter of being under threat of harm; therefore, protecting the vulnerable is primarily a matter of forestalling threatened harms.

Notice that, conceptually at least, the way in which these wounds might come to be inflicted is irrelevant. It makes perfectly good sense to speak of someone's being vulnerable either to manmade threats or to natural ones. Likewise, it makes perfectly good sense to speak of someone's being vulnerable either to harms that come about through others' omissions or neglect or to harms that come about through others' positive actions.[3]

The principle of protecting the vulnerable would, therefore, seem to enjoin more than merely refraining from acting in such a way as to cause others harm. If people can be said to be vulnerable to harms from men or from nature, from actions or from omissions, then protecting the vulnerable must amount to protecting them from *all* these sorts of threatened harms.

As far as the concept of vulnerability is concerned these distinctions do not matter. That they do not matter morally, either, can best be demonstrated by combining a pair of results established previously. Recall, first, my discussion in chapter 2 of the relative strengths of various sorts of duties. Close analysis of conventional morality and codified law revealed that, where special responsibilities (of, e.g., firemen and bodyguards) were concerned, positive duties (duties to aid others) were strictly on a par with negative duties (duties not to harm others); neither was necessarily any stronger or more compelling than the other. Recall, next, the discussion in chapter 4 in which I showed that vulnerability was what really underlay all those standard special responsibilities. If there is no moral importance attaching to the distinction between positive and negative duties (i.e., acts and omissions) for the classic cases of special responsibilities, then there should be none attaching to the distinction for all other responsibilities with the same moral bases. The duty to

---

3. This latter point emerges particularly in relation to such cognate notions as "helplessness" and "dependence." The former is defined as the state of being "unable to help oneself"; the latter as "depending upon, being conditioned or subordinate or subject; living at another's cost; reliance, confident trust." In both these situations, the vulnerability in view is to harms that come about through other people's inactions rather than their actions.

protect the vulnerable is a duty to prevent harm from occurring; it is equally compelling whether it requires positive action or refraining from action. Failing to take positive action to prevent harm from befalling someone who is particularly vulnerable to your actions and choices is morally akin to a bodyguard sleeping on the job.

Having established the various ways in which people might be vulnerable to a threat of harm, and in which we might therefore be responsible for protecting them, I next turn to the nature of the threatened harms. What it may mean for an inanimate object to be vulnerable (as, e.g., a fortress to seige) is perhaps elusive. Where we are talking about people, however, the threatened harm must necessarily be to their "welfare" or "interests," terms which I shall here use interchangeably (Feinberg 1980, chap. 3). It is important to emphasize the variety of ways in which these terms might be construed. (See, e.g., Barry 1965, chap. 10; Parfit 1984, appendix 1.) Some interpretations would be limited to notions of "preference" or "desire"; others would appeal instead to notions of "objective" interests, justifying considerable paternalism in the process. Some would include, and indeed emphasize heavily, "autonomy interests"; others would not. A wide variety of otherwise quite different moral theories can thus be accommodated to the principle of protecting the vulnerable merely by varying the notion of interests accordingly.

Two things, however, are clear. One is that interests must be understood to encompass more than narrowly material ones. After all, some of the most important vulnerabilities have to do with feelings (chap. 4). Various arguments about the importance of self-images and self-respect suggest that we should accord at least as much importance to feelings as to physical/material considerations (Rawls 1971, sec. 67; Goodin 1982b, chap. 5). However we vary the notion of interests, then, the vulnerabilities in view clearly must extend to people's psychological as well as physical senstivities.

The second thing to notice is that in spite of this plasticity of the notion of interests, the principle of protecting the vulnerable does have some specific content. There are certain sorts of things that the principle would require us to do for others no matter what particular standard of interests we adopt. Specifically we would be required to protect people's "needs" or "vital interests": these are "primary goods," things that are in a person's general interests no matter what he (or we) supposes his particular interests to be (Rawls 1971, sec. 15; Miller 1976, chap. 4). The standard list includes food, clothing, and shelter; Rawls would have us add self-respect and civil liberties. If these really are necessary means to any particular ends a person might choose to pursue, then it is clear that protecting the vulnerable (no matter how their vulnerability is interpreted) must be primarily a matter of protecting those people whose vital interests are particularly vulnerable to our actions and choices. In short, the argument for protecting the vulnerable is first and foremost an argument for aiding those in dire need.

Vulnerability implies more than susceptibility to certain sorts of harm, however broadly conceived; it also implies that the harm is not predetermined. Where harm is unavoidable, ''vulnerable'' is too weak a term to describe the situation. It would be odd to say that the condemned criminal was (merely) vulnerable to the hangman, or that houses on the slopes of an erupting volcano were (merely) vulnerable to damage from the lava flowing inexorably toward them. In such cases, some stronger term like ''damned,'' ''cursed,'' or ''condemned'' is required. Vulnerability implies that there is some agent (actual or metaphorical) capable of exercising some effective choice (actual or, as in the case of the dormant volcano, metaphorical) over whether to cause or to avert the threatened harm.

The implication that an agent exists, in turn, implies that ''vulnerability'' is essentially a relational notion. As the *Oxford English Dictionary* reminds us with respect to the cognate notion of ''dependency,'' one depends *upon* someone *for* something.[4] Similarly, references to vulnerability imply two other references. One is *to what* the persons or things are vulnerable. Where do their weaknesses lie? What mechanisms are capable of inflicting harm upon them? The other is *to whom* the persons or things are vulnerable.[5] Who can inflict the harms upon me? Who can protect me against them? One is always vulnerable to particular agents with respect to particular sorts of threats. An airline passenger is dependent upon or vulnerable to his pilot with respect to his physical safety en route to his destination; a debtor is dependent upon or vulnerable to his creditor with respect to the mortgage on his house; and so forth. Any briefer description of the situation would be radically incomplete. Like the notions of power and freedom, that of vulnerability is inherently object and agent specific.[6]

---

4. ''To depend'' is there defined as meaning, *inter alia,* ''to rest entirely *on, upon* . . . for support, or what is needed.''

5. Sometimes we do simply say that someone or something is vulnerable to some particular danger, without mentioning any particular agents who could cause or avert the harm. That, essentially, amounts to employing the description ''vulnerable'' in the context of a game against nature. We say, for instance, that a subsistence farmer is vulnerable to the weather, since either drought or flood would cause him to starve. This just amounts to anthropomorphizing natural forces. For the Greeks, this amounted to vulnerability to the whims of the gods (Nussbaum 1984). Even today we still conceptualize the situation as if we were really playing a game against someone called ''Nature,'' who makes genuine choices; and if Nature chooses drought or flood, the subsistence farmer is in real trouble. It is merely the appearance of a quasi-human chooser, Nature, that warrants the use of the term ''vulnerable'' at all. To prove this, consider a case where there is no uncertainty at all (and hence no illusion of choice) surrounding the outcome. There was a heavy snowfall in the nearby mountains, say, and it is utterly certain to cause serious flooding when it melts. Then, I suggest, we *would* describe the farmer whose land is due to be flooded as ''damned'' rather than merely vulnerable. Insofar as we would still call him vulnerable, that must surely be with respect to some other agents (e.g., neighbors, kin, or government) who are still capable of making some choices of taking actions (e.g., giving him money or food) to alter his plight. One person's vulnerability seems, therefore, to be conceptually linked to the existence of another agent (if only an anthropomorphized Nature) to whose actions and choices he is vulnerable.

6. As Baldwin (1980, 497) says, ''No single change in scholarly writing habits would bring a

The second key notion in my argument is "responsibility," which is ordinarily analyzed in terms of "accountability" or "answerability." To be responsible is, according to the *Oxford English Dictionary*, to be "liable to be called to account, answerable." Whom we are answerable *to* necessarily depends upon social conventions. What we are answerable *for* is less variable. It seems always to be for the *consequences* of our actions and choices: the "event or state of affairs" thereby produced (Feinberg 1970, 25).[7]

Responsibility thus amounts to being held to account for the consequences of your actions and choices. Obviously, the best sort of account that can be rendered is to show that your actions and choices have produced good consequences. That, however, is hardly the context in which questions about responsibility and accountability ordinarily arise. People are rarely called to account for the good they have done; it is their failures that more typically occasion this sort of inquiry. Now, of course, there are various ways of categorizing moral failures of this sort. If a person were truly unable (objectively or psychologically) to foresee the consequences of his actions and choices for the interests of others, then he would be deemed "not responsible" for harm he has done (Roberts 1965, 242). If, instead, he willfully ignored or negligently failed to consider the consequences of his actions and choices for others—if, in other words, he *could* have done otherwise (Chisholm 1966)—then his behavior is deemed "irresponsible." What is important in the present context, however, is that it is always responsibility *for the consequences* of one's actions and choices that is at issue. "Acting responsibly" always consists in acting with due regard for the consequences of one's actions and choices.

The same emphasis upon consequentialistic considerations is apparent in the notion of "a responsibility." Feinberg (1980, 137) notes that a responsibility "unlike a duty . . . carries considerable discretion . . . along with it." But the discretion, notice, consists merely in how best to attain some desired consequence: "A goal is assigned and the means of achieving it are left to the independent judgment of the responsible party."[8] The more discretion we

more dramatic improvement in the clarity and precision of such discussion than the practice of specifying who is dependent on whom in respect of what."

7. This is a proposition familiar to lawyers and philosophers; see, e.g., Hart (1968, 224–25). That it is equally familiar to laymen is evidenced by the report of the Australian Royal Commission on Human Relationships (1977, vol. 1, p. 23), which reads in part: "An act is not responsible unless the consequences of the action are taken fully into account. The consequences of the action should, as far as possible, promote the well-being of all affected by it. Responsibility implies the attempt to make the right choice between alternatives."

8. There is a particularly strong tendency for administrative responsibilities to be accompanied by broad discretionary powers, the limiting case perhaps being the "Henry VIII clauses" that were commonly written into British legislation between the wars, empowering "the appropriate minister to modify the provisions of an act he is called upon to administer so far as may appear to him necessary for the purpose of bringing the act into operation" (Friedrich 1940, 11). So, too, with many of the special responsibilities considered in chapter 4: "we do not approve of the limits of duty being too exactly measured" (Sidgwick 1874, 243). This is particularly true of certain

allow a responsible agent, the more firmly we hold him responsible for the consequences that flow from the exercise of that discretion: "That a man tried his best is more likely to be accepted as an excuse for failure to perform one's duty than for failure to fulfill one's responsibilities. Indeed, the more discretion allowed in the responsibility assignment, the stricter the liability for failure is likely to be" (Feinberg 1980, 137). Essentially, failure to discharge a responsibility is failure to produce the desired consequences, failure to attain the desired goal.

Thus, analytically, the notion of consequences seems central to the notions both of vulnerability and of responsibility. Vulnerability amounts to one person's having the capacity to produce consequences that matter to another. Responsibility amounts to his being accountable for those consequences of his actions and choices.

I f my analysis of these core notions is correct, then the principle of protecting the vulnerable must be fundamentally consequentialistic in form. Its central injunction is to frame your actions and choices in such a way as to produce certain sorts of consequences, namely, ones that protect the interests of those who are particularly vulnerable to your actions and choices. If interests are equated with welfare, the principle is more precisely welfare consequentialistic in form: actions and choices are evaluated on the basis of their consequences, and consequences are evaluated on the basis of their impact on people's welfare (Sen 1979b; Sen and Williams 1982, 4).

Here I am concerned to make two arguments. One is that any welfare-consequentialistic theory (of which utilitarianism is only the most conspicuous example) will necessarily entail the principle of protecting the vulnerable. The second is that, although the principle of protecting the vulnerable is fundamentally consequentialistic in form, the sort of consequentialism it embodies is broadly consistent with all the standard sorts of nonconsequentialist ethics.

The first of these arguments is easily made. The principle of protecting the vulnerable follows straightforwardly from welfare consequentialism, no matter which version of it is considered. To say that one person is particularly vulnerable to another is to say that his interests are strongly affected by the other's actions and choices.[9] On any welfare-consequentialist reckoning, the more strongly and directly our actions affect someone else's welfare interests, the more heavily those effects on that person should weigh with us in deciding

---

special responsibilities, especially those having to do with love and friendship. As Hampshire (1982, 148) says, "the specific realizations of love and friendship seem likely not to conform to a fixed and definite norm . . . and [hence] to principles that can be formulated. One does not normally speak of principles of love and friendship, as of principles of justice and fairness."

9. The word "choices" in this formulation is meant to embrace both "choices to help" and "choices not to help," i.e., to cover both acts and omissions.

our own course of action. From the simple fact that we are in an especially good position to protect those who are particularly vulnerable to us, it follows that we should give them "special consideration" of this sort.[10] If promoting people's welfare is the prime moral imperative, then the mere fact that one person is particularly able to protect another's welfare provides a strong welfare-consequentialistic reason for supposing that he should do so, *ceteris paribus.*[11]

Naturally, other things will rarely be completely equal. We will also have to consider the costs of the act to the Good Samaritan's own welfare, or to that of others he might have helped instead. To decide what he should on balance do, the Samaritan will have to consider how strongly each person's welfare is affected and how strongly the welfare of each should weigh with him. (Utilitarians would have him weigh them all equally; Rawlsians would have him assign priority to the worst-off; etc.) Notice, however, that the only welfare-consequentialist justification for failing to protect one person who is vulnerable to your actions and choices is that it is necessary to fail him in order to protect others (yourself or third parties) whose welfare interests are even more vulnerable to your actions and choices.

Having shown that the principle of protecting the vulnerable is implicit in any form of welfare consequentialism, I must next show that it is also broadly consistent with all the standard forms of nonconsequentialistic ethics. The first thing to notice in this regard is that *non*consequentialism does not necessarily entail (or even ordinarily involve) anything like a thoroughgoing *anti*-consequentialism. To be sure, it is becoming increasingly fashionable to deny that the consequences are everything, morally speaking (Hart 1979). Happily, it is still rare to find anyone who regards consequences as counting for nothing. As C. D. Broad (1916, 44–45) says in his classic essay "On the Function of False Hypotheses in Ethics," "It is thoroughly unreasonable to suppose that the goodness or badness of an action is *entirely independent* of its probable consequences, and no one but a moralist riding a theory to death would maintain this view for an instant" (emphasis added). Such committed non-

---

10. Of course, we are not really giving them special consideration, in the sense of weighing their interests more heavily than anyone else's. Actually, all we are doing is paying greater attention to greater effects. We simply have more opportunities for affecting these people than others. As Sidgwick (1874, 432, 242) rightly replies to Grote (1870, 94–101), the Benthamite dictum that "every man is to count for one, nobody for more than one" must be understood merely as "making the conception of the ultimate end precise—laying down that one person's happiness is to be counted for as much as another's (supposed equal in degree) as an element of the general happiness—not as directly prescribing the rules of conduct by which this end will be best attained. . . . Practically of course the distribution of any individual's services will, even on this view, be unequal: as each man will obviously promote the general happiness best by rendering services to a limited number, and to some more than others."

11. This *ceteris paribus* formulation corresponds well to the "duty of easy [i.e., virtually costless] rescue" that is often enjoined by continental European law, and it is even more often advocated by legal philosophers (Kirchheimer 1942; Kleinig 1976; Weinrib 1980, 268ff.).

consequentialists as Bernard Williams (1973, 90) would nonetheless be prepared to concede it "a mark of sense to believe . . . that there was no type of action" which one should do (or, we might add, refrain from doing) "whatever the consequences." The most that nonconsequentialists can reasonably, or do ordinarily, demand is that moral choices should not be decided *exclusively* on the basis of consequentialistic considerations. That is consistent with consequentialistic reckonings still playing some role, and perhaps even a large one, in moral decision making.[12]

What is distinctive then about nonconsequentialistic moral theories is not their total rejection of consequentialistic considerations but rather the constraints they place upon the operation of such considerations in moral decision making. Essentially, these constraints amount to a prohibition on "doing evil that good may come," and they are ordinarily operationalized through a list of particular kinds of acts that constitute evil and are thus prohibited (Anscombe 1958; Fried 1978, chap. 1). Most conspicuous among the prohibitions are the classic *thou shalt not*'s of the Ten Commandments. Different nonconsequentialists might, however, fill out the list differently.

Now, the first thing to notice about this sort of catalog of prohibited acts is that there is little scope for deriving from it any requirements for positive action, whether to protect the vulnerable or to do anything else. *Thou shalt*'s just do not fall easily out of a list of *thou shalt not*'s. Once the latter have ruled out certain courses of action, all other courses remain merely optional; it is hard to see how you could get from there to making any of them mandatory (unless of course the prohibitions ruled out everything but one course of action, which would be quite extraordinary). Now, nonconsequentialists may well want to embrace a principle like mine of protecting the vulnerable; indeed, Kant himself laid down a duty of mutual aid. Insofar as they do, however, it cannot be for distinctively nonconsequentialistic reasons. Any argument for protecting the vulnerable, whether it comes from a consequentialist or a nonconsequentialist, must make essential reference to the consequences of putting such a principle into operation. "To act beneficently," even in Kantian terms, "is to seek . . . to achieve some of the things that . . . others aim at" in their own lives (O'Neill 1980, 288)—which is to say, to strive to produce consequences of a certain sort.[13] Thus, although my principle of protecting the vulnerable is fundamentally consequentialistic in form, it is not formally at odds with nonconsequentialistic premises in this sense: they offer no alter-

12. Even within Kant's theory, "a man is responsible for what he does to those affected by what he does. . . . This is merely another way of saying that he is responsible for the results of his actions" (Roberts 1965, 223).
13. Similarly, Barbara Herman's (1984) derivation of the Kantian duty of mutual aid from the Categorical Imperative hinges crucially upon the fact that we cannot escape "our shared condition of dependency" and various consequences that follow from that fact. For Herman the reason the Categorical Imperative has the implications it does pertains explicitly to considerations of the possible consequences for necessarily vulnerable others of our acting on a maxim of nonbeneficence.

native grounding for that principle that avoids any essential reference to consequences.

Nor, for the most part, is my principle of protecting the vulnerable inconsistent in its practical implications with the standard nonconsequentialistic constraints. Of course, it is always possible to conjure up wild examples to force a choice. In Bernard Williams's (1973, 98) classic crazy case, Jim can save nineteen vulnerable Indians from death by shooting only by shooting the twentieth himself. There it really might matter whether our principle of protecting the vulnerable was consequentialistic or nonconsequentialistic: a rule of protecting the vulnerable, consequentialistically understood, might lead to the violation of one of the strongest nonconsequentialistic prohibitions.

There is no denying that the implications of consequentialistically based and nonconsequentialistically based principles of protecting the vulnerable do occasionally diverge in these ways. What I would emphasize, however, is how rare the occurrence is. Over the broad range of action implications, there is no such tension between them. Protecting the vulnerable, for the most part, need not entail lying, cheating, stealing, killing, or any other violation of nonconsequentialists' *thou shalt not*'s. It would usually just be a matter of reallocating time, energy, money, and other resources to those who would otherwise suffer grave harms. None of that would violate any of the standard prohibitions that nonconsequentialists place on our actions.[14]

Thus I hope to have shown that although my principle of protecting the vulnerable is undeniably consequentialistic, nonconsequentialists are at least that consequentialistic themselves. If nonconsequentialists embrace a principle of protecting the vulnerable at all (as many of them do), it must be for essentially consequentialistic reasons. Only in the rarest of circumstances are the action implications of that principle incompatible with the *thou shalt not*'s that constitute the core of their doctrine.

The crucial point, I suppose, is that my principle of protecting the vulnerable aspires only to the status of a partial principle of morality. It makes no claim to order the entire moral universe. Hence, a large measure of consequentialism in the realm it does claim to order need not be inconsistent with a hefty dose of nonconsequentialism in other areas of our moral theory.

Allocating Responsibilities

One of the greatest advantages of the vulnerability model is that, at least in its core applications, it allows for the easy allocation of responsibilities to

14. That is to say, there is no nonconsequentialistic objection to laying upon people a *moral* responsibility to do these things. There may still be a nonconsequentialistic objection to backing that with the force of law (Nozick 1974). Even that objection largely falls away when we see the situation as one of compelling people socially to play their part in discharging collective responsibilities. The only really plausible nonconsequentialistic objection here is to publicly forcing people to discharge their private responsibilities. It is almost incoherent to say that people have public responsibilities that are inappropriate for public enforcement. These themes are picked up again in the final pages of this chapter.

particular individuals. Saying that "*A* needs *X*" might imply that *A* should get *X;* but it says nothing about who should be instrumental in *A*'s getting *X.* Vulnerability, in contrast, is a relational notion: a full specification will tell us who is vulnerable to whom with respect to what. Saying that *A* is particularly vulnerable to *B* with respect to *X* clearly fingers *B* as the agent who should be particularly responsible for seeing to it that *A*'s interests in *X* are protected.

Vulnerabilities, and the responsibilities growing out of them, are not only relational but also relative. *A* is more vulnerable to *B* (1) the more control *B* has over outcomes that affect *A*'s interests and (2) the more heavily *A*'s interests are at stake in the outcomes that *B* controls. *B* is defined as having "less control" the more likely it is that the outcome will occur (or not occur) whatever *B* does; this could be either because nobody has much power over the outcome or because lots of people have power to control the outcome and hence the contribution of none of them is particularly crucial.

The basic principle I am advocating can thus be summarized in the following proposition:

First Principle of Individual Responsibility: If *A*'s interests are vulnerable to *B*'s actions and choices, *B* has a special responsibility to protect *A*'s interests; the strength of this responsibility depends strictly upon the degree to which *B* can affect *A*'s interests.

For purposes of this principle and those that follow, I shall assume that, *ceteris paribus,* it is morally good that *A*'s interests should be furthered. This seems to be a fairly uncontentious proposition, at least in the core cases where it is with the interests of people (rather than, e.g., those of animals) that we are concerned (cf. Kleinig 1978, 27–34). Of course, the good involved in furthering one person's interests can come into conflict with other moral goods, and *B*'s responsibility for protecting *A*'s interests is therefore always susceptible to being overridden by *B*'s other moral responsibilities. These may be responsibilities for *B* to protect the interests of some other person *C*. They may be responsibilities for *B* to protect interests of his own. (Where *B* embraces as a centrally important life goal that "*X* be accomplished *by me,*" *B* is uniquely vulnerable to his own actions: by definition, *B* and *B* alone can act so as to satisfy *B*'s interests in that goal.)[15] Finally, these may be moral

---

15. This strikes me as a far better way for *B* to justify favoring his own projects over those of starving Asians than Narveson's (1972) suggestion that *B* appeal (on aesthetic or some other grounds) to the objective superiority of his own projects. Pointing to *B*'s particular vulnerability to his own actions and choices also limits the sorts of situations in which he can give such preference to his own projects, i.e., to those involving projects about which he is in this way "possessive." Not all—indeed, not all that many—of our activities constitute "projects" of that special sort. At most, such notions apply only to our "discretionary activities": it makes little sense to insist that it is *my* project to feed myself, as if that were a goal I freely chose for myself. Even where our discretionary activities are concerned, we are ordinarily more than happy to join coalitions to pursue social goals, to join in partnerships to pursue business ventures, and to join in friendships to pursue personal goals. The fact that others share these projects with us does nothing to diminish their value to us; often it enhances it.

responsibilities connected with moral ideals rather than with anyone's interests. In Barry's (1965) terms, my general scheme is at least formally open to the possibility of an ideal-based rejection of A's want-based claims.

Each individual will thus need to balance one set of responsibilities against others. Some may deny that such balancing can ever be done rationally, saying that these responsibilities are utterly incommensurable. Sartre (1948, 35, 36, 38) offers the classic example:

> A pupil of mine . . . sought me out in the following circumstances. . . . His mother was living alone with him, deeply afflicted by the semi-treason of his father and by the death of her eldest son, and her one consolation was in this young man. But he, at this moment, had the choice between going to England and to join the Free French Forces or of staying near his mother and helping her to live. . . . He had to choose between those two. What could help him to choose? . . . I had but one reply to make. You are free, therefore choose— that is to say, invent. No rule of general morality can show you what you ought to do.

"Sartre's point," according to Charles Taylor (1976, 290–1), "is that there is no way of adjudicating between these two strong claims on his moral allegiance through reason." But, as Taylor goes on to say, if there really were no bases for comparing the claims of kin and country, then the moral dilemma would itself disappear. Neither choice would be right or wrong; there would be no point in agonizing over the options. That, however, is to deny the one thing of which we *are* sure in this case, namely, that it presents the son with a hard moral choice. That fact implies that the competing responsibilities must somehow be commensurable.

The notion of vulnerability, I would argue, can both account for the force of these dilemmas and help us to resolve them. The dilemmas arise because discharging our responsibilities with respect to some of those who are vulnerable to us entails defaulting on our responsibilities with respect to some others who are also vulnerable. Whom we should favor depends, according to this analysis, upon the relative vulnerability of each party to us. We must determine: (1) how strongly that party's interests would be affected by our alternative actions and choices; and (2) whether or not he would be able to find other sources of assistance/protection if we failed him.[16]

---

16. Surely it goes without saying (but perhaps just to be safe I should say, if only in a footnote) that we should also consider *how many* people's interests would be affected by each of our alternative actions and choices. That consideration helps avoid the embarrassing implication, pointed out by David Miller in personal correspondence (1983), that duopolists should according to my argument refrain from undercutting each other's prices. Surely it is true that each duopolist's interests are particularly vulnerable to the other's price-cutting behavior, and surely it does follow according to my argument that each would therefore be responsible for refraining from such behavior, *ceteris paribus*. Among the other things that are not equal here, however, are the effects of the duopolists' price fixing upon the interests of the public at large. No member of the public, taken individually, has as strong an interest in promoting a price war as each duopolist has in avoiding one. Still, lots of little vulnerabilities and responsibilities can combine to trump some larger ones.

Philosophers who have been frightened by the universalism of standard consequentialism have always supposed that any duty to render positive assistance to others must be tightly circumscribed, either by limits on *who* can claim or else by limits on *what* they can claim. Otherwise, they argue, our lives will be interrupted by the constant intrusions of the claims of vulnerable others.[17] To use Thomson's (1971) example, you might have to devote a significant portion of your life to saving a famous violinist with failing kidneys. In the more realistic case for which that one is meant as an analogue, you may be the only one capable of sustaining the life of the uninvited fetus that has taken up residence in your uterus. Both the violinist and the fetus are indeed vulnerable to your actions and choices, and to yours uniquely; so, within the vulnerability model, you have heavy responsibilities in respect of them.[18] How you might best discharge your responsibilities is, of course, left open; and you may even decide, quite properly, that in light of your other responsibilities (including responsibilities to yourself, discussed above), these responsibilities to the violinist or fetus must be sacrificed. That, however, would require serious soul searching, whereas Thomson (1971, 64) stands ready to accept a far simpler reply. To satisfy her, all you need say is that "you are sorry, but you simply cannot see giving up so much of your life to the sustaining of his."[19]

The sort of considerations I have just been discussing should go far toward allaying these fears. The fundamental point, pressed by the classical utilitarians against their earliest critics, is that we rarely are in any very good position to be all that much of a Good Samaritan, to help or to harm very many others in any very significant way. Sidgwick (1874, 434), for example, emphasizes that, "each person is for the most part, from limitations either of power or knowledge, not in a position to do much good to more than a very

17. Walzer (1981, 3), surveying the plight of the Good Samaritan, similarly protests, "My life cannot be shaped by such chance encounters." Fried (1978, 38), echoing Grote's (1870, 94) objection to Mill's utilitarianism, insists that we must be able "to limit and control the number and identities of those who have a privileged call on our help" or else the sense of self itself will disappear. See similarly Slote (1977, 125–26), Fishkin (1982, 14–15, 20–24, 75), and Davis (1983, 268).

18. Thomson (1971, 58), too, briefly canvasses the vulnerability argument, scolding opponents of abortion for "overlook[ing] the possible support they might gain from making out that the foetus is *dependent* on the mother, in order to establish that she has a special kind of responsibility for it." Davis (1984) develops this argument at greater length. Gilligan's (1977) psychological surveys show that it is, in fact, one of the heaviest considerations bearing on the minds of women presented with abortion decisions.

19. If the intrusion were slight, if pregnancy lasted only one hour, say, Thomson (1971, 61) concedes that the refusal to help might be described as "self-centered, callous, indecent." However, it is "not unjust," she argues, since no rights are involved. I quite agree. We should, according to my model, describe such cases in terms of responsibilities rather than rights. As Thomson goes on to acknowledge, however, "the complaints are no less grave; they are just different." Hart (1958, 83) has said in another context that the terms " 'duty' or 'obligation' are too weak, too feeble in condemnatory force, for the blacker moral offenses." The same is true, for much the same reasons, of the term "rights."

small number of persons; it therefore seems, on this ground alone, desirable that his chief benevolent impulses should be correspondingly limited." John Stuart Mill, anticipating Grote's objection, makes just the same point.[20] This is an empirical proposition, to be sure; but, empirically, it does seem highly plausible.

On balance, persons relatively near to us in space and in time probably *will* be rather more vulnerable to us. Their interests are more likely to be affected more heavily by our own actions and choices than are the interests of persons more distant; and our nearer neighbors in space and time are more likely to be depending upon us, more or less exclusively, for assistance and protection. This fact saves my argument from the traditional *reductio* of requiring that we give everything we have to starving Asians or that we forever save everything for infinitely receding future generations or that we have our own lives and projects constantly interrupted to serve others. My analysis would seem to allow (indeed, to require) us, in effect if not in intention, to show *some* bias toward our own "kind," however defined. Still, that bias must not be absolute. The vulnerability of distant others (including a great many of those starving Asians) to our own actions and choices is surely sufficiently large, and how we (and sometimes even we alone) can help is sufficiently clear, to require us to give their interests some substantial weight in reckoning our own responsibilities. Charity may indeed begin at home, but morally it must not stop there.

L ooking at the situation from the viewpoint of the vulnerable party, we must conclude that those to whom he is most vulnerable should have the heaviest responsibilities for protecting his interests. Some people have more or better or exclusive opportunities for inflicting or preventing more or less serious harms. Those to whom a person is relatively more vulnerable have relatively greater responsibilities. Anyone to whom one is uniquely vulnerable—no one else can or will help if he does not—has the greatest responsibilities of all (Brandt 1959, 439).[21]

---

20. "It is a misapprehension of the utilitarian mode of thought, to conceive it as implying that people should fix their minds upon so wide a generality as the world, or society at large. The great majority of good actions are intended not for the benefit of the world, but for that of individuals, of which the good of the world is made up; and the thoughts of the most virtuous man need not on these occasions travel beyond the particular persons concerned, except so far as is necessary to assure himself that in benefiting them he is not violating the rights, that is, the legitimate and authorized expectations, of any one else. . . . The occasions on which any person (except one in a thousand) has it in his power to [produce happiness] on an extended scale . . . are but exceptional; and on these occasions alone is he called on to consider public utility; in every other case, private utility, the interest or happiness of some few persons, is all he has to attend to" (Mill 1863, chap. 2; cf. Grote 1870, 94).

21. Some commentators would balk at acknowledging any special responsibilities simply because others are *unwilling* to help, although they would happily do so if others were genuinely *unable*. Perhaps these commentators have a point. Inabilities are *ex hypothesi* impossible to overcome,

As the magnitudes of the potential harms others might suffer consequent upon my actions or choices diminish, so too do my responsibilities in respect to them. As the connection between my actions or choices and their potential injuries becomes increasingly tenuous, my responsibilities in respect of them are also correspondingly attenuated. Thus, I have less responsibility for rescuing someone drowning on a distant shore than someone drowning at my feet. In the limiting case, I have no responsibility at all for rescuing someone drowning half a continent away; I could not possibly reach him in time.

Let us now look at the situation from the viewpoint of the person upon whom these responsibilities are laid. His first task lies in discovering what his responsibilities are. Who is vulnerable to his actions and choices, and what is he to do to protect those persons?

Our responsibilities are usually defined, by lawyers and philosophers alike, in terms of the expectations of the "reasonable man." Basically, this construct is a useful device for facilitating interactions among a group of anonymous agents. It removes any need for us to know the idiosyncracies of other agents; or they, ours. We can presume that the actions and choices of others will be those of the standardized reasonable man, and presume that they will be making the same presumptions. Coordination is thereby facilitated. Everyone knows what the other expects of him and can plan accordingly.

In many of the core cases of vulnerability, however, the actors are anything but anonymous. The foibles of our families, friends, neighbors, and clients are only too familiar. How might our responsibilities be altered by this intimate knowledge of one another? Of course, in the process of acquiring such knowledge, all sorts of other morally relevant things may have happened. For the moment, however, let us assume these away and concentrate just on the extra information that intimate acquaintance affords.

Suppose your secretary knows that you have a mortal dread of air travel. Yet, knowing this, he has committed you to attending important meetings half a day and half a continent apart, and the only way you can get there is to fly. Now, your fear of flying is quite irrational, so a reasonable man would find nothing wrong with those arrangements. Hence, if we knew nothing about each other, and had simply to proceed on the assumption that everyone was "reasonable" in this regard, there could be no objections to this arrangement—even though, in this case, it might impose a very great burden on the one party. But *knowing* each other's peculiarities, I submit, changes things.

---

whereas simple unwillingness can be overcome though a simple change of heart, which can in turn sometimes be induced by simple moral exhortation. There are various degrees of "unwillingness," however, and in the limiting case "firm resolve" shades into psychological inability to do otherwise. Where other people have firmly committed themselves in such ways to not getting involved, I would argue that the refusal of others to act should simply be taken as a given, as just another background condition against which you must frame your own action plans (D. Regan 1980, 124; Brock 1982, 230). On this point, Bennett's (1981, 90) rhetorical question is compelling: "So long as I am sure that nobody else *will* help . . . , why should it matter whether I think that nobody else *can*?"

Once he was aware of your feelings in the matter, it would be *irresponsible* of your secretary not to consider your sensitivities, however unreasonable.

Where the responsibility for discovering these peculiarities lies is another matter. I am generally inclined to say that the burden should fall upon the actor/chooser to discover *who* might be vulnerable to his actions and choices. But I am also inclined to say that he has discharged his responsibility if, knowing nothing more about them than that they are vulnerable to his actions and choices, he plans protections for them on the assumption they have perfectly ordinary sensitivities. The onus is on the vulnerable party to communicate any peculiar facts about himself. It is your job to tell your secretary about your fear of flying; it is not his to ask. Similarly, it is the patient's responsibility to inform an attending physician of his rare allergy (through a medical bracelet or a card in the wallet, should he be unconscious); in the absence of any indication that the patient might have this rare allergy, the physician who administers a standard treatment that ends up killing him is surely blameless.[22] To allocate this responsibility otherwise would constitute an intolerable barrier to action. Too many patients (with or without allergies) would die while the physician awaits the results of the whole battery of possible tests for allergies.

In practice, putting the onus upon those with peculiar vulnerabilities to tell others what they are may not matter much, because it also seems reasonable to insist that people be responsible for watching for signs of special or unusual vulnerabilities in persons who are particularly affected by their actions or choices. It would, for example, be irresponsible of a physician to administer a drug to an unconscious accident victim without first checking his wallet for possible instructions concerning allergies. With only a little looking, it is easy enough to identify the peculiar sensitivities of groups (be they racial, sexual, occupational, etc.) or, in personal dealings, of particular individuals with whom one is involved. Where such special vulnerabilities are concerned, it is the actor/chooser's responsibility to pick up the signals, however weak they may be.

V ulnerabilities arise in a number of different ways. Some arise from natural causes as in the case of the man drowning at an all-but-deserted beach where there is only one onlooker present to rescue him. Others occur as a consequence of our own actions and choices, as in the case of

---

22. Notice that a similar problem plagues all the standard analyses of "responsibility," "causation," and "blame" because of their reliance upon a notion of the "normal" course of events that straddles "ordinarily predicted" and "morally expected" (Mackie 1955; Hart and Honore 1959; Fitzgerald 1967, 134–35). We think that the normal *will* happen, and we think it *should*. These two ideas are connected: we think it should happen in large part because people are expecting it to, and they are expecting it to because they think it should. This sort of analysis is mildly conservative, but not viciously so. (True, as long as such expectations persist, you are obliged to try to satisfy them; but there is no reason not to try to alter the expectations.) There is, however, something apparently circular about such analyses: what is expected is analyzed in terms of what is right, and what is right is analyzed in terms of what is expected.

giving and receiving promises and other formal commitments. Still others are predicated upon social conventions and the responsibilities thereby assigned to role occupants.

For my analysis, how the vulnerabilities have arisen is not relevant: all vulnerabilities give rise to the same sorts of responsibilities. This position is open to two major lines of attack. One set of critics, focusing upon vulnerabilities that are predicated upon social conventions, would hold that some sort of circularity is involved in deriving responsibilities from vulnerabilities that arise only because some people have conventionally been assigned responsibilities in that regard. Another set of critics would attack my indifference to causal histories more generally. Both of their objections, however, can be met successfully.

C onsider first the "circularity" objection. In some cases a person is by nature vulnerable to another: that is, the other is objectively more capable of helping or harming him. In other cases his vulnerability is induced by societal norms.[23] Furthermore, these socially induced vulnerabilities often result from the very allocation of responsibility which those self-same vulnerabilities are then supposed to justify. Hence the appearance of circularity. For example, a parent has responsiblity for feeding the child because the child is vulnerable to the parent's neglect; the child is vulnerable, in turn, because society assigns the responsibility of feeding children to their parents.

This appearance of circularity is, however, largely an illusion. The only reason it looks as if we are deriving "ought" from "ought" is that we have failed to notice differences between distinct types of prescriptions. In particular, we need to distinguish moral reasons for *having* one particular cooperative scheme rather than another from moral reasons for *following* a scheme once it is in force within our society.

These different sorts of moral reasons provide answers to different sorts of moral questions. Were we debating which cooperative scheme to adopt in the first place, or how to amend the one that we already have, then the former sorts of considerations would be decisive. But those sorts of reasons are appropriate only for that second-order task of deciding which rules to adopt.

---

23. Even where natural vulnerabilities are concerned, there is a feedback relationship at work that might give the appearance of circularity. First, responsibilities are allocated on the basis of natural vulnerabilities. People come to rely upon others discharging responsibilities once allocated. Consequently, they render themselves even more vulnerable to the actions and choices of those who have been allocated the responsibilities, and these responsibilities are therefore reinforced in turn. What is crucial in all this is that, in the first instance, it is the natural vulnerability of one person to the other that generates the initial responsibilities, which then give rise to all the further socially induced vulnerabilities and responsibilities.

Suppose instead it is the first-order task that concerns us: we are simply trying to decide how we should act in some particular situation. Then an utterly decisive reason for following the scheme is that people are relying upon you to do so. Once you have said, "People are relying upon me to follow that rule," it is superfluous to add, "Besides, it is a good rule." That may be important in justifying adoption of the rule in the first place, but it adds nothing to the justification of your following the rule once it is in place and people are relying upon you to follow it. Nor would saying "But it is a nonoptimal rule" detract from the justification of your following it.[24]

This is not to say that whether and how societies allocate responsibilities is a matter of moral indifference. Throughout the following chapters I shall be arguing that certain allocations of responsibility are morally preferable to others. My present point is a more modest one. Here I merely want to say that the existing allocation of responsibilities, whatever its initial basis, should *now* be treated as a "social fact." Whether or not the existing allocation of responsibility itself has any moral warrant, it has made some people vulnerable to others; and *that* fact, if no other, provides a moral warrant for discharging those responsibilities. The pragmatic moral "ought" ("What ought I to do?") attaches to the vulnerabilities, rather than to conventionally defined duties and responsibilities per se. And that "ought" stays attached until and unless responsibilities—and the expectations and vulnerabilities surrounding them—are redefined.[25]

L et us turn now to the more general critique, which suggests it is wrong to focus exclusively upon vulnerabilities and ignore altogether their causal histories. The main alternative to assigning responsibility for protecting the vulnerable to those people to whom they are vulnerable is—to employ a pun that is all too often mistaken for an argument—to assign responsibility to those who are responsible. To unpack that phrase, the alternative is to assign responsibility for the task of getting people out of a jam to those who were causally responsible for getting them into that jam in the first place.

---

24. That assumes, of course, that that rule is better, morally, than none at all. Nevertheless, saying that the others are *relying* upon you to act in accordance with it (rather than merely *expecting* you to) guarantees that it is better, from their point of view, that you act that way rather than not.

25. Sidgwick (1874, 346), considering the duty of parents to children, writes: "We have no doubt about this duty as a part of the present order of society, by which the due growth and training of the rising generation is distributed among the adults. But when we reflect on this arrangement itself, we cannot see intuitively that it is the best possible. It may be plausibly maintained that children would be better trained, physically and mentally, if they were brought up under the supervision of physicians and philosophers, in large institutions maintained out of the general taxes." Still, until this new order is actually instituted, Sidgwick agrees that parents must discharge their conventional duties toward their children. See similarly Brock (1982, 227).

The problems with this move are by now well known. The notion of "causal responsibility" is not the unambiguous, technical term it seems. The ascription of causal responsibility for an outcome represents (as I have just argued) the conclusion of a moral argument, not the premise of one. Sometimes we hold some people responsible for outcomes which they played no causal role in producing, as when we hold an employer vicariously liable for the actions of his servants. At other times we decline to hold responsible those who have made undeniable causal contributions to undersirable outcomes. Had Walter Burley Griffin not designed Canberra as he did, I would have not crashed my car on the Commonwealth Avenue Bridge this morning; but it is my driving, not his design, that is regarded as the cause of the crash. Such examples abound (Hart and Honore 1959; Feinberg 1970, chap. 2).

These familiar difficulties merely reinforce the point that backward-looking notions of causal responsibility are related only imperfectly at best to the forward-looking problem of allocating task responsibility.[26] Sometimes it might happen that the person who "caused" another to be in danger (whatever "caused" might mean) is also best able to help him get out of it. If while we are sailing a two-person boat in a deserted bay, my incompetent handling of the sails caused you to fall out of the boat, then it surely is my responsibility to pull you back out of the water. But that, I would argue, is not so much because I caused you to be in the water in the first place as it is that I am now the only one available to help. Consider a similar case: a speedboat racing past two sailboats produces a wake that, after a minute or two, causes one to capsize. The responsibility for helping the capsized crew surely rests with the crew of the other sailboat still afloat, rather than with the speedboat that is by now long gone.[27] Or, again, consider the plight of the Good Samaritan. "To this Samaritan's 'Why me?' there is no cosmic explanation, and there is no

26. Notice that even Herbert Spencer (1884, chap. 2) sees these as separate issues, although he puts the distinction to characteristically perverse uses. He argues that society, through maladministration of the Poor Law, could be held causally responsible for the plight of the poor. At the end of this discussion, however, Spencer writes, "But now, leaving the question of [causal] responsibilities, however conceived, and considering only the evil itself, what shall we say of its treatment?" In his subsequent discussion, he makes it clear that he thinks task responsibility for alleviating poverty is best assigned to the poor themselves.

27. Davis (1983, 266–67) considers two possible rules: "A: If someone needs your help in particular, he has a right to your help until he no longer needs you in particular"; and "B: If someone needs your help in particular *because of what you have done to him* . . . , he has a right to your help until you can leave him in at least as good a position as you found him." Davis's preliminary conclusion is that "Rule A is not a defensible rule of justice. Rule B certainly seems to be." Then, considering a revised version of the Thomson (1971) kidnapped-violinist case, he relents. Suppose that once you are plugged into the violinist "no one else can be; the shock of unplugging would kill him." Davis then thinks that you would have no right to unplug yourself, and offers this as an example of "a special responsibility falling upon someone who has done nothing to assume it explicitly or implicitly." Although this concession appears to rehabilitate, at least for certain cases, Davis's Rule A—which is, in effect, my First Principle of Individual Responsibility—the rest of Davis's article is written as if the crucial concession had never been made.

better answer than this: 'You are here and therefore in a position to help this victim. Is there a stronger claim upon you now?' '' (Shue 1981, 135–36).[28]

Thus, causal responsibility and task responsibility really are quite distinct notions. They merge in their practical implications only in those (possibly rare) circumstances wherein those who were, in the past, in a position to cause harm will, in the future, remain in a position to provide help. Where that is not true, as it is usually not, responsibility would seem to lie elsewhere. Forward-looking notions of vulnerability, not backward-looking notions tied to causal histories, are what justifies the ascription of responsibilities for present and future action. This principle is nowhere better illustrated than in President Kennedy's (1963, 57) call for arms-control negotiations: "We are not here distributing blame or pointing the finger of judgment. We must deal with the world as it is and not as it might have been had the history of the last eighteen years been different."

Causal histories are thought particularly important insofar as people are vulnerable to themselves—or, more precisely, to their own past actions and choices. It is ordinarily thought that, in such cases, people should bear principal responsibility for protecting themselves. Herbert Spencer (1884, chap. 2) is predictably keen on this point:

> Sympathy with one in suffering suppresses, for the time being, remembrance of his transgressions. The feeling which vents itself in "poor fellow!" on seeing one in agony, excludes the thought of "bad fellow," which might at another time arise. . . . When . . . the miseries of the poor are depicted, they are thought of as the miseries of the deserving poor, instead of being thought of, as in large measure they should be, as the miseries of the undeserving poor. Those whose hardships are set forth in pamphlets and proclaimed in sermons and speeches which echo throughout society, are assumed to be all worthy souls, grievously wronged; and none of them are thought of as bearing the penalties of their own misdeeds.

And even John Stuart Mill (1869, chap. 4; see also 1848, bk. 5, chap. 11, sec. 13) rails against

> unenlightened and short-sighted benevolence, which, taking the care of people's lives out of their own hands, and relieving them from the disagreeable

---

28. From analysis of this case, Shue (1981, 135–36) derives a more general conclusion paralleling my own: "Whoever is . . . in a position to assist the victim has some obligation to do so, regardless of whether he or she was previously involved, unless some stronger obligation overrides. A previous involvement with the case is not required. Call this *responsibility through ability*—ability to make a positive difference." Lest this be thought an overbearingly utilitarian conclusion, however, notice that it is embraced by Kantians as well. Moira Roberts (1965, 245), for example, remarks that "those men we regard as reliable and conscientious are prepared to accept responsibility for many contingencies not due either to their agency or lack of foresight; and anyone in a responsible position has to act on his own initiative in situations which are not all of his own making, and which he might be prepared to interpret and construct in quite a different way were it not for the interests of others entrusted to him."

consequences of their own acts, saps the very foundations of the self-respect, self-help, and self-control which are the essential conditions both of individual prosperity and of social virtue.

It is widely agreed that if people are genuinely unable to protect themselves, responsibility for doing so should devolve upon others (Brewer 1875). But most commentators say that if people are merely unwilling to help themselves, others have no responsibility to do so. Many analysts would apparently stick to that position even when the opportunities for self-help are now in the past, and the only hope of salvation rests in other people.

Similarly, many would say that others have no responsibility—or, anyway, substantially less responsibility—for getting people out of messes of their own making. Here moral philosophers implicitly borrow the legal doctrine of "contributory negligence." The rule of law set forth in Lord Blackburn's 1884 decision "is that if there is blame causing the accident on both sides, however small that blame may be on one side, the loss lies where it falls" (quoted in Heuston 1977, 512). If it could be shown that a plaintiff's negligence contributed in any way to the damage he suffered, then traditionally no one else could be held liable, however much that other person's negligence may have contributed.[29] Suppose, to use a moral philosopher's example, a fully competent adult is floundering in an icy pond merely because he blatantly disregarded a notice reading "No Skating—Thin Ice." Any moral claim he might have on a passer-by to pull him out would, it is said, be reduced by the fact that he got himself into that difficulty through his own irresponsibility. It would arguably be reduced to the vanishing point, moreover, if the skater were incorrigible in this regard, requiring rescue every other day. Even Peter Singer (1977, 45), who is generally strong on our duties to suffering strangers, sees a need to restrict our aid in such cases of gross contributory negligence.[30]

But consider another case where this conclusion is far less compelling. In the course of a 1981 environmentalist protest against a hydroelectric project damming a river at Alta, in northern Norway, a group of young girls chained themselves to some drilling equipment. A particularly unsympathetic foreman, when told by his crew that they could not start the drills without break-

29. This traditional doctrine is now being replaced by a more sensible doctrine of "comparative negligence" which, in its most appealing form, splits liability roughly in proportion to the causal contribution each part made to the final result.
30. Singer (1977, 45), it should be emphasized, does not think that incorrigibly reckless people are any less *deserving* of rescue; it is just a bad investment to waste scarce resources rescuing them rather than others who might learn from their mistakes, which surely is the right response to examples such as those offered by Brock (1982, 232–33). Others, such as Barry (1980, chap. 2; 1982, 221), embrace this same principle but deny that it has the implications commonly claimed for it to cases like famine relief, where the recklessness was usually that of people's parents, ancestors, or governments rather than of the starving peasants themselves.

ing the girls' legs, was reported to have replied, "Well, then, we'll just have to break them." It certainly is true that the protesters brought that risk upon themselves. It is equally clear, however, that it is wrong to say that they would be wholly (or even primarily) to blame for any injuries they might suffer when the drills were switched on. The final choice was that of the construction foreman and his crew, and they, it seems, would have to bear principal responsibility for the consequences.

The more general point is this: People who have failed to take advantage of opportunities to avert harm to themselves may, in some sense, "have themselves to blame" for any harm that befalls them; but they rarely have only themselves to blame. Once all their opportunities for self-help have passed— once the reckless skater is in the icy water, or the chains are locked onto the protesters' legs and the keys thrown away—the situation is beyond their control. Others, however, may still be able to act so as to avert harm to them. To suggest that those others should (or even that they *may*) stand idly by and watch people reap the bitter fruits of their own improvidence is surely absurd. At that point, if not before, those who have gotten themselves into a dangerous situation truly are unable to help themselves. They are, instead, enormously (perhaps uniquely) vulnerable to the actions and choices of particular others for getting them out of the mess. On my analysis, such vulnerabilities generate strong responsibilities.

There is a familiar legal doctrine, the "last clear chance" or "last opportunity" rule, which corresponds to the moral position here being advocated. As explained by Hart and Honore (1959, 205), "The last opportunity rule involves the notion that when one party is no longer in a position to do anything to avoid the harm and when the other knows of his predicament, his negligence 'is exhausted.' . . . [He] may recover if thereafter the other party alone is negligent." In short, whoever has the "last clear chance" to prevent harm is to be held responsible for doing so, regardless of the causal history up to that point.[31] Suppose you are driving down the road. The right-of-way is clearly yours. Suddenly another car turns into your path. Doubtless, the other driver was wrong to make that turn. You, however, have the last clear chance to avert an accident. If, instead, you ram the other car, you are liable for the damages under the "last clear chance" doctrine. Or suppose a locomotive engineer sees a trespasser on the tracks ahead of his speeding train: he is

---

31. In this form, the "last clear chance" doctrine, as Hart and Honore (1959, 206) emphasize, is a doctrine for attributing responsibility, not causation. It crucially presupposes that the individual concerned is conscious of the other's predicament and that it is clear that this is the last opportunity to avert harm. In an effort to overcome the harshness of the traditional contributory-negligence rule, courts extended the last-clear-chance doctrine to many cases for which it was not particularly apt, thereby inviting the wrath of many legal scholars (Williams 1951, chaps. 9–10; Hart and Honore 1959, 201–7; Prosser 1971, 427–33; Heuston 1977, 512–17). Properly circumscribed, however, "last opportunity" considerations remain important even after a rule of comparative negligence has eliminated the need for any such wild extensions (Goodhart 1949).

obliged to whistle and to take all reasonable measures to avert an accident, even though the trespasser is clearly in the wrong. If he fails to do so, he is, under the "last clear chance" doctrine, legally liable for damages. Or, again, if a dock owner pushes away a ship trying to moor illegally at his dock during a storm, he could under the "last clear chance" doctrine be held legally liable for any damage the ship suffers during the storm, although the mooring would clearly have constituted a trespass (Bohlen 1908, 331–32; Posner 1972, 74–75).

Separating task from causal responsibility is open to two objections, both of which are nicely captured in George Bernard Shaw's (1965, 137) observation that the "lazy habit still prevails of tolerating [poverty] not only as an inevitable misfortune to be charitably patronized and relieved, but as a useful punishment for all sorts of misconduct and inefficency that are not expressly punishable by law." The first objection lurking within Shaw's observation is couched in terms of material economic incentives; the other, in terms of moral deserts. Both objections arise from the fact that my rule might tend to encourage improvidence by reassuring people that they can always rely on others to get them out of any jam they might get themselves into.[32]

It is important to emphasize that these objections, although arising out of the same feature of my rule, are really quite distinct. Providing appropriate incentives to encourage prudence or to discourage recklessness is a practical rather than a moral imperative. Material incentives are nothing more than socially necessary bribes and threats. They "have nothing to do with desert," morally understood (Feinberg 1970, 9; see also Rawls 1971, sec. 48).

On this nonmoralized view of incentives, encouraging people to get others out of bad situations is, in principle, just as important as discouraging people from getting themselves into such situations in the first place.[33] Where the emphasis should fall is simply a technical optimization exercise. Donald Wittman (1981) has recently shown that, at least for one important class of cases (i.e., harms resulting from strictly sequential inputs), the optimal incentives for avoiding the harm are created by assigning the bulk of the damage liability to the party with the last clear chance to avert the harm rather than to the party that created the hazardous situation in the first place.[34]

---

32. As Sumner (1883, 24) complains, under a scheme such as mine, "Poverty is the best policy. If you get wealth, you will have to support other people; if you do not get wealth, it will be the duty of other people to support you." See similarly Malthus (1826, bk. 3, chaps. 5–7).

33. By the same token, it is in principle just as important to encourage people to get themselves out of bad situations that others have gotten them into. This, Spencer (1884, chap. 2) would argue, is the position of the poor: although society is causally to blame for their plight, the poor must themselves be responsible for the task of alleviating it. He argues against public relief of socially induced suffering largely on the grounds that it constitutes a disincentive to self-help, which he sees as the optimal remedy. "Much suffering," Spencer argues, "is curative, and prevention of it is prevention of a remedy."

34. Wittman (1981) shows that, optimally, liability for all damages should be assigned to the

Notice, however, that talk of incentives and tort liability for damages is somewhat beside the present point, which is simply one of assigning task responsibility. The latter is a question of deciding who should effect a rescue; the former is a question of who should pay for it. Suppose someone has created a hazard that is now out of his control and will cause harm unless someone else acts so as to prevent that from occurring. It is perfectly possible to conclude that the person who originally created the hazard (for himself or others) should bear its full costs, yet at the same time to conclude that some other party should be the one to take action to avert the harm.[35] Indeed, that is precisely the conclusion dictated by all the standard efficiency considerations to which talk of "appropriate incentives" appeals: if we were to insist that only the person who has created the hazard should bear task responsibility for averting the harm, then once the situation is out of his control no one else will have any responsibility for the task of averting the harm, even if he would prefer to reimburse them for doing so rather than paying for the damages that would occur if they did not. Thus it is clear that even in terms of incentive considerations, whoever can prevent the harm should bear task responsibility for doing so. It is a separate question whether, and to what extent, those originating the hazardous condition should have to reimburse him the costs of performing that task.

There are various reasons for supposing that incentive considerations have little role to play in social welfare policy in particular. For one thing, there is obviously little point in offering incentives to people who have caused unde-

---

person with the last clear chance to avert harm. Others who have contributed to causing the dangerous situation to arise should be held liable only for such extra costs as they create for that person to avoid the accident. Thus, in the case of the driver making an illegal turn into your path, you (being the driver with the last clear chance to avoid the accident) would be liable for all the damages resulting from a crash; the driver making the illegal turn would be obliged to reimburse you only for the costs of slamming on your brakes to avoid hitting him. If someone parked illegally on the roadway, he would be responsible for the extra costs of the evasive maneuvers (braking, swerving, etc.) you would have had to incur in avoiding hitting him; but you, being the driver with the last clear chance to avoid the accident, would be responsible for the damages resulting from hitting his car. This is superior to a comparative-negligence rule, apportioning liability for damages between parties in some way that seems "equitable," taking account of the relative causal contributions of each party, and counting the "last opportunity" having been forgone as just one causal factor among many (Williams 1951, chap. 10; Heuston 1977, 524ff.). That rule provides far stronger incentives against initial recklessness, but it provides wholly inadequate incentives for the person with the last opportunity to avert harm actually to use it. The total value of the damages he could prevent by taking advantage of that opportunity are far greater than the share of damages for which he will be held liable under this rule of "comparative negligence." Consequently, when he is looking at his private balance sheet, he will decide to forgo many opportunities to prevent damages which, looking at total social costs, we dearly wish he had taken. Wittman's rule, assigning him the bulk of the liability, seems to provide far superior incentives in this respect.
35. The Good Samaritan laws of several countries of continental Europe similarly compel people to act as Good Samaritans when they can do so at little risk to themselves, but also allow Good Samaritans to demand reimbursement of their costs from those whom they have helped (Ratcliffe 1966).

sirable outcomes if their opportunities for altering those outcomes have all passed. So, for example,

> the deterrent principles of the Poor Law . . . seem least applicable among the aged. . . . Once the person was old . . . deterrence could not make him less old. Deterrence could usually not hope to "improve" his behavior and return him to the universally acclaimed ideal of self-support (Heclo 1974, 155; see similarly Booth 1892, 223–24).

Or, as Charles Booth (1892, 154) argues more generally, "Sickness, old age, and death are inevitable, not to be avoided by any fear of penalty, nor liable to increase if the troubles they bring are softened. We are therefore free to mitigate these troubles in a way we may" without worrying about disincentives.

Or, again, notice that there is little point in providing incentives with a view to altering the behavior of those who are largely impervious to incentives. There are good reasons to believe that many of the poor are in this position. Theoretically, it is easy enough to see why they should be unresponsive to incentives. Marginal calculations are a costly business, and the poor have more pressing demands on their time and attention. The evidence seems to suggest that the poor are only minimally responsive to incentives, whether positive (e.g., to slack off work when guaranteed a minimal income [Danziger, Haveman, and Plotnick 1981]) or negative (e.g., to avoid hazardous jobs [Viscusi 1979]). Hence, even if the poor were causally completely responsible for their own plight (which is, of course, far from clear) there would be no point in making them "stew in their own juices" as an incentive to alter their behavior. Restricting welfare benefits to the "deserving poor" would probably amount to no more than a gratuitous disincentive brought to bear on a group that is largely oblivious to incentives.

The separate question of moral desert, of course, remains. This presents itself as a counterargument at two points to my proposal for assigning responsibility for protecting the vulnerable to whomsoever is best able to do so, regardless of causal histories. The first problem concerns those who find themselves in difficulty through their own improvidence. Some would say that they had it coming, that they deserve whatever they got and that it would actually be wrong for anyone to help them out of their trouble.[36] The other concerns those who have done nothing to cause another's distress but are (perhaps uniquely) in a position to help relieve it. Some would protest that they have done nothing to deserve this burden, that it would be terribly nice of them if they chose to assume it, but wrong to impose it upon them.[37]

---

36. Social psychologists report a widespread tendency for people to blame the victim. By derogating an innocent sufferer as deserving of punishment, they preserve their image of a "just world" (Lerner 1970, 208; Lerner and Miller 1978; Sorrentino 1981).

37. William Graham Sumner (1883, 131, 136, 138) argued against social welfare legislation on both grounds: "Now, we never can annihilate a penalty. We can only divert it from the head of

Both claims, however, extend the notion of "desert" beyond its proper bounds. Duties and responsibilities are not necessarily (or even characteristically) things that you deserve. More often than not, they are things that just happen to you. Feinberg (1980, 205) rightly remarks on the way in which "so many of the roles we occupy as individuals"—and so many of the moral responsibilities attaching to those roles—are "foisted on us by circumstances, and we occupy . . . as if by default." When walking along a deserted beach, you see a child floundering in shallow water; nothing in your background or character suggests that you deserve to bear the burden of effecting the rescue, but it would be absurd to say that you are therefore morally at liberty to leave the child to drown.

The notion of desert is ordinarily equally out of place in deciding how to judge the improvident. They should be regarded as foolhardy people whose recklessness is to be discouraged through appropriate disincentives, not as evil people whose wickedness deserves to be punished. When dealing with people in precarious situations, questions of fault are simply out of place (Calabresi 1970, pt. 5; Campbell 1974, 16; Singer 1977, 45). Two victims of a traffic accident brought into the hospital emergency room with similar injuries should surely be treated with equal care and attention, even though the one's negligence caused the accident while the other was its innocent victim. The need, dependency, or vulnerability of the victims—not their moral deserts—is what dictates physicians' responsibilities (Goodin 1985a).

A slightly weaker objection in much the same vein might be the following. Perhaps a person who is in distress through some fault of his own might not strictly deserve his fate. A reckless skater who ends up in freezing water because he blatantly disregarded signs warning of thin ice does not deserve to drown; it would not be *wrong* for bystanders to pull him out of the water. Still, we might want to say that the reckless skater has through his actions forfeited any claim he might otherwise have had to our assistance. Thus, while it certainly would be good of others to help him out of the water, they have no duty whatsoever to do so (Barry 1980, chap. 2, sec. 2; Brock 1982, 232–33). But that is to imply that any moral duty we might have to save drowning strangers is fully exhausted by considerations of their moral claims, rights, deserts, entitlements—the accoutrements of "justice," narrowly con-

---

the man who has incurred it to the heads of others [Forgotten Men] who have not incurred it. A vast amount of 'social reform' consists in just this operation. . . . [T]he people who are most uncomfortable in this world . . . are those who have neglected their duties. . . . The people who can be called upon to serve the uncomfortable must be those who have done their duty, as the world goes, tolerably well. Consequently the doctrine which we are discussing turns out to be in practice only a scheme for making injustice prevail in human society by reversing the distribution of rewards and punishments between those who have done their duty and those who have not. . . . [I]t is wrong to preach to the Forgotten Man that it is his duty to go and remedy other people's neglect. It is not his duty. It is a harsh and unjust burden which is laid upon him. . . . The exhortations ought to be expended on the negligent—that they take care of themselves."

ceived. That is simply untrue. Talking of a reckless skater's "forfeiting his claim to be rescued" misses the mark precisely because drowning people do not need to have any particular claims against us in order for us to have a duty to rescue them.[38]

Individual and Collective Responsibilities

So far I have been talking primarily about situations in which one person is vulnerable to some particular other individual. If I am right in my arguments about how responsibilities flow from vulnerabilities, then in such cases that other individual's responsibilities are clear enough. There are other cases, however, in which a person is vulnerable not to any particular individual but rather to others taken as a group. Here I shall tackle the harder question of what responsibilities emerge in such situations.

A person can be vulnerable to a group of others in either of two ways. One of these is disjunctive. In such cases, A is vulnerable to B or to C or to D: any one of them could provide the needed assistance; and if any one of them does, none of the others need to. The paradigm case here is that of the drowning child at the crowded (but unguarded) beach: any one of the bystanders could effect the rescue, and if any one does, the others need not.

One common move in such cases is to lay all the responsibility on whichever individual is "best able to help," somehow defined. Maybe it is the best swimmer. Maybe it is just the person who is standing nearest. Certainly the drowning man is most vulnerable to the person in the best position to rescue him, and therefore that that person must bear primary responsibility for effecting the rescue. Equally certainly, it would be wrong to suppose (as those deploying this move typically do) that that lets all the others off the hook. Should a father fail to wade in to save his drowning child, onlookers cannot excuse their own failure to do so with the plea that it was his job, not theirs. Once it becomes clear that the father is not going to act, responsibility devolves upon the others (Feinberg 1970, 244; Bennett 1981, 84; Fishkin 1982, chap. 10).

Those able to help, albeit not as well as those with primary responsibility, retain a residual responsibility to do so in case the others default; and they also have a continuing responsibility to monitor the situation to see whether or not

---

38. This is true, I think, even when working within the traditional distinction between duties of justice and duties of charity or humanity. Campbell (1974, 16) argues that "a sounder conceptual foundation on which to base the . . . universal obligation to those in need . . . is to identify the obligation to relieve distress, whatever its origin, as one of humanity"; and where duties of humanity or charity are concerned, considerations of moral desert are irrelevant (see similarly Passmore 1979, 28). My aim here, however, is to collapse this distinction and show that both types of duties really derive from the same source, namely, the vulnerability of one person to the other.

their assistance is in fact required.[39] The limit of this responsibility is, quite simply, the limit of the vulnerable agent's needs and of the responsible agent's capacity to act efficaciously—no more, but certainly no less.

It is also common, in such cases, to talk of the "diffusion of responsibility." Since responsibility for the drowning is divided a thousand ways, each of the bystanders is commonly said to be less to blame for the outcome than if he had been the only person available to help. As a psychological proposition, it is undeniable that people are inclined to think this way (Latane and Darley 1970); and as a historical proposition, it is undeniable that often they have acted this way (Spencer 1891, 61). But morally they have no grounds for doing so. The comforting conclusion to the contrary rests upon a most peculiar view of the way the moral books balance: if one death is morally worth a thousand units of bad karma, then the blame, however apportioned, must add up to the same thousand units of bad karma; and if a thousand people share blame equally, each must therefore be charged one unit of bad karma. This is quite explicit in, for example, L. J. Cohen's (1981, 75) remark that "if there are a hundred independent defaulters . . . , and one death, each carries a hundredth of the responsibility, not the whole of it." There is, however, no reason to suppose that the moral books have to balance in this way. To switch metaphors, "responsibility is not a bucket in which less remains when some is apportioned out" (Nozick 1974, 130). Where several people have contributed to an undesirable outcome, we can—and often do—hold each of them fully to blame for it. In tort law, for example, it is traditional to hold defendants jointly and severally liable where harm resulted from their concerted action, or where they all shared a duty which none of them discharged. In such cases, each is fully liable for the entire amount of damages.[40] This practice is no anachronism. Recently, for example, a similar suggestion has been

39. For further elaboration of these "metaduties," and of the subjects treated in this and the following section more generally, see Pettit and Goodin (1985). The conventional wisdom regards these secondary responsibilities as considerably weaker than the primary ones. According to L. J. Cohen (1981, 74), for example, "It is the helmsman, not the engineer, who is responsible for letting the ship go off course, and it is the engineer, not the helmsman, who is responsible for letting its engines overheat. Of course, if the engineer is aware that the helmsman is letting the ship go off course, and does nothing about it, then he is at fault. But his fault is a relatively minor one. He is at fault for letting the helmsman let the ship go off course, not for letting the ship go off course *tout court*. Letting is not a transitive relation." I quite agree that secondary responsibilities are ordinarily weaker than primary ones: primary responsibilities were assigned to the people best able to help in the first place. *Ex hypothesi*, those with only secondary responsibilities have less of the sorts of information or resources that would be required to perform the task, and hence they have less strong responsibilities for doing so.

40. See Pufendorf (1672, bk. 3, chap. 1, sec. 5), Williams (1951, chap. 1), and Prosser (1971, chap. 8). Of course, plaintiffs can collect no more damages than they have actually suffered. If they recover all their damages from one tortfeasor, then they have no claim against any of the others. (Similarly, if the drowning man is pulled out of the water by any one of the bystanders, the responsibilities of the others dissolve.) The point is that, looking at the situation *ex ante* of litigation, the total liability of all tortfeasors would be the total amount of damage done *times* the number of contributing agents, not divided by it.

made that producers, transporters, and storers of toxic wastes should similarly each be liable for any and all damage that might be caused by inadvertent release of those substances into the environment (Anon. 1981). This, I suggest, should be the model for allocating responsibility in cases, such as that of the drowning man at a crowded beach, where any one of many people could prevent harm to some vulnerable individual.

The second way in which one might be vulnerable to a group of others is to be vulnerable to them taken conjunctively. In the previous case, the drowning child was vulnerable to several others individually. Any of them could jump in and single-handedly effect the rescue. Let us now consider cases where someone is vulnerable to several others collectively, in the sense that the cooperation of all is necessary to produce the desired result. A is vulnerable to B and C and D. The model here might be a yachtsman whose boat has capsized in heavy seas and who will drown unless a lifeboat reaches him promptly. The drowning sailor is vulnerable to the actions and choices of the five men of the lifeboat crew jointly or collectively, rather than to each of them separately. No one of the five can, acting alone, rescue the capsized yachtsman. The only way the rescue can be accomplished is by all five working together.[41]

In the disjunctive case, protecting the vulnerable is a matter of making sure that *someone* does what is needed. In the conjunctive, it is a matter of making sure that *everyone* does what is needed. In either case, the task of protecting those who are vulnerable to the actions and choices of several others is (initially, anyway) a task of coordinating the efforts of the various individuals to whom he is vulnerable (Goodin 1976). If responsibilities flow from vulnerabilities, the following proposition emerges:

Principle of Group Responsibility: If A's interests are vulnerable to the actions and choices of a group of individuals, either disjunctively or conjunctively, then that group has a special responsibility to (a) organize (formally or informally) and (b) implement a scheme for coordinated action by members of the group such that A's interests will be protected as well as they can be by that group, consistently with the group's other responsibilities.

Here, as in the case of individual responsibility, the strength of this responsibility depends strictly upon the degree to which A's interests can be affected by the group's actions and choices. As in the case of individual responsibility,

---

41. It is, of course, rare that this would be strictly true. Usually collective endeavours require something less than everyone's cooperation for their success. Indeed, much of the most interesting strategic maneuvering is directed at being among the handful who can shirk their collective responsibilities without spoiling the collective project (Taylor and Ward 1982).

the group's responsibility in respect of *A* can be outweighed by its greater responsibilities in respect of others.

Notice that by my principle groups would be held equally accountable for failures to organize themselves and for what they do or fail to do once organized. Consider the story of the drowning yachtsman. Suppose that in spite of the fact that capsizings are a regular occurrence in the area, the only village within several miles of the sinking ship had either failed to maintain a lifeboat or neglected to crew the one it had. Surely we would hold the community as a whole responsible for deaths resulting from this oversight. Having had every reason to expect emergencies like this, the community was simply irresponsible in not planning for these contingencies. Morally, at least, our conclusions in this regard would seem to be substantially the same whether or not the community itself was organized and whether or not there was a mayor or community council to hold to account for the collective failing.[42] If such emergencies can be foreseen, then those who will be in a position to help when and if they arise must be responsible for organizing themselves to meet them (Held 1970).

In the real world, it is these failures to organize to which collective responsibility most often attaches. Even in the easy case of the drowning swimmer at a crowded beach, it is necessary to coordinate rescue efforts. Otherwise, "the results would be confusing and chaotic, with hordes of rescuers getting in each other's way" (Feinberg 1970, 244).[43] The more realistic the case, the greater the need for coordination. In the case of natural disasters—surely a better analogue for famine relief than Singer's (1972) drowning child—coordination is obviously essential. McKinsey writes,

> For instance, when a flood strikes a community there are many jobs which need to be done: rescue squads need to be dispatched to save those in danger of drowning; doctors and nurses are needed to treat injuries and to innoculate against disease; housing, food and clothing must be supplied to the homeless survivors; engineers and laborers are needed to hold back the still rising waters; and so on. . . . Each person can fulfill his benevolence-obligations in different alternative ways; there is thus no good reason to think that the members of any particular subclass of those in need have any special rights

---

42. Given the obvious hazards involved in crewing on a lifeboat, the community may, of course, be able to give a perfectly adequate accounting of its failure to organize a crew. The argument could be that on balance, the lifeboat is likely to cost more lives than it saves. Or it could be that given the risks, manning the lifeboat must be regarded as a supererogatory act, and there simply were not enough volunteers forthcoming.

43. In that particular case, however, informal coordination techniques will probably suffice. As Feinberg (1970, 244) suggests, we should simply say that "each has a duty to attempt rescue so long as no more than a few others have already begun their efforts. In short, everyone should use his eyes and his common sense and cooperate as best he can. If no one makes any motion at all, it follows that no one has done his best within the limits imposed by the situation, and *all* are subject . . . to blame."

against particular individuals who are in a position to help them. . . . .But the *community* of those in a position to help when a flood strikes is obligated to do *all* of the jobs which need to be done, because taken as a whole the group *can* do these things. (McKinsey 1981, 315, 320; see similarly L. J. Cohen 1981, 73–76)

In the case of the flood, coordination problems arise because there are many ways in which people could act to great effect. Their problem is choosing between them. In a more standard case, coordination might be required because any one person acting alone could do little to help or to harm distant strangers in distress, however great it might be. If nothing else, the uncertainties are too great: we are unsure of what their needs are or of what we can do to help without doing more harm than good. It was with such reasoning that classical utilitarians reassured people that the universalistic obligations they were laying upon them would not be too onerous (Sidgwick 1874, 430–39). Typically, such reassurances are fully warranted from the perspective of people taken individually, but not collectively. Although distant strangers may be largely invulnerable to *each* of us, they can be highly vulnerable to *all* of us. Small effects taken together add up to large effects.

The same is true of information. Uncertainty may be a plausible excuse for individuals, but not for collectivities. With the pooling of facts and resources, the group naturally has both more information and more resources for enhancing information than do any of its members. Besides, what is uncertain from one perspective is often more certain from another. For example, we can know that one thousand people will die this year in traffic accidents without knowing who the victims will be.

Here again, excuses have taken us out of the fire into the frying pan. The price for excusing individual failures in this way is to impose further obligations upon us all to organize collective action. If someone is vulnerable to the actions of several people taken together, then they all share responsibility for organizing to protect him.

Although the organizational responsibility falls equally upon everyone, it will ordinarily be discharged by action by only a handful of political entrepreneurs. Once they have acted, all the rest are relieved of the responsibility, just as bystanders at a crowded beach are off the hook as soon as one of them rescues the drowning man. Until and unless someone else has made those organizational arrangements, however, doing so is a responsibility shared jointly and severally by the entire population.

Ultimately, all group responsibilities must be analyzed in terms of responsibilities of the individuals comprising the group. This is true even where the groups in question are formally organized. Consider the case of the lifeboat crew. Since it is formally organized, we would in the first instance naturally assign the responsibility for rescuing to the collective entity, the crew as a whole. Should it fail, then it will be held to account for its failure. Sometimes that accounting will prove completely satisfactory: the seas were too rough, the wreck too distant, and so forth. Then the crew will be fully exonerated. But sometimes the account will prove unsatisfactory in one way or another. Then there will be blame to be apportioned. Usually that blame falls upon some particular individuals rather than on the crew as a whole.[44] Maybe it will be assigned to someone because he was causally responsible for the failure: he was slow in answering the call to man the lifeboat or forgot to refuel the boat or was a hopeless navigator. Alternatively, someone (usually the captain) may be assigned responsibility for all errors, even if they were made by others—rather as a dog owner is assigned vicarious liability for any damage that his beast may inflict or as a British minister of the crown assumes responsibility for everything that happens within his department even though he has no way of knowing what the thousands of civil servants notionally under his command are doing every moment of the day (Pufendorf 1672, bk. 3, chap. 1, sec. 4; Feinberg 1970, 229). Even when the crew as a whole is, in some sense, held liable, what that really means is that each of the members is jointly and severally liable for the actions of all. Thus, there is nothing mysterious about responsibilities of organized collectivities. In principle, they always amount to responsibilities of identifiable individuals even if in practice it often proves difficult to decide which ones to finger.

A principle of responsibility for individual members of responsible groups can be formulated as follows:

Second Principle of Individual Responsibility: If *B* is a member of a group that is responsible, under the Principle of Group Responsibility, for protecting *A*'s interests, then *B* has a special responsibility:

a. to see to it, so far as he is able, that the group organizes a collective scheme of action such that it protects *A*'s interests as well as it can, consistently with the group's other responsibilities; and

b. to discharge fully and effectively the responsibilities allocated to him under any such scheme that might be organized, insofar as doing so is consistent with his other moral responsibilities, provided the scheme protects *A*'s interests better than none at all.

---

44. Feinberg (1970, 235) thinks otherwise. "Athletic team members must all win or lose together: victory is not the prize of individual merit alone, nor is defeat linked to 'contributory fault.'" My friends who frequent locker rooms assure me that that is utterly untrue in their experience, however. Feinberg (1970, 248) also thinks that there can be "contributory group fault" which is "collective but not distributive." The examples he offers are cases where the group as a whole could have prevented some harm only if some of its members made heroic sacrifices. Then, however, I cannot see how we can hold the group liable at all, except perhaps for not producing heroes when they are needed. In the absence of the hero to act as pump primer, there truly was nothing the group could do.

The strength of this responsibility depends upon the degree to which B's actions and choices can affect A's interests, either directly (under clause b) or indirectly (through his impact upon getting the group to organize a collective scheme to protect A's interests under clause a). The relative resources B should devote to each of these tasks depends upon how efficacious he would be in pursuing each of them, and upon how quick and how certain the results of his various actions would be.[45] The relative resources B should devote to discharging his responsibilities in respect of A depends, once again, upon the relative strength of those responsibilities compared with any competing responsibilities B may have in respect of other people.

One important consequence of deriving individual responsibilities from collective ones in this way is to remove any objection to their social enforcement. Individuals have many moral duties which, for one reason or another, we think society ought not compel them to discharge. However, where the duty is a collective one (at least in the first instance), collective action clearly is in order. Then the collectivity is fully justified in compelling each of its constituents to play its fair role in discharging those duties and responsibilities.

Cooperative schemes for discharging collective responsibilities are usually characterized by some division of labor. Each of us is assigned special responsibility for a narrow range of tasks: feeding our own children, treating our own patients, defending our own clients, protecting our own employees or customers, and so forth. Ideally, a cooperative scheme would be organized in such a way that the larger collective responsibility is fully discharged by everyone performing his own little role. This, indeed, is one of the most common, and most persuasive, justifications for each of us focusing narrowly on our own special responsibilities.

Alas, the organization of such cooperative schemes is rarely perfect. It is characteristically the case that some of those who are vulnerable and stand in need of protection will not, in fact, be protected through the conventional set of special responsibilities. A rule requiring parents to feed their own children leaves orphans to starve. An adversarial courtroom rule directing lawyers to press to the hilt their own clients' claims leaves those without counsel defenseless. And so on. Even if the organization of the schemes were perfect, compliance might not be. Some children are abandoned. Some clients are defended by incompetent counsel.

No one, therefore, is entitled to assume that the cooperative scheme is working perfectly. While the primary responsibility of everyone within such a scheme may be to discharge his own special responsibilities under it, each

---

45. Saying that present payoffs are to be preferred to future ones of the same magnitude is not to say that we should discount for time per se, but merely that we should discount for various factors (risk of death, uncertainty, opportunity costs, etc.) that tend to increase with the passage of time. See Goodin (1982a) and Parfit (1983b).

person also bears certain residual responsibilities under the scheme. One of these is the responsibility to monitor the workings of the scheme to make sure that everyone who is vulnerable is in fact being protected. Another is to lobby for the adjustment, reorganization, or replacement of schemes that prove deficient in that respect. Depending on the circumstances yet another may be to provide interim relief to those who would otherwise go unprotected until the lobbying effort succeeded.[46]

Finally, I should say something about the peculiar dynamics that arise when someone is allocated individual responsibility for discharging group responsibilities. The notion of responsibility implies, as I have said, that of accountability. Holding someone responsible entails holding him to account. We are responsible *to* certain people, and we are responsible *for* actions and choices that have a particular impact upon certain people.

In primitive cases of individual responsibility, it is to the people who are most strongly affected by our actions and choices that we must be primarily answerable.[47] We are not answerable to them alone, however. Otherwise irresponsible parents would be exculpated if their badly raised children, having been moulded by their upbringing, find nothing to object to in it. Irresponsible behavior leading to someone's death would be exonerated because no one left alive has any moral standing to complain. In principle, anyone should be able to complain, not just in the capacity of representative, in some shadowy sense, for those who are vulnerable, but merely as a member of the moral community. (Whether anyone will do so is, of course, another matter: there is a familiar tendency for everyone's business to be no one's.) Although the person most affected by our actions and choices is the person to whom we are principally answerable, anyone and everyone has some secondary, derivative right to hold us to account.

With the advent of the social division of responsibilities and labor, the considerations of to whom and for whom we are responsible are separated out. Where responsibilities have been institutionalized, you are typically responsible *to* one set of people (your superiors and, ultimately, the community

---

46. Sidgwick (1874, bk. 3, chap. 11) writes similarly: "If we consider the duty of parents by itself, out of connexion with this [existing] social order, it is certainly not self-evident that we owe more to our own children than to others whose happiness equally depends on our exertions. To get the question clear, let us suppose that I am thrown with my family upon a desert island, where I find an abandoned orphan. Is it evident that I am less bound to provide this child, as far as lies in my power, with the means of my subsistence, than I am to provide for my own children?" See similarly Frankena (1973, 54).

47. "A man is responsible for what he does to those affected by what he does, or to those who act on behalf of those affected, and thus it is initially by them that he is held responsible" (Roberts 1965, 233). There may be some delay in the accounting. For the same reason that they are vulnerable to us, and we responsible for them, they may presently be unable to assess any account we might render of our actions. This is most conspicuously true of children but may also apply to various other vulnerable agents (unconscious accident victims, etc.).

from which their authority is derived) *for* actions and choices principally affecting a different set (or subset) of people. That is not to say that those most directly affected suddenly lack moral standing to complain themselves. Institutionalization of social responsibilities has not undercut any old claims; it has merely added new ones. Given formal social roles and duties, irresponsible behavior consists in a failure to do one's job. The community as a whole has assigned jobs. The community as a whole is counting on their being carried out. Therefore, it is just as much an injury to the community as to the individual when someone abrogates his duty, and both the injured individual and the community have strong rights (morally, and often legally as well) to complain.

The public servant, like the private citizen, is responsible for the consequences that his actions and choices have for all those whose interests are affected by them.[48] Since it is his job to protect the public interest in certain specified respects, "an official should be as responsible for inaction as for wrong action." As Friedrich (1940, 4) goes on to observe, "certainly the average voter will criticize the government as severely for one as for the other." Holding public servants responsible for the consequences of all their official actions and choices does not, of course, mean that we will necessarily blame them for every bad outcome. It merely means that we will hold them to account. Sometimes, in the course of this accounting, we may well accept excuses (e.g., unavoidable ignorance) which exempt them from blame for the evil outcomes for which they have been held responsible.[49]

The actions and choices of public officials have much greater consequences for many more people than do those of private individuals. Since their capacity to do good or to prevent harm is so much greater, so too must be their responsibilities for doing so.[50] Public servants are surely the sort of people

48. Their principal concern must be with the consequences for their own citizens. That, however, is not because their moral obligations stop at the political boundaries. Rather, it is because decisions of public servants usually have a greater impact on those within their own community than on those outside it. Where the latter impacts are large, we have little hesitation in holding them responsible. Most of us would, I think, describe it as "irresponsible" of the French government to allow the dumping of radioactive wastes in the South Pacific, even if it could be utterly certain that the toxic materials would never return to French shores.

49. Although initially defining "responsibility" in terms of "accountability," Friedrich (1940, 1, 12) subsequently falls into the trap of using "responsibility" to describe only those situations where officials are culpable (because they ignored crucial facts, technical or political).

50. "For private individuals, the duty of beneficence is a modest one, largely because the scope of plausibly effective private action (and hence the scope of moral responsibility) is comparatively small. When, however, an individual assumes responsibility for broad public purposes, and has been granted discretionary command over the substantial powers and resources of the government, the duty of beneficence takes on a markedly different aspect. The difference is partly one of scale. Since the capacity to do things for people is so much greater for public officials than for private individuals, the relative importance of this general duty of beneficence must increase. But the differences seems to be based on the *public* character of the responsibility and the routine use of coercive power in pursuing the good as well. The hope of realizing broad public goals in which

Mill (1863, chap. 2) had in mind when he said that "those alone the influence of whose actions extends to society in general need concern themselves habitually about so large an object" as universal happiness. Much though moralists may extol the virtues of private individuals pursuing some projects of their own regardless of the the larger social consequences, it "seems beyond dispute" that consequentialistic reasoning should be incumbent upon "public officials deciding policy issues" (Moore 1981, 10). Mirrlees (1982, 71) insists:

> I want government ministers to try to maximize utility, even if their personal sense of achievement is gravely compromised, their crazy industrial dreams unfulfilled: the minister's utility deserves no significant weight in our assessments of utility in comparison to the millions who may suffer. To this extent, the morality of economic policy [or, indeed, public policy more generally] is simpler than that of personal life or culture.

In practice, self-indulgence, recklessness, and irresponsibility are some of the most damning charges that can be leveled against any politician.[51]

Within formal organizations there is a strong tendency for the sense of individual responsibility to shrink with every increase the size of the organization, just as the sense of responsibility diminishes with the presence of others in an unorganized group at the seashore (Friedrich 1940). This is largely because the bigger the organization, the more opportunities there are for "passing the buck." That no one wants to take responsibility for administrative actions seems to be an almost universal truism. In assessing "two British errors," P. D. Henderson (1977, 191) points to various features of British administrative procedures (like secrecy and the anonymity or impersonality of interactions) which tend to "weaken and dilute the responsibility" of people in Whitehall; only the most generous would describe that effect as unintended. Aaron Wildavsky (1972, 521–22) describes the even more extraordinary lengths to which a Nepalese civil servant will go to avoid responsibility:

> If a file reaches him calling for a decision, he can try to find some reason it belongs in another jurisdiction. If that fails, he can find a reason to reject any proposal in it that might lead him to take action. He can seek an *ad hoc* committee in which all members can avoid personal responsibility or he can find something that makes the matter such that it will go to a higher authority for signature and thus possible blame. Should all these expedients fail, he will

---

many take satisfaction and the concern about inflicting harm through clumsiness or a deliberate choice to sacrifice some interests to advance others make the duty of beneficence both more important and more difficult than in the private realm" (Moore 1981, 9).

51. Having canvassed all the standard objections to the Anglo-French invasion of Egypt during the Suez crisis, Hare (1957, 23) goes on to say, "Far more important, as it seems to me, . . . it was morally wrong in the same sort of way as it would be morally wrong to drive at sixty miles an hour through a crowded market-place. The action was so foolish, so regardless of the consequences which were almost certain to follow, as to amount to a case of criminal recklessness."

try to hold on to the file as long as possible in the hope it will be forgotten or that events will overtake it. Decisions involving responsibility for money are to be avoided most of all. There can be no spending unless someone wants to take responsibility for it. But history militates against responsibility, that is, against the prospect of taking the blame.

Of course, both the incentives and the opportunities for buck passing are a function of administrative rules and procedures. Without the Official Secrets Act, it would be much more difficult for British civil servants to cover up their irresponsible actions and inactions. Likewise, Nepalese public servants might be less frightened of money-handling responsibilities were it not for the lingering tendency to adhere to the old Rana rule, which dictated that if there were any irregularities "not only your income but those of your children, even unto the seventh generation, would be forfeited" (Wildavsky 1972, 521).

Reforming administrative rules and procedures could help to overcome the problems associated with buck passing. No doubt, some systems for ensuring administrative accountability are superior to others (Hill 1981). Still, reforms would constitute only a partial solution. Administrative lore holds that every attempt to prevent people from "passing the buck" will be countered by an attempt on their part to "cover their asses" in some other way. In less aphoristic terms, every attempt to increase individual accountability within the public service will automatically result in inferior outcomes as risk-averse civil servants waste time and resources on purely self-defensive measures. Unfortunately, this is not merely another groundless administrative myth. It has been found, for example, that student loan funds will be allocated far more efficiently (i.e., to students in greater need) when administrators are guaranteed confidentiality than when they are told they will have to account for their choices to disappointed applicants or funding agencies (Adelberg and Batson 1978).

All this goes to show how difficult it is, in practice, to hold people—here, public servants—responsible for their actions. None of it, however, argues that *morally* they should not be held responsible. The fact that people are psychologically inclined to shirk responsibilities, and are administratively adept at doing so, does not of course mean that it is morally proper (required, or even permissible) to excuse them from those responsibilities. Bearing responsibilities may be distasteful, but it is not beyond the powers of the ordinary psyche. It is, in any case, the very essence of public servants' jobs; those who want less responsible positions should resign. Thus, it is right that public servants should be held responsible for the actions and choices they make on our behalf. Our task is merely to discover which rules and procedures, among all those flawed instruments available to us, are best able to realize that goal.

6

The Extended Implications of Vulnerability

M y argument started from the proposition that we all acknowledge strong "special" obligations to our families, friends, and so on. I went on to show that once we start examining the source of these responsibilities, we discover that there is nothing really very special about them, after all. They are generated by the vulnerability of the others rather than by any voluntary acts of will on our part. Of course, there are many more people vulnerable to us (individually or collectively) than stand in any of the standard special relationships to us. The implication is that our responsibilities for protecting all of these others are strictly analogous to our responsibilities for protecting persons with whom we have any of the standard "special" relationships. These additional responsibilities have the same source and, depending on circumstances, may even have the same strength as those we have always acknowledged to be compelling.

This is, first and foremost, an argument in favor of the welfare state. That institution is the principal mechanism through which we discharge our collective responsibilities to protect our vulnerable compatriots. And that, on my argument, puts public assistance morally on a par with the aid we render to family and friends. The same basic argument would, however, also have important implications for international, intergenerational, and environmental responsibilities. My model promises, therefore, to unify a wide range of moral responsibilities, even if it does not purport to order the whole moral universe.

The Welfare State

The social assistance programs of the welfare state are best seen as devices to protect vulnerable and dependent beneficiaries. That is at one and the same time their intention, their effect, and their justification. Sociologically, protecting the vulnerable is the primary (though not the sole) function of such programs. Historically, that was their advocates' principal (though not sole) argument for them, and it continues to be one of the most prominent arguments offered for their expansion. Morally, that is the most compelling

145

(though not sole) argument that *can* be offered in justification of such social welfare programs.[1]

Here I focus on welfare programs proper, that is to say, social assistance programs explicitly designed to aid those in need.[2] There is nothing novel in describing such programs as devices to protect those who are vulnerable and hence dependent upon state aid. Sometimes the very names of the programs proclaim the fact, as for example, with U.S. Aid to Dependent Children, or, later, Aid to Families with Dependent Children. The provisions of the law usually make it clear, even if the title of the program does not, that social welfare programs strive to aid only those who are necessarily dependent upon state aid. According to the classic criteria Brewer set down,

> It is, strictly speaking, the pauper, and not the poor man, who has claims on public charity. It is not one who is in want merely, but one who, being in want, is unable to remove or prevent such want. There is the idea of help-lessness as well as of destitution. We speak of those whom society must aid, as the dependent classes, not simply because they do depend on society, but because they cannot do otherwise than thus depend. Cold and harsh as the

1. Primary among the other values they are said to serve are autonomy (Weale 1983), equality (Weale 1978), and community (Plant, Lesser, and Taylor-Gooby 1980, chaps. 9 and 10). Notice that all those other values are reducible in part (though none in whole) to considerations of vulnerability—either preventing people from being vulnerable (by equalizing resources or increasing autonomy) or protecting those who are (by increasing fellow-feeling within the community). Notice, furthermore, that my argument for the welfare state focuses upon the community's duties rather than upon the claimant's rights. There are good reasons, to be discussed in chapter 7, for discharging those duties by institutionalizing welfare rights; but that is not to say that, *ex ante*, people have moral rights to welfare (cf. Shue 1980; Brown, Johnson, and Vernier 1981).

2. Most welfare systems—Australia's being a conspicuous exception—also have a large component which is organized (officially, at least) along the lines of insurance, with benefits being paid on the basis of contributions rather than needs. Upon falling ill or becoming unemployed, any paid-up member of an insurance scheme is entitled to claim the benefit whether he needs it or not; insurance benefits by their nature are not means tested (Beveridge 1942, par. 402). Of course, the reason for setting up social insurance schemes—and the reason for making them compulsory—is that people might otherwise be rendered vulnerable or dependent by illness or unemployment. Nonetheless, the goals of these programs are analytically distinct. The programs are aimed not so much at "protecting the vulnerable" as at "preventing vulnerability," a goal which is considered more fully in chapter 7 below.

It should, however, be noted that no social insurance scheme is purely that. The United States Social Security Act of 1935, although basically an insurance scheme for contributory old-age pensions, also included provisions for a markedly noninsurance form of social assistance, Aid to Dependent Children. The ADC payments were to be predicated on need alone rather than on any prior contributions to the social security insurance fund. Even the pension scheme itself was not purely contributory, in that it allowed people to draw out far more than they paid in, not only in the first years of the program but later as well. Indeed, the categories and premium structures in virtually all "social insurance" schemes bear hardly the slightest resemblance to actuarial realities. Letting better risks subsidize poorer ones in this way constitutes a serious deviation from the pure insurance model. "Social assistance" goals of helping the needy (dependent, vulnerable) merely because they are needy have, in this way, been smuggled through the back door into almost all ostensible social insurance programs (Beveridge 1942, par. 26; Titmuss 1974, chap. 7).

statement may seem, it is nevertheless true, that the obligation of the state to help, is limited to those who are *unable* to help themselves. (Brewer 1875, 74–75; see similarly Abbott 1940, 16–19, 97–124; Anderson 1978, 153)

Those standards have now been relaxed. The connection is still sufficiently strong, however, that the secretary general of the Organization for Economic Cooperation and Development continues to characterize social welfare programs generically as "transfers to the vulnerable groups in society" (van Lennep 1981, 10).

Historians see much the same connection. Robson (1976, 21), for example, described the Lloyd George initiatives—old-age pensions, health and unemployment insurance, minimum wage boards, and the like—as "tentative steps . . . to protect the weakest and most vulnerable elements in society such as the aged poor, the unemployed workman, the sweated worker," and so on. Titmuss (1958, 42–43), in his classic lecture on "The Social Division of Welfare," similarly presents the whole history of the welfare state as the increasing recognition of, and the increasing assumption of collective responsibility for, ever more "states of dependency."

Given the background out of which they emerged, it is hardly surprising that modern welfare programs were designed to assist those who were necessarily dependent upon state resources, having nowhere else to turn. The ideology of the Poor Law firmly held that no one should receive public assistance if he was capable of supporting himself. Traditionally it was left to the market to enforce that injunction. Public assistance was made less attractive, in a multitude of ways, than the least attractive job; the laws of political economy then guaranteed that only those who really needed it would apply. Reformers by and large refrained from attacking the general principle: they tended to concede that the public should help only those who were truly dependent upon public assistance and were incapable of helping themselves. What the reformers offered, instead, were independent criteria for identifying these persons, thus eliminating the need to treat recipients badly in order to guarantee that only the truly needy (i.e., the necessarily dependent) applied.

The general pattern of the arguments in favor of expansion of state welfare services was, therefore, first to identify a group in need and then to show that (at least for the great majority of persons in that group) there was nothing that they could have done to alleviate their own distress.[3] Here I shall focus on two

---

3. Naturally, the parallel with my own justification of the welfare state is less than perfect. In practice, we tend to insist that people be *completely* dependent upon state assistance before it is granted, whereas my argument would merely require that the state be the best able to help. Or, again, in practice before granting state assistance, we sometimes insist that there have been nothing people could have done or can now do to alleviate their own distress; whereas in judging their vulnerability and the state's responsibilities, my argument focuses purely upon the forward-looking question of what they can now do. Still, given the well-known obstacles to translating theory into practice, I am inclined to suppose that the fit in this case is really rather impressive.

examples—old age pensions and unemployment relief—to show just how crucial such dependency-based arguments were to the adoption of the programs in question.

The widely acknowledged turning point in the argument for old age pensions in Great Britain came in a paper presented by Charles Booth (1891, 632–32; 1892, 166) to the Royal Statistical Society. First, Booth canvasses the received wisdom on the topic of "state pensions for the aged": "All pauperism no doubt might be said to argue some fault on the part of the pauper. He might have gone less often to the public house; have been more industrious or less lazy; with sufficient care he might have saved; he might have made friends and kept them; if his children had been well brought up they would have taken care of his old age, and so forth." But Booth proceeds to show that, as a general explanation for old age pauperism, this view "is not tenable." In his "Enumeration and Classification of Paupers," the first such systematic survey, 38.4 percent of those over age 65 were classed as paupers. Furthermore, almost 90 percent (eight-ninths) of them "had kept clear of relief" until reaching old age (Booth 1891, 631–32). A few listeners quibbled over Booth's statistics.[4] Most, however, both within the Royal Statistical Society audience and in the larger community, were prepared to concede that "by no reckoning could this proportion of the population be considered undeserving wastrels fit only for the poor law" (Heclo 1974, 162). That they were reliant "on the rates" for support was in itself evidence enough that they could do nothing further to help themselves. Booth's findings suggest that there was, in most cases, nothing they could previously have done either. Thus, the aged were, by necessity, dependent upon the state for support. That was the way the case for old age pensions was made.

The history of unemployment relief programs follows similar patterns. Policymakers instituted programs of public relief only after they had come to realize that those who were out of work might truly have nowhere else to turn. Previously, the presumption was that those out of work could always find a job. According to a central tenet of the political economy of the day, Say's Law guaranteed that no such thing as long-term, structural unemployment

---

4. By far the most worrying for Booth himself at the time was Marshall's (1892, 61) suggestion that paupers might be overstating their age, hoping in that way to reduce the shame that would otherwise attach to their status; but none of the Poor Law Guardians in attendance at the Royal Statistical Society's discussion could confirm this happening from their own experience. There was another source of error, however: Booth was attempting to estimate the total number of persons on Poor Law relief over the course of a year, whereas the preliminary statistics he had available only reflected the number of persons relieved on a single day; and the multiplier he originally used, although appropriate for younger paupers, badly understated the high rates of recidivism among old-age paupers. Booth (1892, 159–65), therefore, was forced to revise his estimates downward. They still remained pretty dramatic: on the revised count 25.9 percent of persons over age 65 were thought to be on relief, five-sixths of them having fallen on relief only in (and presumably only because of) old age. These estimates were borne out by Booth's (1894a, 38; 1894b) later, more thorough surveys.

could exist; at most, there might be some short-term unemployment as the new equilibrium was established. But Say's Law was increasingly discredited throughout the late nineteenth century, and policymakers began to appreciate that people might be unemployed for quite some time while the equilibrium set slowly about reestablishing itself. In its majority report the 1909 Royal Commission on the Poor Law and Relief of Distress conceded that it was no longer possible for the state to

> adopt the simple principle of the [Poor Law] Act of 1834 that, in order to drive men into independent labour, we need only apply a test that shall be sufficiently deterrent. . . . Not only is there cyclical dislocation which recurrently reduces the demand for labour, and issues either in general short time . . . or in workers of all classes and grades being thrown out of employment altogether, but, going on all the time . . . there is the normal underemployment of casual and seasonal workers, and there is the entirely fitful employment of the "unemployables" (Hamilton 1909, pt. 6, paras. 201–2).

Showing that the unemployed worker was thus genuinely dependent upon public assistance made welfare programs increasingly acceptable as a matter of principle. The key to putting the programs into practice, of course, lay in finding some mechanism for distinguishing the genuinely dependent from the merely lazy. As Beveridge complains in his influential *Morning Post* article of July 1907: "The state is forced into the costly and degrading harshness of the Poor Law simply because it has no control or supervision of the labour market. . . . It must rely always on the assumption that the applicant for help could find work if he looked for it because it is never in the position to satisfy itself that there is no work for him" (quoted in Heclo 1974, 80–81). The solution, offered by Beveridge and eventually adopted by the Lloyd George government, was a system of "labour exchanges." Officers of the state would try to bring together workers and jobs. If they failed to find a suitable job for any given worker, then it would be clear that the worker could not support himself through paid employment and therefore presumably had to depend upon the state for support.[5]

This connection between vulnerability and social welfare reforms in Great Britain is replicated in cross-national analyses as well. These show, for example, that the strongest single factor in promoting the growth of the welfare state is industrialization (Jackman 1975, 196). This fact is best explained in terms of the new vulnerabilities which industrialization creates and to which the state must inevitably respond. These are effectively detailed by Heclo (1974, 29–30):

5. Another feature of this scheme which emphasizes its role in protecting those who truly must depend upon the state, and those alone, is that it withholds benefits from those who are somehow at fault for being out of work, either because they have quit without good cause or because they are engaged in a strike.

A new human vulerability was . . . created by these economic changes. . . .
Providing for oneself and one's family increasingly came to depend upon what
one could buy from a variety of other increasingly specialized producers; this
in turn rested on the money income obtained from the sale of labor. More and
more, the individual's *social* security depended upon *economic* security
which, in turn, depended upon *income* security.

This concatenation of vulnerability stemmed not only from wage dependence.
The primary locus of social support, the family, was also changing. . . .
[Deprived of its former labor and leisure functions, the] family in the modern
era has tended to contract into a nuclear group composed of two parents with
one to three children. In this way, the individual member of the family also
became economically more vulnerable by becoming dependent upon fewer
earners and thus more likely to find himself alone in a wage-earning society.

Heclo (1974, 30) goes on to suggest that "one way of looking at" the history
of the welfare state "is as an exploration of how . . . societies . . . create
policies to deal with this new vulnerability."

For yet another indication of the link between welfare programs and perceived dependency, consider the *order* in which social welfare programs tend
to be adopted. Cross-national research reveals the following sequence, substantially invariant across a wide range of countries and periods: first a nation
adopts work-injury programs; and these are then followed by sick-
ness/maternity programs, old age/death/invalidity programs, family allow-
ances, and unemployment insurance in turn (Cutright 1965). For present
purposes, it is important to notice two things about these programs. One is
that they all involve dependencies of one sort of another. The other is that the
sequence proceeds from cases where the dependency is conspicuous to ones
where it is less so. Injured workers are most obviously helpless. Usually there
is little they could have done to avert their injuries; and, in any case, once the
family's wage earner is incapacitated, there is likely to be no other source of
support. While this is arguably true for all the other circumstances listed, and
perhaps even *more* true for some of them, it is (or at least was, according to
the then-prevailing social theories) less obviously true as you progress down
the list. The sequence in which social welfare measures have been adopted,
then, once again suggests that they are designed to protect those who are
perceived to be vulnerable and dependent upon the state for any aid they hope
to receive.[6]

---

6. Of course, none of this explains why the benefits were so often universal in form rather than
being selectively available only to those who were revealed through a "means test" to need
them. A great many of the aged may be truly dependent on the state for support. Not all of them
are, however; some could fall back on savings or families or friends. In the same way, many, but
not all, of the unemployed may be utterly dependent upon state support. If the goal is to protect
the vulnerable and only the vulnerable, why then eschew means tests that would allow us to
accomplish that very goal? No doubt there is some truth in the standard explanation. Thanks to

H aving shown that the general notions of dependency and vulnerability figure largely in the history and rhetoric of the welfare state, I must next show how precisely this fits with my own arguments for protecting the vulnerable. This task falls naturally into two parts. The first derives from the fact that ordinarily the state is (and morally ought to be) the agent of last resort for purposes of promoting a person's welfare. The welfare state discharges residual, secondary, back-up responsibilities. Thus, the first question must be under what conditions should these residual responsibilities be called into play?

The answer, in general terms, is relatively straightforward: the state should become responsible whenever there is no one with primary responsibility, or whenever those with primary responsibility are unable or unwilling to discharge it. I have already alluded to the possibility of failures in collective schemes for allocating primary responsibilities (chap. 5). The strategy traditionally employed in such schemes is to pair up particular vulnerable individuals with particular others who are assigned special responsibilities for protecting them. Thus, parents are conventionally assigned special responsibility for caring for their own children; attorneys, for defending their own clients; and so on. Occasionally this matching strategy fails, and some vulnerable individuals are left without a special protector. In the ordinary scheme of things, no one in particular would have special primary responsibility for protecting those who are without parents or legal counsel. Yet the moral community as a whole has a collective responsibility to see to it that they are, in fact, protected. Secondary duties come into play, then, when no one has been assigned primary responsibility.

An even more common way for secondary responsibilities to be activated is for those with primary responsibilities to prove *unable* to discharge them. Vulnerable children are all too often found in vulnerable families, as both the Carnegie Commission on Children (Keniston et al. 1977) and the Australian Royal Commission on Human Relationships (1977, vol. 1, 63) were quick to emphasize. In Anglo-American law, "it is the family, not the state, which has primary responsibility for child rearing. Despite this predominant pattern, there are about 285,000 children under eighteen . . . for whom the state has assumed primary responsibility" (Mnookin 1973, 600). In the majority of cases, this seems to have occurred because the natural parents were simply

the Poor Law traditions, means tests were widely seen to be (as they were traditionally meant to be) stigmatizing. If the old and unemployed had fallen into need through no fault of their own, then it would have been wrong to subject them to this degrading ritual. Another reason for eschewing means tests may have been simple efficiency. If a vast majority of people in any given category (old, unemployed, etc.) would have passed a means test, then there was little point in applying the test. Administering it would have cost more than it would have saved. Other reasons may have had to do with the hardships that would otherwise have been imposed on families or friends (Schorr 1980; Graycar and Kinnear 1981; Kinnear and Graycar 1982) or with the other moral arguments offered below.

unable to discharge their primary responsibilities, owing either to physical or mental illness of to incapacity or inability to cope with children with emotional problems (Mnookin 1973). Similarly, we ordinarily assign people primary responsibility for providing economic support for themselves and their families. Some people, however, are physically or mentally unable to work; others are precluded from undertaking paid employment either legally (e.g., adolescents, retirees) or by the weight of their other responsibilities (e.g., for child care, where day-care facilities are inadequate); still others are simply unable to find work (Titmuss 1958; Tulloch 1983; 1984). Whichever the cause, people in this position are inevitably forced to default on their special primary responsibility to support themselves and their families. That activates, in turn, the secondary responsibilities of others to support them instead.

Finally, secondary responsibilities might be activated because the persons with primary responsibilities prove *unwilling* to discharge them. This, perhaps, is the most contentious case; and it is far from clear that all instances of sheer unwillingness necessarily activate secondary responsibilities. But some clearly do so. Consider, again, the problem of child care. Of those children in state (i.e., foster) care, a sizable proportion are there because their natural parents have made clear their unwillingness to assume or to continue care. Indeed, something like 8 percent of these children have been literally abandoned or deserted (Mnookin 1973). Some parents, of course, may be unwilling to care for their own children because they are (or can foresee that they will be) unable to do so. Presumably, however, there are lots of cases of unwillingness pure and simple. Those with primary responsibilities in this regard *could* discharge them but refuse to do so. Then we might be inclined to say, "Let their kids starve—it will be on their heads." Indeed, in the United States "a few states go so far as to deny aid to an individual whose relatives have been found capable of supporting him, even if [they] . . . in fact refuse to accept the responsibility" (Burns 1956, 81). But, of course, it is the children who would suffer from such a policy. We are ordinarily, and rightly, reluctant to punish children for the sins of their parents. In such cases, secondary responsibilities to care for children are surely activated as soon as it becomes clear that those with primary responsibility will not, for whatever reason, do so.[7] Various welfare state programs can be justified in this way. Prominent among them is Aid to Families with Dependent Children, which gives subsidies to families whose principal breadwinner has in the vast majority of cases simply deserted them (Steiner 1971, 42).

The second part of my task is to show why it should fall to the state to discharge these secondary responsibilities. In one respect, it might seem ob-

---

7. There are other cases, of course, where we are probably inclined to say that default by those with special primary responsibilities activates no such secondary responsibilities. These cases can probably be characterized generically as those in which the defaulter alone will suffer—but not too badly—from his actions.

vious that it should. These secondary responsibilities are, after all, responsibilities of the moral community as a whole and are thus shared collectively by all its members. Everyone has the responsibility to see to it that a cooperative scheme is set up and operates effectively to protect all the members of the community. Of course, it is not necessary that whole community be actively involved in discharging collective responsibilities. Indeed, in most cases the active agent will be some individual or small group of individuals acting on behalf of the larger community. That is the basic idea behind assigning special primary responsibilities to individuals for discharging what are, at root, collective responsibilities to protect vulnerable children, elders, the ill or accused, and so forth. Secondary responsibilities might be handled in much the same way. Traditionally, godparents were assigned to discharge secondary, back-up responsibilities with respect to their godchildren. Even where the state assumes responsibility for the foster care of children, it is with the hope that some individuals, either natural or adoptive parents, will soon take over. The question, then, is why, where social welfare is concerned, the secondary responsibilities should fall to the state itself.

The basic explanation surely has to do with the argument known today as "deep pockets," the proposition that you should put the burden on whoever is best able to bear it (Calabresi 1970, 21). In terms of my analysis in chapter 5, people are most vulnerable to those who are best able to help them. Sometimes part of the "help" in question comes in the form of affective resources that can only be provided by particular people (parents, friends, etc.) in certain personal relationships; and for that reason we assign special primary responsibility to those who, in purely material terms, might be relatively ill equipped to perform the task. When the question is one of allocating secondary responsibilities, however, that affective component often disappears. Typically the question is one of what to do when those with personal connections have defaulted. Under those circumstances any assistance will of necessity be impersonal, and it will be less satisfactory for that reason;[8] all the more satisfactory options, however, were foreclosed when those with primary responsibilities defaulted. If no one among those to whom we might allocate secondary responsibilities can provide affective support, we might as well allocate those secondary responsibilities purely on the basis of who is materially best able to discharge them. The state has the deepest pockets, and therefore must bear these back-up responsibilities.

8. As Bane (1983, 100) complains of state aid to the elderly, "though sustenance is provided, love, empathy and companionship are not." Sometimes the choice is not quite so stark. Although we still must trade off capacity for rendering affective support against material support, various intermediate combinations of these two goods are available. In some such cases, we decide affective support is more important; e.g., we place abandoned children with adoptive parents whenever we can. At other times, we decide capacity for providing material support is more important; the money may "mean more" if it comes from an unemployed worker's family or friends, but we do not expect them to impoverish themselves to provide it.

Foreign Assistance

In the conventional catalog, special responsibilities to compatriots come right after those to family and friends (Shue 1980, chap. 6; Parfit 1983b, 35). Indeed, in a metaphorical sense they are seen to be one and the same. "The common idea of a nation no doubt contains the survival of the familiar conception of kinship as the normal bond for holding men together in a political society: accordingly in popular talk it is often assumed that the members of a Nation are descended from the same stock" (Sidgwick 1897, chap. 14, sec. 32).

False analogies aside, it is hard to see how any special claims of our compatriots can be morally grounded. Once our moral vision has expanded sufficiently to recognize our duties to *all* of our compatriots—once we have come to appreciate the moral case for the welfare state—it is logically very difficult indeed not to be drawn "beyond the welfare state" (Myrdal 1960) and extend similar protections to the needy worldwide. It would prima facie seem as arbitrary to deny someone assistance on the basis of the color of his passport as on the basis of the color of his skin.[9] Nonetheless, there remains the persistent "underlying intuition . . . that citizens owe some sort of special obligation to the less fortunate members of their own society that is capable of overriding their general obligation to improve the prospects of less advantaged groups elsewhere" (cf. Beitz 1979b, 163).

My strategy in this section will be first to undermine arguments against foreign assistance that are couched in terms of special obligations to compatriots. That negative task accomplished, I shall then explore alternative positive justifications for international transfers, first in the narrower terms of duties of justice and secondly in the broader terms of duties of humanity, benevolence, or charity. Although I would argue that both justifications are, at root, vulnerability-based notions, the latter is conspicuously so. And it is the latter that provides the more adequate justification for systematic transfers from rich nations to poor ones.

F ar and away the most standard objection to foreign aid is the notion that charity begins at home. Any moral duties we may have with respect to needy foreigners are allegedly overridden by our stronger special responsibilities with respect to our compatriots. These, in turn, are ordinarily predicated on the values of "community."[10] Certain kinds of social relations

9. John Rawls (1971, sec. 58) himself includes knowledge of one's nationality among the morally arbitrary facts that should be denied people behind the veil of ignorance. For an early contractarian argument reaching similar conclusions by a different route, see Christian Wolfe (1764, chap. 2).

10. Sometimes this is phrased as "the liberty to form communities." Rawls (1971, sec. 58), for example, thinks that "one consequence" of his equal liberty principle is "self-determination, the right of a people to settle its own affairs without the intervention of foreign powers." Rawls has

are possible only among people who are committed to one another and who share certain things (histories, values, objects, traditions) among themselves (Sidgwick 1897, chap. 14, sec. 2; Parry 1982). Such communities are valuable, both intrinsically and extrinsically, and should be fostered. Part of what it means to be involved in such communities is that members should, before all else, honor claims arising out of these associations. That is what loyalty is all about.[11]

Political communities have traditionally been regarded as being essentially clubs. This emerges most clearly in discussions of the right of states to control immigration into their territories. This is not surprising, since one of the most cherished rights of any club is to control its own composition. Walzer (1981, 32) writes, for example: "Admission and exclusion are at the core of communal independence. They suggest the deepest meaning of self-determination. Without them, there could not be *communities of character,* historically stable, ongoing association of men and women with some special commitment to one another and some special sense of their common life." From this principle follow all the standard principles of the international law of immigration: a state must be empowered "to exclude inhabitants of other States altogether from its territory, without violation of duty"; and should it decide to admit them, "a State must obviously have the right to admit aliens on its own terms, imposing any conditions on entrance or any tolls on transit, and subjecting them to any legal restrictions or disabilities that it may deem expedient" (Sidgwick 1897, chap. 15, sec. 2). It is precisely this sort of argument that was used to defend the notorious "white Australia" policy. As one minister for immigration, Sir Alexander Downer, explained "We seek to create a homogeneous nation. Can anyone reasonably object to that? Is not this the elementary right of every government, to decide the composition of the nation? It is just the same prerogative as the head of a family exercises as to who is to live in his own house" (quoted in London 1970, 98).

On the now-standard want-regarding theories of community attachments, such propositions would seem irrefutable. If morality were just a matter of respecting people's choices, then we would be obliged to respect their choices of associates. *Ceteris paribus,* according to this model people should be allowed to eat with whomever they want, live with whomever they want, do business with whomever they want—all the way up to associating with whomever they want in the affairs of state. But of course the reverse side of

---

been roundly criticized for concentrating on the standard formalisms of international law (nonaggression, etc.) and failing to face up to the consequences of his theory for international distributive justice (Barry 1973, chap. 12; Danielson 1973; Amdur 1977, 452–58; Singer 1977, 42, 50; Beitz 1979b, pt. 3). Actually it seems that Rawls is merely being true to earlier arguments for the priority of liberty; and if his critics are right (as I think they are) to bemoan the international implications, then they should be equally concerned with the domestic ones.

11. See, e.g., Royce (1908), Walzer (1970; 1981), Gorovitz (1977), and Oldenquist (1982).

"to each as he is chosen" is that those who are not chosen can rightly be excluded (Goodin 1982b, 77–78).

One obvious implication of models of community as a "cooperative venture for mutual advantage" is that

> Those who do not belong to a given political community—that is, those who are not its citizens—cannot, under this theory, be given, *for purely altruistic reasons,* the property of those who do belong to it; such giving could not, by definition, serve the common good of the community. . . . Government may take from citizens and give to foreigners when doing so serves the common good of the citizens, but it may not do so if (as the doctrine of altruism assumes) all advantage will accrue to foreigners and none to citizens. (Banfield 1962, 24)

In short, so long as we cling to models of community as a cooperative venture for mutual advantage, "our political philosophy does not give our government any right to do good for foreigners" (Banfield 1962, 24). Similarly, in the Humean version of Rawls' theory of justice, we would have obligations under such cooperative schemes only to partners whom we have chosen (or would have chosen behind the veil of ignorance) to join us in them. Any individual or group so weak as to constitute a net drain on the scheme's resources would rationally have been excluded from such ventures (Barry 1978; 1979b, 68–69). Consequently, we would have no obligations to them, or at least no obligations of this stronger "special" sort. The model of special obligations as self-assumed thus reemerges at this point to justify the enormous international differences between rich and poor.[12]

There are various ways to try to escape such conclusions. One is to maintain that honoring our duties to aid general others would not destroy those values that our special duties are supposed to serve. Beitz (1979b, 157–58) argues that there is no reason to believe that the simple redistribution of primary goods, as required by applying Rawlsian distributive principles to the world at large, would seriously undermine local community sentiments. What makes this suggestion plausible, I think, is, our intuitive sense that different sorts of things are exchanged among friends and among strangers. Giving money is one thing; giving affection, another. All that a theory of international distributive justice would require us to do is to transfer money. However much money it may demand of us, our reserves of affection remain untouched.

---

12. See, e.g., Danielson (1973), Nelson (1974, 424–29), Amdur (1977, 452–58), Passmore (1979, 30–33), and Beitz (1979b, pt. 3). Of course, people can be said to have an "interest" in their moral duties being discharged; and hence, if they can be shown to have a moral duty to aid the needy regardless of nationality, then a government's foreign aid program might further the interests of its citizens (Shue 1980, 141–42). However, there is no easy way to show, within this model, that people *do* have the moral duty in question.

There are however various replies to this sort of argument.[13] The most powerful one is that it neglects this crucial fact: a profession of loyalty implies a propensity to action. "What is loyalty," Gorovitz (1977, 134) asks, "if not a special sort of favoritism—the singling out of a subset of the population that one is justified or perhaps even obligated to count as being of greater importance than persons generally?" It would be difficult for us, individually, to be at all persuasive in professing a loyalty that we never manifest in action. And it would be even more difficult for us persuasively to profess a collective loyalty to our fellow-citizens if it never manifested itself in any action at all, or if it only manifested itself in the private actions of isolated individuals within the group. In practice it will surely prove well nigh impossible to sustain a community composed purely (or even largely) of people who are loyal but never show it in the ways that matter. Flag waving is just not enough. Symbolic acts implicitly promise subsequent action, and the symbolism will rightly be regarded as empty if the implied follow-up is never forthcoming (Goodin 1980, chap. 5).

This is not to say that in order for the values of free association and community to be preserved, our special duties to members of our own communities must always take absolute priority over general duties to the world at large. It is surely possible to make some cross-community redistribution without destroying the bonds of community altogether. Equally certainly, however, if community values are to be preserved, the special duties owed to members of one's own community must be given some priority over general duties. This rejoinder to the communitarian defense of special duties to compatriots can, then, be only partially successful.[14]

---

13. One rejoinder, offered by Fishkin (1982, 75), points to how *very much* you would have to give. If we give full weight to the facts of world poverty and our general duty to relieve it, "we would . . . each be morally required to give up our entire way of life and devote ourselves full time to the amelioration of world poverty, disease and overpopulation." But while our "way of life"—understood as our present standard of living—may have to go, it is my no means clear why our "community attachments" more narrowly defined should depend in any way whatsoever on our wealth or material possessions.

14. Communitarians would argue that there is one good in particular which cannot be reallocated without undermining the community, namely, membership in that community. Walzer (1981, 20, 19), for example, argues that "there is one group of needy outsiders whose claims cannot be met by yielding territory or exporting wealth, but only by taking people in. This is the group of refugees whose need is for membership itself, a nonexportable good. . . . Some places in the world will still be more desirable than others, either to individual men and women with particular tastes and aspirations, or more generally. Some places will still be uncomfortable for at least some of their inhabitants. Hence immigration will remain an issue even after the claims of distributive justice have been met on a global scale." Suppose, however, that material resources have been completely equalized throughout the world, by moving those resources that can be moved and compensating for those (such as climates) that cannot. Then the only reason people would have for wanting to immigrate would be that they share (or want to share) our values; and it is far from clear how admitting them would constitute a threat to the "sense of relatedness and mutuality" that is said to characterize community attachments (Walzer 1981, 21; see also Sidgwick 1897, chap. 14, sec. 4; Parry 1982).

Another rather more successful challenge to the communitarian defense of special obligations to compatriots focuses on the notion of "community" used in such arguments. There is a plethora of definitions of the word, not all of which have moral significance. According to the two definitions most commonly employed in arguments for restricting international assistance, however, we appear to be more nearly members of a single worldwide community to a larger extent than is commonly supposed.

The first notion of "community" invoked by champions of special obligations toward our compatriots is that of a "moral community," what Shue (1980, 135–39) calls a "community of principle." By that is meant a group of people who acknowledge reciprocal rights and duties with respect to one another. Now, in one sense, this definition amounts to pure question begging: it makes true by definition what the argument is supposed to prove, namely, that foreigners have no rights or duties with respect to one another. In another sense, it is simply wrong to say that foreigners, naively understood, are not members of the same community thus defined. Legal rights and duties, which are presumably a subspecies of moral ones, *can* cross national boundaries. Individuals can sign contracts with foreigners. So, too, can states sign treaties with one another, thereby incurring promissory obligations every bit as strong under customary international law and morality as personal promissory obligations are under our conventional domestic law and morality. Indeed, the giving of foreign aid has the result (and typically the intention as well) of establishing bonds of moral obligation between benefactor and beneficiary.[15] We can *make* them members of our own moral community, in this sense, by offering them aid. Hence, refusing to aid foreigners on the grounds that they are not part of our moral community would amount to a prophecy that is unacceptably self-fulfilling, to an excuse that is intolerably self-justifying.

The other sense of "community" used in this connection is that of a "cooperative venture for mutual advantage"—the Rawlsian-Humean analysis. If that is what we mean by the concept, then the simple fact of widespread foreign trade is sufficient to prove that the community and the consequent moral obligations extend far beyond present national boundaries (Beitz 1979a, 62–63; 1979b, 151; cf. 1983, 595). As a positive argument for more international assistance, this analysis is less than decisive: it ignores distinctions between various types of social cooperation for mutual advantage, some of which seem to generate moral obligations while others do not;[16] it leaves

15. See, e.g., Morgenthau (1962) and McKinley and Little (1977; 1978).
16. Barry (1982, 233) maintains that, "trade, however mulitlateral, does not constitute a cooperative scheme of the relvant kind [because] . . . trade . . . is not . . . the kind of relationship that gives rise to duties of fair play. To the extent that justice is involved it is . . . justice as requital, that is, giving a fair return. Justice as fair play arises not from simple exchange but from either the provision of public goods that are collectively enjoyed . . . or from quasi-insurance schemes for mutual aid." See similarly Barry (1980, chap. 5, sec. 6) and Walzer (1981, 103), and on the notion of obligations of fair play arising out of cooperative ventures for mutual advantage more generally, Hart (1955, 185–86) and Rawls (1958).

unprotected some very poor nations, and some very poor people in virtually all nations, who have nothing of value to trade with anyone else (Geertz 1977); and it constitutes a virtual invitation to the rich to evade their moral responsibilities merely by withdrawing from trading relations.[17] Still, this argument is more than enough to succeed, negatively, in showing that it is wrong to reject any and all international redistribution on the basis of special obligations tied to communities of this sort.

From the foregoing discussion it is clear that no particularly good arguments *against* international redistribution can be found in communitarian notions of special obligations. Having undermined those objections to foreign aid, I shall now explore positive arguments in favor of it. Among the many such arguments that could be offered, the vulnerability model makes the best case for systematic international redistributions.

Consider the alternatives. There is, for example, some scope for arguing for a certain measure of international redistribution on the grounds of justice, even narrowly understood. First, there is the argument couched in terms of restitution. To some extent, the rich nations are rich today precisely because they exploited the poor countries in the past. Imperial powers gave an unfair return for the resources they extracted from their former colonies. Transnational corporations arguably persist in that practice to this day (Moran 1978; Bergsten, Horst, and Moran 1978). Insofar as this is true, the case for international redistribution to remedy this historical injustice is incontestible.[18] Even Nozick (1974) would have to agree. This is a powerful argument so far as it goes but, alas, it does not go very far. First, there is the problem of determining what a "fair return" for extracted resources would have been.[19] Then

---

17. Beitz (1979b, 160–61) considers the possibility of withdrawing from trading relationships, but for different purposes. He is quite right in maintaining there that it is no reply to allegations of injustice to say that the disadvantaged states could always have withdrawn from the relationship; that was never really an option. He ignores the more important problem of what a rich state's withdrawing would do to his theory.

18. Barry (1980; 1982, 227–29) and Lichtenberg (1981). The classic argument has always been couched in terms of paying an unfair price for resources extracted. It can be equally well, and in many respects better, cast in terms of imposing unfair burdens on foreigners. Perhaps the best example is the export of hazardous products and production processes. United States consumers "pay lower prices, suffer less inflation, etc., because the health costs of the retention of the less safe technology are now borne by [e.g.] the Mexican workers and Mexican society" (Shue 1981, 136). "It is true," Shue concedes, "that most of us did not ask to have this arrangement made. But once we understand it, we are no longer unwilling (because unknowing) beneficiaries. We must now choose whether to continue to accept these benefits on these terms." Shue (1981, 136) calls this "responsibility through complicity—complicity by continuing acceptance of benefits." Notice that where trade is concerned "the benefits are not just received, but sought after; they are integral, not just incidental, to one's aims" (Lichtenberg 1981, 84). Hence, obligations really do follow from receipt of these benefits.

19. Lichtenberg's (1981, 84) formulation is that "A owes something to B if A gets from B more than A gives." That pretty clearly trades on some notion of a "just price" fixed, if not exactly in heaven, then at least outside the preference structures of A and B. A voluntary trade would never have taken place unless A valued what he received from B more than what he gave in return, and

there is the problem of deciding how much compensation—if any at all—is required for past wrongs. Are we liable for the injustices done by our fore-fathers? Are other people entitled to compensation for injustices done to theirs? (Beitz 1979a, 60–61). In some measure, these problems can be over-come by moving the action into the present and focusing on continuing pat-terns of power politics embedded in ongoing trade relations. That is the strategy of the *dependencia* theorists. But their arguments still beg the crucial question about the causation of world poverty. In any claim for reparations for harms caused by our acts, whether past acts or present ones, it is crucial to establish the relevant counterfactual condition. Injured parties can claim no compensation if they would have ended up in exactly the same position had we (or our ancestors) not interfered with them.[20] It is ordinarily quite difficult for claimants to prove otherwise; and of course it is they who must bear the burden of proof in such matters. Finally, the restitution argument is in any case inadequate to justify any *systematic* aid from rich to poor. Some poor peoples have never been abused, and some rich ones have never been guilty of abuse (Beitz 1979a, 61–62).

Second, claims of international distributive justice might be grounded in the premise that no one has a properly *moral* claim to the purely natural resources that made him rich. On this point, Barry's argument explicitly par-allels Hart's (1955) argument for natural rights. Claims to natural resources, Barry argues, stand logically prior to any claims based upon what people subsequently did with them; "therefore everyone has an equal right to enjoy their benefits" (Barry 1982, 235; see similarly Barry 1980, chap. 6 and Beitz 1979b, 136–43). Such arguments hinge on the proposition that people's ordi-nary entitlements to particular objects are "inextricably bound up with what they *have done*"; but natural resources, if they are purely natural, "are not the results of individuals' past actions." Therefore, claims to them "can have nothing to do with desert," and hence there can be no grounds for supposing that anyone has any greater claim to them than anyone else (Steiner 1977, 44–45).

Attractive though this argument is, it unfortunately contains a potentially

---

vice versa. Perhaps that is precisely the point: the exchange was *not* voluntary; the inequality of the terms of trade is simply evidence of that involuntariness; and it is the injustice of that coercion that justifies us in mending bad bargains. It seems to me, however, that the argument works far better run the other way: it is easier to find evidence of coercion, and to build a case for the rectification of past injustices on that, than it is to infer injustice merely from the pattern of distributive outcomes. On the difficulties lying within the notion of an "unequal exchange" between rich nations and poor, see more generally Barry (1979, 62–69; 1980, chap. 5; 1982, 227–29).

20. Sher goes further still: you might not have to compensate someone even if an injury were done to him, provided he has changed sufficiently between then and now to be in some significant respect a different person (Sher 1979); and the less compensation you will need to pay, the more the uncertainty about how well off the aggrieved party would now have been had you not injured him (Sher 1981).

fatal flaw. Certainly it is true that people have done nothing to *create* purely natural resources. By definition, the resources would have existed even in our absence. It is equally certain, however, that some people *have* done something to render those preexisting resources useful to mankind, if only by discovering them. Whether or not you are morally entitled to a finder's fee that runs to the full value of the thing you have found is, perhaps, an open question. But at least it is clearly wrong to say that you have *done nothing* and for that reason have no entitlement whatsoever to the resource.

The practical consequences of an equal right to natural resources are, in any case, indeterminate. The basic idea is that we should put the full value of unimproved natural resources into some sort of international kitty, to be shared out equally among all the people of the world. Before we can do that, however, we would need to decide what portion of the value of each product is due, respectively, to labor inputs, capital inputs, and the natural resources per se. This is a highly contentious issue in which economists differ violently. Given the present state of the economic sciences, there appear to be no nonarbitrary way of performing this task and hence implementing this scheme.

What all of this argument and counterargument seems to suggest is this: There may be various other partial arguments, supporting *some* aid from *some* of the world's rich to *some* of the world's poor; and, negatively, the communitarian argument clearly provides no good grounds for priority to special duties to compatriots. For a positive argument in support of systematic international transfers from rich to poor per se, however, we have to fall back on a more general duty of humanity, by which our duties to give foreign assistance are traced directly to the vulnerability of needy foreigners to our actions and choices, and to that alone.

This sort of argument as applied to international aid has been developed most fully in the literature surrounding Peter Singer's 1972 article, "Famine, Affluence and Morality." In attempting to frame a moral response to the circumstances surrounding the 1971 Bengal famine, Singer (1972, 23) comes to the conclusion that "if it is in our power to prevent something bad from happening, without thereby sacrificing anything of comparable moral importance, we ought, morally, to do it." He likens the Bengali famine victims to a drowning child: "If I am walking past a shallow pond and see a child drowning in it, I ought to wade in and pull the child out. This will mean getting my clothes muddy, but this is insignificant, while the death of the child would presumably be a very bad thing." To move from this case to that of the starving Bengalis, Singer must of course add that "the principle takes no account of proximity or distance. It makes no moral difference whether the person I can help is a neighbour's child ten yards from me or a Bengali whose name I shall never know, ten thousands miles away." And he must add furthermore that "the principle makes no distinction between cases in which I am the only person who could possibly do anything and cases in which I am just one among millions in the same position'' (Singer 1972, 24; see also Singer 1977; 1979, chap. 8).

Those anxious to avoid Singer's implication usually seize upon the last point as the weak link in his argument. The proper analog, they say, is to a child drowning at a *crowded* beach, where any of a great number of people are equally well placed to save him. As I have argued in chapter 5, that does nothing whatsoever to diminish the responsibility of each and every one of them to effect the rescue. While it is true that they would all be off the hook if any one of them acted, it is equally certain that they all remain firmly on the hook so long as none act.[21]

Singer's opponents may try to avoid his conclusion by rejecting the argument about the irrelevance of proximity. It is sometimes said, for example, that "one could not be expected, nor would it be desirable to try, to treat those whom one sees and knows just as one treats those whom one does not'' (Lichtenberg 1981, 97; cf. Singer 1977, 42; and Bennett 1981, 88). What makes such propositions appealing is, paradoxically, our aversion to arbitrariness of any kind in moral affairs. The problem is that as individuals we can help only a handful from among a multitude of equally needy strangers, whose moral claims upon us are indistinguishable. There is no nonarbitrary way for us to select which to help and which to shun; we therefore choose to concentrate our attention on needy acquaintances, who are fewer in number and can therefore all be helped without the need to choose arbitrarily among them. Arbitrariness undeniably makes us uncomfortable—but unjustifiably so, I would argue, where (as here) our choice is between arbitrariness in the course of fulfilling our duties or failing to fulfull those duties altogether.[22] In such a choice, arbitrariness seems the lesser sin. Besides, at some level, it is equally arbitary to help only those we have happened to meet.[23] Our meeting may not have been purely by chance, but it cannot be said to have been *morally* dictated. From a moral point of view, the meeting, and the acquaintance following from it, was surely just as arbitrary as our choice of which starving Bengali stranger to feed.

The most effective replies to Singer's application of the ''save a drowning child'' principle to the case of famine relief are, I think, of the form ''it makes no difference whether or not I do it.'' In the terms of my argument, the poor and starving of the Third World are not all that vulnerable to people in the First World, taken individually. That, in turn relieves us of individual responsibility for helping them.

---

21. See further Feinberg (1970, 244), Bennett (1981, 84), Barry (1982, 222), and Fishkin (1982, chap. 10).
22. In saying this, I am assuming: (1) that our duty of humanity requires that we aid those most in need first; and (2) that those whom we know personally are (sometimes) less needy, and hence less deserving of aid on this principle, than those we do not know.
23. It is also a very *demanding* principle, having, as Bennett (1981, 88) points out, ''strenuous implications for the moral effects of, say, a brief stopover in Bombay.''

Glover (1975) and Singer (1979, 170) both denigrate such excuses. They agree that it makes no difference to the overall level of world poverty whether or not I contribute to Oxfam. My contribution would indeed only be a ''drop in the bucket''—if reducing overall levels of world poverty were the bucket in question. But, they emphasize, it is not. My contribution certainly would make an enormous difference to the one or few individuals rescued by my aid from grinding poverty. It is that, they rightly point out, that really matters.

This argument, however, rests on an empirical claim that strikes me as uncertain, if not untrue. The great and familiar flaw in person-to-person aid programs—Adopt a Child and the like—is that they neglect the larger economic and social context of the aided individual. Therefore these programs can, and often do, end up doing as much harm as good to both the putative beneficiaries and those around them. To make sure that our well-intentioned gifts have the desired results—and results that are as good as they possibly can be—they must be part of some reasonably comprehensive, well-integrated scheme for restructuring the recipient's whole community. That requires a kind of coordination well beyond anything that isolated individual donors could reasonably hope to accomplish. It requires coordination well beyond anything that large-scale charitable organizations could reasonably hope to accomplish. Indeed, it requires coordination beyond anything that isolated national governments (whether as donors or as recipients of aid) could reasonably hope to accomplish (Hoffman 1966).

Hence I conclude that we do have a responsibility to aid distant peoples in distress but that it is a collective rather than an individual responsibility (McKinsey 1981; Shue 1983, 601 n.). While people in the Third World may not be vulnerable to us in the First World as individuals, they are enormously vulnerable to us as a collectivity.[24] Saying that the responsibility is a collective one does not exempt individuals from responsibility: it merely changes the character of their responsibilities. Individual members of the collectivities in question have a responsibility to cooperate in whatever schemes are organized to discharge collective responsibilities (McKinsey 1981).[25] They also

24. Perhaps, as is sometimes claimed, some of the very poorest nations are *not* particularly vulnerable to our choices because their position is so hopeless whatever we do. Triage is not popular, personally or philosophically (Singer 1979, 174–79). For what it is worth, however, I must say that it seems to me indisputably correct to concentrate our relief efforts on those who are most capable of benefiting from them. One of the reasons for the common revulsion to triage, and one that applies with particular force to the international application, is that we can rarely be completely sure that a case is hopeless. Great vulnerability shades imperceptibly into invulnerability at the neediest end of the spectrum; and whenever there is any doubt at all about which side of the line people are on, we had best err on the side of caution and treat the very needy as if they were extraordinarily vulnerable.

25. Some of the most promising collective schemes do, in fact, leave lots for individuals to do. In order to make individual citizens feel psychologically a part of the foreign-aid program, Hirschman and Bird (1968, 15), for example, propose that individual taxpayers should be allowed to ''elect to use a limited portion of their income-tax obligation for contributions to one or several [multilateral] World Development Funds,'' rather like the tax checkoff now operating to finance the presidential campaign fund in the United States.

have a responsibility to undertake political action—at the national and/or international level, depending upon where they can be most efficacious—that is designed to ensure that such schemes are in fact organized.[26] For the time being, then, our principal responsibility must be that of taking political action (Narveson 1972, 530).[27] We are obliged to campaign for our governments to organize generous and well-intergrated multilateral schemes for foreign assistance.[28]

Ideally, everyone who shares in these collective responsibilities would bear a fair share of the costs of discharging them. My argument not only tends toward that conclusion but also legitimates the coercive intervention of the collectivity to ensure that result. Imposing in this way like burdens on the entire population would go a long way toward countering the "excessive burden" objection (Beitz 1983, 599). Inevitably, some people will manage to evade their responsibility to participate (or to participate fully) either in the relief efforts themselves or in the political campaigns required to organize them. Hence the question arises whether one person's delict is sufficient to excuse another's—and ultimately, everyone else's. Within my model, it is clear that it does not.[29] Our obligation is, quite simply, "to cooperate with whomever else is cooperating, in the production of the best consequences possible given the behaviour of non-cooperators" (D. Regan 1980, 124).

26. Here there is a threat of infinte regress: our obligation to organize the coooperative scheme for discharging our collective responsibilities to aid the needy is itself a collective responsibility, which is best (perhaps only) capable of being discharged through another cooperative scheme of concerted political action. What forestalls the threat of infinite regress is that, in practice, some people are keener than others on discharging their responsibilities; and the contributions of the keenest in effect "prime the pump," reducing the marginal costs enough for the next keenest to be willing now to do his duty, and so on down to the least keenest (M. Taylor 1976).

27. Until these political campaigns actually bear fruit, we may also have some subsidiary responsibility to give aid ourselves. Singer, for example, argues that "perhaps it is more important to be politically active in the interests of the poor than to give to them oneself—but why not do both?" (1979, 180); and besides, "I doubt whether preaching what one does not practice would be very effective" (1972, 32). If personalized aid giving is as futile (or indeed counterproductive) as I fear, then we would have no such duty, even as an interim measure. If I am wrong in that, if things are not *quite* that bad, I still insist that our principal duty is the political one. Coordinated public aid would be *so* much more effective that that duty vastly overshadows the duty of personal aid-giving. Where resources devoted to one purpose are resources denied to the other (as inevitably they are), it is obviously wrong to denote any resources at all to personal aid-giving except for purposes of relieving the most urgent necessities, if that.

28. Multilateral schemes are to be preferred not only because they are a much more successful solution to the problems of coordination but also because they minimize the opportunity for any particular donor to exploit power over any particular recipient (Andreas 1969, 172; Gergen and Gergen 1971; 1974; McKinley and Little 1977; 1978). The moral significance of that result is discussed in chapter 7 below.

29. The "generalization" argument—"what if everyone did likewise?"—can be used both to stimulate the giving of aid and to restrict it. The results of generalizing a rule that "people not give aid to those in need" is morally unacceptable. The same argument can, however, also be used to restrict the amount of aid any one of us is morally obliged to give to the amount we would be required to give in a world where everyone did give aid. But the classic rejoinder—that not everyone *will* do likewise (Broad 1916)—undercuts any such excuse for restricting our aid to that amount (Singer 1972, 25–26).

In deciding who has primary responsibility to help whom, two considerations should predominate. One is what sort of assistance the recipient needs and how badly. The other is what sort of assistance the donor is capable of giving and at what cost. Certain sorts of assistance can only come from certain sorts of donors. If the need is for food, then only those with a surplus of food can supply it. If the need is for money, then only those with a surplus of capital can supply it. Perhaps, in the family of man, just as in our individual families, there may be certain sorts of affective needs as well as material ones. Then, once again, only those with the relevant affinities can supply the things required.

On the other side, donors differ in their capacity to provide the needed assistance. Some do not have the goods in question. Some can provide them only at great sacrifice. Others can provide them at relatively little cost to themselves. People who are in a position to provide the needed resources have a collective responsibility with respect to those in need of those resources. People within each donor group are also vulnerable to one another, however. Each donor is vulnerable to the defaulting of others, since that would oblige him to bear still higher costs of assisting those in need. Each recipient is similarly vulnerable to the activities of other recipients, since the more aid any one of them attracts from the relatively fixed pool of aid, the less there is left for the others. Donors and recipients therefore have responsibilities to each other, growing out of these vulnerabilities, to organize cooperative schemes for allocating the benefits and burdens of aid among themselves. Coordination, while not the prime moral imperative, is nonetheless crucial to seeing to it that the prime imperative is honored (Goodin 1976; Fishkin 1982, 169–70).[30]

Finally, notice that coordinated collective efforts can better overcome all the standard practical obstacles to effective international assistance. It may well be true that as individuals, "we are in a better position to judge what needs to be done to help a person near to us than one far away, and perhaps also to provide the assistance we judge to be necessary. If this were the case, it would be a reason for helping those near to us first," as Singer (1972, 24) and virtually all his utilitarian predecessors would happily concede.[31] Perhaps Singer is right to suppose that "instant communication and swift communication have changed the situation" completely, even for the isolated individual. But be that as it may, national governments and other collective organizations certainly are in a very good position to collect a great deal of relevant informa-

---

30. Notice that I talk in terms of "people" rather than of "nations," as is more ordinary. The reason is simple. Having shown above that no moral importance attaches to communities, national or otherwise, the state has no moral significance except as a coordination mechanism. It is a dreadfully stunted one at that, since the need for coordination so clearly transcends the boundaries of nations.

31. See similarly Mill (1863, chap. 2), Sidgwick (1874, bk. 4, chap. 3, sec. 3), Banfield (1962, 23–24), Bennett (1981, 90), Brock (1982, 227), and Fishkin (1982, 73).

tion and to arrange for the provision of whatever resources are needed. Uncertainty may excuse (or might once have excused) individuals for failing to act so as to relieve distant suffering, but it cannot excuse collectivities.

The one practical obstacle that remains to generous international assistance, even when that assistance is organized on a collective basis, is the alleged "disincentive effect." Richards (1971, 139), for example, supposes that

> creating immediate equality of wealth by such transfers may have such adverse effects on the wealthy economy (on the exercise of superior managerial and scientific talent which the wealthy economy makes possible, and thus on productive efficiency, rates of investment, research, and development) as to lower the rates of economic growth of all nations, through reduced trade, investment, and invention, and even reduce the life prospects of desire satisfaction of the least advantaged class over several generations in an underdeveloped country, as compared with a situation of inequality of wealth.

Similar objections are widely acknowledged by both economists (Hutt 1970, 36) and philosophers (Beitz 1979b, 162; Carson 1982, 243). The implication seems to be that if we are to maximize the absolute well-being of the poor, then we may well have to sacrifice equality to do it (Rawls 1971, sec. 13; Richards 1971, 139).

It is important to be clear about the moral status of this argument. The claim is not that rich people are right to reduce their productive efforts in response to higher marginal tax rates, or even that they are within their rights to do so. Quite the contary, where their taxes are needed to honor collective moral responsibilities that the rich share, such behavior is blatantly *immoral*.

In the short term, we must simply take the delict of the wealthy as given and frame a plan to discharge our common responsibilities as best we can in light of it. In the longer term, we must try to make our schemes less sensitive to such delicts. One way is to transfer to the developing countries "the specialized managerial and scientific talents which were previously the monopoly of developed countries" (Richards 1971, 140). That step would make the poor less vulnerable to blackmail by the rich. We should also explore alternative administrative arrangements for extracting taxes from the rich, to see if there might not be some way to get more monies for international aid with less deleterious impact on overall ouput.

In the end, there is only one way of morally justifying the proposition that the rich should be excused from moral duties to aid the poor, either domestically or internationally. This relies upon a peculiar variant of the proposition that "ought implies can," the doctrine that it makes no sense to say that people ought to do what they cannot do. Here, however, "cannot" takes on a curious cast. The argument is that there are some acts, morally desirable thought they may be, which cannot be made morally obligatory because doing so would ask more of people than they are psychologically capable of bringing themselves to do. That is how Urmson (1958) and Sidgwick (1874, 220–

21, 492–93) before him distinguish supererogation from strict moral duties. Shue (1983, 606–8), borrowing from Rawls (1971, 175–82), supposes that such psychological "strains of commitment" place constraints on our obligation to transfer to the world's needy. That is also among the considerations that underlie the "cutoff for heroism" that Fishkin (1982, chap. 4) offers to spare us any serious obligation to aid the world's poor.

There are powerful rejoinders to this argument, however. One is that it takes an unreasonably static conception of human psychology. This, indeed, was Sidgwick's (1874, 227) own reply: "Even when it is beyond our power to realise virtue immediately at will, we recognize a duty of cultivating it and seeking to develop it." Analogously, our ignorance of certain relevant facts may excuse our failure to act on them at present; but we surely are liable to blame for our past failure in not having acquired or for our present failure to take steps to acquire facts we need to know in order to discharge our moral obligations (Goodin 1982b, chap 7). How much of a duty people are psychologically able to bear is not fixed but malleable. On this point, I find Singer's (1972, 29-30) analysis compelling:

> Given a society in which a wealthy man who gives five percent of his income to famine relief is regarded as most generous, it is not surprising that a proposal that we all ought to give away half our incomes would be thought to be absurdly unrealistic. In a society which held that no man should have more than enough while others have less than they need, such a proposal might seem narrow-minded. What it is possible for a man to do and what he is likely to do are both, I think, very greatly influenced by what people around him are doing and expecting him to do. (See similarly Beitz 1979b, 155-56)

In philosophical discussions of our duties with respect to foreigners, questions of cash transfers ordinarily take pride of place, and of course it is right that they should. For the purpose of illustrating my vulnerability model, however, two other cases are also interesting.

One concerns our duty to refugees. It has been a long-standing principle of normative international law that "by nature the right belongs to an exile to dwell anywhere in the world" (Wolff 1764, sec. 147). The rationale provided by Christian Wolff (1764, secs. 147, 150) for this principle very much parallels my own: "exiles have been expelled from the place where they had domicile. . . . They have no fixed abode. . . . They cannot free themselves from this evil with which they are afflicted. . . . Therefore we ought to be compassionate toward exiles."[32] Exiles, and refugees more generally, are in Wal-

---

32. Elsewhere Wolff (1764, secs. 149, 148) draws back, saying that while exiles must be "allowed to seek admittance elsewhere, . . . if admittance is refused, that must be endured." Apparently, however, that is merely a *prudential* "must," deriving from the fact that powerful governments are always in a position to enforce their (possibly immoral) will upon defenseless individuals.

zer's (1970, 146–7) words, "stateless persons, radically dependent on their hosts and unable to look backward to any protecting authority"; they exhibit "a special kind of helplessness and pathos." Such dependence, I argue, gives rise to special responsibilities.

Responsibilities for refugees fall upon anyone and everyone who is in a position to provide them with sanctuary. Often, many nations will be in such a position; the responsibilities then will be collective ones, shared by all of them alike. The appropriate manner of discharging those responsibilities would be to organize a cooperative scheme for sharing out refugees, or the cost of accommodating them, among all the nations that are under the responsibility.

Suppose that no other nation is prepared to share the refugees (or the costs). Then our nation would be under a peculiarly strong responsibility, a sort of international equivalent of an individual responsibility, to offer them sanctuary. This principle finds particularly clear expression in British immigration rules: "the criterion for the grant of political asylum is that a person should not be required to leave the United Kingdom 'if the only available country to which he might be sent is one to which he is unwilling to go owing to well-founded fear of being persecuted for reasons of race, religion, particular (social) group or political opinion' " (Wade and Phillips 1977, 424). Analogously, consider the strong personal responsibility falling upon the German householder to shelter from the Nazis the Jewish family hiding in his attic. It is widely agreed that this is such a strong and obvious moral obligation as to justify violation of otherwise absolute moral prohibitions, or to discredit any absolute moral norms if they cannot be bent to accommodate it (Fried 1978, 69–78; Barry 1979a, 644–46).

The second application of my vulnerability model is suggested by the discussions of the *dependencia* school, which trace the poverty of the Third World to its dependency on the First World. This dependency was brought about partly by the design of ex-colonial powers and their corporate collaborators and partly through accidents of economics, history, and geography.[33] For the purposes of my argument, it is the consequence rather than the cause of the dependency that really matters: namely, that Third World peoples are particularly sensitive to our own actions and choices. For that reason, if no other, we have strong responsibilities to frame our own actions with their impact upon the Third World firmly in mind. When choosing macroecomonic strategies, for example, we should give serious consideration to their effects on economies dependent upon our own. For another example, when deciding upon health and safety regulations, we should frame our regulations in such a way as to protect foreign workers and consumers who can be protected by us and us alone. "It is no good merely to say, 'Let their own governments look

---

33. See Bergsten, Horst, and Moran (1978), Moran (1978), Galtung, O'Brien, and Preiswerk (1980); and Lichtenberg (1981, 91).

after them', if isolated or even allied groups of governments of poor countries could not in fact control the more powerful firms'' (Shue 1981, 135).

Future Generations

According to the conventional moral wisdom, our special relationships to our contemporaries require us to give priority to their interests and to discount accordingly the interests of future generations. Parfit (1983b, 35–36; 1984, 485), for example, observes that

> According to commonsense morality, . . . there are certain people to whose interests we *ought* to give some kinds of priority. . . . Such a view naturally applies to the effects of our acts on future generations. Our immediate successors will be our own children. According to common sense, we ought to give their welfare a special weight. We may think the same, though to a reduced degree, about our obligations to our children's children. . . . Such claims might suggest a . . . kind of discount rate, . . . discounting here, not for time itself, but for degrees of kinship.

The consequence of discounting of this sort is, of course, to inflate the claims of those nearer to us in time and to reduce correspondingly the claims of those further from us. It leads, in Smart's phrase, to another form of "localized benevolence." When this benevolence "is localized in space we get the ethics of the tribe or the race: When . . . localized in time we get an ethic of the present day and generation" (Smart 1973, 63).

Discounting the claims of our descendants, of course, flies in the face of any theory of intergenerational justice. Alas, theories of intergenerational justice have until recently gone undeveloped. Before Rawls (1971), virtually no modern philosopher had devoted any sustained attention to the problem. Even since then, it has been discussed very largely in connection with the issue of overpopulation.[34] Thus, the question of what we owe future generations turns into a question of whether we owe them anything at all, even life itself. Casting the question in those terms gives the opponents of intergenerational justice an argumentative advantage. They need simply to deny the possibility of purely potential people's having any claims in terms of rights (or hence of justice) that they can lodge against us. Advocates of intergenerational justice are then forced to devote most of their time to the necessary moral preliminaries of establishing the moral standing of merely potential people. Only after showing that it is possibile to have obligations toward unborn people can we turn to the subsidiary question of *what* these obligations might be and *why*.

As far as I am concerned, this foundational question has been conclusively

---

34. See Bayles (1976), Sikora and Barry (1978), Kavka (1982), and Parfit (1982a,b; 1983a; 1984, pt. 4).

answered by Feinberg's (1980, 159–84) penetrating essay on "The Rights of Animals and Unborn Generations."[35] Feinberg's argument is twofold. First he demonstrates that "the sorts of beings who *can* have rights are precisely those who have (or can have) interests" (Feinberg 1980, 167). Then he goes on to show that,

> whoever these [future] human beings may turn out to be, and whatever they might reasonably be expected to be like, they will have interests that we can affect, for better or worse, right now. That much we can and do know about them. The identity of the owners of these interests is now necessarily obscure, but the fact of their interest-ownership is crystal clear, and that is all that is necessary to certify the coherence of present talk about their rights (Feinberg 1980, 181).

Future people are thus the sorts of agents that can have, although not make, moral claims.[36] In any case, it is clear enough that they are the sorts of agents in respect of whom we may have moral duties; and that is all that matters here. Given that, the question then becomes one of what their claims or our duties are and how we can justify them. This harder question has, surprisingly, attracted scant philosophical attention.

C onsistent with the voluntaristic ethos of the age, most of the arguments that have heretofore been offered for intergenerational rights and duties have been contractualist in some sense or another. None of them, however, has been particularly successful. Vulnerability-based arguments provide a far firmer foundation.

35. Golding (1972, 64) offers a far more odious solution to this problem: he argues that "whether someone's claim confers an entitlement for him to receive what is claimed *from me* depends upon my moral relation to him, on whether he is a member of my *moral community.*" Then he goes on to define "moral community" extraordinarily restrictively: "the determination depends . . . on what he is like and what are the conditions of his life" and, more specifically, on whether "the good that I acknowledge [is] . . . good for him." If I can show that "my conception of the good is not relevant to him," then Golding thinks that justifies the conclusion that " 'his kind' do not [and, morally, should not] count" from my point of view (Golding 1972, 68). His kind may have claims, but not against me and mine. On this account, "whether or not we have any obligations to future generations depends on whether we expect them to live in ways that would lead us to regard them as part of our 'moral community'. If we think they will develop in ways we disapprove of, we have no obligations to them." Having thus summarized Golding's view, Barry (1977, 272) snorts, "This view is obviously a diachronic version of the common American view that famine need only be relieved in countries with the right attitude to capitalism." The more telling criticism, to my mind, is that this is simply not how moral claims work among contemporaries. I cannot wiggle out of my debt to a creditor by showing that his conception of the good does not match my own. How can I wiggle out of my debts to future generations any more easily? Rights *in rem*—rights against the world rather than against some particular individual—are rights against the *whole* world. For those purposes, we must all be part of a single moral community.
36. Steiner (1983) argues that future generations cannot have rights, because they are logically incapable of exercising the sorts of choices that rights entail. Although it is quite enough for my purposes that we merely have duties with respect to future generations, I see nothing in Steiner's argument logically disqualifying future generations from having rights, too. After all, court-appointed guardians exercise the rights of infants and idiots even though these are just as incapable as future generations of exercising choices themselves.

John Rawls's (1971, sec. 44) version of the contractualist case for intergenerational justice is the most famous. His argument admits of various interpretations, but it succeeds in none of its possible variations. Rawls himself prefers to imagine that everyone in the "original position" is drawn from a single generation; the veil of ignorance merely prevents people from knowing their generation's place, early or late, in the history of its society (Rawls 1971, secs. 24, 44). For the Kantian interpretation of the theory, that may be enough. Each generation would prefer that its predecessors had saved; universalizing that rule, in Kantian fashion, would therefore require that each generation should itself similarly save for future ones. On the Humean version of the theory, however, this argument is of no consequence. Each generation will reason as follows: surely we wish that our predecessors had saved for us; but since we are all members of the same generation, making rules only for ourselves, we must simply take what they have done as a given; and however much or little they might have saved, we contemporaries will be better off now if we ourselves save nothing (Rawls 1971, sec. 44).

All that Rawls can do at this point to save the Humean version of his theory is to alter the motivational assumptions, saying that although people are "mutually disinterested" in the pains or pleasures of their contemporaries, they will internalize the pains and pleasures of their children.[37] As he sometimes puts it, mutual disinterestedness obtains between households, but benevolence obtains within them (Rawls 1971, sec. 24). Intergenerational transfers are just, on this account, merely because people are (or know, as a firm psychological law, that they will be) generously inclined toward their immediate successors (cf. Hubin 1976).

There are many things wrong with this response, not least of which is that it ignores "sleeper effects" (Barry 1977, 279; Richards 1983, 137–38). Intergenerational benevolence can secure some protection for the next generation, and perhaps even the one following it. But it cannot stop us from doing something now that will inflict damage, however certain and severe, on the fifth generation to come. People are not very attached psychologically to their great-great-great grandchildren (Barry 1977, 279).[38] The worst thing about

37. The alternative, to drop the Humean version and go with Kant alone, may be the only viable option; and Rawls, in his later work (none of which, however, focuses on this precise problem), seems to be pursuing that course. By taking this course Rawls would sacrifice the enormous advantages of the two-pronged attack showing that all metaethics lead to the same substantive conclusions. Rawls's conclusions then whould be no stronger than the weakest link in the Kantian chain.

38. Passmore (1980, 88–89) tries to avoid this outcome with the following argument: "Love, no doubt, extends only for a limited distance in time. Men do not love their grand-children's grand-children. They cannot love what they do not know. But in loving their grand-children . . . they hope that those grand-children, too, will have grand-children to love. They are *concerned*, to that degree, about their grand-children's grand-children. . . . Such a degree of concern for one's grand-children's grand-children is a natural consequence of one's love for one's grand-children; it is as it were, an anticipation of *their* love. . . . By this means there is established a chain of love and concern running throughout the remote future." Of course, the question is just *how much*

this approach, however, is that it is such an ad hoc response. As Barry (1977, 249) rightly complains, "The only justification offered for the 'motivational assumption' is that it enables Rawls to derive obligations to future generations. But surely this is a little too easy, like a conjurer putting a rabbit in the hat, taking it out again and expecting a round of applause."

What Rawls should have done, and what his follower David Richards (1971, 81; 1983, 137–39) does do, is to forsake the Humean version of his theory altogether at this point and go with Kant alone. Then he could say that the just arrangement is the arrangement that would command "universal hypothetical assent" among all people, present and future. In Rawlsian terminology, the people who are being asked to choose social institutions from behind the "veil of ignorance" could best be thought of as representatives of *all* generations, not just of a single one (Barry 1977, 268; 1978, 239).

Rawls himself considers the possibility of interpreting his theory this way and rejects it, saying that it would "stretch the fantasy too far" (1971, sec. 24). It is not altogether clear what he means by this. Perhaps the problem Rawls sees here is just a matter of rhetoric and persuasion. What David Richards (1983, 139) calls "the gap between the reader's intuitive moral reflections and the demands of abstract moral theory" will be reduced if the Rawlsian mind game demands merely that we imagine ourselves negotiating with our contemporaries, instead of asking us to imagine ourselves negotiating with everyone who ever has lived or ever will live. That might be a good reason, strategically, for Rawls to opt for the narrower interpretation. Philosophically it is no kind of reason at all.

The only real philosophical problem in stretching the fantasy that far was pointed out by Barry (1977, 280–82): How are we to conceptualize people who would have been born if one course of action were chosen but not if others were pursued instead? Rawls allows us only two options. One is to imagine an "original position" that is a convocation of all possible people, present and future. But then we would have to face the prospect that some of the people who join us in our deliberations in the original position might, in consequence of those deliberations, never be born. That smacks uncomfortably of making deals with ghosts. "Not to be born after you have already attended a meeting of representatives takes on too much of the aspect of dying extremely prematurely" (Barry 1977, 282; see also Hubin 1976, 74). Surely we all share Barry's disquiet at this result.[39] The alternative is to imagine an

---

concern is involved. Suppose each generation does, to some extent, internalize the utlities of each successive generation—weighting them, say, at X percent of their own in their utility functions. Then the weight that the present generation will attach to the nth generation down the line is X^n. If, for example, the weighting is 0.1, the fifth generation's utilities will weight in our present calculation at only $(0.1)^5$, or 0.00001 of our own. Passmore's chain therefore has lots of slack— and the more so the more remote the generation in question happens to be. The criticism stands.

39. Taking account of the *interests* of those who might have been born is easy enough. That is

original position that is a convocation only of people who are certain to become actual people. Yet this is no more satisfactory. The problem here is that which particular individuals (indeed, which classes of "representative individuals," in Rawls's [1971, 64] terms) become actualized depends in part upon what is choosen in the original position. It is logically incoherent to suggest that a group of people should make a choice when the composition of the group doing the choosing is itself determined by the choice.[40] The convocation of all generations is specious under either interpretation, and the Rawlsian approach to intergenerational justice is therefore untenable in any form.

Another variation on the contractualist theme holds that "the parents . . . hand down to their children the return for all which they had themselves inherited from their ancestors" (Sumner 1883, 73). This theme finds its fullest expression in modern moral philosophy in a 1970 article by Peter Laslett. In his schema, we discharge our debts to our parents through the aid we render to our children. "In the ethical exchange between procreational generations then, duties meet rights; but not in respect of the same persons" (Laslett 1970, 48). Future generations are, in this way, seen as just another instance of that familiar jurisprudential phenomenon, the third-party beneficiary.

Now, there is nothing incoherent in saying that you can sometimes discharge your obligations to one person by performing actions that benefit someone else. What is, on some accounts, incoherent is to say that those who would benefit in such circumstances themselves have any claim against you. The duty, after all, is owed to the second party, even if it is the third that would benefit from its being discharged (Hart 1955, 180). In the context of Laslett's analysis of intergenerational justice, this would have the counterintuitive consequence that past rather than future generations have claims on the present generation to do something to benefit its successors. This is hardly the way we ordinarily conceive of the situation.[41] In practical terms, however,

---

how Parfit (1976a, b; 1982; 1983a) gets around the analogous problem he has set for himself. Both Feinberg (1980, 181) and Richards (1983, 140) argue that intergenerational moral claims are predicated on the presumption that there will be future generations with interests, even if we do not know very much in particular about the individuals that will populate the future world. This sort of argument is even easier to carry off if you are looking only at that narrowly circumscribed set of interests that appear to people behind a Rawlsian "veil of ignorance," for then all peculiarities of different people's differing tastes would be filtered out. None of this, however, can help Rawls himself. The Rawlsian mind game requires not only that we know the interests of future people but also that we imagine ourselves locked in negotiations with them. Imagining yourself communing with nonexistent people is hard enough in the case of people who are merely not yet born; it is enormously more so in cases of people who *never will* be born.

40. Brian Barry, in personal correspondence (1983) clarifying the point of his 1977 article, likens this to saying that "the person who wins the lottery should be given the job of picking a number out of the hat to determine who wins."

41. One further problem is this. Laslett must presuppose that the obligations owed to our parents

the differences may not matter much: neither past nor future generations are in a position to press their claims. Besides, other legal philosophers have pointed out that third-party beneficiaries can have (Feinberg 1980, 131–32), and on some accounts must have (David Lyons 1969), the same sorts of claim rights as the second party has.

Nevertheless, the duty of the present generation (to whomever it may be owed) derives from the actions of past generations. The real problem in Laslett's analysis is how to justify the proposition that children have obligations to their parents by virtue of benefits their parents foisted upon them. This proposition has been rejected (chap. 4) in the context of the child's putative duty to support aged and infirm parents. The selfsame counterarguments could also be offered here, where the demand is that children discharge their duties to their parents by helping not the parents but rather their own children. In both cases, the crucial question is why children should be thought to have any duties to their parents in the first place. It is a well-established principle, in law as well as morals, that uncovenanted benefits confer no rights on the benefactor and no duties on the beneficiary. The children clearly have entered into no formal convenant with their parents; if we try to found these rights and duties on implicit, hypothetical convenants, then we run into problems identical to those found in Rawls's theory of intergenerational justice. Whichever way Laslett turns, he must inevitably meet insurmountable obstacles.

Another, more plausible version of three-generation analysis is captured in the concept of "trusteeship," which has been alluded to by various authors but perhaps best developed philosophically by Annette Baier (1980; see similarly Barry 1978, 242–44; 1982). In the trusteeship model, once again, it is the actions and choices of previous generations that impose moral constraints on how the present generation can treat its own successors. Our forefathers have passed on to us goods which they intended not only for us to use and enjoy but also to pass on in turn to our successors.[42] While our duties derive

are owed to them whether alive or dead. Otherwise, we would have no obligation toward our children if their grandparents happened to be dead. Yet it is far from clear that those who are already dead can have any interests or claims, or we any duties or obligations to them. Feinberg (1980, 173) admits that in this application his "interest principle" is "stretched near to the breaking point." Setting out the case against this extension, Feinberg writes, "A dead man is a mere corpse, a piece of decaying organic matter. Mere inanimate things can have no interests, and what is incapable of having interests is incapable of having rights." Although Feinberg himself eventually comes down slightly in favor of posthumous rights, Partridge (1981) carries this argument against them forward to its compelling conclusion.

42. This suggests that perhaps we are not *merely* trustees. Barry (1983b, 24), e.g., suggests that we may use up all the capital we have inherited if those who produced it did so with the intention that it should be used in precisely that way, i.e., to improve our (but not our successors') standard of living. Perhaps there is a more general case to be made for believing that we, along with all of our own successors and successors' successors, should be construed as joint heirs, each entitled to consume some share of the estate for our own purposes. How to divide up the estate among an indeterminate and maybe almost infinite set of beneficiaries is obviously an enormous problem, however.

from the actions and choices of our predecessors, the duties are owed to both our predecessors and our successors. As trustees, we have duties both to the benefactor who created the trust and to the intended beneficiaries of the trust.

This version of the contractualist analysis, while far more satisfactory than Laslett's, still contains substantial difficulties. The most serious derives from the fact that the trusteeship relationship has never been formally established. Our parents, individually or collectively, did not stipulate any such conditions as these when passing down their estates to us. We, for our part, never agreed to act as trustees when accepting their bequests. Both facts trouble the trusteeship theory of intergenerational obligations.

In principle, the problems inherent in the trusteeship model need not be insurmountable. We have plenty of experience in disposing of the effects of people who die intestate: we just attribute to them "standard preferences" regarding the disposition of their estates. We assume, for example, that had they taken the trouble to write out a will, most people would have preferred their spouses over their children, their children over their siblings, and so on. We might similarly assume that most people would want to impose some sort of trusteeship condition, requiring that their children pass on their inheritance in much the same form to their grandchildren, and so on. This can legitimately be presumed only if it were a very standard preference indeed, however. Many people leave at least some of their property to charity; but the practice is not nearly universal enough for us to suppose, in the absence of a written testament, that all would want to do so. Hence, the crucial question is just how standard might be the preference that one's heirs should receive one's bequest only on condition that they hold it in trust for their successors. That is an empirical question, to be sure. Empirically, however, the preference that heirs act as mere trustees seems not nearly universal enough for it to be imposed in this way.

Equally severe problems arise from the fact that none of us have agreed to act as trustees in this respect. Of course, that agreement need never have been made explicit. It would be enough if trusteeship were simply a widely understood condition for receiving an inheritance, with "inheritance," for these purposes, being construed to include any and all benefits created by previous generations. If, however, we expand the notion of inheritance widely enough to guarantee that the duty to provide for future generations falls on all in the present (as we firmly believe it should), then we will almost certainly have made the notion of an inheritance so broad that people have no choice but to "accept." It is by now almost universally accepted that no quasi-obligations follow from the receipt of a benefit which could not have been declined.[43] A

---

43. Baier (1980, 79) concedes that "the taking begins to occur too early to be by choice." She analyzes these as role obligations; but she goes on to say that, like "the most fundamental ones," these are not self-assumed. Here, then, as throughout chapter 4, the challenge is to explain the binding force of role obligations without recourse to notions of "self-assumed obligations." My solution emphasizes vulnerability and dependency. Baier (1980) hints at this solution herself.

further problem, less fundamental but in practice more important, is that the requisite "understanding" is not in fact "widely shared." We in the present generation have not been given "due notice" that accepting benefits from previous generations will entail trusteeship obligations with respect to future ones. Hence, no such obligations will in fact have been incurred.

A final brief in support of the claims of future generations might go as follows. Even if we have no duty to save things for our descendants, we have no right to destroy things either. Advocates of this model would argue that a Hohfeldian "no-right" is, for practical purposes, almost as good as a duty. If we have no right to destroy things, we have no recourse but to save them.

Natural resources provide the clearest example to which the above argument might be applied.[44] These resources were created by no one but were, in the first instance, merely appropriated by somebody. Picking up acorns does not give you title to destroy them wantonly, as Locke (1690, sec. 31) himself emphasizes. But the implications of this principle extend far beyond examples involving natural resources. If at most you have the right to destroy what you yourself have created, then no one can have the right to destroy capital acquired in trade or inherited from predecessors (Barry 1983b, 22–24; Page 1983, 50–52).

This approach, however, just amounts to the familiar old game of "shift the presumption." Traditionally, it is presumed to be morally permissible for property owners to do whatever they like with their property unless they have specific duties to do otherwise. The present argument protects resources for future generations by merely shifting that presumption. Here, it is presumed to be morally impermissible for property owners to destroy property unless they have some specific right to do so. Good reasons need to be given for setting the presumption one way or the other. To date, no very powerful reasons have been given for either point of view. Advocates on both sides seem to spend most of their time discrediting the opposite presupposition, as if theirs could win by default. But of course it cannot. Logically there is an intermediate possibility to be considered: it is perfectly possible that there should be no presumption either way. Indeed, the weight of arguments against either way of setting the presumption seems to support this stand. The consequence of setting no presumption is that everyone would be at liberty to destroy whatever they wished: no one would have a right to do so, but neither would anyone need such a right. Hence, unless conservationists can give much stronger positive arguments for their preferred presumption, despoilers win by default.[45]

44. See, e.g., Barry (1978, 242; 1979b, 73–78; 1980, chap. 5; 1982; 1983b).
45. Notice, furthermore, that many of the arguments that might be given to undermine the right of people to *destroy* what they did not create could also undermine their rights to do all sorts of *other* things to it or with it as well. Hence, this may turn out to be an attack on property rights as a whole. Many of those arguing this case would be pleased to argue that one as well. It should, nonetheless, be seen to be a very much larger and more difficult task.

N o analysis of intergenerational justice that is cast even vaguely in terms of reciprocity can hope to succeed. The reason is the one which Addison (1714, 594) puts into the mouth of "an old Fellow of a Colledge, who when he was pressed by the Society to come into something that might redound to the good of their Successors, grew very peevish. 'We are always doing', says he, 'something for Posterity, but I would fain see Posterity do something for us.' "

Various contemporary philosophers have remarked upon the impossibility of reciprocity in relationships between generations, and some important philosophical insights have emerged from the clash between the obvious reality of intergenerational obligations and the obvious impossibility of intergenerational reciprocity.[46] Barry (1978), for example, uses this to discredit the Humean-Rawlsian analysis of "the circumstances of justice," according to which there would be no obligations (of justice, anyway) other than those growing out of relationships of mutual advantage (Hume 1777, appendix 3; Rawls 1971, sec. 22).

Yet, by and large, these philosophers have overlooked the possibility of deriving intergenerational obligations from precisely the fact that we enjoy "unilateral power" over the generations that succeed us (Barry 1977, 270). Obviously, we can help or harm them in a way that they will never be able to help or harm us.[47] In many respects they are completely dependent upon us for providing help or for averting harm. Whatever we destroy or use up will be unavailable for future generations to enjoy. Indeed, the only way they will have anything at all (beyond that which they can create for themselves out of thin air) is for us to leave it to them. The vulnerability of succeeding generations to our actions and choices seems to be the strongest basis for assigning to present ones strong responsibilities for providing for them.[48]

46. See, e.g., Laslett (1970), Golding (1972, 65), Hubin (1976), Barry (1977, 280, 273; 1979b, 69–72), Baier (1980), and Parfit (1982, 114).

47. This conclusion is predicated on my rejection above of notions of "posthumous interests/rights." Even if we admit such notions, the relationship is still not one of reciprocity. As Barry (1977, 270) points out, even if future generations "control a resource which may matter to us, we have no way of negotiating an agreement with them to the effect that they will treat our reputations [or posthumous interests more generally] in a certain way if we behave now in a certain way."

48. Philosophers occasionally acknowledge this point in passing but fail to appreciate its real force. David Richards (1983, 146), perhaps, comes closest when remarking that future generations "are uniquely vulnerable and powerless, much more so than the stigmatized groups (for example, blacks or women) singled out for special protection under American constitutional concepts of equal protection." Although he argues for extending such constitutional rights to future generations, his justification for that seems to derive from a kind of Kantian-Rawlsian contractualism rather than from the fact of this vulnerability itself. Passmore (1980, 98), too, observes that "we now stand, if the more pessimistic scientists are right, in a special relationship to the future; unless we act, posterity will be helpless to do so. This imposes duties on us which would not otherwise fall to our lot." The truth of this proposition is nowise predicated upon the accuracy of any *particularly* pessimistic forecasts; indeed, it is an absurdly *optimistic* forecast that would predict future generations to be utterly invulnerable to our present actions and choice. Baier (1980, 179, 174) also partially recognizes the moral importance of vulnerability when she

In tracing the implications of this argument for responsibilities to future generations, little more needs be said than has already been said in connection with the previous applications to the welfare state and foreign aid. Responsibilities toward future generations should also be seen primarily as collective ones. The duty falls upon everyone in the present generation to organize and participate in coordinated schemes for protecting the interests of succeeding generations. Some people will inevitably fail to discharge these duties, but the delict of some does not excuse the others from doing their duty. As long as there remains something we (individually or collectively) can do to protect the interests of vulnerable future generations, we should do it, *ceteris paribus*.

Here, again, there may be affective as well as material vulnerabilities. Specifically, there may be affective links between us and our children and our children's children that will be missing between us and the tenth generation. Such affective links mean that we should provide assistance to our particular successors in proximate generations, even if in purely material terms others were marginally better able to do so. A further consequence is that my argument will, in light of these affective vulnerabilities, permit us to give more to our nearer temporal neighbors and less to our distant descendants than would have been justified in the absence of such links. But here again, the bias introduced by such considerations is necessarily slight and easily overridden by considerations arising out of vulnerabilities of a more material sort.

There may be various other reasons for supposing that people will be less vulnerable to us, and our responsibilities towards them correspondingly weaker, the more distant from us they are in time. First, risk and uncertainty tend to increase with distance (in space or time) from the event we are trying to influence. Second, if people in the future continue to get richer and richer whatever we do, then they will be less and less vulnerable to our present savings decisions. The implications of both these arguments is the progressive weakening of our responsibilities to the future generations. Both arguments, however, turn upon highly contestable empirical propositions. They may not be true at all; this seems especially likely with respect to the claim that future generations will be ever richer. Alternatively, both claims may be true in general but not for any particular case. Furthermore, even if they are generally true, they are unlikely to be true in the form that would justify ordinary discounting procedures, whereby the present value of future payoffs diminishes in a geometrical progression with the time it takes for them to accrue (Goodin 1982a). Therefore, although the vulnerability argument may allow for some discounting of the future, it does not allow for anything like the dramatic discounting that is practiced at present.

---

writes that "the relations that form a moral community, and which, once recognized, give rise to obligations, all concern dependency and interdependency." Yet in analyzing intergenerational obligations, she chooses to focus merely on the fact that future generations depend "on some representative . . . . empowered to speak for them" in the present generation. Actually, of course, they are dependent upon us for far more than *that*.

Environmental Protection

As with unborn generations, so too with animals, plants, and other fixtures of the natural environment: the moral argument has hardly gotten past first base. The main preoccupation is still with establishing the moral status of the objects in question. This issue is further complicated, in the case of animals especially, by a fixation on their rights rather than on our duties with respect to them.

Nearly everyone agrees that rights can be predicated only of agents possessing "interests."[49] Although there are still a few hold-outs against animals having interests (e.g., Frey 1980), the main protagonists in this dispute— McCloskey (1965, 122–27) and Feinberg (1980, 159–84)—now agree that animals do have interests in the morally relevant sense. Having conceded that point, McCloskey (1983, chap. 6) quite rightly goes on to query whether having interests is a sufficient rather than only a necessary condition of having rights. Curiously enough, almost all the earlier discussions seemed to suggest that it was sufficient.[50] Surely it is not: as McCloskey emphasizes, all sort of things can have interests without having rights. Thus, the argument for animal rights remains incomplete.[51]

---

49. The sequence of argument and counterargument that led to this conclusion was as follows. The opponents of animal rights maintained that (1) rights are claims; (2) animals are incapable of making claims; (3) therefore animals are incapable of having rights. This conclusion drew the obvious reply: one need not *make* claims to *have* claims. All sorts of human beings who indisputably have rights (e.g., underage heirs) are in no position to claim them. We appoint guardians to represent their interests, and there is no reason in principle why we could not appoint a human mouthpiece to enunciate animals' claims. Medieval practice seems to have done just that; one sixteeth-century source holds that "even rats have a right of counsel" (Clark 1977, 20). Contemporary lawyers are arguing that we should do the same for trees (Stone 1972). What *is* true, however, is that "representing" clients (be they heirs or hares) must necessarily be a matter of representing their *interests*. Hence the conclusion that only things with interests capable of representation can be accorded the status of right holder. For the best exposition of this position, see Feinberg (1980, 159—84). The only alternative seriously mooted is Regan's (1979): that we should ascribe rights to anything with inherent value. That, however, would have consequences that even the most sensitive environmentalist would probably find absurd. On that account, for example, we would have violated rights every time we made an arithmetic error, assuming, as most people surely would, that "truth" (including the necessary truths of mathematics) is of intrinsic value.
50. See, e.g., Frey (1980, 5); Attfield (1981), and Mish'alani (1982, 137).
51. Feinberg (1980, 166) passes from the proposition that animals can have rights to the proposition that they do have them with this simple and unsatisfactory argument: "ask ourselves for whose sake ought we to treat . . . animals with consideration and humaneness. . . . If we hold . . . that we ought to do so for the animals' own sake, . . . then it follows that we do ascribe rights to animals." It is not at all clear to me, for one, that the claims of animals do in fact "pass this phenomenological test." Argument is required; Feinberg offers only intuitions. Notice that I say merely that the case for animal rights is not yet proven. It should be emphasized that arguments *against* them are equally indecisive. One of the more famous is that line initiated by Ritchie (1900) and pursued by Passmore (1980, 116, 216): "If it is essential to a community that the members of it have common interests and recognise mutual obligations then men, plants, animals and soil do not form a community. Bacteria and men do not recognise mutual obligations nor do they have common interests. In the only sense in which belonging to a community generates ethical obligation, they do not belong to the same community." But, of course, neither

The whole question of animal rights is, however, of far less significance than is ordinarily supposed. Animal lovers have overstretched themselves in striving to establish full-fledged rights for animals. They could equally well— indeed, far better—argue for the same results if, following Hume's (1777, sec. 3, pt.1) lead, they couched their case in terms of our duties rather than of animals' rights. As a modern champion of the cause of animals says: "Let it be that animals have no *rights;* they can still be wronged" (Clark 1977, 29; see similarly Frey 1980, 12; Passmore 1980, chap. 5). That fact is what provides the real force behind objections to the mistreatment of animals.

Sometimes the language of rights is employed to highlight the fact that our objection to the mistreatment of animals is a distributional one, an objection to our using them for our benefit (T. Regan 1980). Of course, assigning real rights to animals would be one way of grounding such a distributional objection, but it is not the only one. There are a great many ways of describing the wrongness of the (mal)distribution of pains and pleasures between man and beast without recourse to notions of rights. One version of the argument asks us to universalize our moral principles over all sentient creatures, either by imagining ourselves to be in their places (Godlovitch 1971) or by choosing our principles from behind a veil of ignorance so thick as to preclude our knowing whether we are man or beast (VanDeVeer 1980). Another version of the argument for the decent treatment of animals turns upon the principle of equal consideration of interests, animals' and ours alike (Singer 1975; 1980).

What is crucial for all those arguments—and what will prove to be crucial for mine as well—is that animals possess morally significant interests. As long as this is true, considerations of animals' interests could be quite sufficient to impose on us strong responsibilities with respect to them, whether or not rights are involved.

It is unclear what might go into making interests morally significant or, perhaps more important, what might preclude them from being morally significant. For the sake of my earlier arguments, I make a relatively noncontentious assumption that the interests of human beings are *ipso facto* morally significant. There may well be more dispute where the interests of animals are concerned. But those who deny their moral importance should bear the burden of justifying differential treatment of agents' interests depending upon whose interests they are. Favoring human interests over animal interests for no other reason than that they are ours surely constitutes a morally impermissible form of "human chauvinism" (Routley and Routley 1979). For present purposes, therefore, let us proceed on the provisional assumption that interests per se are morally significant, no matter whose interests they are.

---

infants nor mental incompetents recognize mutual obligations. The fact that they are incapable of discharging duties does not prevent them from having certain rights, in their role as "wards of the moral community" (Mish'alani 1982, 132). Animals and even inanimate objects clearly could, and perhaps should, be regarded similarly.

By my analysis, what gives rise to our special duties to protect animals from pain and suffering is their peculiar vulnerability to us. Although that vulnerability may be to individuals—to the hunter or the factory farmer, for instance—it usually also extends to us collectively, since the animals are dependent on the collectivity's legislating against the cruel practices of individuals who might contravene merely moral duties in this regard. Animals are also vulnerable to us collectively even where they are not particularly vulnerable to any one of us individually: much of the damage we do to their interests is through the cumulative effects of many actions by many people, each of which is independently of little consequence. Individually or collectively, then, we can have a strong impact on their interests, which fact alone is sufficient to give rise to strong responsibilities on our part in respect of them.

This point is often recognized, but usually in passing. John Stuart Mill (1848, bk. 5, chap. 11, sec. 9), tracing the limits of the "non-intervention principle," touches on the case of "defenceless creatures" such as slaves and animals. Reflecting on cruelty to such creatures he writes, "The domestic life of domestic tyrants is one of the things which it is the most imperative on the law to interfere with." Feinberg (1980, 161, 189) quotes repeatedly and approvingly John Chipman Gray's injunction that we should "preserve the dumb brutes from suffering." McCloskey (1983, 122) canvasses the possibility that "helpless animals . . . would need protection similar to that needed by helpless infants." Steven Clark (1977, 17, 22, 30), in his discussion of "man's prerogatives" vis-à-vis animals, asks us to "suppose for a moment that . . . animals, and children, and the old, the sick, the defenceless and our posterity have no rights at all. Are we . . . ready to assert that we may decently do as we please with them?" He concludes that "they may justly resent our conduct when they lay at our mercy" and offers in partial explanation of that claim the proposition that "those that are weak deserve our especial care. . . . A powerful, amiable, useful male citizen is in little danger of oppression: it is the unamiable, the powerless, who need protection against the strong." None of these statements amount to much more than comments-in-passing on the vulnerability model's argument for the protection of animals, however.[52]

---

52. Some evidence of animals' vulnerability as the grounds for our duties with respect to them might be found in connection with laws regulating hunting and the treatment of domestic pets. We are almost universally prohibited from shooting sitting ducks or from using a spotlight at night to blind and hence "freeze" our prey. One reason we impose such rules on hunters may be that under those circumstances the prey (sitting ducks, fawns caught in a spotlight, etc.) would be completely helpless, without any chance whatsoever of escaping; and even hunters are obliged to protect the interests of creatures who are so completely vulnerable to them. The same, I think, might be said of the "special claims" our domestic pets are said to have against us, under both our conventional moral and legal codes. Ritchie (1900, 388) is no doubt partly right in thinking that these follow from their "quasi-human character"; in giving my dog a personal name, I grant him honorary human status, with all the rights and duties appertaining thereto. Another even more important consideration in generating special moral duties toward domestic pets is that, by domesticating them, we have deprived them of much of their capacity (and most of their will) to

A s we move down the order of nature from animals to vegetables to rocks, it becomes increasingly doubtful that the objects in view can have interests of their own which command our respect. Feinberg (1980, 168) for example, concludes that trees are morally different from "the higher species of animals" because, "having no conscious wants or goals of their own trees cannot know satisfaction or frustration, pleasure or pain." Interests, Feinberg goes on to argue, "are compounded out of *desires* and *aims,* both of which presuppose something like *belief,* or cognitive awareness." This is precisely what trees lack. Certainly they have natural propensities, for example, to seek water and light; but "mere brute longings unmediated by beliefs . . . are altogether different from the sort of thing we mean by 'desire' " (Feinberg 1980, 168–69).[53]

As we move still further down the natural order, it becomes ever more doubtful that the objects in view can have interests of a morally significant kind. Where animals are concerned, Feinberg regards it as a debatable proposition and decides in the affirmative (cf. Frey 1980). Where trees are concerned, Feinberg still regards it as debatable but decides in the negative.[54] Where rocks are concerned, the question of morally significant interests is not even debatable. Rocks might be "morally considerable" on various other grounds (Goodpaster 1979), on more of which later; but as far as interests go, it is just as obvious that they lack them as it is that humans possess them.

For Feinberg's purposes, these questions concerning morally significant interests are crucial for deciding whether animals, trees, on so on, are capable of possessing rights. Here I have shunned the language of rights. The same questions about interests, however, remain as crucial for my purposes as for his. Only things with interests of their own can qualify directly, in and of themselves, for protection under the principle for which I have been arguing. The phrasing of that principle is important: we have special responsibilities to

---

protect themselves against cruel masters. That renders them peculiarly vulnerable to their owners, and according to my argument would give rise to peculiarly strong responsibilities on the part of the owners to protect them.

53. Presumably Feinberg would insist even more firmly upon this conclusion with regard to things like ecosystems or babbling brooks which, while possessed of a "teleology" in some sense or another, could not conceivably be said to be possessed of any form of consciousness whatsoever. Other writers, of course, deny the importance of "self-consciousness," arguing, for example, that a "self-ameliorative competence" is quite sufficient to ground interests (Mish'alani 1982, 136–40; see also Goodpaster 1979). Stone's (1972, 471) rejoinder, although less subtle, is in many ways more powerful. To those who claim that the interests of the environment are incapable of being communicated or hence represented, he says: "I am sure I can judge with more certainty and meaningfulness whether and when my lawn wants (needs) water, that the Attorney General can judge whether and when the United States wants (needs) to take an appeal from an adverse judgment by a lower court. The lawn tells me that it wants water by a certain dryness of the blades and soil—immediately obvious to the touch—the appearance of bald spots, yellowing, and a lack of springiness after being walked on; how does the United States communicate to the Attorney General?"

54. Cf. Stone (1972), Goodpaster (1979), and Attfield (1981).

protect those who have morally important *interests* that are particularly vulnerable to our actions and choices. Under that principle, we can have special responsibilities only in respect of things that have interests of their own. On the basis of Feinberg's careful analysis, animals might qualify for direct protection, while trees, rocks, landscapes, and landmarks would not.

Admittedly, this is not a particularly pleasing result. Surely there is something wrong with flooding the Grand Canyon or the southwest Tasmanian wilderness. Intuitively, what is wrong seems to be closely related to such considerations as I have been discussing.

One way to accommodate these cognate intuitions within my model would be to recast the principle in terms of "intrinsic values" rather than interests. The obligation would then be to protect the *value* of things that are particularly vulnerable to our actions and choices. The values to be protected would then be not only subjective (interests) but also objective (Tribe 1974). Among the things that are ordinarily thought to have objective value are truth and beauty. Arguments against "faking nature" often invoke aesthetic principles to distinguish the "fake" from the "genuine article";[55] and just such considerations figure largely in appeals to preserve all sorts of natural wonders— forests, waterfalls, canyons, coral reefs, and so forth—in their pristine, natural form.[56] Arguments for protecting endangered species (or the "last of its kind" more generally) often seem to appeal to similar values, albeit more obliquely. In the end, however, this amounts to little more than an analogy. No particularly powerful arguments can be adduced for it; either you "see it," or you do not (Elliot 1980, 16).

Even if this analogy between works of art and works of nature does not hold, the Grand Canyon is still not totally bereft of protection under my principle. Although it might not be entitled to any protection directly, in its own right, it may still have an enormously strong indirect claim by virtue of the interests of hundreds of thousands of people worldwide in preserving such a spectacular natural landscape. Ritchie (1900, 388), for example, argues that although we loosely speak of such duties "as owed to inanimate things, . . . our duties to an ancient building, a beautiful landscape, an historic oak, a family heirloom . . . are really and strictly owed to humanity." If so, legislation designed to protect such objects should not be construed as legislation protecting *their* interests, but rather "as legislation protecting the interests human beings may have in them" (Feinberg 1980, 169). Whetwell's

---

55. See, e.g., Benn (1977), Passmore (1980, 101), Elliot (1982), and Goodin (1983).
56. The best example of this sort of argument is Passmore's (1980, 124–25, 217) allusion to the notion of "vandalism." This points to a principle to which we are all firmly committed: "it is wrong unnecessarily to destroy"; "the moral onus is on anyone who destroys." This notion of vandalism applies paradigmatically to human artifacts, and most especially to works of art; "it is very natural to extend it to the destruction of nature as well. . . . The man who cuts his name on a redwood is being a vandal, just as much as the man who scratches his initials on the portico of Wells Cathedral."

remarks concerning laws against the bear baiting may well apply to legal measures designed to protect the natural environment more generally: "Such laws are enacted to prevent what is repugnant to the general feeling of the English public"—no more, no less (quoted in Clark 1977, 12; see similarly Sagoff 1974).

Tying our duties to protect the natural environment to the interest we happen to take in it makes my argument for those duties uncomfortably contigent: if it so happens that we have no interest in nature, then we will have no moral responsibilities with respect to it. Much of the discomfort associated with that result can be removed by reflecting upon the fact that the "we" in question is composed of a virtually infinite series of future people.[57] As I have argued elsewhere, if there is a chance that we or any of our successors will come to regard an object as irreplaceable, one for whose loss they could not be compensated, then in purely want-regarding terms it is prima facie wrong to destroy it (Goodin 1983). Protecting what future generations will (or even might) come to value is, then, just a special case of protecting the interests of future generations. Understood broadly, that principle can have roughly the same practical implications as a principle of protecting the natural environment in its own right.

What must be emphasized, in connection with my larger argument, is that even according to this more modest interpretation, our responsibilities to protect natural environments are still predicated upon "nature's *vulnerability* to human depredations" (Passmore 1980, 176, emhasis added). Here "vulnerability" is used in a broader sense than before. It no longer refers to the fact that somethings' own interests are vulnerable to our acts but instead to the fact that their states are easily altered by our interventions. Those alterations matter morally only because people's (or perhaps animals') interests are sensitive, in turn, to such alterations in the natural environment. Unless *both* types of vulnerability—state based as well as interest based—were present, we would have no particularly strong responsibilities to protect the environments in question. Such responsibilites come into play only when we can make a difference that makes a difference, so to speak.

The role of vulnerability in generating environmental obligations emerges most clearly through various allusions to our trusteeship or stewardship relation vis-à-vis nature (Sax 1970; Attfield 1983, chap. 3). Originally, of course, these duties were grounded in theology. In one seven-

---

57. On duties to protect our own future selves, see Goodin (1982b, chap. 3). Regan (1984) offers a similar object for preserving natural objects: we can (indeed, by his argument "should") "learn about and take pleasure in" them even if we do not do so at present. If people can have "posthumous" claims, then the class of claimants expands still further. Many arguments for environmental stewardship do indeed take the form "we owe it to our forefathers to pass down intact what we inherited from them"; but that attributes "posthumous interests" to people, which is of course contentious (Feinberg 1980, 173; Partridge 1981).

teenth-century text, for example, we find Chief Justice Sir Matthew Hale arguing, "The end of man's creation was, that he should be the viceroy of the great God of heaven and earth in this inferior world; his steward, *villicus* [farm manager], bailiff or farmer of this goodly farm of the lower world" (quoted in Passmore 1980, 30). Even to this day, a quasi-theological residue remains in such arguments. Barry (1977, 284), for example, traces his "strong conviction that we would be wrong to take risks with the continuation of human life" not to human interests but rather to "a sense of its cosmic impertinence—. . . we should be grossly abusing our position by taking it upon ourselves to put a term on human life and its possibilities."

It is not at all clear how we can ground stewardship obligations without recourse to theology. Certainly no analysis of these as self-assumed obligations will suffice. "We made no decision individually or collectively to fill the role of superintendent of nature. Like so many of the roles we occupy as individuals, this one was foisted on us by circumstances, and we occupy it as if by default" (Feinberg 1980, 205).

I suggest that the notion of "vulnerability" provides the firmest foundations for obligations of environmental stewardship. Vulnerability, of course, generates responsibilities only in conjunction with some theory of interests or values; and it is not altogether clear whether we should focus on the interests of humans (past, present, or future), or more generally on the interests of animals, or more generally still on intrinsic values. Whatever the conclusion at this stage of the argument, the next step always remains the same. The emphasis there is always upon duties that follow from "the requirements of our unique station as rational custodians of the planet we temporarily occupy" (Feinberg 1980, 205). What really matters, at one crucial point in the argument at least, is the vulnerability of the earth and its inhabitants to our actions and choices.

Sometimes nature is vulnerable to the actions and choices of a particular individual. Domestic pets are especially (if not exclusively) vulnerable to the action and choices of their owners; the southern shores of Lake Michigan were especially (although hardly exclusively) vulnerable to the actions and choices of Elbert Gary, back in the days when Judge Gary *was* United States Steel. Such vulnerabilities impose strong personal responsibilities on those particular individuals.

More often, however, environmental degradation results from the combination of many people's actions and choices, no one of which is particularly crucial in itself. No single individual (or small group of individuals) can be said to have strong personal responsibility to protect an environment that is largely invulnerable to his particular actions or choices. The environment *is,* however, vulnerable to the actions and choices of many people taken together. Indeed, since ecosystems embody various threshold and multiplier effects, the damage done by the whole community will far exceed the damage done by the sum of its parts. This, of course, constitutes the classic rationale for enforceable social rules as mere coordination devices (Harrod 1936, 148; Goodin 1976, chaps. 3–5).

People are, as I have shown in chapter 5, under a strong collective responsibility to organize and participate in cooperative schemes to protect that which is vulnerable to them collectively. The environment qualifies for protection under this principle. The details of possible protective schemes may vary greatly, along with the moral and pragmatic considerations that guide us in choosing between them (Goodin 1976, 144–98).[58] Nevertheless, the obligation to organize cooperative schemes to protect vulnerable environments is clear, at least in broad outline. For present purposes, that is enough.

Conclusion

In this chapter I have explored the extended implications of vulnerability. I have shown that the principle of protecting the vulnerable gives rise not only to the standard special responsibilities (to our families, friends, clients, etc.) but also to strictly analogous special responsibilities toward vulnerable compatriots, foreigners, future generations, animals, and natural environments. More often than not, these newly discovered responsibilities are collective rather than individual ones. They are none the less compelling.

The more special responsibilities there are, the greater the risk of conflict between them. I have shown that all these special responsibilities can be traced back to the same fundamental principle, making their attendant moral demands at least theoretically commensurable. But that is not to say that all the responsibilities will necessarily, or even probably, have the same weight. Therefore, the question of how to adjudicate between conflicting responsibilities becomes particularly important.

In chapter 5 I laid down some principles for settling such conflicts. There I suggested that vulnerabilities and correlative responsibilities were greater the more strongly and directly others were affected by your actions and choices or the more limited their alternative sources of assistance. These two considerations go some way toward reducing the relative urgency of our responsibilities with respect to people distant in time or space. No doubt such considerations

58. One complication is well worth noting, however. It is rarely strictly necessary for absolutely everyone to take part in the cooperative scheme if our goal is simply to protect vulnerable environments. We can usually afford a few free riders; and there will inevitably be a fair bit of jockeying for that privilege (Taylor and Ward 1982). Unfair though free riding assuredly is, I would argue that our preeminent concern should be with the protection of the vulnerable—here, vulnerable environments. The objection that a cooperative scheme is less than universally respected and suffers from a few free riders is a decisive objection only if the participants are thereby precluded from achieving their goal of protecting the vulnerable. Thus, for example, Kennan (1970) quite rightly suggests that a "club" of rich nations should band together to protect the environment internationally: "it is they whose economies produce the pollution problem," and action by them alone is quite sufficient to solve that problem on an international scale (see also Goodin 1976, chap. 17).

are invoked far too often, to justify far too much stinginess with aid to distant peoples or future generations. Still, to the extent that genuine risks or uncertainties are present, we must discount the anticipated benefits of our actions accordingly (Goodin 1982b, chap. 9).

Notice, however, that we are still giving equal weight to everyone's interests in such calculations. We do not discount the pains and pleasures of distant peoples but merely our estimates of the ways in which our present actions and choices might affect them. Where human beings—present or future, near or far—are concerned, the proper principle is indeed "each counts for one, none for more than one" (Goodin 1982b, 16–18, 162–83).

Where animals are concerned, I am much less confident of that judgment. From the Stoics forward, we constantly hear the complaint that

> human life . . . could become quite impossible if men thought of themselves as governed in their relationships with animals by [the same] moral considerations [as govern relationships with other men]. It would then be quite wrong to kill animals for food, to harness them for work in the fields, to use them as beasts of burden. And that would mean the collapse of civilisation—"we shall be living the life of beasts once we give up the use of beasts" (Passmore 1980, 113).

Now, of course, the complaint as stated cannot stand: that result does not follow merely from letting "moral considerations" govern our relationships with animals; it does not even follow from letting the *same* moral considerations govern them; it follows instead (if at all) only from one particular way of weighting the claims of animals within those principles. That risk can become a serious one only if we weight the claims of animals the same (or nearly the same) as our own. There I may well hesitate, joining MacIver (1948, 65) in the judgment that "if I tread wantonly on the woodlouse, I do wrong . . . but it is only a small wrong, and to exaggerate its wrongfulness is sentimentality. Little wrongs have to be done in order that greater wrongs may be avoided. If I kill a Colorado beetle, I do wrong by the beetle; but, if I fail to kill it, I do wrong by all the farmers and consumers of potatoes, and their interests are vastly more important." Since I can offer no mechanism to help us decide how much more heavily their interests should weigh, I shall simply leave the matter there.[59]

59. I must, however, note that a pair of extreme alternatives both prove unsatisfactory. Stanley Benn (1977, 407) would give animals' interests *no* weight, on the grounds that animals have none of the sorts of "projects, plans, etc." that impart moral significance to human lives. By that token, however, it would be permissible for a trustee to embezzle funds from a trust set up for a human vegetable, who has equally few plans, projects, etc. That will not do. Nor will Peter Singer's (1979, chaps. 3–4) suggestion that we should give equal consideration to all interests, be they of humans or of animals. He tries to reassure us that his will not lead to the result Passmore fears, because other animals are capable of less suffering than are humans (especially that

My theory is admittedly imcomplete at the margins, where its implications for animals and the natural environment are concerned.[60] But it should be emphasized that these considerations are indeed marginal ones and that even there the uncertainty does not relate to *whether* they deserve protection but merely to *how much* they deserve.

---

associated with the anticipation of suffering). His argument here is, however, predicated upon some very demanding interspecies utility comparisons (Singer 1979, 88–90). It is hard enough to imagine yourself in the position of certain other people (cf. Sen 1979a); when you try to imagine yourself in the position of animals, I deeply suspect that the results will be nothing more than pure imagination. Elsewhere (Goodin 1982b, 16–18) I have argued that the only proper way to perform interpersonal utility comparisons is to stipulate, by moral edict, how much each person's sum-total utility (or ''most preferred state,'' if you prefer that language) is to count for, compared with everyone else's. The same goes for animals, too, at least until such time as we get a reliable hedonometer that is calibrated to register reliably the utilities of both man and beast.

60. I must also admit that I am inclined to attach more importance to the preservation of some whole species than to the preservation of any particular human individual. I am also inclined to extend that principle to cover any particularly spectacular and unique natural landscape. What that points to is, I think, a more general inclination to ''let each kind count for one, and none for more than one.'' How exactly we differentiate kinds is, of course, tricky. For certain purposes we are prepared to treat such natural wonders as Yosemite or the Grand Canyon as ''one of a kind,'' and make considerable sacrifices (of human life, if necessary) to protect them. For other purposes, we are prepared to think in terms of different kinds of animals, and accordingly protect endangered species—again, sometimes at substantial cost (Clark 1977, 171). For still other purposes, we regard each different human culture or community as ''one of a kind,'' and that explains why we object to ''genocide,'' over and above our objections to the killing of the individuals who carry that culture. For yet other purposes, we treat each human individual as unique and irreplaceable, ''one of a kind.'' If we are to ''let each kind count for one and none for more than one,'' then how we differentiate ''kinds'' is obviously going to make a big difference in the weights assigned various considerations in policymaking. To decide what is the proper weight, we therefore need a strong theory to guide us in switching between various criteria of different ''kinds.'' Having no such theory to offer, I am once again incapable of providing any detailed guidance on the proper weighting of environmental versus human values. Nevertheless, I can indicate what such a theory would look like in broad outline, and perhaps even roughly what conclusions such a theory should reach.

7

Invulnerability as an Alternative

John Stuart Mill deemed it "the great error of reformers and philanthropists . . . to nibble at the consequences of unjust power, instead of redressing the injustice itself" (1848, bk. 5, chap. 11, sec. 9). This complaint echoes into our own day. "Social democrats are sensitive to the effects of exploitation on people, but not to the fact of exploitation itself. They want to succour the exploited while minimizing confrontation with those who exploit them" (G. A. Cohen 1981, 14). Such complaints may well be lodged against my previous chapters.[1] There I have been primarily concerned with what morally follows from the fact that someone is in a weak, vulnerable, dependent position. Repeatedly, my argument has been that those to whom one is vulnerable and upon whom one depends are morally bound to do what they can to protect one.

In this chapter I turn to the moral evaluation of that antecedent condition itself. Having shown that if people are vulnerable we must protect them, I now ask whether it is morally proper for people to be in a vulnerable position in the first place. Logically, this is a separate question.[2] It is also an extremely

---

1. This is particularly true, perhaps, because of my continuing emphasis upon people's duties with respect to those who are vulnerable, rather than vulnerable people's rights against them. Rodman (1973, 493) picks up this theme in his plea for "children's rights" in particular: "Except for the institutionalized, who live in a state of enforced childishness, no other group is so totally dependent for its well-being on choices made by others [as are children]. Obviously this dependency can be explained to a significant degree by the physical, intellectual and physiological incapacities of (some) children which render them weaker than (some) older persons. But the phenomenon must also be seen as part of the organization and ideology of the political system itself. . . . The basic rationale for depriving people of rights in a dependency relationship is that certain individuals are incapable or undeserving of the right to take care of themselves and consequently need social institutions specifically designed to safeguard their position. It is presumed that under the circumstances society is doing what is best for the individuals. Along with the family, past and present examples of such arrangements include marriage, slavery and the Indian reservation system."
2. Certain modal logics may imply that the one does inevitably follow from the other: the norm that "we ought to help people who have been robbed" presupposes that there actually are people who have been robbed; so that seems to suggest that the former norm implies another, namely, that people *ought* to be robbed. In the present context, we might infer from the norm that we ought to protect people who are vulnerable a further proposition that people *ought* to be vulner-

important one in practice. Quite possibly, a better response to a situation of vulnerability or dependency is not to protect the person but to free him from his condition and hence from any need for special protection (Gaylin 1978, 30).

T his option arises only insofar as dependencies and vulnerabilities of others lie within our power to alter.[3] At first brush, it appears that they do not. The circumstances that make people vulnerable and dependent are, paradigmatically, things like physical and psychological incapacities. In one sense, these clearly are "natural" rather than "social" states: they relate to objective rather than socially constructed features of people's physical and mental states.

For purposes of this argument, however, that is not enough. Dependency or vulnerability is "natural" in a sense that relieves us of responsibility only if it is by nature fixed, inevitable, and immutable. That is not completely true in the case of disabling mental or physical illness. Which and how many people become ill is in part a function of existing social arrangements. Which people recover and how quickly is also in part a function of society's choices in allocating resources to the task. How much independence is secured in the process of recovery is also in part a function of the way we organize certain crucial social institutions. Social psychologists studying the behavior of patients show that hospital staff and routines encourage and reward "learned helplessness" (Seligman 1975; Raps et al. 1982), and the same seems to be true for institutions caring for the aged (Townsend 1981, 13–23; Booth et al. 1983; Gibson 1984).

Most important of all, however, is the fact that how disabling any given physical or mental condition will turn out to be also depends in part on existing social arrangements. Inability to climb stairs is no handicap if all buildings are provided with wheelchair ramps, and so on. The same is also true of those other ostensibly natural dependencies, conceded as such by Titmuss (1958, 42) himself, connected with childhood, childbearing, and extreme old age. Even if the physical states are truly inevitable and immutable, the social disadvantages attaching to them can obviously vary, depending on the choices made by a society. As philosophers have long realized and as social scientists

---

able. No one, however, is willing to embrace that conclusion. On the contrary, this so-called Good Samaritan paradox has always been thought to discredit the logical systems that give rise to it. Logicians have, by now, found several alternative formulations of model logic that would avoid any such paradox. See, e.g., Prior (1958, 144), Nowell-Smith and Lemmon (1960), Routley and Nozick (1962), Castañeda (1975, chap. 7), and Vermazen (1977).

3. In the desert-based argument for welfare services, it is crucial to show that society is to blame for people's misfortunes and hence should be responsible for ameliorating them. Most writers have therefore pursued backward-looking questions ("to what extent is society responsible for creating the dependency in the first place?"). See, e.g., Titmuss (1958); Rein (1965, 89–92). Here, however, I emphasize the forward-looking question ("what can society do to relieve dependency?").

are now coming to realize, "socially contrived dependencies shape, supplement and balance natural and unavoidable dependencies" (Baier 1980, 179).[4]

All of this goes to show that any dependency or vulnerability is arguably created, shaped, or sustained, at least in part, by existing social arrangements. None is wholly natural. We can go further still: some of the most important dependencies and vulnerabilities seem to be almost wholly social in character. "Apart from injury, disease and innate incapacity," Titmuss (1958, 3) argues, " 'man-made' dependencies . . . now constitute the major source of instability in the satisfaction of basic needs." Among these manmade dependencies he lists "unemployment and under-employment, . . . compulsory retirement from work, the delayed entry of young people into the labour market, and an infinite variety of subtle cultural factors ranging from the right trade union ticket to the possession of status symbols."

Titmuss sees all of the above conditions producing dependency by affecting incomes. All entail "some degree" of "destruction, curtailment, interruption or frustration of earning power in the individual." Indeed, many dependencies arising out of the quasi-natural conditions of childhood, childbearing, old age, and so forth, can be traced fairly directly to outright "workforce exclusion" (Tulloch 1983). With the advent of industrialization, it came to be the case that "the individual's *social* security depended upon *economic* security which, in turn, depended upon *income* security" (Heclo 1974, 29). Those who are themselves precluded from holding paid employment are thus forced to depend for support on others who do. Yet notice that the young, the pregnant, and the old are excluded from the work force by choices of society rather than by facts of nature. They are not physically unable to perform any and all tasks for which they might receive remuneration, although there certainly are some jobs they would be unable to do. They are instead excluded from the work force on account of social conventions—sometimes explicit edicts (e.g., compulsory retirement policies) but more often masquerading as impersonal market forces ("labor force demands")—which prevent them from holding even those jobs for which they would be physically and mentally suited.[5]

None of this is necessarily an argument against these social policies. Child labor laws, for example, are not necessarily a bad thing.[6] I am here merely arguing against the proposition that dependencies are ever wholly beyond the

4. See similarly Rousseau (1762a, bk. 2), Wollstonecraft (1792), and Mill (1869).
5. See, e.g., Marks (1975), Skolnick (1975), Gaylin (1978, 29–30), Kane and Kane (1979), Graycar and Kinnear (1981, 50–55), Passmore (1981, 34–35), Townsend (1981, 10–13), and Walker (1980; 1982).
6. The argument in favor of them is presumably this. Certain characteristics that *are* naturally associated with childhood—limited information, understanding, sophistication, etc.—make children inevitably vulnerable (i.e., incapable of protecting their own interests) in ordinary labor markets. Their natural vulnerability in these respects is so severe that the only way to protect them adequately is to prohibit child labor altogether.

power of society to control. Having outlawed child labor by social edict, we can hardly turn around and say that those children who could otherwise have been working to support themselves are "naturally" dependent upon their parents or other adults for support.

D ependencies and vulnerabilities are all largely created or exacerbated by existing social arrangements. By altering those arrangements, we could mitigate if not necessarily eliminate those conditions. Two things bear emphasizing, however. One is that we can probably never eliminate all forms of dependency. On the personal level, Rein (1965, 87) persuasively argues that it is

> far more profitable to view economic dependence as biologists view ecologic dependence: we are all involved with one another. Life is interdependent— and the most fruitful understanding of it can come from examining degrees and conditions of interdependency, rather than from isolating . . . a dichotomy between the dependent and the independent. (See similarly Smith 1955, 10–11)

The same is true of interdependencies on a collective level. Arthur Schlesinger (1981, C1) brilliantly traces the failures of postwar foreign and economic policies of the United States to the mislearned lessons of Pearl Harbor and the Great Depression:

> we were determined to make sure that the United States would never again be vulnerable to devastating surprise attack. As the traumatic experience of the Great Depression led to the resolution to make the economy depression-proof, so the traumatic experience of Pearl Harbor led to the resolution to make the nation war-proof.

Of course, both goals were sheer folly. Absolute invulnerability is an impossible ideal, as a number of Third World countries have also painfully discovered.[7] It is now accepted dogma among development specialists anxious to preserve the prerogatives of newly sovereign states that "self-reliance is not the same as self-sufficiency" (Galtung 1980b, 27). As Galtung (1980a, 356) points out,

> "dependence" has two negations in English, both of them implicit in the idea of self-reliance: *in*dependence and *inter*dependence. The meaning of independence is autonomy, that invaluable combination of self-confidence, a high level of self-sufficiency and fearlessness out of which invulnerability is forged. The meaning of interdependence is equity, which means a style of cooperation that does not engender new patterns of dependence.

For most purposes, it is clearly this interdependence with which nations, like individuals, must make do.

---

7. See, e.g, Nyerere (1968, chap. 8), Biersteker (1980), and Galtung, O'Brien, and Preiswerk (1980).

The second point I wish to emphasize is that it is not at all clear that we should necessarily seize any and all opportunities to reduce or remove vulnerabilities. Not all dependencies are necessarily undesirable (Rein 1965, 87–88). In some cases, people willingly render themselves vulnerable to a variety of other people for a variety of purposes. Upon reflection, we have to concede that it is morally proper that they should do so.

Consider, first, personal relationships. As Wilson (1978, 315) remarks, "A world in which no one had power over another, and in which no one was vulnerable, a world in which people could be moved to action by force or reasons alone, would be a world without love, an inhuman world." Love—that most salient of all personal relationships—can, Wilson shows, most plausibly be analyzed in terms of "putting yourselves in one another's power." Lovers undoubtedly render themselves vulnerable to one another. There may be some question about the "willingness" of that action. (The imagery of "falling in love" seems to suggest that perhaps the parties "could not help themselves.") But whether willingly incurred or not, there can be no doubt that the resultant vulnerabilities are morally permissible—yea, morally desirable.

Much the same is true of a great many wider social involvements. Consider, for example, commercial transactions. Interdependence is the essence of trade and hence of all mutually profitable business ventures, as economists since before Adam Smith have perceived. Similarly in politics, interdependence forms the basis of all alliances and coalitions.[8] We may well take moral offense at the particulars of any exchange or alliance; but surely we would not object to such arrangements *merely* on account of the vulnerability and dependency which they reflect and, indeed, exacerbate.

The implication is that we do not object to a person's dependency or vulnerability as such. Our objection lies instead in the fact that "power resides implicitly in the other's dependence" (Emerson 1962, 32).[9] The attendant risks of the power being abused underlies our moral objections to vulnerability and dependency relationships. What is really wrong with them is that they necessarily create opportunities for the strong to exploit the weaknesses of those who are vulnerable and dependent.[10]

8. See generally Baldwin (1980).
9. See also Blau (1964), Keohane and Nye (1977, chap. 1), Caporaso (1978), Hirschman (1978), and Baldwin (1980).
10. Notice, for example, how the Tanzanians' Arusha Declaration represents "the policy of self-reliance" as a means of achieving the deeper goal of an "absence of exploitation" (Nyerere 1968). Wilson (1978) similarly traces our objection to using people to the notion of exploitation. He toys with the idea of arguing that "it is unfair to take advantage of someone's loneliness, or destitution, or love, or in any other way to derive disproportionate benefit from a position of power with regard to another." However, he rejects that, saying that a skeptic could well ask,

The objection to exploitation is rooted in notions of fairness. Essentially, exploitation amounts to taking unfair advantage of other people.[11] One way to do that would be to obtain benefits from others on the pretense that they will later be repaid and then failing to so so: that is the form of unfairness emphasized in the classic reciprocity model (Rawls 1971). Another way, more to the present point, would be to turn the other's disadvantages to our own advantage. That is what we do when we use our unequal bargaining power to strike "unconscionable contracts" with others (Leff 1967). Taking advantage of that sort of structural weakness of other parties to a bargaining game is, at root, what talk of economic exploitation is all about (Elster 1978; 1982; see also Scott 1975; 1976).[12] Similarly, on a more personal level, we would say "it is *unfair* to exploit the deficiencies of the imbecile, . . . just as it would be unfair, and not just ordinarily dishonest, to steal from a blind man" (Benn 1967, 71).

The objection, notice, is that people in a vulnerable position are exploitable—not necessarily that they are exploited. It is, *ceteris paribus,* immoral to tolerate a serious risk of immoral outcomes (e. g., exploitation) even if that risk never actually becomes a reality; and this is true whether what prevents the immoral outcome is an act of will or a stroke of luck. Suppose you have a choice between two courses of action: by one an immoral outcome would be rendered impossible; by the other that outcome would remain possible, but assuming everyone abided by the moral law, it would not in fact occur. The former must surely be the morally preferable alternative, certainly in those

---

"Why should one be fair?" He prefers voluntaristic grounds for our obligations not to exploit others: "by deriving advantage from his plight, freely and knowingly, I give him a legitimate claim against me" (Wilson 1978, 309–10). This takes us back to my critique of self-assumed obligations in chapters 3 and 4 above. There, just as here, I argue that someone is not excused from moral blame for doing grave damage to another just because he derived no benefits from the other's plight, much less because he did not derive such benefits "freely and knowingly." For present purposes, perhaps it is enough to note that the same argument Wilson offers against the unfairness interpretation could be offered against his own. The thoroughgoing skeptic could equally well ask, "Why should I honor my commitments?"

11. In his early paper, "Justice as Fairness," Rawls (1958, 178) alludes to this more general formulation: "a practice will strike parties as fair if none feels that, by participating in it, they or any of the others are taken advantage of." Although this notion has dropped out of Rawls's later work, it remains central to subsequent work on the notion of exploitation (Coleman 1983; Feinberg 1983).

12. This point emerges also in philosophical discussions of Braithwaite's *Theory of Games as a Tool for the Moral Philosopher* (1955). The problem there is how to divide fairly the playing time between two musicians living in adjoining nonsoundproof rooms; and many people object to the fact that Braithwaite's scheme would allow one party (the trumpeter, who does not so much mind the pianist next door playing at the same time he does) to exploit his stronger bargaining position to obtain a greater share of playing time (Lucas 1959, 9–10; Sen 1970, 120–23; Rawls 1971, 134–35, n. 10). The point is not really that people should refrain from threatening to harm one another, though it is often phrased that way; it is instead that the stronger party should not benefit from the other's weakness (Barry 1983a, chap. 3).

cases where the payoffs of the two alternatives are otherwise identical and probably in most cases where they are not.[13] After all, in the latter there is a chance that (through ignorance, incompetence, or weakness of will) the immoral outcome will come about. In the former, there is no chance of this occurring.

Whether exploitation actually occurs depends not only upon how many opportunities people have to exploit one another but also upon whether or not they decide to take those opportunities. Arguably, at least, the fewer opportunities people have to exploit one another, the less inclined they will be to use them. In his *Subjection of Women*, John Stuart Mill makes the following claim:

> Even the commonest men reserve the violent, the sulky, the undisguisedly selfish side of their character for those who have no power to withstand it. The relation of superiors to dependents is the nursery of these vices of character, which, wherever else they exist, are an overflowing from that source . . . .
> We know that the bad propensities of human nature are only kept within bounds when they are allowed no scope for their indulgence. . . . [P]ower seeks out and evokes the latent germs of selfishness in the remotest corners of his nature—fans its faintest sparks and smouldering embers—offers to him a licence for the indulgence of those points of his original character which repress and conceal, and the repression of which would in time have become a second nature. (Mill 1869, ch. 2)

What I must emphasize at this point, however, is that some dependency or vulnerability relationships pose greater threats of exploitation than do others. The risk of exploitation arises, and the dependency or vulnerability relationship therefore becomes morally objectionable, only insofar as the relationship displays the following characteristics:

1. The relationship embodies an *asymmetrical* balance of power.

2. The subordinate party *needs* the resources provided by the relationship in order to protect his vital interests.

3. For the subordinate party, the relationship is the *only source* of such resources.

---

13. There may also be something to Postow's (1978–79) argument that your self-respect suffers when you are subject to the arbitrary will of another: it is demeaning that you must count on the good grace and moral rectitude of another to provide you with what you need. Lane's (1982, 12) review of the psychological evidence on this point reveals that an *earned income* is among the strongest correlates of self-esteem, although it is unclear whether this is a universal feature of the human psyche or whether it is just an artifact of our own culture. Held (1974, 175) is surely on firmer ground in tracing our objection to exploitation to the notion of respect for persons. "To respect another person,"she writes, "is to renounce the use of coercion against that person even when he or she is powerless or not inclined to resist."

4. The superordinate party in the relationship exercises *discretionary control* over those resources.

To the extent that a dependency or vulnerability relationship fails to display any of these features our moral objection to the relationship is diminished.

P erhaps the most striking fact about those dependency relationships which we are intuitively inclined to find morally unproblematic is that they involve *inter*dependencies. In debates in the House of Lords, the Archbishop of Canterbury makes precisely this point about modern marriage relations: they embody, he says, a morally desirable sort of "symmetry and complementarity" (Coggan 1976, 1258). The same is true of all those other political and commercial relationships which, although they undeniably embody dependencies, we nonetheless regard as morally unobjectionable. They are "relations of reciprocal dependence" (Held 1974, 178; Keohane and Nye 1977). The vulnerabilities are mutual; each party depends on the other. That fact seems to be crucial in explaining why we are so untroubled by these circumstances.

Mutuality is important because, insofar as each party is dependent upon the other, there is that much less risk of exploitation. The exploitably dependent person is one who "seeks something for nothing [and] is therefore powerless to modify the conditions of his existence" (Gouldner 1973, 270). Those who have something others want or need, in contrast, have the capacity to negotiate terms and conditions with others in society.

Consider the limiting case, one where each is *equally* dependent upon the other. We may still want to say that a "power relation" of some sort exists between these two parties. If dependencies or vulnerabilities were perfectly reciprocal, however, the power relation would be a balanced one. Any threat one could make the other could match. Exploitation would therefore be impossible. Only *asymmetrical* power relations, only *unilateral* dependencies, create opportunities for one side (the stronger) to exploit the other (the weaker).[14]

Such observations have led a variety of commentators to insist that any dependencies or vulnerabilities should be completely mutual or reciprocal.[15] Wilson (1978, 315), for example, writes that "it is both inevitable and right that people should be in one another's power, though it would be best, per-

14. Barry (1976, 93) remarks similarly: "By 'asymmetry' I mean simply that one party stands to gain more out of the relationship than the other, because it is in a position to exploit the weakness or necessity or vulnerability of the other." See similarly, Keohane and Nye (1977, 8–19), Caporaso (1978), Hirschman (1978), Baldwin (1980).

15. Held (1974, 177) would distinguish between a relation of reciprocal power and one of true mutuality, the latter being "characterized by a mutual renunciation of the use of power. Equality of power may be a precondition for any such satisfactory, voluntary, extended renunciation," but the two are only contingently connected at most. See similarly Pateman (1981).

haps, if . . . every power were balanced by an equal and opposite one.'' Early feminists put the point more bluntly. William Thompson's (1825, 203) ideal society is one of ''mutual co-operation'': ''women here are no more dependent on men, or on any individual man, than men are on women.'' Translated into my terminology, that would seem to amount to a demand that the vulnerabilities be perfectly symmetrical, that is, that each party depend on the other in exactly the same measure. In this context ''symmetry'' must, of course, be subjectively defined. What each party gains from the relationship (or, equivalently, what each would lose were it terminated) must have an equal importance in each party's overall life plan.

Demanding *complete* symmetry in any relationship is wildly unrealistic. That condition would be satisfied in virtually no trading relation, in virtually no alliance, and if you come right down to it, in probably very few personal relationships either (Keohane and Nye 1977, 10–11). In all these cases, both parties may depend upon each other in some way or another and to some extent or another. Both may be vulnerable to each other, in that each would stand to lose if the other were to withdraw from the relationship. However, there is nothing in that to suggest that each needs the other equally, that the gains from the relationship are (or the losses from terminating it would be) perfectly symmetrical.

What, then, might constitute the minimum conditions of an acceptable dependency or vulnerability relationship? For a start, each party must get something out of the relationship (or equivalently, each should stand to lose something if it were terminated). That, however, is obviously not enough. It would still permit grossly unequal bargaining power and all the inequitable outcomes deriving from that. The strong might have enough power to exploit the weak mercilessly without quite enjoying the sort of monopoly of power that would allow them actually to enslave their victims. Hence, the interdependency condition needs to be supplemented with some other condition designed to guarantee that the power relations will not be *too* asymmetrical. The way to do that is by analyzing how dependent upon others a person is and what he depends upon others for.

Barry (1976, 93) observes that ''there is a close connection, *though not a perfect one,* between asymmetry and unfairness'' (emphasis added). Several factors go into making this connection less than perfect. The most obvious ones have to do with the capacity of the notionally subordinate party to *withdraw* from the relationship altogether. As long as the subordinate party can withdraw without severe cost, the superordinate cannot exploit him.[16] Femi-

---

16. In the game theoretic tradition, someone is said to be ''exploited'' only if he receives less than he could expect to obtain by withdrawing from the game altogether. In my model, one is exploited precisely because one cannot withdraw. This appeals to a notion of exploitation as taking unfair advantage, which Elster (1982) shows to be distinct from and preferable to Roemer's (1982a; 1982b, chap. 7; 1982c, 275–84) ''hypothetical withdrawal'' formulation.

nist writers see this quite clearly: "Women must have enough economic, social, political and psychological independence to be able to subsist satisfactorily without this relationship [with men]. . . . Otherwise the actual relation between man and woman becomes subverted into a relation of dominance and submission" (Held 1974, 177; see similarly Mill 1848, bk. 5, chap. 11, sec. 9). Several commentators have similarly observed that the relations of dominance and submission between nation-states is explained by one side's "dependency," understood as its inability to withdraw from the relationship without extraordinary cost to itself.[17]

This capacity to withdraw has two important aspects. One has to do with the relative importance to the notionally subordinate party of the resources controlled by the superordinate one. The other has to do with the alternative sources of supply of those resources available to the notionally subordinate party.[18]

Julius Nyerere (1968, 151) writes that "a self-reliant individual is one who cooperates with others, who is willing to help others and be helped by them, but who does not depend on anyone else for his food, clothing or shelter." This emphasis on the basic necessities of life is well placed. Suppose that one party has an absolute monopoly of power over some particular resource. Suppose, furthermore, that that party is himself utterly self-sufficient. Then there will exist what may fairly be called an asymmetrical power relationship: others depend upon him for their supply of the resource in question; he depends upon them for nothing. Yet this will give real power to the party with the monopoly only if the resources are ones that matter to others.[19] Suppose instead that others regard the resources simply as frills which they could easily, and would happily, do without. (I might, for example, depend upon some particular gamekeeper for my supply of plover eggs without caring all that much about plover eggs.) Then the monopolist would enjoy no real power, no real threat

---

17. See, e.g., Keohane and Nye (1977, 8–19), Caporaso (1978), Hirschman (1978), Beitz (1979b, 146–47), Baldwin (1980), and Galtung (1980a).

18. Baldwin (1980, 499) offers the following illustration: "If state *B* must forego warm homes, fully employed factories, adequate transportation systems, and high living standards, when state *A* stops exporting oil, state *B* is dependent on state *A* for oil. If, on the other hand, state *B* can easily get its oil elsewhere or if it is indifferent to warm homes, etc., it is not very dependent on state *A* with respect to oil." Harry Frankfurt (1973, 71–72) offers another: "the butcher has the customer in his power . . . when . . . two . . . conditions are satisfied. First, the customer is *dependent* on the butcher for meat: he cannot readily obtain it from another source. Second, the customer *needs* meat: it is essential either for preventing what he would regard as a significant deterioration of his welfare or for preventing his continuation in what he would regard as an undesirable condition." Frankfurt goes on to say that these two conditions allow the butcher to "*exploit* the customer's dependence and need, . . . demand[ing] for his meat an unfair or improper price," by making a coercive threat to withdraw from the trading relationship. See similarly Emerson (1962), Blau (1964, 118–25), Caporaso (1978), Hirschman (1978), Gibson (1984), and Tulloch (1984).

19. See, e.g., Emerson (1962), Blau (1964, 118–25), Caporaso (1978), Hirschman (1978), Baldwin (1980), Galtung (1980b, 21), Gibson (1984), and Tulloch (1984).

advantage. If he threatened to cut off supply of the resources unless others paid some exorbitant price, they would simply reply, "Go right ahead."[20]

It is merely the intensity of the subordinate's desire for a resource that gives whoever controls that resource power over him. If the subordinate wants the resource very badly—if, in Emerson's (1962, 32) terms, he has a high "motivational investment" in it—then the superordinate can extract a very high price from him.

The condition of a morally acceptable dependency relationship is stated above in terms of *needs* rather than of desires. These two are not unrelated. What you need you usually desire intensely; or at least you *would* ordinarily come to desire it with increasing intensity, the more you were deprived of it. The correlation, however, is far from perfect. There are, in particular, a great many things that we desire intensely but can hardly be said to need. Hence, the two are not strictly equivalent expressions, and I must say something more to justify my preference for a condition phrased in terms of needs rather than of intense desires.

The justification is, quite simply, that it is within a person's power to change his preferences, in a way that it is not within his power to change his needs.[21] Whether someone should have to change his preferences is, perhaps, debatable.[22] Moral philosophers are, however, increasingly regarding preferences as matters for moral deliberation and choice, rather than as things which are somehow externally given. They say, therefore, that people must take "responsibility for self," for the bundle of goals, preferences, and character traits that they choose to display (C. Taylor 1976). Rawls (1982, 170-71), too, supposes that it is the duty of citizens to adjust their preferences so as "to moderate the claims they make on their social institutions" in accordance with their fair allocation of primary goods. As he adds in one purple passage, "the fact that we have a compelling desire does not argue for the propriety of

20. Strictly speaking, the only supplier of plover eggs might not be a true monopolist if there are close substitutes for that commodity. My point is that even if he were a monopoly supplier of a commodity for which there were no close substitutes, he would have no great power to exploit your dependence upon him for that commodity provided you regard the commodity as a luxury you could (fairly easily) do without.

21. Perhaps there are a few preferences that are beyond our power to change. But the reason would, invariably, turn out to be connected to the fact that they serve to satisfy certain physical or psychological needs of some sort.

22. We are substantially less hesitant to ask people to change their preferences to protect themselves, however, once we realize that those preferences were not themselves fully autonomous. They were often implanted, often intentionally, by the selfsame agents who controlled the resources required to satisfy them. Dommen (1980) shows that the South Pacific islanders were able to remain self-reliant only as long as they retained their traditional values and preferences and resisted Western cultural penetration. Galtung (1980b, 21) argues more generally that one important aspect of the fight of peripheral peoples to attain "self-reliance" is "the struggle for independent taste-information, being less susceptible to 'tastes' generated from the centre and satisfiable with centre goods only."

its satisfaction any more than the strength of a conviction argues for its truth'' (Rawls 1982, 171).

Both Taylor and Rawls are, of course, demanding that people choose or change their preferences in light of *moral* considerations, whereas in the case at hand it is being suggested that they should change them for purely prudential reasons. The important point remains that they *can* change them. Where it is within people's power to protect themselves—here, to protect themselves from the power of superordinates by restructuring their own preferences—we ordinarily expect them to do so.

Needs, in contrast, are unalterable. No one has it within his power to waive claims to those resources which are required to protect his vital interests. These notions of need and vital interests might be interpreted in a variety of ways. The traditional formulation is in terms of ''immutable biological and psychological imperatives.'' The more modern one is in terms of ''primary goods,'' those things which constitute preconditions for whatever else we might desire to do or to be.[23] The constant element running throughout all definitions of needs is, however, immutability. Where one person controls a resource that others need to protect their vital interests, those others cannot deprive him of power over themselves merely by changing their preferences.

That I *need* what another supplies is a necessary but not sufficient condition of his having any great power over me. It is also crucial that he be a *monopolist,* that he be my only source of supply of those goods. Much though I need food to sustain life, no particular greengrocer enjoys any power over me so long as there are plenty of others to whom I can turn should he become difficult. Were he my only source of supply of necessities, he would indeed have enormous power over me.[24] Stipulating that the resources constitute necessities guarantees that I cannot possibly do without them. Stipulating that he is my only source of supply guarantees that I cannot satisfy my needs elsewhere. The conjunction of those two conditions provides him with a substantial threat advantage over me: he can, at little cost to himself, terminate the relationship; I cannot, except at enormous cost to myself. That, in turn, gives him tremendous power over me which he could (if he so chose) exercise very exploitatively indeed.

Notice, however, that there is one further condition which is necessary in order for one person to have the power to exploit the other. What would be crucial in giving a monopolistic greengrocer a threat advantage over me is the

23. See Rawls (1971, sec. 15; 1982), Miller (1976), Shue (1980, chap. 1). I have argued elsewhere that, at root, these both amount to the same thing. ''What makes 'primary goods' or 'needs' instrumental toward any possible end in any possible world is that they are connected to something inherent in the nature of man, which, in turn delimits what can count as a possible variation on our world'' (Goodin 1982b, 171).

24. See, e.g., Blau (1964, 118–25), Caporaso (1978), Hirschman (1978), Baldwin (1980), Gibson (1984), and Tulloch (1984).

fact that he can afford to withdraw from our relationship and I cannot. In more general terms, he must enjoy *discretionary power* over the resources which I need and which I can obtain from him alone. It must lie within his power to choose whether to give them to me or to withhold them. Suppose this were not the case. Suppose the monopolist *has* to give them to me (or that he *cannot* give them to me, even if he wants to do so). Then however much I might need the goods, and however impossible it might be to get them anywhere else, he would have no threat advantage over me. Thus, the superordinate has no power to exploit subordinates unless he can dispose of the resources at will.[25]

In most dependency relationships, this question probably does not arise. Ordinarily, superordinates enjoy substantial (if not quite complete) discretion over the disposition of the goods that are within their control.[26] There are however cases wherein one party needs resources which the other has no choice but to supply him. The first example that comes to mind is the relation between a sole seller and a sole buyer.[27] Better examples would be those in which the superordinate's control over resources is hedged by institutional constraints. Putting my money in a bank rather than under my bed might seem to render me vulnerable to my bank manager: he has control over something that I need and can obtain nowhere else. But I am not really vulnerable to him in any way that morally matters, since he cannot refuse to honor my checks so long as I keep enough money in my account to cover them. His discretionary control over those resources is legally circumscribed.[28] Since it is, there is no chance of his abusing his position of asymmetrical power to exploit me.

S o far I have been talking largely in terms of the limiting cases. The most morally objectionable dependency or vulnerability relationship would exist where one party has discretionary control over resources that the other needs and cannot obtain elsewhere, yet no such dependency exists on the part of the first party to the second. A relationship lacking these features

25. Rousseau (1762a, bk. 2) is firm on this point: "If there is any cure for this social evil [of dependence of men on men], it is to be found in the substitution of law for the individual; in arming the general will with a real strength beyond the power of any individual will. If the laws of nations, like the laws of nature, could never be broken by any human power, dependence on men would become dependence on things; all the advantages of a state of nature would be combined with all the advantages of social life in the commonwealth."

26. Recall from chapter 5 that even the moral responsibilities shown above to follow from another's vulnerability themselves entail broad areas of discretion, specifying goals while leaving the choice of means largely open.

27. Upon closer analysis, however, we find that here the first condition stated above is not met: the power relationship between a sole seller and a sole buyer is not genuinely asymmetrical.

28. For an example that may be of rather more practical importance for social policymakers, welfare officers will have no power to exploit the vulnerability of claimants once the claimants have been vested with a "right to welfare" that denies welfare officers any discretionary power over payments. On this, see Smith (1949, 288; 1955, 3, 17, 30).

would be the most morally acceptable dependency or vulnerability relationship—if indeed it could still be called by that name.

Most actual relationships, of course, fall somewhere between the extremes. Relationships are more or less asymmetrical. One party may have a greater or lesser need for the resources in question. It may be more or less difficult for him to find alternative sources of supply. The superordinate may have more or less discretion in his control over those resources.

It is far from clear how all these factors should be mixed in some composite index representing the moral badness of a dependency or vulnerability relationship. The conventional wisdom would, I think, attach far greater weight to asymmetry than to any other consideration in this index. The rationale would be that symmetrical dependencies admit of no abuse. Where each party depends equally (or approximately equally) on the other for the satisfaction of basic needs, neither can exploit the other through a plausible threat to terminate the relationship on which they both depend so heavily.

Notice, however, that there are two strategies for trying to solve the moral problems posed by interpersonal dependencies and vulnerabilities. One strategy is to guarantee each party the capacity to *defend* itself against the other. That is what those who emphasize symmetry hope to accomplish. In perfectly symmetrical relationships, each side can give as good as it gets in any fight. That is also the aim of those who emphasize the importance of the capacity to withdraw from the relationship (either because parties can do without the resources altogether or because they can get them from elsewhere). Both are essentially guarantees of a good self-defense.

That strategy is deeply flawed. Even if parties have no differential threat advantage over one another, they can—and on many accounts rationally should—still try to threaten each other. And when one of them does so, the onus (and the costs) of self-defense would on this account have to fall to the threatened party. That is an unhappy but an inevitable consequence of this strategy.

The alternative strategy for coping with the moral problems posed by dependency relationships is to try to *forestall* the threat of exploitation rather than merely trying to defend against it. This is best accomplished by making sure that the superordinate party has no discretion over the disposition of the resources needed by the subordinate one. Those who have no choice about whether to supply resources cannot even *attempt* to control others by threats to withhold those resources. Preventing superordinates from being in a position to use exploitative threats in the first place is preferable to giving subordinates the capacities which we hope (but cannot guarantee) will allow them to defend themselves (although not costlessly) against threats that have been made. Accordingly, I would attach the highest priority to depriving superordinates of discretion in the disposition of needed resources. That is by far the best way to deprive dependencies of their moral sting.

L et us return to the question of whether it is better to protect the vulnerable or to render them invulnerable. The discussion above has shown that complete invulnerability, total independence, is an illusory ideal. Indeed, it is doubly so. In the fullest sense that state is not possible: some vulnerabilities are inevitable and immutable. Even insofar as it is possible, total independence is not ideal: often people voluntarily render themselves vulnerable to others, and at least under certain conditions it is morally right that they should do so.[29] Vulnerability then, will remain a feature of social life, even in the ideal world.

In this ideal world, however, the vulnerable would seem to be in need of no special protection. The conditions that go into making dependency or vulnerability relationships morally acceptable go a long way toward guaranteeing that those who are vulnerable can be put under no threat or that they can perfectly well protect themselves. If he has no discretionary control over resources, a superordinate cannot threaten to deny use of them to a subordinate; in a symmetrical power relationship, each party could meet any threat from his opposite number with an equally compelling counterthreat of his own; where basic needs are not at stake, each can always withdraw from the relationship if the other gets too demanding; and so on.

What, then, is the status of the injuction to "protect the vulnerable"? Certainly it has an important role as a stopgap or second-best rule of morality. It finds important interim application to all those morally unacceptable vulnerabilities and dependencies which we should, but have not yet managed to, eliminate. If we cannot (or will not) eliminate feudal power relations, then the least we can do is to retain the feudal code of *noblesse oblige* that goes along with them. Besides, not all dependencies and vulnerabilities are entirely within the power of society to control. Many are, at least in part, genuinely "natural," inevitable and immutable. It is sometimes unavoidable that one party will enjoy a measure of asymmetrical, discretionary control over resources that the other needs and can obtain nowhere else. In this second-best world, all we can do is to insist that people must bear especially strong reponsibilities to protect those who are inevitably vulnerable to and dependent upon them. In these cases, the moral requirements are not redundant: they provide the only protection that is enjoyed at all by those who are, and by natural necessity must remain, in positions of unilateral vulnerability and dependency.

Even in the ideal case, where vulnerabilities and dependencies are completely reciprocal, the injunction to protect the vulnerable still has an important and distinctively moral role to play. At worst, the injunction might be

---

29. An element of voluntarism remains in my model. Compared with the conventional model of self-assumed obligations, however, the locus of voluntarism has shifted significantly. In my model, it would be perfectly permissible for you to render yourself vulnerable to others if you so prefer. You may, in other words, choose to place yourself in a weak position. What you may not do is opt out of the obligations which follow from the fact that you enjoy a strong one.

said to be motivationally redundant: a person has strong nonmoral (i.e., prudential) reasons for refraining from trying to exploit those who have the same power over him as he has over them; there is no need to spell out moral reasons as well.[30] Redundancy of this sort does not deprive the principle of its moral force. An action can be both prudent and morally proper at the same time.

30. Even there the injunction is not completely redundant. People who are perfectly capable of protecting themselves may fail to do so. Once their opportunities for self-help are past, others to whom they are vulnerable should step in to protect them, as I have argued in chapter 5 above.

8
Conclusion

The aim of this book has been partly proscriptive and partly prescriptive. What I have argued against is the way in which certain narrowly defined "special duties" run riot over any general duty we may have to aid others in need. My objection is precisely to the narrowness with which those duties are ordinarily defined. I do not deny that we have special duties toward family, friends, clients, compatriots, and so forth. Nor do I deny that those duties are particularly compelling ones. I do deny that that conventional catalog exhausts the category of people who are morally entitled to special protection from us.

For practical purposes, we usually just take the conventional catalog as given, without inquiring too deeply into what lies behind it. Some would say that nothing lies behind it—that there is just a random assortment of special responsibilities having an intuitively obvious but rationally groundless claim on us. Others would say that what stands behind it all is a model of self-assumed obligations. On either of those accounts, there would be no good grounds for moving beyond the standard set of special responsibilities.

My arguments have, however, shown both claims to be incorrect. There is a common thread unifying all those special responsibilities, but it is not one of self-assumed obligations. That model fails to account fully for all the morally important features of the special responsibilities which we all so readily acknowledge. That model is not so much wrong as radically incomplete. What really underlies our special responsibilities, I have argued, is the peculiar vulnerability of someone else to our actions and choices. Self-assumed obligations are just a special case of that: people ordinarily come to rely upon the promises and contracts of others, and it is for that reason (rather than any special moral significance attached to the "will binding itself") that those obligations are especially strong.

Self-assumed obligations are, according to this analysis, just one of many sorts of responsibilities growing out of the peculiar vulnerabilities of people to one another. Those other responsibilities have the same moral basis and, depending upon circumstances, perhaps even the same strength as those found in the conventional catalog. Merging self-assumed obligations into the larger vulnerability model in this way has two important consequences. The first is that many other responsibilities that may have less immediate intuitive appeal are thereby elevated to the high status previously enjoyed by self-assumed duties alone. Second, and perhaps more important, those new responsibilities circumscribe the operation of self-assumed obligations, depriving things like "unconscionable contracts" (ones which exploit someone else's vulnerability) of their moral force.

In other words, my argument is that we should protect *all* those who are particularly vulnerable to our actions and choices, rather than restricting our attention to the narrowly circumscribed subset enshrined in conventional morality. My basic prescriptions can be summarized as follows:

Preventing exploitable vulnerabilities: No one should be forced into a vulnerable or dependent position, insofar as this can be avoided. If people are placed in such a position (either through personal choice or natural or social necessity), vulnerabilities/dependencies should be reciprocal and, ideally, symmetrical among all those who are involved. In no case should they be so severe and asymmetrical that one party has exclusive, discretionary control over resources that the other needs to protect his vital interests.

Protecting the vulnerable: Where people are particularly vulnerable to or dependent upon you, for whatever reasons, you have a special responsibility to protect their interests. Where they are vulnerable to you individually, you must seek to produce this result directly through your own efforts. Where they are vulnerable to a group of you, the group as a whole is responsible for protecting their interests; and you as an individual within that group have a derivative responsibility to help organize and participate in a cooperative scheme among members of that group to produce that result.

That leaves the problem of how to apportion resources between those tasks: between preventing people from becoming vulnerable and protecting those who already are; and within the realm of collective responsibilities, between organizational efforts and direct assistance. Beyond that is the further problem, and pragmatically the more vexing one, of how to apportion assistance between all the particular people who are vulnerable to us in so very many ways.

In principle, the solution to such problems is easy enough. All that balancing should be done simply by considering who is most vulnerable to us, and which action plans are most efficacious in protecting them. In practice, however, those calculations are bound to be enormously difficult. What particular policies we should pursue, individually and collectively, to discharge these responsibilities is largely an empirical question, turning upon what the actual effects of various alternative policy interventions might be. Pending further empirical investigations into those matters, that must necessarily remain an open question. Still, the moral principles are there all ready to go, once the empirical details have been filled in. More important, the moral principles are there to tell empirical researchers what they should be looking for, what matters morally and what does not. That in itself is no mean accomplishment.

The principles developed in this book can thus have some real policy relevance. Some of the more central implications are sketched in chapter 6, and some of the more topical are developed elsewhere (Goodin 1985b) in reply to current attempts to force "self-reliance" to supplant the welfare state. Although much more clearly needs to be done to explore the full ramifications of this line of analysis, these preliminary indications suggest that the basic vulnerability model will prove fruitful for a broad range of policy choices.

References

Abbott, E. 1940. *Public assistance.* Chicago: Univ. of Chicago Press.

Addison, J. 1714. *The Spectator,* no. 583 (August 20). In *The Spectator,* ed. D. F. Bond, vol. 4:592–95. Oxford: Clarendon, 1965.

Adelberg, S., and Batson, C. D. 1978. Accountability and helping: when needs exceed resources. *Journal of Personality and Social Psychology* 36:343–50.

Allport, G. W. 1954. *The nature of prejudice.* Cambridge, Mass.: Addison-Wesley.

Amdur, R. 1977. Rawls' theory of justice: domestic and international perspectives. *World Politics* 29:438–61.

American Bar Association (ABA). 1969. Code of professional responsibility. In Pirsig 1970, pp. 373–438.

American Law Institute (ALI). 1970. Uniform marriage and divorce act. In *Uniform laws annotated,* vol. 9A:91–221. St. Paul, Minn.: West, 1979.

———. 1976. Uniform commercial code. *Uniform laws annotated,* vols. 1–3A. St. Paul, Minn.: West, 1976.

American Medical Association (AMA). 1957. Principles of medical ethics. In *Medical ethics,* ed. C. J. McFadden. Philadelphia: Davis, 1967.

Anderson, M. 1978. *Welfare.* Stanford, Calif.: Hoover Institution Press.

Andreas, C. 1969. "To receive from kings . . . ": an examination of government-to-government aid and its unintended consequences. *Journal of Social Issues* 25:167–80.

Anon. 1928. Reciprocity of rights and duties between parent and child. *Harvard Law Review* 42:112–15.

Anon. 1981. Allocating the costs of hazardous waste disposal. *Harvard Law Review* 94:584–604.

Anscombe, G. E. M. 1958. Modern moral philosophy. *Philosophy* 33:1–19.

———. 1967. Who is wronged? *Oxford Review* 5:16–17.

Arrow, K. J. 1974. Government decision making and the preciousness of life. In Tancredi 1974, pp. 33–47.

Ashford, N. A. 1976. *Crisis in the workplace: occupational disease and injury.* Cambridge: MIT Press.

Atiyah, P. S. 1979. *The rise and fall of freedom of contract.* Oxford: Clarendon.

Attfield, R. 1981. The good of trees. *Journal of Value Inquiry* 15:35–54.

———. 1983. *The ethics of environmental concern.* New York: Columbia Univ. Press.

Australia. Royal Commission on Human Relationships. 1977. *Final report.* Canberra: Australian Government Publishing Service.

Baier, A. 1980. The rights of past and future persons. In Partridge 1980, pp. 171–83.

Baldwin, D. A. 1980. Interdependence and power: a conceptual analysis. *International Organization* 34:471–506.

Ballantine, H. T. 1979. Annual discourse: the crisis in ethics, AD 1979. *New England Journal of Medicine* 301:634–38.

Bane, M. J. 1983. Is the welfare state replacing the family? *Public Interest* 70:91–101.

Banfield, E. C. 1962. American foreign aid and doctrines. In *Why foreign aid*, ed. R. A. Goldwin, 10–31. Chicago: Rand McNally.

Barry, B. 1965. *Political argument*. London: Routledge & Kegan Paul.

————. 1973. *The liberal theory of justice*. Oxford: Clarendon.

————. 1976. Power: an economic analysis. In *Power and political theory*, ed. B. Barry, 67–102. London: Wiley.

————. 1977. Justice between generations. In *Law, morality and society*, ed. P. M. S. Hacker and J. Raz, 268–84. Oxford: Clarendon.

————. 1978. Circumstances of justice and future generations. In Sikora and Barry 1978, pp. 204–48.

————. 1979a. And who is my neighbor? *Yale Law Journal* 88:629–58.

————. 1979b. Justice as reciprocity. In Kamenka and Tay 1979, pp. 50–78.

————. 1980. Rich countries and poor countries. Department of Political Science, University of Chicago. Mimeo.

————. 1982. Humanity and justice in global perspective. In *Nomos XXIV: ethics, economics and the law*, ed. J. R. Pennock and J. W. Chapman, 219–52. New York: New York Univ. Press.

————. 1983a. Fair division and social justice. Division of Humanities and Social Sciences, California Institute of Technology, Pasadena. Mimeo.

————. 1983b. Intergenerational justice in energy policy. In MacLean and Brown 1983, pp. 15–30.

Barsh, R. L., and Henderson, J. Y. 1980. *The road: Indian tribes and political liberty*. Berkeley: Univ. of California Press.

Bayles, M. D., ed. 1976. *Ethics and population*. Cambridge, Mass.: Schenkman.

————. 1979. A problem of clean hands: refusal to provide professional services. *Social Theory and Practice* 5:165–81.

————. 1981. *Professional ethics*. Belmont, Calif.: Wadsworth.

Becker, G. S. 1982. *A treatise on the family*. Cambridge: Harvard Univ. Press.

Beitz, C. 1979a. Global Egalitarianism: can we make out a case? *Dissent* (Winter):59–68.

————. 1979b. *Political theory and international relations*. Princeton: Princeton Univ. Press.

————. 1983. Cosmopolitan ideals and national sentiment. *Journal of Philosophy* 80:591–600.

Benn, S. I. 1967. Egalitarianism and the equal consideration of interests. In *Nomos IX: equality*, ed. J. R. Pennock and J. W. Chapman, 61–78. New York: Atherton.

————. 1977. Personal freedom and environmental ethics: the moral inequality of species. In *Equality and freedom*, ed. G. Dorsey, vol. 2:401–24. New York: Oceana.

Bennett, J. 1981. Morality and consequences. In *The Tanner lectures on human values*, ed. S. M. McMurrin, vol. 2:45–116. Cambridge: Cambridge Univ. Press.

————. 1983. Positive and negative relevance. *American Philosophical Quarterly* 20:185–94.

Berger, F. R. 1975. Gratitude. *Ethics* 85:298–309.

Berger, P. L. 1974. *Pyramids of sacrifice*. New York: Basic Books.

————. 1976. In praise of particularity: the concept of mediating structures. *Review of Politics* 38:399–410.

Bergsten, C. F.; Horst, T. O.; and Moran, T. H. 1978. *American multinationals and American interests*. Washington, D.C.: Brookings Institution.

Berkowitz, L., and Daniels, L. R. 1963. Responsibility and dependency. *Journal of Abnormal and Social Psychology* 66:429–36.

Berlin, S. B., and Jones, L. E. 1983. Life after welfare: AFDC termination among long-term recipients. *Social Service Review* 57:378–402.

Beveridge, W. H. 1907. Labour exchanges and the unemployed. *Economic Journal* 17:66–81.

————. 1942. *Social insurance and allied services*. Cmd. 6404. London: His Majesty's Stationary Office.

Biersteker, T. J. 1980. Self-reliance in theory and practice: transforming Tanzanian trade relations. *International Organization* 34:229–64.

Blackmun, H. A. 1971a. Opinion of the U.S. Supreme Court. *Graham v. Richardson*. 403 U.S. 366–82.

————. 1971b. Opinion of the U.S. Supreme Court. *Wyman v. James*. 400 U.S. 309–27.

Blackstone, W. 1783. *Commentaries on the laws of England*. London: Strahan.

Blau, P. 1964. *Exchange and power in social life*. New York: Wiley.

Blum, L. A. 1980. *Friendship, altruism, and morality*. London: Routledge & Kegan Paul.

Blum, L.; Homiak, M.; Houseman, J.; and Scheman, N. 1975. Altruism and women's oppression. *Philosophical Forum* 5:222–47.

Blustein, J. 1979. Child rearing and family interests. In O'Neill and Ruddick 1979, pp. 115–22.

————. 1982. *Parents and children: the ethics of the family*. New York: Oxford Univ. Press.

Bohlen, F. H. 1908. The moral duty to aid others as a basis of tort liability. *University of Pennsylvania Law Review* 56:217–44, 316–38.

Bok, S. 1978. *Lying*. New York: Pantheon.

Booth, C. 1891. Enumeration and classification of paupers, and state pensions for the aged. *Journal of the Royal Statistical Society*, ser. A, 54:600–43.

————. 1892. *Pauperism and the endowment of old age*. London: Macmillan.

————. 1894a. *The aged poor in England and Wales*. London: Macmillan.

————. 1894b. Statistics of pauperism in old age. *Journal of the Royal Statistical Society*, ser. A, 57:235–45. Reprinted in Booth 1894a, pp. 1–54.

Booth, T. A.; Barritt, S.; Berry, S.; Martin, D. N.; and Melotte, C. 1983. Dependency in residential homes for the elderly. *Social Policy and Administration* 17:46–62.

Bowie, N. E. 1979. Changing the rules. In *Ethical theory and business*, ed. T. L. Beauchamp and N. E. Bowie, 147–50. Englewood Cliffs, N.J.: Prentice-Hall

Braithwaite, R. B. 1955. *The theory of games as a tool for the moral philosopher*. Cambridge: Cambridge Univ. Press.

Brandt, R. B. 1959. *Ethical theory*. Englewood Cliffs, N.J.: Prentice-Hall.

————. 1964. The concepts of obligation and duty. *Mind* 73:374–93.

————. 1976. The psychology of benevolence and its implications for philosophy. *Journal of Philosophy* 73:429–53.

Braucher, R., and Farnsworth, E. A., reporters. 1981. *Restatement (second) of the law of contracts*. St. Paul, Minn.: American Law Institute.

Brennan, W. J. 1977. Opinion of the U.S. Supreme Court. *Smith v. Organization of Foster Families*. 431 U.S. 816–56.

Brewer, D. J. 1875. Opinion of the Kansas Supreme Court. *Griffith v. Osawkee Township*. 14 Kansas 418. Reprinted in Abbott 1940, 73–80.

———. 1908. Opinion of the U.S. Supreme Court. *Muller v. Oregon*. 208 U.S. 416–23.

Briggs, A. 1961. The welfare state in historical perspective. *Archives Européennes de Sociologie* 2:221–58.

Broad, C. D. 1916. On the function of false hypotheses in ethics. *International Journal of Ethics* 26:277–97. Reprinted in Broad 1971, pp. 43–62.

———. 1953. Self and others. In Broad 1971, pp. 262–82.

———. 1971. *Broad's critical essays in moral philosophy,* ed. D. Cheney. London: Allen & Unwin.

Brock, D. W. 1982. Utilitarianism and aiding others. In Miller and Williams 1982, pp. 225–41.

Brown, P. G.; Johnson, C; and Vernier, P., eds. 1981. *Income support: conceptual and policy issues*. Totowa, N.J.: Rowman & Littlefield.

Brown, P. G., and Shue, H., eds. 1977. *Food policy*. New York: Free Press.

———. 1981. *Boundaries: national autonomy and its limits*. Totowa, N.J.: Rowman & Littlefield.

Buchanan, A. E. 1982. Philosophical foundations of beneficence. In *Beneficence and health care,* ed. E. E. Shelp, 33–62. Dordrecht: Reidel.

Burns, E. M. 1956. *Social security and public policy*. New York: McGraw-Hill.

Calabresi, G. 1970. *The costs of accidents*. New Haven: Yale Univ. Press.

Campbell, T. D. 1974. Humanity before justice. *British Journal of Political Science* 4:1–16.

Caplow, T. 1982. Christmas gifts in kin networks. *American Sociological Review* 47:383–92.

Caporaso, J. A. 1978. Dependence, dependency, and power in the global system. *International Organization* 32:13–43.

Cardozo, B. 1915. Opinion of the New York Court of Appeals. *People v. Crane*. 214 N.Y. 154; 108 N.E. 427.

Carson, T. L. 1982. Utilitarianism and world poverty. In Miller and Williams 1982, pp. 242–52.

Cass, B. 1982. Family policies in Australia. SWRC Reports and Proceedings, no. 21. Social Welfare Research Centre, University of New South Wales, Sydney. Mimeo.

Castañeda, H.-N. 1975. *Thinking and doing*. Dordrecht: Reidel.

Chisholm, R. M. 1966. Freedom and action. In *Freedom and determinism,* ed. K. Lehrer. New York: Random House.

Clark, H. H., Jr. 1968. *The law of domestic relations*. St. Paul, Minn.: West.

Clark, S. R. L. 1977. *The moral status of animals*. Oxford: Clarendon.

Coggan, F. D. 1976. The family in Britain today. *Hansard's Parliamentary Debates*. House of Lords. 5th ser. 371:1257–68.

Cohen, G. A. 1981. Freedom, justice, and capitalism. *New Left Review* 126:3–16.

Cohen, L. J. 1981. Who is starving whom? *Theoria* 47:65–81.

Coleman, J. L. 1983. Liberalism, unfair advantage, and the volunteer armed forces. In *Conscripts and volunteers,* ed. R. K. Fullinwider, 109–25. Totowa, N.J.: Rowman & Allanheld.

Cooper, J. M. 1977. Aristotle on the forms of friendship. *Review of Metaphysics* 30:619–48.

Cottingham, J. 1983. Ethics and impartiality. *Philosophical Studies* 43:83–99.

Cutright, P. 1965. Political structure, economic development, and national social security programs. *American Journal of Sociology* 70:537–50.

Daniels, N. 1979. Wide reflective equilibrium and theory acceptance in ethics. *Journal of Philosophy* 76:256–82.

Danielson, P. 1973. Theories, intuitions, and the problem of world-wide distributive justice. *Philosophy of the Social Sciences* 3:331–40.

Danziger, S.; Haveman, R.; and Plotnick, R. 1981. How income transfer programs affect work, savings, and income distribution. *Journal of Economic Literature* 19:975–1028.

Darwin, C. 1874, *The descent of man.* New York: Modern Library, 1948.

Davis, M. 1983. Foetuses, famous violinists, and the right to continued aid. *Philosophical Quarterly* 33:259–78.

Davis, N. 1980. The priority of avoiding harm. In *Killing and letting die,* ed. B. Steinbock, 172–214. Englewood Cliffs, N.J.: Prentice-Hall.

———. 1984. Abortion and self-defense. *Philosophy and Public Affairs* 13:175–207.

Demos, J. 1970. *A little commonwealth: family life in Plymouth Colony.* New York: Oxford Univ. Press.

Devlin, P. 1965. *The enforcement of morals.* London: Oxford Univ. Press.

Dicey, A. V. 1905. *Lectures on law and public opinion in England.* London: Macmillan.

Dixon, J., and Jayasuriya, D. L., eds. 1983. *Social policy in the 1980s.* Canberra: Canberra College of Advanced Education.

Dommen, E. 1980. Self-reliance in a benign environment: the South Pacific. In Galtung, O'Brien, and Preiswerk 1980, pp. 269–82.

Douglas, W. O. 1965. Opinion of the U.S. Supreme Court. *Griswold v. Connecticut.* 381 U.S. 479–86.

Durkheim, E. 1903. *Moral education.* Trans. and ed. E. K. Wilson and H. Schnurer. Glencoe, Ill.: Free Press, 1961.

Dworkin, R. M. 1977. *Taking rights seriously.* London: Butterworth.

Edwards, J. 1765. *The nature of true virtue.* Ann Arbor: Univ. of Michigan Press, 1960.

Edwards, P., ed. 1968. *Encyclopedia of philosophy.* London: Collier-Macmillan.

Eisenstadt, S. N. 1956. Ritualized personal relations. *Man* 56:90–95.

Eliot, T. S. 1942. *Little Gidding.* London: Faber.

Elliot, R. 1980. Why preserve species? In *Environmental Philosophy,* ed. D. Mannison, M. McRobbie, and R. Routley, 8–29. Canberra: Department of Philosophy, RSSS, Australian National University.

———. 1982. Faking nature. *Inquiry* 25:81–94.

Elster, J. 1978. Exploring exploitation. *Journal of Peace Research* 15:3–17.

———. 1982. Roemer versus Roemer: a comment of Roemer 1982c. *Politics and Society* 11:263–73.

———. 1983. *Sour grapes.* Cambridge: Cambridge Univ. Press.

Emerson, R. M. 1962. Power-dependence relations. *American Sociological Review* 27:31–41.

Engels, F. 1845. *The conditions of the working class in England.* Trans. and ed. W. O. Henderson and W. H. Chaloner. Oxford: Blackwell, 1958.

English, J. 1979. What do grown children owe their parents? In O'Neill and Ruddick 1979, pp. 351–56.

Epstein, R. A. 1980. *Modern products liability law.* Westport, Conn.: Quorum.

Erskine, H. G. 1961. The quarter's polls. *Public Opinion Quarterly* 25:657–65.

Ewin, R. E. 1981. *Co-operation and human values.* Brighton: Harvester.

Ewing, A. C. 1947. *The individual, the state, and world government.* New York: Macmillan.

Feinberg, J. 1970. *Doing and deserving.* Princeton, N.J.: Princeton Univ. Press.
————. 1980. *Rights, justice, and the bounds of liberty.* Princeton, N.J.: Princeton Univ. Press.
————. 1983. Noncoercive exploitation. In *Paternalism,* ed. R. Sartorious, 201–35. Minneapolis: Univ. of Minnesota Press.
Fellner, C. H., and Marshall, J. R. 1981. Kidney donors revisited. In Rushton and Sorrentino 1981, pp. 351–65.
Fishkin, J. S. 1982. *The limits of obligation.* New Haven: Yale Univ. Press.
————. 1983. *Justice, equal opportunity, and the family.* New Haven: Yale Univ. Press.
Fitzgerald, P. J. 1967. Acting and refraining. *Analysis* 27:133–39.
Flathman, R. E. 1972. *Political obligation.* New York: Atheneum.
Fletcher, G. P. 1968. Legal aspects of the decision not to prolong life. *Journal of the American Medical Association* 203:65–68.
————. 1972. Fairness and utility in tort theory. *Harvard Law Review* 85:537–73.
————. 1976. Criminal omissions: some perspectives. *American Journal of Comparative Law* 24:703–17.
————. 1978. *Rethinking criminal law.* Boston: Little, Brown.
Foot, P. 1978. *Virtues and vices.* Oxford: Blackwell.
Frankel, T. 1983. Fiduciary law. *California Law Review* 71:795–836.
Frankena, W. K. 1973. *Ethics.* 2d. ed. Englewood Cliffs, N.J.: Prentice-Hall.
Frankfurt, H. G. 1973. Coercion and moral responsibility. In *Essays on freedom of action,* ed. T. Honderich, 63–86. London: Routledge & Kegan Paul.
Freeman, R. B., and Medoff, J. L. 1982. *What do unions do?* New York: Basic Books.
Frey, R. G. 1980. *Interests and rights: the case against animals.* Oxford: Clarendon.
Fried, C. 1970. *An anatomy of values.* Cambridge: Harvard Univ. Press.
————. 1974. *Medical experimentation.* New York: American Elsevier.
————. 1976. The lawyer as friend: the moral foundations of the lawyer-client relation. *Yale Law Journal* 85:1060–89.
————. 1978. *Right and wrong.* Cambridge: Harvard Univ. Press.
————. 1979. Correspondence regarding Taurek (1977) and Parfit (1978). *Philosophy and Public Affairs* 8:393–95.
————. 1980. Review of Atiyah (1979). *Harvard Law Review* 93:1858–68.
————. 1981. *Contract as promise.* Cambridge: Harvard Univ. Press.
Friedrich, C. J. 1940. Public policy and the nature of administrative responsibility. *Public Policy* 1:3–24.
Fuller, L., and Perdue, W. R., Jr. 1936–37. The reliance interest in contract damages. *Yale Law Journal* 46:52–96, 373–420.
Galtung, J. 1980a. The politics of self-reliance. In Galtung, O'Brien, and Preiswerk 1980, pp. 355–86.
————. 1980b. Self-reliance: concepts, practice and rationale. In Galtung, O'Brien, and Preiswerk 1980, pp. 19–44.
Galtung, J.; O'Brien, P.; and Preiswerk, R., eds. 1980. *Self-reliance: a strategy for development.* London: Bogle-L'Ouverture for Institute of Development Studies, Geneva.
Gaylin, W. 1978. In the beginning: helpless and dependent. In *Doing good,* 1–38. New York: Pantheon.
Geertz, C. 1977. The judging of nations. *Archives Européennes de Sociologie* 18:245–61.
Genovese, E. D. 1974. *Roll Jordan roll.* New York: Random House.

Gergen, K., and Gergen, M. 1971. International assistance in psychological perspective. *Yearbook of World Affairs* 25:87–103.

———. 1974. Understanding foreign assistance through public opinion. *Yearbook of World Affairs* 27:125–40.

Gibson, D. M. 1984. The dormouse syndrome: restructuring the dependency of the elderly. *Australian and New Zealand Journal of Sociology*. Forthcoming.

Gilligan, C. 1977. In a different voice: women's conceptions of self and morality. *Harvard Educational Review* 47:481–517.

Gilmore, G. 1974. *The death of contract*. Columbus: Ohio State Univ. Press.

Ginnow, A. O., and Gordon, G. eds. 1978. *Corpus juris secundum*. St. Paul, Minn.: West.

Glendon, M. A. 1977. *State, law, and family: family law in transition in the United States and Western Europe*. Amsterdam: North-Holland.

Glover, J. 1975. It makes no difference whether or not I do it. *Proceedings of the Aristotelian Society, Supp.,* 49:171–90.

———. 1977. *Causing death and saving lives*. Harmondsworth: Penguin.

Godlovitch, R. 1971. Animals and morals. *Philosophy* 46:23–33.

Godwin, W. 1793. *Enquiry concerning political justice*. London; G. G. J. & J. Robinson.

Golding, M. P. 1972. Obligations to future generations. *Monist* 56:85–99. Reprinted in Partridge 1980, pp. 61–72.

Goldman, A. H. 1980. *The moral foundations of professional ethics*. Totowa, N.J.: Rowman & Littlefield.

Goode, W. J. 1963. *World revolution and family patterns*. Glencoe, Ill.: Free Press.

Goodhart, A. L. 1949. The "last opportunity" rule. *Law Quarterly Review* 65:237–55.

Goodin, R. E. 1976. *The politics of rational man*. London: Wiley.

———. 1980. *Manipulatory politics*. New Haven: Yale Univ. Press.

———. 1982a. Discounting discounting. *Journal of Public Policy* 2:53–72.

———. 1982b. *Political theory and public policy*. Chicago: Univ. of Chicago Press.

———. 1983. The ethics of destroying irreplaceable assets. *International Journal of Environmental Studies* 21:55–66.

———. 1985a. Negating positive desert claims. *Political Theory*. Forthcoming.

———. 1985b Self-reliance versus the welfare state. *Journal of Social Policy* 14: 25–47.

Goodpaster, K. E. 1979. On being morally considerable. *Journal of Philosophy* 75:308–25.

Gorovitz, S. 1977. Bigotry, loyalty, and malnutrition. In Brown and Shue 1977, pp. 129–44.

Gouldner, A. 1973. The importance of something for nothing. In *For sociology*, 260–99. London: Allen Lane.

Graycar, A., and Kinnear, D. 1981. The aged and the state. SWRC Reports and Proceedings, no. 5. Social Welfare Research Centre, University of New South Wales, Sydney. Mimeo.

Green, T. H. 1881. Liberal legislation and freedom of contract. In *Works,* ed. R. L. Nettleship, vol. 3:365–86. London: Longmans, Green, 1888.

Grote, J. 1870. *An examination of the utilitarian philosophy*. Ed. J. B. Mayor. Cambridge: Deighton, Bell.

Grotius, H. 1625. *The law of war and peace*. Trans. F. W. Kelsey; ed. J. B. Scott. New York: Oceana, 1964.

Guest, A. G. 1979. *Anson's law of contract*. 25th ed. Oxford: Clarendon.

Gummer, B. 1979. On helping and helplessness: the structure of discretion in the American welfare system. *Social Service Review* 53:214–28.

Haksar, V. 1979. *Equality, liberty, and perfectionism*. Oxford: Oxford Univ. Press.

Halberstam, M. J. 1974. Professionalism and health care. In Tancredi 1974, pp. 231–52.

Hamilton, G., chairman. 1909. *The public organisation of the labour market*. Majority report of the Royal Commission on the Poor Law and Relief of Distress. Cmd. 4499. London: His Majesty's Stationary Office.

Hamilton, W. H. 1931. The ancient maxim, *caveat emptor*. *Yale Law Journal* 40:1133–87.

Hampshire, S. 1982. Morality and convention. In Sen and Williams 1982, pp. 145–58.

Hardin, R. 1982a. *Collective action*. Baltimore: Johns Hopkins Univ. Press.

———. 1982b. Exchange theory on strategic bases. *Social Science Information* 21:251–72.

Hare, R. M. 1957. Reasons of state. In *Applications of Moral Philosophy*, 8–23. London: Macmillan, 1972.

———. 1981. *Moral thinking*. Oxford: Clarendon.

Harman, G. 1975. Moral relativism defended. *Philosophical Review* 84:3–22.

Harrod, R. F. 1936. Utilitarianism revisited. *Mind* 45:137–56.

Hart, H. L. A. 1955. Are there any natural rights? *Philosophical Review* 64:175–91.

———. 1958. Legal and moral obligation. In Melden 1958, pp. 82–107.

———. 1961. *The concept of law*. Oxford: Clarendon.

———. 1968. *Punishment and responsibility*. Oxford: Clarendon.

———. 1979. Between utility and rights. In *The idea of freedom*, ed. A. Ryan, 77–98. Oxford: Clarendon.

Hart, H. L. A., and Honore, A. M. 1959. *Causation in the law*. Oxford: Clarendon.

Heath, A. 1976. *Rational choice and social exchange*. Cambridge: Cambridge Univ. Press.

Heclo, H. 1974. *Modern social politics in Britain and Sweden*. New Haven: Yale Univ. Press.

Hegel, G. W. F. 1821. *Philosophy of right*. Trans. T. M. Knox. Oxford: Oxford Univ. Press, 1952.

Heisterman, C. A. 1934. Removal of nonresident state-poor by state and local authorities. *Social Service Review* 8:289–301.

Held, V. 1970. Can a random collection of individuals be morally responsible? *Journal of Philosophy* 67:471–81.

———. 1974. Marx, sex, and the transformation of society. *Philosophical Forum* 5:168–83.

Helps, A. 1845. *The claims of labour: an essay on the duties of the employers to the employed*. 2d ed. London: William Pickering.

Henderson, P. D. 1977. Two British errors: their probable size and some possible lessons. *Oxford Economic Papers* 29:159–94.

Herman, B. 1984. Mutual aid and respect for persons. *Ethics* 94:577–602.

Heuston, R. F. V. 1977. *Salmond on the law of torts*. 17th ed. London: Sweet & Maxwell.

Hill, L. B. 1981. Bureaucratic monitoring mechanisms. In *The public encounter*, ed. C. T. Goodsell, 160–86. Bloomington: Indiana Univ. Press.

Hill, T. E., Jr. 1980. Humanity as an end in itself. *Ethics* 91:84–99.

Hirsch, F. 1976. *Social limits to growth*. Cambridge: Harvard Univ. Press.

Hirschman, A. O. 1978. Beyond asymmetry. *International Organization* 32:45–50.

Hirschman, A. O., and Bird, R. M. 1968. Foreign aid—a critique and a proposal. Essays in International Finance, no. 69, Department of Economics, Princeton University. Mimeo.

Hobbes, T. 1651. *Leviathan.* London: Andrew Crooke.

Hodgson, D. H. 1967. *Consequences of utilitarianism.* Oxford: Clarendon.

Hoffman, M. L. 1966. Aid coordination. Paper presented to the Ditchley Conference on Improving the Effectiveness of Aid for Overseas Development, Ditchley Park, Oxfordshire, England, June 3, 1966.

Hollis, M. 1977. *Models of man.* Cambridge: Cambridge Univ. Press.

Hubin, D. C. 1976. Justice and future generations. *Philosophy and Public Affairs* 6:70–83.

Hughes, G. 1958. Criminal omissions. *Yale Law Journal* 67:590–637.

Hume, D. 1739. *A treatise of human nature.* London: John Noon.

————. 1777. *An enquiry concerning the principles of morals.* London: Cadell.

Hunt, L. 1975. Generosity. *American Philosophical Quarterly* 12:235–44.

Hutt, W. H. 1970. Immigration under "economic freedom". In *Economic issues in immigration,* ed. C. Wilson et al., 17–44. London: Institute of Economic Affairs.

Hutter, H. 1978. *Politics as friendship.* Waterloo, Ontario: Laurier Univ. Press.

Jackman, R. W. 1975. *Politics and social equality.* New York: Wiley.

Jevons, W. S. 1883. *Methods of social reform.* London: Macmillan.

Jonas, H. 1969. Philosophical reflections on experimenting with human subjects. *Daedalus* 98:219–47.

Kahn-Freund, O. 1967. A note on status and contract in British labour law. *Modern Law Review* 30:635–44.

Kamenka, E., and Tay, A. E.-S., eds. 1979. *Justice.* London: Edward Arnold.

Kane, R. L., and Kane, R. A. 1979. Alternatives to institutional care of the elderly: beyond the dichotomy. RAND Paper P-6256. Santa Monica, Calif.: RAND.

Kant, I. 1797. *Lectures on Ethics.* Ed. L. W. Beck. New York: Harper & Row, 1963.

Karst, K. 1980. Freedom of intimate association. *Yale Law Journal* 89:624–92.

Kavka, G. S. 1982. The paradox of future individuals. *Philosophy and Public Affairs* 11:93–112.

Kekes, J. 1981. Morality and impartiality. *American Philosophical Quarterly* 18:295–303.

Keniston, K., et al. 1977. *All our children.* New York: Harcourt Brace Jovanovich.

Kennan, G. F. 1970. To prevent a world wasteland: a proposal. *Foreign Affairs* 48:401–13.

Kennedy, J. F. 1963. What kind of peace do we want? Speech at American University, Washington, D.C., June 10, 1963. In *The burden and the glory,* ed. A. Nevins, 53–58. New York: Harper & Row, 1964.

Keohane, R. O., and Nye, J. S. 1977. *Power and interdependence.* Boston: Little, Brown,

Ketchum, S. A. 1977. Liberalism and marriage law. In Vetterling-Braggin, Elliston, and English 1977, pp. 264–76.

Kinnear, D., and Graycar, A. 1982. Family care of elderly people. SWRC Reports and Proceedings no. 23. Social Welfare Research Centre, University of New South Wales, Sydney. Mimeo.

Kirchheimer, O. 1942. Criminal omissions. *Harvard Law Review* 55:615–42.

Kleinig, J. 1976. Good samaritanism. *Philosophy and Public Affairs* 5:382–407.

————. 1978. Crime and the concept of harm. *American Philosophical Quarterly* 15:27–36.

Krebs, D. L. 1970. Altruism: an examination of the concept and a review of the literature. *Psychological Bulletin* 73:258–302.

Kronman, A. T. 1981. A new champion for the will theory: review of Fried (1981). *Yale Law Journal* 91:404–23.

———. 1983. Paternalism and the law of contracts. *Yale Law Journal* 92:763–98.

Lane, R. E. 1982. Government and self-esteem. *Political Theory* 10:5–31.

Laslett, P. 1970. The conversation between the generations. In *The proper study,* ed. G. Vesey. Royal Institute of Philosophy Lectures, vol. 4:172–89. London: Macmillan. Reprinted in Laslett and Fishkin 1979, pp. 36–56.

Laslett, P., and Fishkin, J. S., eds. 1979. *Philosophy, politics, and society.* 5th ser. Oxford: Blackwell.

Latane, B., and Darley, J. M. 1970. Social determinants of bystander intervention in emergencies. In Macaulay and Berkowitz 1970, pp. 13–27.

Leff, A. 1967. Unconscionability and the code: the emperor's new clause. *University of Pennsylvania Law Review* 115:485–559.

Lerner, M. J. 1970. The desire for justice and reactions to victims. In Macaulay and Berkowitz 1970, pp. 205–30.

Lerner, M. J., and Miller, D. T. 1978. Just world research and the attribution process. *Psychological Bulletin* 85:1030–51.

Lewis, G. C. 1841. *An essay on the government of dependencies.* London: John Murray.

Lewis, W. D. 1932. *Restatement of the law of contracts.* St. Paul, Minn.: American Law Institute.

Lichtenberg, J. 1981. National boundaries and moral boundaries: a cosmopolitan view. In Brown and Shue 1981, pp. 79–100.

———. 1982. The moral equivalence of acts and omissions. In *New essays in ethics and public policy,* ed. K. Nielsen and S. C. Patten. Calgary: Univ. of Calgary Press.

Locke, J. 1690. *Second treatise of government.* Ed. P. Laslett. Cambridge: Cambridge Univ. Press, 1960.

London, H. I. 1970. *Non-white immigration and the "white Australia" policy.* Sydney: Sydney Univ. Press.

Luban, D. 1984a. The adversary system excuse. In Luban 1984b, pp. 83–122.

———, ed. 1984b. *The good lawyer.* Totowa, N.J.: Rowman & Allanheld.

Lucas, J. R. 1959. Moralists and gamesmen. *Philosophy* 34:1–11.

Lyon, D. W. 1976. The dynamics of welfare dependency: a survey. RAND Paper P-5769. Santa Monica, Calif.: RAND.

Lyons, Daniel. 1969. The odd debt of gratitude. *Analysis* 29:92–97.

Lyons, David. 1969. Rights, claimants, and beneficiaries. *American Philosophical Quarterly* 6:173–85.

———. 1982. Benevolence and justice in Mill. In Miller and Williams 1982, pp. 42–70.

Macaulay, J. R., and Berkowitz, L., eds. 1970. *Altruism and helping behavior.* New York: Academic Press.

Macaulay, T. B. 1837. Notes on the Indian penal code. In *Complete Works,* ed. Lady Trevelyan, vol. 7:429–558. London: Longmans, Green, 1875.

McCloskey, H. J. 1965. Rights. *Philosophical Quarterly* 15:115–27.

———. 1983. *Ecological ethics and politics.* Totowa, N.J.: Rowman & Littlefield.

MacCormick, N. 1972. Voluntary obligations and normative powers. *Proceedings of the Aristotelian Society, Supp.,* 46:59–78.

MacDonnell, J. 1908. *The law of master and servant.* 2d ed. London: Stevens.

MacIntyre, A. 1968. Egoism and altruism. In Edwards 1968, vol. 2:462–66.
_____. 1983. The magic in the pronoun "my": review of Williams (1981). *Ethics* 94:113–25.
MacIver, A. M. 1948. Ethics and the beetle. *Analysis* 8:65–70.
Mack, E. 1980. Bad samaritanism and the causation of harm. *Philosophy and Public Affairs* 9:230–59.
Mackie, J. L. 1955. Responsibility and language. *Australasian Journal of Philosophy* 33:143–59.
_____. 1977. *Ethics: inventing right and wrong.* Harmondsworth: Penguin.
McKinley, R. D., and Little, R. 1977. A foreign policy model of U.S. bilateral aid allocation. *World Politics* 30:58–86.
_____. 1978. A foreign-policy model of the distribution of British bilateral aid, 1960–70. *British Journal of Political Science* 8:313–32.
McKinsey, M. 1981. Obligations to the starving. *Nous* 15:309–23.
MacLean, D., and Brown, P. G., eds. 1983. *Energy and the future.* Totowa, N.J.: Rowman & Littlefield.
Macneil, I. R. 1980. *The new social contract.* New Haven: Yale Univ. Press.
McNeilly, F. S. 1972. Promises de-moralized. *Philosophical Review* 81:63–81.
Maimonides, M. 1168. *The code of Maimonides (Misheneh Torah).* Trans. I. Klein. New Haven: Yale Univ. Press, 1979.
Maine, H. S. 1861. *Ancient law.* London: John Murray.
Malthus, T. R. 1826. *An essay on the principle of population.* 6th ed. London: John Murray.
Marks, F. R. 1975. Detours on the road to maturity: a view of the legal conception of growing up and letting go. *Law and Contemporary Problems* 39 (Summer):78–92.
Marshall, A. 1892. Discussion of Mr. Booth's (1891) paper. *Journal of the Royal Statistical Society,* ser. A, 55:60–63.
Marshall, J. 1831. Opinion of the U.S. Supreme Court. *Cherokee Nation v. Georgia.* 5 Peters (30 U.S.) 1–20.
Marshall, T. 1979. Opinion of the U.S. Supreme Court. *United States v. Rutherford.* 442 U.S. 546–59.
Masters, R. D. 1975. Is contract an adequate basis for medical ethics? *Hastings Center Report* 5 (December):24–28.
Mather, C. 1710. *Bonifacius, an essay upon the good.* Boston: Samuel Garrish.
Matthews, S. 1886. Opinion of the U.S. Supreme Court. *Choctaw Nation v. United States.* 119 U.S. 25–41.
May, W. F. 1975. Code, covenant, contract, or philanthropy. *Hastings Center Report* 5 (December):29–38.
Melden, A. I., ed. 1958. *Essays in moral philosophy.* Seattle: Univ. of Washington Press.
Mellows, A. R. 1977. *The law of succession.* 3d ed. London: Butterworth.
Mill, J. S. 1848. *Principles of political economy.* London: Parker & Son.
_____. 1863. Utilitarianism. In *Mill: Utilitarianism and other writings,* ed. M. Warnock. Glasgow: Collins, 1962.
_____. 1869. *The subjection of women.* Oxford: Oxford Univ. Press, 1975.
Miller, D. 1976. *Social justice.* Oxford: Clarendon.
Miller, H. B., and Williams, W. H., eds. 1982. *The limits of utilitarianism.* Minneapolis: Univ. of Minnesota Press.
Miller, S. F. 1885. Opinion of the U.S. Supreme Court. *United States v. Kagama.* 118 U.S. 375–85.

Mirrlees, J. A. 1982. The economic uses of utilitarianism. In Sen and Williams 1982, pp. 63–84.

Mish'alani, J. K. 1982. The limits of moral community and the limits of moral thought. *Journal of Value Inquiry* 16:131–42.

Mnookin, R. H. 1973. Foster care—in whose best interest? *Harvard Educational Review* 43:599–638.

Montaigne, M. 1580. Of friendship. In *The complete essays of Montaigne*, trans. D. M. Frame, 135–44. Stanford, Calif.: Stanford Univ. Press, 1958.

Moore, M. H. 1981. Realms of obligation and virtue. In *Public duties*, ed. J. L. Fleishman, L. Liebman, and M. H. Moore, 3–31. Cambridge: Harvard Univ. Press.

Moran, T. H. 1978. Multinational corporations and dependency: a dialogue for dependentistas and nondependentistas. *International Organization* 32:79–100.

Morgenthau, H. 1962. A political theory of foreign aid. *American Political Science Review* 56:301–9.

Myrdal, G. 1960. *Beyond the welfare state*. New Haven, Conn.: Yale Univ. Press.

Naegele, K. D. 1958. Friendship and acquaintances: an exploration of some social distinctions. *Harvard Educational Review* 28:232–52.

Nagel, T. 1970. *The possibility of altruism*. Oxford: Clarendon.

———. 1977. Poverty and food: why charity is not enough. In Brown and Shue 1977, pp. 54–63.

———. 1980. The limits of objectivity. In *The Tanner lectures on human values*, ed. S. M. McMurrin, vol. 1:75–139. Cambridge: Cambridge Univ. Press.

———. 1982. The limits of partiality: review of Williams (1981). *Times Literary Supplement*, 7 May, 501.

Narveson, J. 1972. Aesthetics, charity, utility, and distributive justice. *Monist* 56:527–51.

Nelson, W. N. 1974. Special rights, general rights, and social justice. *Philosophy and Public Affairs* 3:410–30.

Newson, E. 1978. Unreasonable care: the establishment of selfhood. In *Human values*, ed. G. Vesey. Royal Institute of Philosophy Lectures, vol. 11:1–26. Hassocks, Sussex: Harvester.

Norman, R. 1979. Self and others: the inadequacy of utilitarianism. In *New essays on John Stuart Mill and utilitarianism*, ed. W. E. Cooper, K. Nielsen, and S. C. Patten, 181–201. Guelph, Ont.: Canadian Association for Publishing in Philosophy.

Nowell-Smith, P. H., and Lemmon, E. J. 1960. Escapism: the logical basis of ethics. *Mind* 69:289–300.

Nozick, R. 1974. *Anarchy, state, and utopia*. Oxford: Blackwell.

Nussbaum, M. C. 1984. *The fragility of goodness: luck and rational self-sufficiency in Greek ethical thought*. Cambridge: Cambridge Univ. Press.

Nyerere, J. K. 1968. *Ujamaa-essays on socialism*. Dar es Salaam: Oxford Univ. Press.

O'Driscoll, L. H. 1977. On the nature and value of marriage. In Vetterling-Braggin, Elliston, and English 1977, pp. 249–63.

Oldenquist, A. 1982. Loyalties. *Journal of Philosophy* 79:173–93.

O'Neill, O. 1979. Begetting, bearing, and rearing. In O'Neill and Ruddick 1979, pp. 25–38.

———. 1980. The moral perplexities of famine relief. In *Matters of life and death*, ed. T. Regan, 260–98. Philadelphia: Temple Univ. Press.

————. 1982. Prerogatives of the premature. *Times Literary Supplement*, 26 March, 332.

O'Neill, O., and Ruddick, W., eds. 1979. *Having children.* New York: Oxford Univ. Press.

Orwell, G. 1949. Reflections on Ghandi. In *Collected essays, journalism, and letters,* ed. G. Orwell and I. Angus, vol. 4:463–70. London: Secker & Warburg, 1968.

Page, T. 1983. Intergenerational justice as opportunity. In MacLean and Brown 1983, pp. 38–58.

Paine, R. 1969. In search of friendship: an exploratory analysis in "middle-class" culture. *Man* 4:505–24.

Parfit, D. 1976a. On doing the best for our children. In Bayles 1976, pp. 100–15.

————. 1976b. Rights, interests, and possible people. In *Moral problems in medicine,* ed. S. Gorovitz et al., 369–75. Englewood Cliffs, N.J.: Prentice-Hall.

————. 1978. Innumerate ethics. *Philosophy and Public Affairs* 7:285–301.

————. 1979a. Correspondence regarding Fried (1979). *Philosophy and Public Affairs* 8:395–97.

————. 1979b. Prudence, morality, and the prisoner's dilemma. *Proceedings of the British Academy* 65:539–64.

————. 1982. Future generations: further problems. *Philosophy and Public Affairs* 11:113–72.

————. 1983a. Energy policy and the further future: the identity problem. In MacLean and Brown 1983, pp. 166–79.

————. 1983b. Energy policy and the further future: the social discount rate. In MacLean and Brown 1983, pp. 31–7. Reprinted in Parfit 1984, pp. 480–486.

————. 1984. *Reasons and persons.* Oxford: Clarendon.

Parry, G. 1982. Tradition, community, and self-determination. *British Journal of Political Science* 12:399–420.

Parsons, T., and Shils, E. A., eds. 1951. *Toward a general theory of action.* New York: Harper & Row, 1962.

Partridge, E., ed. 1980. *Responsibilities to future generations.* Buffalo, N.Y.: Prometheus.

————. 1981. Posthumous interests and posthumous respect. *Ethics* 91:243–64.

Passmore, J. 1979. Civil justice and its rivals. In Kamenka and Tay 1979, pp. 25–49.

————. 1980. *Man's responsibility for nature.* 2d ed. London: Duckworth.

————. 1981. *The limits of government.* Sydney: Australian Broadcasting Corp.

Pateman, C. 1979. *The problem of political obligation.* Chichester, Sussex: Wiley.

————. 1981. The shame of the marriage contract. Department of Government, University of Sydney. Mimeo.

Paton, H. J. 1956. Kant's theory of friendship. *Proceedings of the British Academy* 42:45–66.

Pellegrino, E. D., and Thomasma, D. C. 1981. *A philosophical basis of medical practice.* New York: Oxford Univ. Press.

Pettit, P., and Goodin, R.E. 1985. The possibility of special duties. *Canadian Journal of Philosophy.* Forthcoming.

Pinker, R. 1979. *The idea of welfare.* London: Heinemann.

Pirsig, M. E., ed. 1970. *Cases and materials on professional responsibility.* St. Paul, Minn.: West.

Plant, R.; Lesser, H.; and Taylor-Gooby, P. 1980. *Political philosophy and social welfare.* London: Routledge & Kegan Paul.

Pollock, L. 1981. *The freedom principle.* Buffalo, N.Y.: Prometheus.

Posner, R. A. 1972. *Economic analysis of law.* Boston: Little, Brown.

Postow, B. C. 1978–79. Economic dependence and self-respect. *Philosophical Forum* 10:181–205.

Pound, R. 1916. Individual interests in the domestic relations. *Michigan Law Review* 14:177–96.

———. 1945. Individual interests of substance—promised advantages. *Harvard Law Review* 59:1–42.

Prior, A. N. 1958. Escapism: the logical basis of ethics. In Melden 1958, pp. 135–46.

Prosser, W., reporter. 1965. *Restatement (second) of the law of torts.* St. Paul, Minn.: American Law Institute.

———. 1971. *Handbook of the law of torts.* 4th ed. St. Paul, Minn.: West.

Pufendorf, S. 1672. *Of the law of nature and nations.* Trans. B. Kennett. 3d ed. London: Sare, 1717.

———. 1682. *On the duty of man and citizen according to the natural law.* Trans. H. F. Wright. New York: Oxford Univ. Press, 1927.

Quine, W. v. O. 1961. *From a logical point of view.* 2d ed. Cambridge: Harvard Univ. Press.

Ramsoey, O. 1968. Friendship. In Sills 1968, vol. 6:12–17.

Raps, C. S.; Peterson, C.; Jonas, M.; and Seligman, M. E. P. 1982. Patient behavior in hospitals: helplessness, reactance, or both? *Journal of Personality and Social Psychology* 42:1936–41.

Ratcliffe, J. M., ed. 1966. *The good samaritan and the law.* Garden City, N.Y.: Anchor.

Rawls, J. 1951. Outline of a decision procedure for ethics. *Philosophical Review* 60:177–97.

———. 1958. Justice as fairness. *Philosophical Review* 67:164–94.

———. 1971. *A theory of justice.* Cambridge: Harvard Univ. Press.

———. 1974. The independence of moral theory. *Proceedings and Addresses of the American Philosophical Association* 48 (November): 5–22.

———. 1982. Social unity and primary goods. In Sen and Williams 1982, pp. 159–86.

Raz, J. 1972. Voluntary obligations and normative powers. *Proceedings of the Aristotelian Society, Supp.* 46:79–102.

———. 1982. The claims of reflective equilibrium. *Inquiry* 25:307–30.

Reeder, J. P., Jr. 1982. Beneficence, supererogation, and role duty. In *Beneficence and health care,* ed. E. E. Shelp, 83–108. Dordrecht: Reidel.

Regan, D. 1980. *Utilitarianism and cooperation.* Oxford: Clarendon.

———. 1984. Duties of preservation. In *The preservation of species,* ed. B. G. Norton and H. Shue. Totowa, N.J.: Rowman & Allanheld.

Regan, T. 1979. An examination and defense of one argument concerning animal rights. *Inquiry* 22:189–219.

———. 1980. Utilitarianism, vegetarianism, and animal rights. *Philosophy and Public Affairs* 9:305–24.

Rein, M. 1965. The strange case of public dependency. In Rein, *Social policy,* 85–99. New York: Random House, 1970.

Richards, D. A. J. 1971. *A theory of reasons for action.* Oxford: Clarendon.

———. 1983. Contractarian theory, intergenerational justice, and energy policy. In MacLean and Brown 1983, pp. 131–50.

Ridley, M., and Dawkins, R. 1981. The natural selection of altruism. In Rushton and Sorrentino 1981, pp. 19–39.

Ritchie, D. G. 1900. The rights of animals. *International Journal of Ethics* 10:387–89.

Roberts, M. 1965. *Responsibility and practical freedom.* Cambridge: Cambridge Univ. Press.

Robson, W. A. 1976. *Welfare state and welfare society.* London: Allen & Unwin.

Rodman, H. 1973. Children under the law. *Harvard Educational Review* 43:487–514.

Roemer, J. E. 1982a. Exploitation, alternatives, and socialism. *Economic Journal* 92:87–107.

———. 1982b. *A general theory of exploitation and class.* Cambridge: Harvard Univ. Press.

———. 1982c. New directions in the Marxian theory of exploitation and class. *Politics and Society* 11:253–87.

Rorty, R. 1983. Postmodernist bourgeois liberalism. *Journal of Philosophy* 80:583–89.

Ross, E. A. 1907. *Sin and society: an analysis of latter-day iniquity.* Boston: Houghton Mifflin.

———. 1921. *Principles of sociology.* New York: Century.

Ross, W. D. 1930. *The right and the good.* Oxford: Clarendon.

Rousseau, J.-J. 1762a. *Emile.* Trans. B. Foxley. London: Dent, 1974.

———. 1762b. *Social contract.* Trans. and ed. J. R. and R. D. Masters. New York: St. Martin's, 1978.

Routley, R., and Nozick, R. 1962. Escaping the good samaritan paradox. *Mind* 71:377–82.

Routley, R., and Routley, V. 1979. Against the inevitability of human chauvinism. In *Ethics and problems of the twenty-first century,* ed. K. Goodpaster and K. Sayre, 36–59. Notre Dame, Ind.: Notre Dame Univ. Press.

Royce, J. 1908. *The philosophy of loyalty.* New York: Macmillan.

Rushton, J. P., and Sorrentino, R. M., eds. 1981. *Altruism and helping behavior.* Hillsdale, N.J.: Lawrence Erlbaum Associates.

Rydell, C. P.; Palmerio, T.; Blais, G.; and Brown, D. 1974. Welfare caseload dynamics in New York City. RAND Report R-1441-NYC. New York: New York City RAND.

Ryle, G. 1973. Negative "actions". *Hermathena* 115:81–93.

Sagoff, M. 1974. On preserving the natural environment. *Yale Law Journal* 84:205–67.

Salmond, J. W. 1957. *Jurisprudence.* Ed. G. Williams. 11th ed. London: Sweet & Maxwell.

Sandel, M. J. 1982. *Liberalism and the limits of justice.* Cambridge: Cambridge Univ. Press.

Sartre, J.-P. 1948. *Existentialism and humanism.* Trans. P. Mairet. London: Methuen.

Sax, J. L. 1970. The public trust doctrine in natural resource law. *Michigan Law Review* 68:471–566.

Scheffler, S. 1982. *The rejection of consequentialism.* Oxford: Clarendon.

Schelling, T. C. 1963. *The strategy of conflict.* Cambridge: Harvard Univ. Press.

Schlesinger, A. M., Jr. 1981. Unlearning the lessons of Pearl Harbor. *Washington Post,* 6 December, sec. C, pp. C1 and C3.

Schorr, A. L. 1960. *Filial responsibility in the modern American family.* Washington, D.C.: Government Printing Office.

———. 1980. ". . . Thy father and thy mother . . .": a second look at filial responsibility and family policy. SSA publication no. 13-11953. Washington, D. C.: Government Printing Office.

224   References

Schrag, F. 1976. Justice and the family. *Inquiry* 19:193–208.
Scott, A. W., reporter. 1959. *Restatement (second) of the law of trusts.* St. Paul, Minn.: American Law Institute.
Scott, J. C. 1975. Exploitation in rural class relations: a victim's perspective. *Comparative Politics* 7:489–532.
————. 1976. *The moral economy of the peasant.* New Haven, Conn.: Yale Univ. Press.
Searle, J. R. 1969. *Speech acts.* Cambridge: Cambridge Univ. Press.
Seavey, W. A., reporter. 1958. *Restatement (second) of the law of agency.* St. Paul, Minn.: American Law Institute.
Seavey, W. A., and Scott, A. W., reporters. 1937. *Restatement of the law of restitution, quasi contracts, and constructive trusts.* St. Paul, Minn.: American Law Institute.
Seligman, M. E. P. 1975. *Helplessness.* San Francisco: Freeman.
Sen, A. 1970. *Collective choice and social welfare.* San Francisco: Holden-Day.
————. 1979a. Interpersonal comparisons of welfare. Reprinted in *Choice, welfare, and measurement,* 264–81. Oxford: Blackwell, 1982.
————. 1979b. Utilitarianism and welfarism. *Journal of Philosophy* 76:463–89.
————. 1982. Rights and agency. *Philosophy and Public Affairs* 11:3–39.
————, and Willaims, B., eds. 1982. *Utilitarianism and beyond.* Cambridge: Cambridge Univ. Press.
Sesonske, A. 1957. *Value and obligation.* New York: Oxford Univ. Press, 1964.
Shanley, M. L. 1979. Marriage contract and social control in seventeenth century English political thought. *Western Political Quarterly* 32:79–91.
Shaw, G. B. 1965. *The complete prefaces of Bernard Shaw.* London: Paul Hamlyn.
Sher, G. 1979. Compensation and transworld identity. *Monist* 62:378–92.
————. 1981. Ancient wrongs and modern rights. *Philosophy and Public Affairs* 10:3–17.
Shue, H. 1980. *Basic rights.* Princeton: Princeton Univ. Press.
————. 1981. Exporting hazards. *Ethics* 91:579–606. Reprinted in Brown and Shue 1981, pp. 107–45.
————. 1983. The burdens of justice. *Journal of Philosophy* 80:600–608.
Shultz, M. M. 1982. Contractual ordering of marriage: a new model for state policy. *California Law Review* 70:204–334.
Sidgwick, H. 1874. *The methods of ethics.* 7th ed. London: Macmillan, 1907.
————. 1897. *The elements of politics.* 2d ed. London: Macmillan.
Sikora, R. I., and Barry, B., eds. 1978. *Obligations to future generations.* Philadelphia: Temple Univ. Press.
Sills, D. L., ed. 1968. *International encyclopedia of the social sciences.* London: Collier-Macmillan.
Simmons, A. J. 1979. *Moral principles and political obligation.* Princeton, N.J.: Princeton Univ. Press.
Singer, P. 1972. Famine, affluence and morality. *Philosophy and Public Affairs* 1:229–43. Reprinted in Laslett and Fishkin 1979, pp. 21–35.
————. 1975. *Animal liberation.* New York: New York Review Press.
————. 1977. Reconsidering the famine relief argument. In Brown and Shue 1977, pp. 26–53.
————. 1979. *Practical ethics.* Cambridge: Cambridge Univ. Press.
————. 1980. Utilitarianism and vegetarianism. *Philosophy and Public Affairs* 9:325–37.
————. 1981. *The expanding circle.* Oxford: Clarendon.

Skolnick, A. 1975. The limits of childhood: conceptions of child development and social context. *Law and Contemporary Problems* 39 (Summer):38–77.

Slote, M. A. 1977. The morality of wealth. In *World hunger and moral obligation,* ed. W. Aiken and H. LaFollette, 124–47. Englewood Cliffs, N.J.: Prentice-Hall.

———. 1979. Obedience and illusions. In O'Neill and Ruddick 1979, pp. 319–26.

Smart, J. J. C. 1973. An outline of a system of utilitarian ethics. In Smart and Williams 1973, pp. 3–74.

Smart, J. J. C., and Williams, B. 1973. *Utilitarianism, for and against.* Cambridge: Cambridge Univ. Press.

Smith, A. 1766. *Lectures on justice, police, revenue, and arms.* Ed. E. Cannan. New York: Kelley & Millman, 1956.

Smith, A. D. 1949. Public assistance as a social obligation. *Harvard Law Review* 63:266–88.

———. 1955. *The right to life.* Chapel Hill: Univ. of North Carolina Press.

Smith, H. M. 1983. Intercourse and moral responsibility for the fetus. In *Abortion and the status of the fetus,* ed. W. B. Bondeson et al., 229–45. Dordrecht: Reidel.

Sorrentino, R. M. 1981. Derogation of an innocently suffering victim: so who's the "good guy?" In Rushton and Sorrentino 1981, pp. 267–83.

Spencer, H. 1884. *Man versus the state.* London: Williams & Norgate.

———. 1891. Railway morals and railway policy. In *Essays,* vol. 3:52–112. London: Williams & Norgate.

Stampp, K. M. 1963. *The peculiar institution.* New York: Knopf.

Steiner, G. Y. 1971. *The state of welfare.* Washington, D.C.: Brookings Institution.

Steiner, H. 1977. The natural right to the means of production. *Philosophical Quarterly* 27:41–49.

———. 1983. The rights of future generations. In MacLean and Brown 1983, pp. 151–65.

Stevens, C. M. 1974. Selecting health care systems. In Tancredi 1974, pp. 253–70.

Stewart, P. 1978. Dissenting opinion. *Cagan v. Mohammed.* 441 U.S. 380, 401–17.

Stocker, M. 1981. Values and purposes: the limits of teleology and the ends of friendship. *Journal of Philosophy* 78:747–66.

Stone, C. D. 1972. Should trees have standing? *Southern California Law Review* 45:450–501.

Stone, L. 1977. *The family, sex, and marriage in England, 1500–1800.* London: Weidenfeld & Nicholson.

Stouffer, S. A. 1949. An analysis of conflicting social norms. *American Sociological Review* 14:707–17.

———, and Toby, J. 1951. Role conflict and personality. In Parsons and Shils 1951, pp. 481–96.

Strawson, P. F. 1974. *Freedom and resentment and other essays.* London: Methuen.

Streib, G. F. 1958. Family patterns in retirement. *Journal of Social Issues* 14, no. 2:46–60.

Sumner, W. G. 1883. *What social classes owe to each other.* New York: Harper.

Sundstrom, G. 1982. The elderly, women's work, and social security costs. *Acta Sociologica* 25:21–38.

Tancredi, L. R., ed. 1974. *Ethics of health care.* Washington, D. C.: National Academy of Sciences.

Taurek, J. M. 1977. Should the numbers count? *Philosophy and Public Affairs* 6:293–316.

Taylor, C. 1976. Responsibility for self. In *The identities of persons,* ed. A. O. Rorty, 281–300. Berkeley: Univ. of California Press.

Taylor, M. 1976. *Anarchy and cooperation*. London: Wiley.

Taylor, M., and Ward, H. 1982. Whales, chicken, and collective action. *Political Studies* 30:350–70.

Telfer, E. 1970–71. Friendship. *Proceedings of the Aristotelian Society* 71:223–42.

Thompson, W. 1825. *Appeal of one half of the human race, women, against the pretensions of the other half, man, to retain them in political, and thence in civil and domestic slavery*. London: Longmans.

Thomson, J. J. 1971. A defense of abortion. *Philosophy and Public Affairs* 1:47–66.

Titmuss, R. M. 1958. The social division of welfare: some reflections on the search for equity. In *Essays on "the welfare state"*, 34–55. London: Allen & Unwin.

———. 1974. *Social policy*. London: Allen & Unwin.

Toulmin, S. 1981. The tyranny of principles. *Hastings Center Report* 11, no. 6 (December):31–39.

Townsend, P. 1957. *The family life of old people*. London: Routledge & Kegan Paul.

———. 1981. The structured dependency of the elderly: a creation of social policy in the twentieth century. *Ageing and Society* 1:5–28.

Tribe, L. H. 1974. Ways not to think about plastic trees: new foundations for environmental law. *Yale Law Journal* 83:1315–48.

Trivers, R. L. 1971. The evolution of reciprocal altruism. *Quarterly Review of Biology* 46:35–57.

Tulloch, P. 1983. Workforce exclusion and dependency. In Dixon and Jayasuriya 1983, pp. 23–37.

———. 1984. Gender and dependency. In *Unfinished business: social justice for women in Australia*, ed. D. Broom. Sydney: Allen & Unwin.

United Nations. General Assembly. 1959. Declaration of the rights of the child. Reprinted in O'Neill and Ruddick 1979, pp. 112–14.

Urmson, J. O. 1958. Saints and heroes. In Melden 1958, pp. 198–216.

van Lennep, E. 1981. Opening address. In *The welfare state in crisis*, 9–12. Paris: OECD.

VanDeVeer, D. 1980. Animal suffering. *Canadian Journal of Philosophy* 10:463–71.

Veatch, R. M. 1972. Medical ethics: professional or universal? *Harvard Theological Review* 65:531–59.

———. 1981. *A theory of medical ethics*. New York: Basic Books.

Vermazen, B. 1977. The logic of practical "ought"-sentences. *Philosophical Studies* 32:1–71.

Vetterling-Braggin, M; Elliston, F. A.; and English, J., eds. 1977. *Feminism and philosophy*. Totowa, N.J.: Littlefield, Adams.

Viscusi, W. K. 1979. *Employment hazards*. Cambridge: Harvard Univ. Press.

Wade, E. C. S., and Phillips, G. G. 1977. *Constitutional and administrative law*. Ed. A. W. Bradley. 9th ed. London: Longmans.

Wakley, R. 1846. Speech on the Ten Hour Bill. *Hansard's Parliamentary Debates*. House of Commons, 3d ser., 86:1045–50.

Walker, A. 1980. The social creation of poverty and dependency in old age. *Journal of Social Policy* 9:49–75.

———. 1982. Dependency in old age. *Social Policy and Administration* 16:115–35.

Walker, A. D. M. 1980–81. Gratefulness and gratitude. *Proceedings of the Aristotelian Society* 81:39–56.

Walzer, M. 1970. *Obligations* Cambridge: Harvard Univ. Press.

———. 1981. The distribution of membership. In Brown and Shue 1981, pp. 1–35, 101–5. Reprinted in Walzer 1983, pp. 31–63.

———. 1983. *Spheres of justice*. New York: Basic Books.

Warnock, G. J. 1971. *The object of morality*. London: Methuen.
Wasserstrom, R. 1975. Lawyers as professionals: some moral issues. *Human Rights* 5:1–24.
_____. 1984. Roles and morality. In Luban 1984b, pp. 25–37.
Weale, A. 1978. *Equality and social policy*. London: Routledge & Kegan Paul.
_____. 1983. *Political theory and social policy*. London: Macmillan.
Weinrib, E. J. 1980. The case for a duty to rescue. *Yale Law Journal* 90:247–93.
Weitzman, L. J. 1974. Legal regulation of marriage: tradition and change. *California Law Review* 62:1169–1288.
_____. 1981. *The marriage contract*. New York: Free Press.
Wigmore, J. J. 1897. The pledge-idea: a study in comparative legal ideas. *Harvard Law Review* 10:321–50, 389–417; 11:18–39.
Wildavsky, A. 1972. Why planning fails in Nepal. *Administrative Science Quarterly* 17:508–28.
Williams, B. 1973. A critique of utilitarianism. In Smart and Williams 1973, pp. 75–150.
_____. 1981. *Moral luck*. Cambridge: Cambridge Univ. Press.
Williams, G. L. 1951. *Joint torts and contributory negligence*. London: Stevens.
_____. 1961. *Criminal law*. 2d ed. London: Stevens.
Williston, S., reporter. 1932. *Restatement of the law of contracts*. St. Paul, Minn.: American Law Institute.
Wilson, J. R. S. 1978. In one another's power. *Ethics* 88:299–315.
Winkler, E. R. 1982. Utilitarian idealism and personal relations. *Canadian Journal of Philosophy* 12:265–86.
Winston, M. P., and Forsher, T. 1971. Nonsupport of legitimate children by affluent fathers as a cause of poverty and welfare dependence. Santa Monica, Calif.: RAND.
Wittman, D. 1981. Optimal pricing of sequential inputs: last clear chance, mitigation of damages, and related doctrines in the law. *Journal of Legal Studies* 10:65–91.
Wolf, E. R. 1966. Kinship, friendship, and patron-client relationships in complex societies. In *The social anthropology of complex societies,* ed. M. Banton, 1–22. London: Tavistock.
Wolf, S. 1982. Moral saints. *Journal of Philosophy* 79:419–39.
Wolfenden, J. F., chairman. 1957. *Report of the Committee on Homosexual Offences and Prostitution*. Cmnd. 247. London: Her Majesty's Stationery Office.
Wolff, C. 1764. *Jus gentium methodo scientifica pertractatum*. Trans. J. A. Drake. 2d ed. New York: Oceana, 1964.
Wollstonecraft, M. 1792. *A vindication of the rights of women*. 2d ed. London: Johnson.

Index